SIMPSON'S WORLD

JOHN SIMPSON

SIMPSON'S WORLD

DISPATCHES FROM THE FRONT LINES

miramax books

HYPERION

NEW YORK

ISBN 1-4013-0041-3

First Edition
10   9   8   7   6   5   4   3   2   1

SIMPSON'S
WORLD

INTRODUCTION

I am a traveler by profession, and commute to work; but my job tends to be carried out in outlandish and difficult places—Afghanistan, the Middle East, the darker parts of Africa and Latin America. As a result I have had a rather larger acquaintance with deranged dictators, ethnic cleansers, bandits and terrorists than seems altogether reasonable. Quite a number of them will make an appearance in these pages: Ayatollah Khomeini refusing to shake my hand, Osama bin Laden offering a disturbingly small amount of money to have me killed, Fidel Castro assuring me he would abdicate soon, Colonel Gadhafi breaking wind loudly and determinedly throughout our television interview.

I have endured these things, and worse, in service of the organization that I joined in 1966 at the tender age of twenty-two: the British Broadcasting Corporation, which to my surprise and that of everyone who works for it has now emerged as the world's largest and most powerful television organization. The British, who pay for it through the license-fee system, know it, with a certain affection, as Auntie; its staff never call it that, preferring the Broken Biscuit Company or, more briefly, the Beeb.

Like a fifty-eight-year-old who still lives with his parents and explains it away by saying it makes financial sense, I always feel called upon to explain this long BBC habit of mine. It is true that I have done other jobs concurrently—for six years, after 1990, I was associate editor of the *Spectator* magazine, then moved to the *Sunday Telegraph*, where I write a weekly column on foreign affairs—yet I have always been in essence a BBC man.

Like every long-term Beeber, I have suffered for it. It first became clear that this might be the case one May morning in 1970, on my very first assignment as a BBC radio reporter, when an equally new and inexperienced news editor suggested I should try to ask a question of (or "doorstep," in journalistic parlance) the then British prime minister, Harold Wilson. The idea was that I should ask him if it were true, as the newspapers were reporting, that he was planning to hold a snap election. Wilson was going to Euston Station in London to take a train to his constituency at Huyton, and Downing Street suggested that any news organization that wanted to get some pictures of him was welcome to send someone round there.

Wilson proceeded down Platform 7 like a pudgy Roman emperor in a cloud of officials and minders; and realizing that none of the waiting journalists would do anything more than smile ingratiatingly at him, I decided it was my duty to step forward with my trusty tape recorder and ask him the question of the moment.

"Excuse me, Prime—"

That was as far as I got before my world exploded. The chief executive of my country punched me hard in the stomach and tried to wrestle the microphone out of my hand. I doubled up; he might not have been much as a political leader, but he had a good left hook. And as he wrestled and punched he hissed that my behavior was outrageous, that the BBC's director-general knew he didn't do these things, and that he would make the strongest complaint about me directly he reached Huyton. Then he and his courtiers swept on.

The other journalists gathered round me, grinning.

"You can't just doorstep the PM like that, sonny," said one of the older reporters, patting me comfortingly on the shoulder.

He was right. In 1970, the attitude of a journalist to senior politicians was still one of deference and respect: They were the masters. In a single generation, of course, all that has changed—and good riddance to it. Today, a British prime minister who physically attacks a journalist in front of the cameras will probably have resigned by the end of the day; but in May 1970, although every photographer and cameraman present had pictures of the incident, not a single one ever appeared, and there was no mention whatever of it in the next day's papers.

A famous colleague of mine, the infinitely older and more experienced Alistair Cooke, once described how shocking it was for him to report on the American Democratic Party's convention of, I think, 1944, when President Roosevelt revealed to the world that he was a sick man, and could only walk with crutches. All the more senior American journalists had known about his illness for years, yet no one had ever thought this might be a subject of any interest to the public at large. In other words, there was a comfortable little conspiracy between the press and the government to keep it hidden.

Within just a few years, all that was swept away. Journalists in Britain and the United States no longer saw themselves as junior partners in the business of government, and it became perfectly acceptable to call out tricky questions to prime ministers. Margaret Thatcher, to her credit, was the first to answer them, and she used the technique cleverly and well; I became something of an expert at doorstepping her, though she never liked me. It was partly personal and partly because I worked for the BBC, and entirely mutual. But not liking her wasn't the same as not admiring her; she was, after all, as close as I'm likely to get to Queen Elizabeth I, even if (as Noel Coward said of Winston Churchill, or Churchill said of de Gaulle, or someone else said of someone entirely different) she had more Achilles heels than are usual in a biped.

Anyway, standing on Platform 7 at Euston Station trying to get my breath back, I looked at my watch: it was only five past eleven in the morning of my first working day, and I seemed to have lost my job already.

But I hadn't. Calmer counsels must have prevailed on the express as it headed northward, and no complaint was made about me.

As I say, it was a different world; and one of the compensations for growing older is to understand how much it has changed. In fact, thanks to the job that I didn't after all lose, I have been privileged to see, first-hand, the kinds of changes that were utterly unthinkable that May morning on Platform 7: the collapse of entire empires, of whole systems of thought and behavior. I have been present at thirty-four wars, revolutions and insurrections, and have picked up the odd scar along the way. And not just physically: one marriage and one long-term relationship also appear on the casualty list. A good divorce lawyer would probably have cited the BBC as co-respondent.

I have been blown up and shot at and bombed and arrested and threatened with violent death more times than I can easily remember; and yet the initials BBC, on whose behalf these things happened to me, have often been enough to protect me from further harm. You'd be surprised how many robbers, drug barons, secret policemen and dictators watch and listen to its programs; among them my own inexpensively produced, shoestring *Simpson's World,* which attracts an unthinkably large audience: 240 million, according to one estimate. Colonel Gadhafi, King Abdullah II of Jordan and the emperor of Japan rather like it; Saddam Hussein, I have been told on good authority, watched it but often criticized it. Which sounds ominous.

It has enthusiasts lower down the social scale, too. In June 2001, on the night of the presidential election in Iran, my camera crew and I were rescued from the hands of some very nasty cops indeed by a police general who watched *Simpson's World* regularly. Even the Taliban in Afghanistan, who were so violently hostile to television on the grounds that it created graven images of everyone and everything (contrary to the Holy Koran) that they hanged television sets from the lampposts like convicted felons, were not immune to the BBC's attractions; during a meeting with their foreign minister, Dr Mutawakil, he accidentally let slip that he often watched the program.

It is always a serious mistake, however, for any broadcaster to think that this kind of recognition has anything to do with his or her personal abilities. It is the medium, not the particular messenger, that is responsible. It is the BBC that these people watch, and I just happen to be one of the shadows that pass briefly across its screen. Anyone who gets carried away by a sense of personal significance is an idiot. Like the Roman general celebrating a triumph in the crowded Forum, we would do well to have (at least in our imaginations) a red-painted slave standing behind us in our chariot, whispering in our ear that it is all just luck—that in reality we are utter failures who couldn't present a decent weather report on Kinshasa

Television, and that if we weren't the one in front of the camera it would be someone else, who would probably do the job rather better.

It helps to have worked in radio for twelve years, as I did. No matter how good you are, no one recognizes a radio reporter in the street, and you are the better for it. There is something unpleasantly self-referential about us television performers, as you have no doubt been thinking to yourself as you read my words. No matter how dull and cowardly we are, we know that the viewers invest us with all sorts of qualities we will never possess: brains, sensitivity, kindness, honesty, courage. Journalists in general are not a lovable breed, but television journalists are worse than most.

Some years ago the cartoon strip *Doonesbury* mocked us savagely and with precision, when it showed the standard TV reporter returning from an arduous assignment in Lebanon and going to the local washeteria to launder his clothes.

"I'm a television war correspondent," he confides to another of the strip's standard characters, a clever, sharp-tongued young woman, who is also there doing her laundry.

"I guessed."

"How?"

"I think it was the epaulettes on your underwear," she says.

Exactly. I don't like wars, I don't like the people who do like them, and I particularly don't like being called a war correspondent. It reeks of epaulettes and red scarves knotted around the neck and suede boots with commando soles. One of the best war correspondents I know looks like a Post Office clerk, and one of the best combat cameramen I have ever worked with dresses like a bank manager. During the terrible siege of Sarajevo, which began in 1992, a correspondent who was based there for a long time used to drive around with cardboard signs on his car saying WE WHO ARE ABOUT TO DIE SALUTE YOU and YOU CAN'T KILL ME, I'M IMMORTAL. It was with a certain guilty enjoyment that I heard he'd been shot, fortunately not seriously, and had at once packed his bags and left for home.

It has often been necessary, of course, for someone like me to report on conflict and violence; as you will have noticed, there is a certain amount of it around. Yet there are plenty of other news stories to concentrate on as well—some of them are even moderately encouraging, even if we don't seem to read so much about them. Not just those painful, unrealistic good-news items that you see on television news, where the people speak sentences of five curtailed words and every emotion and motive is so simplified as to be grotesquely caricatured; but interesting, valuable accounts of the lives and efforts of real people.

Television news isn't famous for doing this kind of reporting, any more than it is famous for explaining complicated changes and underlying motivation. But the job can be done, if the will is there. The trouble is, if audience size is the only consideration, and the real arbiters of news values are the dull, suited characters who sit in their offices studying the findings of focus groups and audience surveys, then the result will always be the homogenized, locally obsessed pap that passes for news in so many cities and countries: Newzak, as glitzy, well-produced and empty of meaning or understanding or genuine value as—well, as most television news programs.

It is, I must say, a great relief to work for an organization whose income isn't dependent on the market, and where the judgment of news is based on its significance, not on whether some former rubber-goods salesman thinks it will appeal to a focus group made up of people whose main qualification is that they don't know a lot. The BBC is very far from being perfect, God knows, and its domestic news programs are increasingly under criticism for being too much concerned with British affairs—the dull, trivial mix of consumerism, socio-medicine, crime and small-time local politics that you get on the television services of so many countries. But we have two things in our favor: the largest network of foreign correspondents of any broadcasting organization in the world, and an eighty-year-old tradition of serious news reporting.

If, of course, you are broadcasting primarily to your own national audience, domestic news has to take a certain precedence. Yet on BBC World, our international television service, there is only one criterion: getting the real news to people, the news about their world, in as much breadth and depth as possible. For someone like me, working for it is a genuine liberation.

There is a depressing downward spiral in domestic television news, which is most obvious in the United States but exists everywhere. The less you tell people about the outside world, the less they are interested. The less they are interested, the less they demand. The less they demand, the lower the ratings for anything that falls outside their interest and experience. So you tell them less, and they demand less, and you end up telling them almost nothing about the world they inhabit. The reporting of international news has almost vanished from the American television networks, and, with a few honorable exceptions, American television journalists have become rarities at news stories in the outside world. And then, one fine day, the world comes out of the blue and hits your audience in the face, and they start complaining that you didn't warn them it was going to happen.

Of course you have to take an audience's interests into consideration when you broadcast to them; it's no good boring people or talking over their heads. But you have a certain duty to tell them what they should know, as well as what they want to know. And if this word duty sounds too *dirigiste*, too arrogant, too elitist, I'm sorry. But I don't suppose that if you were going into the hospital for an operation you would expect the surgeons to check out their procedures beforehand with a focus group, or ask you to tick a box for the kind of treatment you would like to have. The real world, as the United States discovered on 11 September 2001, can be a very weird and dangerous place, and those of us who are aware of that have a duty to inform and warn the rest.

Even after the attacks of that day, the main U.S. networks often seemed to ignore reporting from Pakistan or Afghanistan in favor of their State Department and Defense Department correspondents who simply reported, mostly uncritically, on what officialdom wanted them to know. As a direct result of the way the American media reported these events, the BBC's audience in America increased hugely. (Worldwide, it rose at times to 350 million: a third of a billion people.) That such numbers would turn to a foreign television station to tell them what was going on is a pretty powerful indictment of the domestic broadcasters; and in the case of American viewers the BBC received enormous quantities of letters and e-mails, many of them talking about a breath of fresh air.

Wars of any kind, even wars against an abstract noun like terrorism, are always difficult for journalists from the countries involved. Should you act as a cheerleader for your side, keeping up civilian morale and supporting the government of the day in spite of your own private misgivings and the evidence that things may not be going altogether well— or do you try to stay objective, so that your viewers, listeners and readers can make up their own minds about what is going on? I suppose the very way I have framed the question shows what I believe the answer should be. In the case of the United States, where there is a huge reservoir of thoughtful, intelligent people who long for more and better information, the national media acted as a cheerleader to a disturbingly large extent, and left the genuine seekers of information out in the cold.

These are the times when journalists have to stand up and be counted. It's perfectly easy to show an Olympian judgment, balanced and principled, when it's a matter of someone else's war. If the war is your own, it becomes a great deal harder. That, believe me, is the time for sticking to your principles, gritting your teeth, putting your head down and going for it. The majority of people at the time will dislike you for doing it; but afterward, when the emotion has faded and the memory of the government pressure has evaporated, they will thank you. And even if they don't, you will be able to look at yourself in the shaving mirror with no more than the usual amount of distaste.

During the early years of World War II, when the very existence of Britain as an independent nation was in question, the BBC came in for much criticism from government and the public because of its irritating habit of informing people accurately about the battles that British troops were losing, the British cities that were being destroyed and the British ships that were being sunk. The BBC even boasted that it reported these things before the German and Japanese propaganda services could do so. It was no way to court popularity—and yet the BBC became hugely popular, and its news reporting proved to be a remarkable validation for a country that claimed to be fighting for the basic values of democracy. And the way the BBC reported on the war gave it a reputation around the world that has lasted to this day.

You must remember, when you read all this, that I am paid to sing the praises of the outfit, like some antique harpist in the halls of an Irish

chieftain describing the virtues of his host's clan. Yet if it weren't true, I would sing a different set of words; after all, if I can't be honest about the BBC, why should I be honest about anything else I report on? I have often been in trouble with my bosses for criticizing the Beeb, just as I have often been in trouble with British governments for my reporting. No one joins the BBC in order to have an easy time, any more than they join it to get rich. Because it's a public corporation, it pays peanuts and is always under attack from somebody; but, as one of Raymond Chandler's lesser detectives says somewhere, Trouble is my business.

No one forces me or my colleagues to do what we do; we could always get a job presenting the news in a nice, warm, safe studio somewhere if we chose, or go and base ourselves in Switzerland. It just wouldn't be nearly so enjoyable. After all, doing something like taking a walk into Taliban-occupied Kabul ahead of the Northern Alliance forces in November 2001 with only my BBC colleagues for company might have been frightening, but it also was as exhilarating as anything I have ever done. The same, you could say, was true of being forced to swim a river in darkest Amazonia on a moonless night, seven days' journey from the nearest town, or visiting a cocaine market in the depths of Colombia with only a bunch of very nasty guerrillas who didn't care whether we lived or died for protection from the dealers, or rooting around in the deep freeze of the cannibal Emperor Bokassa, who allegedly ate the leader of the opposition in the Central African Empire; or even being bombed by the American air force in Baghdad and Belgrade. It may not have been particularly enjoyable at the time, but it was fine afterward.

This, then, is a book about how I have enjoyed myself over the years. What follows is a distillation of four volumes about my life and hard times, which I published in Britain during the past decade: *The Darkness Crumbles* (1992), *Strange Places, Questionable People* (1998), *A Mad World, My Masters* (2000), and *News from No Man's Land* (2002). My gratitude to all the editors, researchers and others who labored on them with me; to all the cameramen, sound-recordists, picture-editors, producers, translators, fixers and drivers who helped me to report on the events in the pages which follow; to my wife Dee, who is the producer of *Simpson's World* and happily travels with me to the nastiest of places; to her sister

Gina Nelthorpe-Cowne, who (with generous help from her husband Mark) organizes our lives for us; and to their mother Adele Krüger, who allowed me to take over almost her entire house in South Africa for the writing and assembling of this book. It has, you see, become a family enterprise.

—Johannesburg, January 2003

PART ONE

PART ONE

1
Walking to Kabul

What the British public wants first, last and all the time is News.
Remember that the Patriots are in the right and are going to win.
The Beast *stands by them four square. But they must win quickly.*
The British public has no interest in a war which drags on indeci-
sively. A few sharp victories, some conspicuous acts of personal brav-
ery on the Patriot side and a colourful entry into the capital. That
is The Beast *Policy for the war.*
                                    —EVELYN WAUGH, *Scoop*, 1937

The city lay below us in the dawn, as vulnerable as an oyster on the half shell. The date was Tuesday, 13 November 2001.

Kabul, at last. Standing there in the cold, with my flak jacket weighing heavily on me, I couldn't take my eyes off it. For the past three months I had been directing almost every thought, every effort to getting back there.

I had last been in the city in September 2001, just before the attacks on the World Trade Center in New York and the Pentagon in Washington. Then, on 9 September, the Taliban ordered me out and I left, even though they were so disorganized that I could probably have stayed on for a while. It wasn't the finest decision I have ever made. Having been in the right place and left it unnecessarily, I felt that I had something to prove to myself.

Now, after all this waiting, Kabul was only a short walk away.

But there was a problem: the Northern Alliance army, which we had traveled with, had been ordered to stop there on the outskirts of the city rather than enter it. It was clear to me that we would have to disobey these orders and head down into Kabul, even though it was still occupied by the Taliban and their foreign allies, Al-Qa'ida. Would my BBC companions come with me? After living alongside them for so many weeks, I felt pretty certain they would. But it might be risky.

A tough-looking Northern Alliance soldier stood in the roadway, with a red scarf tied around his head and an RPG-7 rocket grenade launcher cradled in his arms. His back was to Kabul, his face toward us. He had orders not to let anyone pass. And yet he wasn't the main obstacle; that was the man in charge of the Northern Alliance advance on Kabul, General Gul Haidar. He had been told by his political bosses that, after smashing through the Taliban front line, he must halt his men at the gates of Kabul and allow a trained force of policemen to enter the city to restore law and order there. The Northern Alliance didn't want a repeat of the street-by-street fighting that went on in Kabul when the mujaheddin were in charge of it last time. No one else, us included, would be allowed in.

Gul Haidar was a pleasant, noisy, ebullient man in his early forties, short and bulky, with a rolling walk like a sailor going down a village high street. He probably had the walk even before he lost his leg to a landmine. When the mad dash of the Northern Alliance to the gates of Kabul was halted, a few minutes earlier, we filmed him haranguing his men, shouting at them and warning that if any of them disobeyed him and headed into Kabul he would kill them. Sulkily, they agreed.

But we weren't Gul Haidar's men. We were free agents, and all we had to do was persuade him to let us pass. After that, we would see if the Taliban would fire on us as we entered the city. I thought probably not, as long as they could see we were journalists and unarmed; but there was no way of finding out, except to try it.

I looked round. In the glorious reds and oranges of dawn arching over us, the vehicles in which the advance party of the Northern Alliance drove down were halted awkwardly all round. We were standing in an open, desert area, where the road went down between some low hills and revealed Kabul below us. It was chilly, and we needed our flak jackets for warmth rather than protection against enemy fire. There was no enemy fire, and we hadn't heard any since the battles of the previous day. Up here, the Taliban had vanished altogether, except for those who were lying dead in the road. The rest were presumably down there in Kabul.

There were eight of us from the BBC altogether, and apart from Anthony Loyd from the *Times* and a freelance photographer, Seamus Murphy, who had been living alongside us for the previous month, I could only see three other journalists: Tony Davis, a wise and wiry Australian who knew the country well and had been a useful source of ideas and advice for me over the past few weeks; and the attractive and dashing Barbara Jones from the *Mail on Sunday,* plus her large, bearded American photographer. Eight Brits, an Irishman, an Australian, an Afghan and a couple of Americans. Maybe, in the tailback of Northern Alliance vehicles, there were other journalists; there were stories about a French photographer—though in my experience there always are stories like that. The world's media had gathered in Afghanistan for the culmination of the entire campaign, but we were the only ones on hand, now that the key moment had arrived.

It wasn't just chance. All of us had shared a determination to be there first rather than to keep with the herd, and we had each in our way sacrificed everything to that determination. In the case of the BBC people, plus Loyd and Murphy, we had lived rough for an entire month close to the front line, in a dirty, cold, shattered building which had been used for years as a public latrine. To be here now represented our reward for all that.

A small red car came screaming up the hill in low gear from the direction of Kabul. It had taken several bullets—in the doors, through the roof. It stopped close to us, and a familiar, dark, hairy head poked through the window on the driver's side: Hajji Bari, the Northern Alliance commander who had been our landlord throughout the previous month. He had been trying to negotiate the surrender of the Taliban in Kabul, and it didn't look as though he'd had much luck.

Hajji was the BBC's secret weapon in this whole enterprise. It was an extraordinary piece of good fortune to have linked up with him. Even the fact of paying him so much money for the privilege of living in his disgusting building counted in our favor now. We had nicknamed him "Hajji Dollar," but he had consistently looked after us and made absolutely sure we were with him and the rest of the Northern Alliance's spearhead force on this morning's mad dash to Kabul. He even gave us his official jeep to make sure no one would stop us.

Instead of his jeep, therefore, he had been driving the little red car, and as Gul Haidar's second in command, he had driven it down the hill into Kabul about twenty minutes earlier, alone except for a single guard, to see if he could ensure a peaceful entry into the city for the Northern Alliance. The bulletholes were the Taliban's response. Hajji was lucky to have escaped with his life, and his eyes were as red as the bodywork with fatigue and fury.

So now we knew what to expect. I turned to the rest of the BBC team: Would they, even so, take a walk with me into the city?

I had been fortunate enough to have the services of two cameramen on this trip. One was Peter Jouvenal, the doyen of Afghan combat journalists: an impressive-looking ex-army man constructed along the general lines of a Victorian explorer-adventurer. I knew what his response would be, because I had been with him on so many other visits to Afghanistan. It was Jouvenal who, against all common sense, accompanied me to Kabul in 1989 when the Communists were in power and the people who smuggled us into the city claimed to have infiltrated the secret police there. They had, but it was a close call. Jouvenal was a careful man and didn't take silly risks, but I couldn't imagine him waving me goodbye as I headed off down the hill alone.

"No point in getting killed," he said as he thought it through.

"Absolutely not. But if we walk down there they'll see we aren't Northern Alliance, and they might not fire at us."

I could see he was tempted. He had often told me about being in the lead helicopter into Kabul in 1992, when the mujaheddin captured the city from the pro-Communist forces. If he comes with me now, I thought, he can make it a set.

I cast around for a way of clinching it, and realized that Joe Phua was standing near us: he was the other cameraman working with me. I had come to like and admire Phua immensely. He belonged to a famous clan of Singapore Chinese television news cameramen: his uncles, cousins and father were all in the business. He had come close to death a couple of weeks ago when a Taliban missile landed right beside his car, but characteristically he had kept on filming. I knew what he was going to say, even before I asked him.

"Sure, no problem."

Yet there was a problem, a serious one. A week or so before, while clambering through a window, Joe had fallen and injured his ankle. It got so bad that we had to call in the local Afghani bone setter several times to sort it out. Joe had been hobbling around ever since, filming away; nothing could stop him. I had been feeding him with the ferocious painkillers my doctor had given me before I left England, and he insisted he was feeling fine. But there was no real way of knowing with Joe; was he really up to a long, fast walk carrying his gear, with Taliban gunmen prepared to open fire on him?

I looked at him as he stood there, tall and rangy, a scarf tied around his head like a pirate from the South China Sea. I honestly didn't think his ankle could take it, but I knew he'd be devastated if I ordered him to stay behind. And he'd probably follow us down the road anyway, which wouldn't do anyone any good.

Then there was Kate Clark, the BBC Kabul correspondent who had been thrown out by the Taliban the previous March because of her reporting. That, of course, was a badge of honor, and yet Kate had something to prove too. Kabul was her patch, and she was determined to get back there, with or without the approval of the Taliban. The reason I had been in Kabul at the beginning of September was to try to persuade them to accept her back. They refused point-blank; so the only way she would be able to return to her office was with the help of the Northern Alliance army. She had endured the hardships of Hajji Bari's boarding house near the front line for an entire month, and she certainly wasn't planning to go back there tonight. She, I knew, would come with us.

Peter Emmerson, standing close to her, checking his recording equipment, was a BBC radio engineer whose skills—diplomatic and journalistic as well as technical—had brought him considerable seniority in the BBC. A quiet, peaceable man in his early forties, with a neatly trimmed beard that reminded me slightly of Napoleon III, he nevertheless hinted at another side of his personality by driving a sky blue Morgan when he was in London. Not that he was in London much. He was always traveling for the BBC to the big international news stories and he didn't just choose the easy ones that involved staying in five-star hotels. Peter was here in Afghanistan because he wanted to be; and beneath the graying beard and gentle, slightly nerdish engineer's appearance there was real grit. No doubt about him.

Nearby, recording the sounds of the occasion on his tape recorder, microphone held high above his head, was the correspondent for domestic radio, Ian Pannell. Thirtyish, pleasant and well-read, he typified the new BBC. In the distant past we used to appoint tough, assertive people to the job of reporter, but gradually we found that those who stayed the course better were not the big, swaggering egos but thoughtful, reflective, intelligent people with a touch of irony and a good sense of humor. Pannell was just such a one. He was a good quarter century younger than me, but I had enjoyed his companionship greatly over the previous month; even at the worst and most uncomfortable of times he had been cheerful and amusing. He had a young family back in London, and I felt I must ask him to think carefully before he agreed to come down into the city. No shame would attach to anyone who felt on reflection that it wasn't a good idea, I told him. I was wasting my breath. Before I had half finished the sentence he was nodding vigorously.

No doubts, either, about the last but one member of the team. John Jennings was a completely different character from the rest of us, with a completely different background. He wasn't even employed by the BBC. He was an American freelance writer, and a former member of the U.S. Marine Corps who nowadays worked in an ER unit at a New York hospital. I knew him through Jouvenal: he used to live in Peshawar, on the North-West Frontier of Pakistan, and was an expert on Afghan politics. He spoke good Dari, and had been our translator when we hunted down an Afghan warlord who was responsible for many crimes and had come to settle in, of all places, Mitcham, in southeast London. Jennings was an ideal member of the team. He could translate for us, and if we got hurt, he could patch us up.

The final member of the group was our Afghan translator, Khalil. Kate

Clark had bumped into him on the street, in a little town we passed through on our way southward from the Tajikistan border a month ago. Khalil was a medical student whose studies were brought to an end by the arrival in power of the Taliban. His English was pretty good, and he had a relaxed and easy way about him which meant he never grumbled about the privations and dangers of working on the front line. He would certainly come with us now. I looked at him: He nodded.

Eight of us, and we were all in agreement. Having come so far and stuck together so long, no one felt like dropping out. But there was the slight problem of the armored personnel carrier parked across the road, and the man with the RPG-7 who had orders not to let anyone pass. There had been, it was true, a certain leakage from the Northern Alliance forces who had gathered there at the entrance to the city. Every now and then you could see individual soldiers wrapping their long *patous*, their dun-colored blankets, around themselves and slipping past the sentry down the road into the city. Perhaps they were Kabulis who were planning to lose themselves in the crowds and quietly rejoin their families. But there weren't many of them.

This was the critical moment. If we were stopped here now, it could be hours before we got down to Kabul. The vast army of journalists, based well behind the lines, would have a chance to catch up with us, and our month-long effort to be in the vanguard would be squandered.

And then Gul Haidar's car drove slowly past us, and he made the mistake of winding down the window.

"Hullo, Peter," he said.

For him, Jouvenal was always the chief among us.

"Go on, Peter," I hissed. "Tell him we want to go into Kabul."

Peter was crucial as far our relations with Gul Haidar were concerned. The two men knew each other extremely well. When they had first met, in the early 1980s, Jouvenal was merely a young and inexperienced photographer, but Gul Haidar was already a first-class guerrilla leader in the mujaheddin resistance. Before the Russians invaded Afghanistan in December 1978, he had been a butcher in Kabul. Afterward he turned himself into a butcher of Russians. It was his habit to creep into Soviet bases during the night, slit the throats of the unfortunate sentries, and bring out their weapons. On one occasion he trod on a landmine on his way in and lost his leg. Jouvenal, even though he had very little money in those days, paid for him to be brought to London and fitted with a prosthetic leg. Possession of this leg gave Gul Haidar greater prestige than ever among the Afghani mujaheddin. He rose quickly in the estimation of the leaders, and now he was the general in charge of the assault on Kabul. Being an Afghan, he could never forget a debt of honor.

Sitting in the passenger seat of his car, he pursed his lips. I could tell what he was thinking.

"He says it's too dangerous," said Jouvenal.

"But will he stop us if we go on foot?"

Jouvenal put the question to him. Gul Haidar puffed out his cheeks and spread his thick butcher's hands, the hands that had slit so many Russian throats.

"Well, if you're going to go on foot . . ."

He couldn't refuse Jouvenal. Leaning farther out of the window, he shouted an order: a soldier would go with us, to give us a bit of protection.

Maybe I should have invited the other newspaper journalists to go too, but I didn't. Although I liked them a lot, I didn't intend to share our good luck—Gul Haidar's debt of honor to Jouvenal, for instance, or our links with Hajji Dollar—with anyone else. My job was to make sure we were the unquestioned leaders. The BBC would be in Kabul first.

As it happened, the BBC was there already. One of Kate Clark's predecessors as Kabul correspondent, William Reeve, had managed to use his contacts with the Taliban to get them to allow him back in a few days earlier. Willie, a polo player and a definite eccentric, had done two difficult tours of duty in Kabul and knew the Taliban well. In the meantime, Rageh Omaar, a correspondent who had previously worked in the outfit of which I am the nominal head, the BBC's World Affairs Unit, had persuaded a group of Muslims to take him to Kabul as well. Rageh had been brought up and educated in Britain, but his family came from Somalia. He was charming and well read but with an underlying toughness, like the rest of the new breed of correspondent. He had taken a big risk by mobilizing his Muslim links to get him to Kabul, and it had paid off handsomely. With the two of them was another cameraman I enjoy working with, Fred Scott, a quiet, extremely witty Californian who lived in London.

The three of them had had a difficult time once they got to Kabul; a nearby house had been hit by an American bomb just as Willy Reeve was in the middle of an on-camera broadcast from the BBC office. The pictures were spectacular: the wall and ceiling seemed to be coming in, and Willy shouted, "Jesus Christ!"—quite restrained under the circumstances, people felt. The enterprise and drive which had gotten two correspondents and a cameraman into Kabul had been the BBC's best single achievement in the entire series of events that had begun on 11 September.

All of us who worked for the organization abroad knew by this stage, 13 November 2001, that the crisis that had begun two months earlier had pitchforked the BBC into a position of outright dominance in the business of international television news. The audience for *BBC World*, the poorly funded yet most admired jewel in our broadcasting crown, had swelled to a third of a billion people worldwide. What was required now, I felt, was some sort of capstone on the entire achievement; and here it was. We would go ahead of the Northern Alliance into Kabul and join our colleagues there.

It wasn't the moment for making a Shakespearean speech. I set off down the hill, confident that the others would follow me and that no one would stop us. I grinned at the man with the RPG-7, and he stood aside to let us pass. The road ran steeply downward between two bald, dusty hillocks. There was Kabul lying before us, a colorless sprawl of mud brick innocent of suburbs or high-rise buildings, looking like a monochrome steel engraving in an early Victorian travel book. This must have been Kabul precisely as Alexander Burnes had seen it when he reached this point in 1839. Bokhara Burnes was a famous Central Asia explorer who was destined to die in the Afghan uprising of 1841, when the British Army of India was wiped out. *Absit omen*, I told myself.

But I had no sense of foreboding. Instead, I felt as though the burdens of the past two months had lifted off me. My heavy flak jacket scarcely weighed on me at all now; I had shed twenty-five years and was a young man again, with everything to play for.

This first part of the road was pretty steep, and we headed down it at quite a rate. It was obvious to me that the others weren't tamely going to let me go first: it was turning into a kind of race. There were a few local people around, standing and watching us, cheering and shouting as they realized who we were and what organization we represented. Seventy-five percent of the population of Afghanistan listened to the Farsi and Pashtu services of the BBC, and when they understood how we came to be walking down this road, they started going crazy, shouting and waving their arms and trying to shake our hands. I turned to look at Ian Pannell, who was striding alongside me, holding up his radio mike to record the noise of greeting.

"Get a shot of him," I shouted to Joe Phua, who was hobbling down the hill as fast as he could, keeping up with Ian and filming him. I was determined that this should be a BBC achievement—no point in all our travails together if it was turned into something personal, and something exclusively about television.

The crowds were getting bigger and noisier, and I could hear them shouting "BBC London," both greeting us and explaining to each other who this strange regiment of people were. They knew from the fact that we were there that the Northern Alliance must be close behind us, and that they had been liberated from the rule of the Taliban. Hands reached out to grab me, shake my hand, touch my flak jacket.

After all the waiting, all the fear, all the anxiety about failure and being beaten by our opposition, a superb sense of elation built up inside me, and I raised my arms to greet the crowds, forcing my way through them. A bus was stuck in the throng, and everyone inside it who could get an arm through the windows tried to touch me. I grabbed as many hands as I could, laughing with the relief and pleasure of it all. To be the first journalists out of so many to enter the most closed and difficult city on earth—it was a superb moment.

Ahead, I could see the sign in the middle of the road that marked the boundary of the city. Peter Emmerson was a little ahead of me, as he had been for much of our walk. I sped up, wanting to be the first to pass it.

Childish, of course; after all, what did it matter which of us got past the marker first? But I was still in the grip of the fierce will to win, which we had all experienced and which had brought us all here, far ahead of our competitors.

My legs were becoming painful with the effort of walking downhill so fast, so laden with body armor and the rest of my gear. A small piece of jagged blue lapis lazuli, which I had bought in the Charikar market a few days ago and brought with me partly for good luck and partly so the Afghans wouldn't steal it back at our base, was making a painful bruise where it rubbed on my thigh. No matter: these small pains merged into the wider sense of freedom and achievement. I looked at my watch: 7:53 A.M. Kabul was no longer a Taliban city, and no one had fired a shot at us.

2
Wandering

After a long and toilsome march, weary of the way, [the wanderer] drops into the nearest place of rest to become the most domestic of men. . . . But soon the passive fit has passed away; again a parox-ysm of ennui coming on by slow degrees, Viator loses appetite, he walks about his room all night, he yawns at conversations, and a book acts upon him as a narcotic. The man wants to wander, and he must do so, or he shall die.
—Sir Richard Burton, *Personal Narrative of a Pilgrimage to El-Medinah and Meccah,* 1855

Overhead the clouds were as dark and bunched as a boxer's fist, and just as threatening. There was a rich, hot dampness in the atmosphere. Drops of darkish water hung on the lush bushes from the last down-pour. I had to watch where I walked: the road surface was crumbling away, and some of the puddles were deep. My hair hung limply over my forehead, and I could feel the drops of sweat working their way down my back.

I was covering the war in Angola—this was in 1976—from the side of the Marxist MPLA in Luanda, and having a difficult time of it. Most military regimes impose tight controls on the movement of journalists, and with so many advisers from East Germany, Cuba and the Soviet Union, the MPLA had become particularly good at it. Slipping out of Luanda at a time of siege took careful planning and a certain amount of luck, therefore, since they thought we were all spies. Not long before I arrived, an American journalist had been thrown out for sending a mes-sage to his office:

Everything short here. Send bottled water, as shaving in Coca-Cola difficult.

The head of the government information service, an intelligent but rather sinister man named Luis de Almeida, decided that this could only be a coded message to the CIA.

I managed to get a lift to the outskirts of Luanda. The word was that the Cuban troops who were in Angola had a base out here somewhere, just a mile or so from the edge of Luanda. It would, I thought, make an interesting story. I was always getting ideas like that.

The soldiers who were guarding the bridge ahead of me were relaxed. They grinned at me. Their uniforms were tattered, and their boots, unlaced as ever, were too big for their skinny ankles. One of them held out a beer bottle to me and gestured with his other arm that I come and join them. I grinned back without accepting; you never knew what these Angolan soldiers put in beer bottles.

In Africa soldiers usually treat you pleasantly and do what you ask them. It may cost a cigarette or two, but that's all. There is a natural politeness and deference to the foreigner. When things go wrong, it's another matter.

A big sergeant stood on the bridge, his olive green MPLA fatigues black with sweat under the arms and across the chest. There was nothing remotely polite or deferential about him. He shifted a bottle from hand to hand and watched me, red-eyed, as I toiled up the slight incline toward him.

Below the bridge a river swirled slickly along, gathering branches and leaves and bits of detritus as it went. The waters were a paler version of the red earth all around us.

"*Bom dia*." This exhausted most of my stock of Portuguese.

The sergeant merely grunted. I looked round: taking their cue from him, the soldiers looked less friendly now. They gathered to listen.

The sergeant asked me for something I couldn't understand. Money? A cigarette? Since I had no cigarettes and little money, all of which I wanted to keep, I played for time. I reached for my accreditation, an oblong of plastic with an unconvincing photograph of me on it and an official's illegible signature underneath. The sergeant scarcely looked at it. He gestured for more. This was when I made my big mistake. I gave him my passport.

There was something about it that the sergeant didn't like. Maybe it was the royal coat of arms on the front, maybe it was the little paper windows for my name and the passport number. He opened it contemptuously and flicked through it. Sometimes he held it upside down: not a good sign. Then he jammed my Angolan press accreditation inside it, and flicked it deftly over his shoulder.

"But . . ."

I watched the little dark blue book spin up into the damp air, opening as it went and releasing the accreditation. Then they both fell together and hit the reddish brown water of the river a few inches apart. There was scarcely a splash. They tumbled over and over each other, and disappeared behind a rock.

"*Molt' obrigado.*" That represented virtually the last of my Portuguese, and I put as much irony into it as I could.

The sergeant ignored me. His men laughed loudly and obsequiously, as though he had done something particularly witty. By his standards, perhaps he had. I made a play of writing it all down in my notebook, as though I were getting together the material for an official complaint, but it was wasted on them. So was the shouting I did; they just laughed even louder.

I was devastated. At that stage in my life I still believed that there was powerful magic in a passport—that it somehow represented my identity, my selfhood. Maybe I also believed that pompous little coda on the inside front cover about Requesting and Requiring in the Name of Her Majesty. I probably even thought that if I got into trouble abroad, the British Embassy would try to do something about it. I was inexperienced in those days.

There really is nothing very significant about a passport. When the old hard-backed dark blue version began to be phased out during the 1980s in favor of the smaller, softer red European one, many British people were outraged. They felt their national as well as their personal identity had been weakened and somehow compromised.

This merely showed how much we have forgotten about our own

national past. From the end of the Napoleonic Wars in 1815 to the outbreak of the First World War a century later, it was the chief distinguishing mark of British citizens abroad that they didn't carry a passport. They went where they wanted, merely announcing themselves at border crossings and being allowed through because they were British.

In 1875 Frederick Gustavus Burnaby, the biggest and strongest soldier in the British Army, traveled across Russia to the forbidden central Asian city of Khiva, carrying an out-of-date *laissez-passer* from the Russian embassy in London, but no passport. He started his journey at Victoria Station, and when his train reached the German-Russian border, he and the others in his compartment, who included a Russian diplomatic secretary, had to get out.

> A few minutes later I found myself, with the rest of the passengers, in a large high hall, set aside for the examination of luggage and inspection of passports.
>
> It was not a pleasant thing to be kept waiting in a cold room for at least three-quarters of an hour, whilst some spectacled officials suspiciously conned each passport. The Russian secretary himself was not at all impressed with the wisdom of his Government in still adhering to this system, which is so especially invented to annoy travellers. "What nonsense it is," he remarked; "the greater scoundrel a man is the greater certainty of his passport being in the most perfect order. Whenever I go to France, and am asked for my passport, I avoid the difficulty by saying, 'Je suis anglais; no passport;' and the officials, taking me for an Englishman, do not bother me, or make me show it."

So the way you demonstrated that you were British was by not being able to prove it. As Thomas Paine said about the wearing of clothes, the carrying of a passport is simply a sign of our fall from grace; and in the case of British people it is a very real come-down: a sign of Britain's fall in the world, rather than something to boast about.

That most British of twentieth-century statesmen, Ernie Bevin, understood this perfectly well. Shortly before his death in 1951 the *Spectator* asked him about his foreign policy. He answered, "My policy is to be able to take a ticket at Victoria Station and go anywhere I damn well please." In other words, just like Frederick Gustavus Burnaby three quarters of a century earlier, Bevin meant he wanted a world without the paraphernalia of modern controls: this at a time when Central and Eastern Europe was closed to Westerners, and China had turned Communist (and had been recognized reluctantly by Bevin himself, who famously said afterwards, "I didn't ought never to have done it.") Passports, visas, the compulsory possession of a return ticket, and so on are simply the ways by which international bureaucracy stops us going anywhere we damn well please.

It was in Africa that I first began to understand these things.

When I got back in Luanda after the loss of my passport, Luis de Almeida shrugged his shoulders, and ticked me off for going out alone.

"At least they didn't take your tape recorder."

I wished they had; I could cross borders without a tape recorder.

At the British embassy there was a big chain and padlock on the embassy gates when I went there, and a sign advising British citizens to seek help from the Swiss embassy. There was a chain and padlock on the Swiss embassy too, but no sign. Back at the Angolan foreign ministry the officials were pleasant but scarcely helpful. If they gave me a piece of paper to travel with, one of them reasoned, it would be tantamount to accepting that something had happened to my passport.

"But it has."

Again the smile, the shrugged shoulders, the expressive hands held out, palms upward. I began to think I might have to stay in Angola for a very long time.

That evening one of the other correspondents, hearing of my problem, told me that somewhere in Luanda there was still a solitary Western honorary consul: a Dutchman, he thought. I looked up the name in a pre-war phone book and drove out to meet him. He was indeed the honorary Dutch consul, and he turned out to be in his mid-fifties, stout, inclined to sweat heavily, and very jolly. He had stayed behind when all the other Westerners left, he said, because he liked the place: no other reason. Oh, yes, and he could still make money. An attractive young *mestis* woman in a T-shirt and shorts brought in a tray with tiny cups of excellent Angolan coffee. He winked.

"Maybe there are some other reasons too." He pronounced it "udder."

Reaching into an untidy drawer he pulled out a sheet of official note paper.

"We make dis look good."

He put it into an old-fashioned typewriter. Sweat made splashes on the desk as he hammered at the keys, sometimes pausing and going back over what he had already written. In the end he did that satisfying trick, now obsolete in the days of word processors and printers, and pulled the paper out of the carriage with a ripping sound and the sense of something achieved.

"Dere you are."

It wasn't merely good; it was magnificent. Her Majesty the Queen of the Netherlands greeted whomever might read this document and assured them that Mr. John Cody Fidler-Simpson, a representative of the British Broadcasting Corporation, was a citizen of the United Kingdom, being a member of the European Economic Community, and should be accorded any help he might request; by the power vested in the Hon. Consul as Her Majesty's Representative in Angola, etc., etc.

There was no photograph to be countersigned by a justice of the peace, no date of birth, no place to write in my next of kin, and no rules about who, precisely, could be a British citizen and why people who had always thought they were could no longer claim the full package. It was just a piece of paper.

"Do you think I'll really be able to travel with this?" It sounded ungrateful.

"I don't see why not."

He was right. I traveled across Africa and Europe for more than a month after that, producing my increasingly tattered and furry piece of paper at each border crossing and having it accepted without question everywhere I went. Eventually one of the eight segments into which it was folded separated from the rest and I lost it. That meant that part of the honorary consul's signature was gone, and at least a quarter of his official stamp. It still didn't matter: I was allowed out of Germany and back into Britain on the basis of the remaining seven-eighths.

The immigration officer at Heathrow peered at a couple of the stamps.

"You seem to have been traveling round quite a lot."

I half expected him to call for help, or put me on a plane to somewhere else. Instead he folded the paper carefully, and handed it to me with a wry look.

"It might be easier to get the real thing."

It was, of course. I wrote a long letter to the Passport Office explaining everything, and put my dog-eared *laissez-passer* away in a drawer somewhere. It might have been falling apart, but it was still valid; the Dutch consul in Luanda had forgotten to put an expiration date on it.

There are three bad times: the night before you leave for somewhere difficult, and you sit with your lover or your family trying to behave entirely normally in order to show how safe everything is going to be; the following morning, when the car comes to take you to the airport; and the moment when the plane touches down at your destination. Of all these moments, the last is by far the worst. It is also more unpleasant than anything you are likely to experience later.

Even if you find yourself under long, intensive shelling, which is the nastiest thing I know, or are attacked by an angry crowd, which is the second nastiest, it never quite matches that dreadful sense of foreboding when the plane jolts, the tires scream, and the trip begins to unfold: the separation from the comfortable, safe, familiar world of an aircraft, the cold air, the uncertainty of standing in line at the immigration desk, defenseless against all the fears you have been suppressing. And of course if shelling, arrest, or angry crowds materialize—and they usually don't—you are much too busy to worry about the outcome.

All of this is a kind of comfort in itself. Knowing that your arrival is likely to be the worst thing that happens makes everything easier. You become phlegmatic, relaxed, undisturbed.

"Aren't you excited about going?" my wife, Dee—the Memsahib, as I call her—asks me; or alternatively, "Aren't you worried?"

She has worked alongside me for newspapers and television in all sorts of difficult places, from Bosnia to Nigeria, and before she met me she covered the South African townships for the BBC, and they can be more dangerous than almost anywhere else on earth. Nowadays she is the producer on my program for BBC World, called *Simpson's World*, and therefore she goes with me almost everywhere, whether pleasant or dangerous. (Not long ago I had an angry letter from a mullah in Egypt, who wrote: "Always you are calling this world your world. You must know the world belong only to GOD. To say Simpson World is dishonor to GOD.") Traveling with Dee has brought an entirely new dimension of enjoyment to my job. But she still asks me if I am excited or worried.

The answer is that I am not, because things so rarely turn out as you expect. I have arrived in Baghdad, expecting to be taken hostage or even executed, and have found myself treated with the greatest courtesy. I have been on a routine trip to China, looking forward to an interesting few days of diplomatic reporting, and found myself still there a month later, lying in a gutter with bullets cracking a foot or two above my head.

The trouble with real life, as you may have noticed, is that it isn't like the movies. Happy endings usually turn out to be neither happy, nor proper endings. This is one of the reasons why, like the movies, tabloid journalism bears no relationship to life as we know it; it is too extreme, too lacking in complexity. There are too few categories of existence. The people the tabloids write about are either two-dimensionally glamorous or successful, or they are victims, or they are "evil"; and the characters in the heartwarming stories that the tabloids love have to live happily ever after.

None of us ever looks as good or acts as well as we would like. And when we find ourselves in danger, there is no low, disturbing minor-key music on the soundtrack to warn us that something is just about to happen. We are just as likely to get into trouble on a bright spring morning as on a dark night, and the people we meet along the way will probably smile at us and wave. Until, that is, the trouble starts.

So if the only thing you know is that you cannot know anything about what will happen, it has a remarkably calming effect. You become like some grizzled sergeant-major, an old campaigner who prepares for the worst and actively relishes every quiet, pleasurable moment that comes his way. As Mr. Salter tells William Boot in *Scoop*: "There are two invaluable rules for a special correspondent—Travel Light and Be Prepared. Have nothing which in an emergency you cannot carry in your own hands. But remember that the unexpected always happens."

The dull sameness that afflicts the shopping malls of the world has not yet started to seep into airports. Not, at any rate, too much. Heathrow is haphazard and utterly unplanned, yet manages at times to be surprisingly stylish. Charles de Gaulle is built around a single concept, which sometimes makes life easier and sometimes not, and it is the only major airport I know to have a fully stocked antiques shop. Miami has three times as many stalls selling ice cream as bookshops, there are no baggage trolleys because the porters won't permit them, and it is horribly difficult to make an international phone call. At JFK I have had to carry two heavy suitcases half a mile between terminals in the summer's heat because the porters refused to do it and I couldn't find a taxi driver who was prepared to take me. Smaller American airports—Minneapolis, for instance, or Dallas-Fort Worth—are usually charming.

At Rio de Janeiro you can doze for hours in comfortable seats (even if you can't talk your way into one of the airline lounges). You can have a shave and a haircut for almost nothing, borrow books to while away the time from the excellent bookshop, and sip *caipirinhas*, those wonderful Brazilian cocktails whose name means "little country girls," and smoke the strange, sometimes wayward Brazilian cigars. I would rather spend a day in Rio de Janeiro Airport than any other airport on earth. For that matter I would rather spend a day in Rio than anywhere else.

There are dreadful airports like Delhi and Beijing, neat and agreeable ones like Helsinki and Amsterdam, graceless ones like Frankfurt, and ludicrously planned ones like Munich. One or two, in the words of the Michelin guide, *vaut le voyage*—they are worth a journey in themselves: Singapore, Barcelona and Kansai in Japan for instance. A pleasant and interesting airport like Buenos Aires or Bogota is a pleasure to pass through. They're not particularly fast or well organized, but the shops are interesting, the food is edible, and the system works in an easy-going kind of way.

The most exciting airport in the world used to be Kai Tak at Hong Kong. Even though I dislike being trapped in an inside seat on a long journey, I always used to ask for "window" rather than "aisle" on a Hong Kong flight. Arriving there was the great flying experience. As the plane came in over the crowded suburb of Mong Kok, the highrise buildings crowded in on either side until you were actually looking up at the inhabitants on their minuscule balconies, watching them hanging out the washing. The noise in that narrow canyon was mind-numbing.

"How can you bear to live here?" I asked a man in Mong Kok shortly before Kai Tak Airport was closed down forever. He was a cook, and wore a white coat with orange and brown stains down the front. His English was scarcely comprehensible, but he was the only person on the whole street who seemed able to speak it.

I had to repeat the question, because another plane went overhead so close I felt I could read the small print on the wings or recognize the passengers' faces at the windows, strained or excited like riders on a fairground ride.

"It is very comfortable," said the cook. "We know every plane. When they are not flying, it feels different—not so good. If you live here, you live with aeroplanes."

For the pilots, Kai Tak was the last really interesting place in the world to land. The captain traditionally took control as soon as Hong Kong appeared in front of the plane, and he would know exactly when to heel over and raise one wing high, allowing for the difficult crosswinds.

Of course it couldn't last. Nothing in Hong Kong does—not even the skyline, not even the view from the Peninsula Hotel, not even British rule. The terminal building at Kai Tak, an excellent example of 1950s airport architecture, was eventually closed. Nowadays the new airport at Chek Lap Kok, on Lantau Island, is a larger version of Stansted Airport, rational and quiet and pleasant, a kind of genetically modified airport created with the help of focus groups and in-depth passenger surveys. The taxi journey, across some of the world's most exciting bridges, is extraordinary; so is the price. Chek Lap Kok is closed much more often than Kai Tak ever was, thanks to the winds, and landing there can be just as alarming but lacks the charm.

Things happen at airports. At the one in Kinshasa, a terrible place, I hid in the disgusting lavatories from the white mercenaries who were hunting for me. At Frankfurt Airport I encountered a Soviet agent who—to my surprise—told me his whole story on camera. At Brussels Airport, deserted and late at night, I realized I had left my passport behind and was only able to catch the last plane by crawling on my hands and knees below the eyeline of the immigration officer, who was reading a sex magazine. At Blantyre Airport in Malawi the soldier searching me found I had 2,000 times the amount of money I was permitted to take out of the country, but he let me keep it because I worked for the BBC. At Lima Airport we were warned privately by the Peruvian vice president that a government agent was going to plant cocaine on us as we left, but we made such a public fuss about the possibility that nothing happened.

In 1989, I spent six weeks in Afghanistan, living rough and traveling across mountainous country to reach Kabul, where the cameraman Peter Jouvenal and I stayed for three days and then escaped shortly before the security police could capture us. On our way back through the mountains, a mujaheddin leader, in tribute to our escape, gave me a Russian bayonet as a keepsake. I tucked it into my kitbag and forgot about it.

We had a harrowing drive through the snow-covered mountains along the border with Pakistan, and I thought I was a dead man several times before we finally made it to the Khyber Pass, and safety. At Peter's house in Peshawar I stripped off my stinking clothes and prepared to wash in hot water for the first time in a month and a half. It was a pleasure simply watching the steam rising from the shower. I introduced my right foot into the hot water.

Then the phone rang.

"It's your office in London," Peter shouted. "They say they want you back there as quick as possible."

Struggling with a towel, I took the phone. There was a stream of instructions from the other end: times of planes, road distances, estimates of possible arrival. The only things I grasped properly were that the plane was full except in first class, and that I would have to leave right away. I turned the shower off without getting into it, and put my filthy clothes back on. They, and I, still hadn't been washed for six weeks.

The taxi journey to Islamabad Airport lasted an hour and a half, and was a nightmare. The Grand Trunk Road, straight and tree lined, is a splendid route for a lover of Kipling, but by night it can be terribly dangerous, with unlit cars, trucks and cyclists suddenly rearing up in the headlights. I had borrowed a very large banknote from someone, and every time the driver slackened his pace I would fold it up in a marked kind of way, put it in my pocket, and say, "What a pity you aren't going to earn this now." But he did earn it. He got me there thirty-five minutes before the Swissair flight was supposed to leave.

Running through the airport with my heavy kitbag took time, and made me sweatier and if anything smellier than ever. I threw it onto the X-ray machine, went through the metal detector and stood waiting for it.

Someone shouted something in Urdu. Someone else translated.

"You have some kind of large knife. This is a dangerous weapon. We must report it."

I explained, still out of breath: Russian bayonet—given me by mujaheddin leader—no problem—pacifist myself—desperate to get to London for BBC—couldn't they just overlook it?

Dubiously, they agreed that they could overlook it as long as I promised not to get it out of my kitbag during the flight. God bless the British Raj, I thought, and promised with enormous sincerity.

"Sir, you'll have to run now. You might just be able to get on board."

I picked up the kitbag, which seemed heavier than ever, and stumbled out across the tarmac. Ahead of me, they were just starting to wheel the steps away from the aircraft.

"Hey! Stop! I'm coming! I have to catch the flight! Please!"

Maybe the sight of this wild creature, clothes fluttering, carrying a kitbag the size and weight of a dead body in his arms and smelling like a detachment of mujaheddin affected them with pity: I had clearly been touched by Allah. They pushed the steps back up. I stamped my way heavily up them, completely done, and reached the top. A Swissair stewardess stood there. She looked as though everything she had ever worn had been ironed three times before she put it on, and she didn't like the look of me.

"We are closing this flight," she said disapprovingly.

"First class," I said, and I didn't mean it as a term of approval.

The stewardess reacted as though I had confided to her that I owned

Blenheim Palace. But I was still gripping the wonderful red boarding pass, and she could see that.

"Well, I suppose—"

She let me on board.

Heads still turned to look at me. Having stuffed the kitbag into a cupboard, I stretched out at full length in my seat. I was breathing pretty heavily, and such sweating as I had done before was a mild trickle to what I did now. The Swiss businessman beside me looked as though a dog had fouled the seat.

"Hot, isn't it?" I said with an engaging smile.

Actually, since it was February, there was snow on the runway. He looked away with a shudder, and moved as far away as a first-class seat will allow; a lot farther, that is, than a tourist-class seat, but still within smelling range. I grabbed the glass of champagne which the stewardess brought me, and drank it down in one gulp.

"First drink in six weeks," I confided to the cabin at large, and laughed from pure relief. Even to my own ears I sounded a bit loud.

The Swiss businessman reached up and pressed the call button.

"I would like another seat," he said.

I have, of course, had plenty of bad flights in my time. Once, setting off for a trip in a small plane in Mexico, my colleagues and I solemnly shook hands with one another in case we didn't get the chance again, and to show that there were no hard feelings. We were going to fly over difficult territory with a pilot who was a lapsed alcoholic.

In Brazil I flew in a single-engine plane over the jungle with the sole survivor of a team of seven pilots. Each time one of them had crashed, he said, he had replaced parts of his own plane from the wreckage.

"So you're a mechanic?"

"No, not at all," he answered, and hooted with laughter.

At such a time, looking out at the forest canopy as it reaches unbroken for hundreds of miles in every direction like the surface of the ocean, you find yourself listening very carefully to the note of the engine.

During the Iran-Iraq War I flew over the Mesopotamian desert in a helicopter belonging to the Iranian air force. Before we left, the pilot had tried to keep down the payload by turning people away, but they merely dodged around to the other side and climbed on there; so he eventually shrugged and ignored the problem. Most of us were Western journalists who had to get back to file our material, though there were also at least a dozen injured soldiers who needed urgent medical care.

The helicopter was an ancient American one for which the Iranians had received no spares for a long time. It shook and shuddered as it took off, and ran much farther down the improvised runway than usual. At the end was a grove of palm trees, and we flew so low over them that I could see the individual dates clustered under the fronds.

It was late afternoon, but still appallingly hot. We were all crushed in together, and my left foot was twisted painfully underneath my right leg. The only good thing was that I could see out of the window.

"If I ever get out of this alive, I'll sink a couple of really cold beers," said the Australian cameraman jammed in beside me.

"Islamic beers," I answered sourly.

Islamic beer is the disgusting nonalcoholic malt drink you get in Iran. Alcohol is forbidden.

"I forgot," he said.

The helicopter ground along for another three-quarters of an hour. We were safe by now from Iraqi anti-aircraft guns, and were flying too low to be in danger from fighters. I could see the ridges of sand rippling away to the horizon, an angry yellow red in the dying sunshine.

"Only about another fifteen minutes," said the cameraman who wanted a cold beer.

"Thank God," said someone, probably me.

I was still looking down. The ridges of sand seemed somehow less precise now. I stared at them, trying to work out what it was. Maybe my eyesight was blurring? Or had the window become smeared?

"Christ, quite a sandstorm starting up down there," said the cameraman.

It seemed to mount toward us as we flew on, a body of thick, reddish cloud that wrapped around us like a sheet and penetrated the helicopter so that our eyes became sore and the grains of sand grated between our teeth.

On the flight deck, which was open, the three crew members were starting to shout at each other. By twisting my head and easing one leg round I could watch them.

"Bloody pilots falling out among themselves," said the cameraman. "All we need."

My limited Farsi indicated that they were blaming each other for allowing so many of us to climb aboard. Then the argument became fiercer. It seemed as though they were trying to decide whether to put down in the desert at once, or attempt to make the final thirty miles or so to the air force base. One of them shouted into the radio, then pushed his mike aside in disgust: we had lost radio contact. If we crashed now, no one would even know where we were.

The note of the rotor blades suddenly seemed to be different. The sand was obviously clogging the engine. More angry discussion among the crew. Then two of them raised their hands: they were voting, and the navigator, who wanted to put down here in the desert, lost. He buried his head in his hands.

"*Allah-u akbar!*" shouted the pilot.

It didn't instill confidence.

We limped on heavily, losing height. We all thought now that we would crash before we got anywhere near the base.

Strangely, there is a kind of comfort in being up against it to this extent. There is, after all, nothing you can do. I couldn't even find the room to move, let alone wrest the controls out of the pilot's hands. There was no point in wracking my brain for some kind of solution, because there was no solution. Either we got there, or we didn't: the next ten minutes would tell.

I thought idly about the arrangements I had always planned to make about my funeral, and had never got around to: where it was to take place, the guests for dinner afterward, the instruction to everyone to enjoy themselves and remember the good times. I was just starting to imagine how the different mourners would behave, when the pilot shouted out again.

"*Allah-u akbar!*"

This time it sounded different. He was pointing through the windscreen at something. It could only be the base.

"Looks as though we're nearly there," I said to the cameraman.

He looked as emotionless and flat as I felt.

"Oh, great."

"You still won't be able to get a beer."

"That's what I was thinking."

I like the atmosphere of a big hotel: the neat young women at the reception desk, the older porters who walk on the sides of their shoes, the watchful managers, the discreet chambermaids, the room-service waiters who pretend to be surprised when you tip them. Except for the very worst and the very smallest, there is a basic similarity between hotels, regardless of size and cost. The people who work in them tend to believe in what they are doing (this can include even the ghastly old Soviet-era hotels of provincial Russia) and when times are hard they can show a remarkable devotion to the ideal of service.

At the Holiday Inn in Sarajevo in the dreadful winter of 1992 the waiters wore dinner jackets and white shirts with bow ties even though there was no water, no soap and no way of drying anything; and they made their way to and from work to the accompaniment of the sniper's rifle and the mortar bomb. At the Commodore in Beirut in 1982 the housekeeper made sure every guest had clean laundry every morning, despite the constant artillery barrage. At the Europa in Belfast, the most-bombed hotel in the world, they kept the nightclub going throughout the 1970s as though they were in the South of France, and the kitchen provided an excellent room-service steak only twenty minutes after each new bomb scare.

The telephonists at the Laleh Hotel in Tehran would stay up all the night trying to get international calls for the guests. At the Mandarin Hotel in Jakarta, during the disturbances of 1998, Chinese members of staff continued to arrive for work and were unfailingly polite and cheerful to the hotel guests, even though a few hundred yards away the mobs were burning Chinese people to death in the streets. At the Carrera in Santiago in the 1980s the waiters pretended not to notice when you staggered in after an anti-Pinochet rally, stinking of tear gas and dripping with water heavily laced with sewage, and demanded a stiff gin and tonic. You can forgive a hotel the odd overbilling or the occasional lost sock if it rises to the occasion like this.

Sometimes, though, you feel the staff are not on your side. In the summer of 1992, I arrived at the Tequendama Hotel, close to the dangerous old center of the Colombian capital, Bogota, and was kept awake for some time during the night by the sound of automatic fire and the occasional *crump* of a mortar. In the morning I went down to breakfast, and met the stony-faced assistant manager in the lobby.

"Bit of noise last night, eh?"

"Señor?"

"You know, rat-a-tat-tat. Guns. Bombs."

"No, *Señor.*"

"But there were. I heard them. I saw the flashes."

"No es posible, Señor."

The reception desk at the InterContinental in Lusaka, the capital of Zambia, used to be known as the Wailing Wall because, no matter what documentary proof you might have of your reservation, the staff behind the counter would always deny its existence. Once when I was there a middle-aged German businessman, stout and hairy, was told that there was no record of his having booked a room there, even though he was holding their telex confirmation of his booking in his hand.

"Very well," he shouted, "I shall spend the night here in the lobby. I shall undress here, and sleep on that couch."

A group of us gathered around sympathetically. He took off his jacket, his tie, his shirt, his shoes, and finally his trousers. It wasn't a particularly pretty sight, but it was only when he hooked his thumbs in the elastic of his underpants, encouraged by us, that the manager came running out. They had found him a room.

There are hotels that routinely tell the security police who you have seen and the calls you have made. On the whole, though, I like to think that the people who work in hotels prefer not to do that kind of thing. At the Al-Rashid in Baghdad, in the run-up to the first Gulf War, I tried to persuade the staff at the reception desk to let me have a particular room because of its view and its closeness to my colleagues. Although I knew this room was available, the woman behind the counter refused to let me have it. In the end I had to make do with something I felt was distinctly inferior. It turned out later that the room I had been demanding had a little camera fitted into its television set so the security people could watch what the occupants did. The receptionist had wanted to protect me from their attentions.

In a war, a revolution, or a crisis, there is usually one hotel that the journalists settle into with the swarming instinct of bees. This place then takes on a completely different life of its own. The lobby is perpetually crowded with camera crews carrying their battle equipment in or out: flak jackets, metal boxes full of equipment, aluminium stepladders for crowd work. The business center will be taken over by newspaper journalists, plugging in their computers and sending faxes. The roof will be occupied by satellite dishes and tents where the engineers sit and talk all day, no matter how fierce the weather.

Local politicians will come in to be interviewed at the rooftop camera positions, and will give impromptu press conferences in the coffee shop or on the front steps of the hotel. The stairs from the uppermost floor to the roof, dingy and undecorated and normally used only by the hotel's maintenance staff, will now be the main thoroughfare for sharply dressed television journalists combing their hair, adjusting their ties, and running through the points they will shortly be asked about, live on air. Downstairs, meanwhile, the bars and restaurants will be full at all hours, and the staff will have to find extra supplies of food and alcohol where they can.

The more dangerous the situation in the streets, the rowdier the journalists' parties in their chosen hotel. In the run-up to the Gulf War the team from TV-AM, which supplied breakfast news to commercial television in Britain until it undeservedly lost its franchise, held a famous party one Saturday night on the eleventh floor of the Al-Rashid Hotel. The hotel had been built during the Iran-Iraq war and was designed to protect its guests from missiles: concrete baffles sheltered the windows on every floor. During the course of the party an Australian cameraman, out of his skull with drink, weaved slowly across the room, went to the open window, climbed onto the sill and jumped out.

In the horrified silence, everyone rushed over to look. He was hanging by his arms from the concrete baffle immediately below, swinging gently like an orangutan. And after a while, because he was a strong little man, he hoisted himself up and climbed back inside. The relief was intense, and when he did exactly the same thing a few minutes later (perhaps having forgotten) scarcely anyone bothered to look out; though his correspondent, a tough lady from South Africa, was sufficiently annoyed to pour a glass of wine over his head as he hung there in the Baghdad night.

People who do a dangerous or stressful job are liable to let off steam noisily. It is unpleasant for other guests—though at times of crisis the businessmen and tourists all disappear anyway—and can be annoying for the staff. On the other hand, when the caravan moves on and a new crisis somewhere else takes over from the old one, the people at the hotel miss the excitement badly. For long afterward they will recall the time when they were at the center of the world's attention, and yearly on the vigil the names of the most famous broadcasters will be as familiar in their mouths as household words. Nothing will seem quite so much fun again. Sometimes the only reason a hotel survives at a time of crisis is because of all the room service and the phone calls and the bar bills that are generated by the journalists; but what the people who work there remember most is how exciting it all was.

"You look so beautiful," Woody Allen tells Diane Keaton in *Manhattan* as they are being taken somewhere by taxi, "I can hardly keep my eyes on the meter."

In a really expensive hotel, you can hear the meter ticking all the time. I have stayed in some splendid hotels over the years: the Raffles in Singapore, the Four Seasons in Hamburg, the Beverly Hills Hotel, the Regent in Hong Kong, the Copacabana Palace in Rio, the Waldorf-Astoria in New York. But if you are essentially bourgeois, as I am, you can never entirely forget that every single minute is costing you serious money, and merely opening the door of the minibar provokes a major guilt attack.

I have a weakness for old, grand places. Latin America is full of them: the Carrera in Santiago, the Victoria Plaza in Montevideo, the Plaza and the Claridge in Buenos Aires. Architecture is more important to me than a recent coat of paint, and a friendly front desk is better than glitzy furniture in the lobby. The Pera Palace in Istanbul, once the stamping ground of the Duke of Windsor and Agatha Christie, is a favorite of mine for these reasons. I used to stay at the Nacional in Havana, another of the Duke of Windsor's watering holes, until the package tourists drove me out and I discovered the pleasantly restored Santa Isabel in the old part of the city. This is so beautiful that it more than makes up for its barely post-Soviet staff.

The American Colony Hotel in the Arab part of Jerusalem is one of the pleasantest places in the world to stay, and a dinner with good company in the open courtyard is mandatory. George, the head porter, combines just the right degree of deference with a sense that he is superb at his job. Once, on Christmas Day, the kitchen staff even cooked a Christmas pudding for me. It was surprisingly good.

I have fond memories of the Grand Hotel Terme in Brindisi, even though I have spent only a single night there, on my way to Albania. It seemed so drab and gloomy when I arrived late at night that I thought nothing of its vast ceilings and its paneling. It was only in the morning that I discovered that this was where, from the 1870s onwards, travelers from Britain took ship for India. The hotel is on the waterfront, and a gangplank ran from the first floor directly onto the small, fast steamships which the P & O operated down to the Suez Canal. (They acted, wrote Kipling, "as though 'twere a favour to allow you to embark," which shows that means of transport may change, but the cabin crews stay the same.)

For something of the same reason I like the old Imperial in Delhi better than the expensive, modern, air-conditioned places; and every time I go to Pakistan I try to arrange a trip to Peshawar so as to be able to stay at the Pearl Continental. This, though unpretentious, is my favorite hotel in the world: the level of service and politeness is unrivaled. A great deal has happened to me there, from meeting spies and drugs traffickers to walking through the lobby unconvincingly disguised as an Afghan, in *shalwar kameez* and turban. The assistant manager and head porter, while knowing exactly who I was, politely pretended they had never seen me in their lives before.

In Moscow I prefer the National. Nowadays it has been thoroughly overhauled and modernized, but I always used to stay there in the old Soviet days, when there were grand pianos and vast chandeliers in many of the rooms, and tiny single beds in an alcove. That hoary old traveler's tale about the British/American/French journalists/businessmen/diplomats who came back to their room drunk was invented about the National: they decided to search for the microphone, you remember, found it under the carpet, unscrewed it—and heard the chandelier crash to the floor in the ballroom below.

Late one night, when a friend of mine and I were searching hungrily for a meal (not necessarily an easy thing to find in Soviet days) we peered in from the street through the windows of the National's dining room and saw a few last guests finishing their meals. The main street entrance was shut, so we went into the lobby of the hotel and tried to get in that way. An old man in a hotel uniform was half asleep on a stool by the doorway.

"Let's give it a try," said my friend, and started to push past him.

The old man scarcely moved. He simply reached out a hand and gripped my friend by the testicles.

"*Ne mozhne,*" he said. It was the watchword of Soviet officialdom: Not possible.

My friend let out a strange noise, like a newborn lamb bleating. After that he didn't feel so hungry anyway.

Everyone who travels for business thinks he knows what a city is. We arrive there at an airport, take a taxi through the sprawling suburbs, and stay at a hotel somewhere in the old center. If it's nighttime this center will be largely empty; while we were coming in the inhabitants were heading in the other direction, out to the suburbs. By morning the center will be full again, as the tide of population flows back in and floods the empty shell.

None of this makes much sense; it's just how most of us have come to expect things to be, except perhaps in Paris, which has always stayed more or less true to the old way. There, now as in the past, you never need to leave your own particular quarter. On the street where I stay, there is a baker's shop opposite the front door, a butcher's and a hairdresser's within twenty yards, a launderette and fishmonger within thirty yards, and a bank, a vegetable market, a lawyer, a taxi rank, a police station and a dozen bars and restaurants within forty yards.

But for most Westerners, living in a city really means living in its suburbs; and we have come to think that this is how cities naturally are.

Not necessarily.

Managua, the capital of the Central American country of Nicaragua, strange, beautiful and seismic, possesses no city center. The terrible earthquake that devastated it nearly thirty years ago destroyed an area as large as Hyde Park in London; only it was packed with little streets and shops and houses.

The entire world was shocked. I remember donating ten pounds, which I couldn't afford, to help the suffering of Managua, and around the world seventy million pounds was raised altogether: a great deal of money for the early 1970s.

The president, an old-style Latin American dictator called Anastasio Somoza, thanked the world with tears in his eyes and put the whole lot in his Swiss bank account. Not a pound, a dollar, a franc or a mark ever went to relieve the suffering of the homeless or to build a new city center. It was one of the reasons why he was overthrown by the Sandinistas soon afterward.

Somoza belonged to the old generation of Cold War tyrants who could always rely on American support, on the "I know he's a bastard, but he's *our* bastard" principle. In fact it was Somoza who was the bastard in question. In some remote geological period a massive earthquake enclosed a large coastal inlet, and the sharks, swordfish, seahorses and other marine animals caught up in it had to adapt their physiology as this new lake gradually changed from salt water to fresh. (Something of the same thing happened to the Amazon, which once flowed from east to west; when a seismic upheaval blocked it off from the Pacific it flowed into the Atlantic instead, and the seagoing dolphins trapped in the delta also adapted to fresh water, and swim in several parts of the river today.) Anastasio Somoza's idea of a good time was to get a party of friends together, stock one of his American-supplied helicopters with plenty of beers and automatic rifles, and fly over Lake Nicaragua shooting up the freshwater sharks and dolphins. Sometimes, as an alternative diversion, he would pick up a political prisoner or two and drop them into the nearby volcano.

Somoza was the dictators' dictator: he was a stage villain, crazy and violent, yet (according to those who knew him) oddly in need of friends and drinking companions. During the revolution he would sometimes turn up at the main press hotel, the charming Camino Real, and get amazingly drunk with the foreign journalists there.

Once he shouted, "Go on, if you all hate me so much, shoot me now," and slammed his silver-handled revolver down on the bar in front of a friend of mine.

His bodyguards, who were a very nasty bunch indeed, stiffened. When my friend explained that he didn't go in for that kind of thing, Somoza burst into tears and staggered off into the darkness, the body-guards backing out after him.

The Sandinistas didn't have the money to rebuild the city center after they threw Somoza out, so it was left to run wild. When I first visited Managua in 1984, the entire area of the old city was covered with bushes as high as my waist, and families of beggars lived in the ruins. It was like the fall of the Roman Empire: the cathedral, its frontage cracked and ruined, emerged from the surrounding greenery with the suddenness of a deserted temple. Now the cathedral has been properly repaired, and the area is more under control. But Managua still doesn't have a real center; what were once the inner suburbs constitute the city.

It also has a hallucinogenic system for finding addresses. If there are officially sanctioned street names, they are never used. Instead people say things like "I live two blocks up toward the mountain from the place where Somoza's mistress used to have a hat shop, and four blocks toward the lake from the old tree that was hit by lightning." If you don't live in Managua, you can't possibly work it out for yourself.

Strange though this system is, it is not unknown elsewhere. The black township of Soweto, outside Johannesburg, is a city that used not to exist officially, since under the insane old apartheid system it was expected to wither away as the races separated. So although it was one of the biggest cities in Africa and had one of the largest hospitals in the world, Soweto wasn't mentioned on the maps, and there were no signposts to it.

Nor were there any street signs inside Soweto itself. Even now when you go there you have to find your way by stopping people and asking for directions. I once wanted to find Nelson Mandela's house, and drove up and down the little streets with their thick brown dust and their neat four-room bungalows, some with superbly tended gardens, calling out to passers-by.

"Two more blocks that way, then turn left and ask again."

It was like a relay race: I found Mandela's house after being passed from person to person seven or eight times. It was bigger and nicer than the others around it, and the great man grinned, shook my hand and laughed to hear of my experience.

In Russia, cities have suddenly appeared on the maps after decades during which their existence was a secret; usually they were involved in the arms industry or the space race, or were large prison towns. Sometimes they were merely known by numbers. Millions of people lived there, without being able to tell the outside world where they were or what they were called. Now anyone can visit them; and yet the only thing of interest when you get there is that they were once unknown. In every other way they are exactly like every other Russian city. Their centers are occupied by old Party buildings and an Intourist hotel. Farther out, charming, decaying old Tsarist wooden bungalows battle for territory with 1960s and '70s office buildings.

And beyond that? Vast, ugly suburbs full of tower blocks where the workers live. The very existence of these places might have been hidden from us, but they still echoed the pattern of our own cities, all the same.

There are cities like Brasilia or Canberra or Abuja in Nigeria, purpose-built capitals with no life whatsoever and no reason for existing, where no one wants to be and which everyone leaves as quickly as they can. There are cities like Lagos and Tehran and Mexico City, which are so huge and dysfunctional that most suburbanites never make the journey to the center and few drive across it from one side to the other. Once, leaving Tehran for a tour of the country lasting a week or two, I realized I had left my passport behind at the house where I had been staying. By this stage we had gone right through the city from north to south, and had emerged onto the motorway to the holy city of Qom. Thinking it over, I felt it would be better to talk my way through any problems that might arise rather than put the driver through the business of going all the way back and coming all the way out again—a process that could have lasted four or five hours. It was a bit of a gamble, but it turned out to be the right decision: rather like Fred Burnaby's contemporaries in 1875, I just announced that I was British (or, on occasion, Irish) and policemen, revolutionary guards, soldiers and hoteliers just accepted it. I got back to Tehran nearly two weeks later.

The most dysfunctional city in the world, until November 2001, was probably Kabul. When the United Nations, at the urging of President Clinton, imposed sanctions on the Taliban regime in Afghanistan because it refused to hand over Osama bin Laden, civilized life became very hard indeed to sustain. Those of us who had our doubts about the wisdom and morality of holding ordinary citizens to ransom for the actions of their government (isn't that, after all, what terrorists do?) had particular trouble with the policy of grinding the poorest country in the world even farther into the dust.

There was little fuel in Kabul, and no electricity. Walking through the streets at nine o'clock at night, I realized that the stars in the sky were the city's brightest lights, and that by nine thirty, when a curfew came into force, the loudest noise was the barking of dogs. Cities must have been like this throughout human civilization, until street lighting was first recorded in Baghdad in the eighth century (Paris and London had to wait until the fifteenth). But it was strange to stand in Kabul under the brilliant stars of central Asia, and reflect that this, too, was a city.

3
Journeys

To pass from the cold and snow into such a village and its warm houses, on escaping from want and suffering, to find such plenty of good bread and fat sheep as we did, is an enjoyment that can be conceived only by such as have suffered similar hardships, or endured such heavy distress . . . passing from distress to ease, from suffering to enjoyment.

—BABUR, founder of the Moghul Empire, on his journey
from Chakhcharan to Yakawlang in Afghanistan, 1506–7

Real traveling, of course, is done the hard way. Planes merely get you to the general area; to penetrate to the difficult places you have to go by four-wheel drive or by horse or by boat. Or you can walk.

It is the expeditions that stand out most in the memory: being driven across the North African desert by bedouin who relied on the sky and the look of the sand dunes rather than instruments, and who arrived at precisely the right place at precisely the time they had promised; or heading out from Yekaterinburg, the former Sverdlovsk, to visit Boris Yeltsin's home village of Butka, on a morning so cold that the road was a slick ribbon of ice and the driver had to peer through a strip of clarity two inches wide on the windscreen; or leaving the Ugandan capital, Kampala, to drive into Rwanda, stopping at the equator to take photographs of ourselves, and shredding three tires along the way; or hiring a marvelously colorful bus, which drove us to the nastiest and most frightening of the Peruvian drug towns in relative safety because it never occurred to the drug dealers or their allies, the military, that we would arrive in this fashion.

I have sailed on the *Queen Mary* and the *QE2* in my time, and flown on Concorde with a BBC executive in the seat beside me swearing me to eternal secrecy about it, even though it had only cost us the same as a business-class flight. I've been chauffeur-driven to the Taj Mahal, and airlifted from the South Pacific to Hawaii in a superbly fitted executive jet with a gorgeous hostess dispensing champagne and lobster. But it wasn't serious. Serious traveling is never comfortable or safe, and is very rarely accompanied by champagne; unless, that is, you have brought your own. Serious traveling is difficult, and the enjoyment is in direct proportion to the degree of difficulty. By which I mean it only starts to be really enjoyable once it's over.

Our journey to the forest of Tai had not started well. Before we had even left the outskirts of Abidjan, the capital of Ivory Coast, a policeman in a khaki uniform with lanyards and a sergeant's stripes noticed that I wasn't wearing a seat belt and waved us down. A long negotiation followed, and we had to pay a fine of 10,000 francs: $15. If it hadn't been for our guide, who shouted at the policeman in raucous French, we would have paid much more.

The police in Ivory Coast, once a model of enlightenment in West Africa, were starting to become noticeably more corrupt. They swaggered around at roadblocks every few miles, always on the lookout for ways of getting money off us, yet still not quite at the stage where they would demand it whether or not we provided them with any excuse.

We were traveling in moderate comfort: our *quatre/quatre*, or four-wheel drive, was well set up, and though our driver looked like any other skinny young hang-out in Abidjan in his T-shirt and jeans, he was excellent. He never did anything remotely risky, he drove at a steady sixty miles an hour, and he didn't fall asleep at the wheel. In Russia, in Iraq, in Colombia, in the former Yugoslavia I have had to keep my eyes fixed on those of the driver, ready to nudge him savagely the moment his eyelids started to droop. This time, there was no need; I could allow my own eyelids to droop instead.

We began with a motorway, decaying a little and yet clearly inspired by Western Europe. Then we turned off onto a side road, whose surface was still mostly good but was beginning to break up in places, so that the rich red-brown earth erupted through the tarmac like boils, leaving craters deep enough to send us spinning off the road if we hit one at speed. We traveled most of the width of the Ivory Coast on this road, before branching off along a reddish dirt track.

Shortly before we reached the little town of Tai, next to the forest, the rain began. I could see it coming, rushing toward us like a tidal wave down the darkened road and striking us heavily enough to check the powerful engine for an instant. The huts of clay, roofed with palm fronds, were engulfed like rocks beside the sea, and half-naked figures, their bodies glistening in the streaming rain, hurried about and put up shutters to keep the weather out.

In some ways it was a relief to enter the forest. Threatening and black, it closed over us like a tunnel. Above, the canopy was so thick that the heavy rain scarcely seemed to penetrate it. The *quatre/quatre* ploughed on through the reddish mud, its lights picking out the troughs and pools of water on the little-used track ahead. On either side of us the trees shut us in. The lights rested on fallen branches, strange root systems, dead leaves. Small animals ran in front of us, their frightened eyes yellowish red in the lights. Once a bat flew across the track, a few feet above the ground.

What the producer and cameraman felt, I didn't know. Our translator, an endlessly talkative African woman, had fallen silent; she had told us often enough how the forest scared her. I rather shared her feelings. Panic, or more properly panic fear, is the terror which the god Pan instills in anyone who strays into his domain, and often when I was a boy, wandering through the woods of my childhood, I would be overcome by this sense of panic and would run terrified through the undergrowth for safety.

A tree with fronds instead of branches lay across our path, and we had to stop sharply. The cameraman got out to see what could be done, and swore quietly: He had walked into a thorn-bush and cut his face. The sight of blood in this of all places made us feel a little uneasy, as though a gap had opened up in our defenses. The Ebola virus was endemic here, and we had come to film the efforts of scientists to isolate it.

By now it was nearly nine o'clock, and we had been on the road for more than eleven hours. The rain started easing off, and I had brought a bottle of single malt and some good Havanas in my knapsack to share around. There were a couple of German scientists working at the little station in the middle of the woods. Maybe they would cook something for us; anyway, they were bound to want a little new company in all this darkness and silence.

The road turned, and a parked Land Rover outside a darkened building reflected our headlights back at us. Everybody in the vehicle stirred with anticipation: we were there. We drove a little farther, past some huts built in the heart of the forest, and then ahead of us in the darkness we could see the faint gleam of two candles shining out. We parked, slowly extricated ourselves from the positions we had been in for hours, and started pulling out our gear. We made a lot of noise.

It was at that stage that I realized we were not going to get the welcome we had anticipated. There were five of us, three men and two women; and one of the women was remarkably good-looking. The two German scientists, specialists in different kinds of frogs, had been in the forest for six months, during which time their only company had been that of a French Ebola specialist and his three locally hired assistants. I was certain they would fawn on the blonde producer and then perhaps ask us to play bridge with them, and I wouldn't know how; in the jungle your mind tends to turn to the ethos of the Somerset Maugham short story.

But these two were out of a different book altogether. One, a pleasant-faced, chubby man in his early thirties, with a pair of granny spectacles on his nose, was standing over the gas stove, cooking something; the other, much darker and more saturnine, was hunched over the table doing something that even from a distance looked pretty obsessive. Around them were glass cases in which little jewel-like frogs, green and orange, climbed the sides with their suctionpads and peered out sadly, trying to work out why the air had solidified and trapped them inside.

Neither of the Germans acknowledged our arrival: one carried on stirring, the other remained hunched over the table.

"Hello," said the producer pleasantly.

The cook made an embarrassed sound. The stirring continued. He seemed a little sane still, though the following night I watched him slip into his room in another building to get a bottle of Campari, then smuggle it over to his obsessive friend, presumably on the assumption that we would take it from them if we saw it.

The obsessive took no notice of her whatever. She went closer to see what he was doing. At first she was worried that she might find him cutting up frogs, but in fact he was chopping a pineapple into pieces the size of tiny dice, and piling them up in some meaningful pattern beside him. When he had finished doing that he began cutting up a grapefruit, extracting the pips one by one and piling them up too. He didn't speak or turn around.

Outside, the rain had let up. The trees around the camp soared up fifty feet or more into the darkness. Somewhere out there were forty-six different types of bat, two hundred and fifty types of bird, and more than three hundred different types of snake. One or other of them were likely to be carriers of Ebola, and the big black-and-white monkeys that might catch it and pass it on to humans were asleep in the trees.

The candles burned down, the frog-loud darkness closed in on the little station. And still the German scientists kept on cutting up pineapples and taking the pips out of grapefruit, drinking Campari and taking no notice of the arrivals from the outside world.

The forest had gotten to them.

By day it seemed rather less menacing than it had done the previous night. Still, being there was like scuba diving: you could never forget that you were completely out of your element, and you must always think about everything you did with extreme care.

Even when the sun shone down so hard that the beams looked as solid as pillars, you could see no more than twenty or thirty feet through the trees. If you slipped away and mistook your way back, you might be lost forever here. It was, to quote *Heart of Darkness*, "like traveling back to the earliest beginnings of the world, when vegetation rioted on the earth and the big trees were kings."

In a tropical forest, more than anywhere else, you are aware of the extraordinary diversity of life on the planet. I had seen this in the most distant parts of Brazil; here in West Africa the awareness was reinforced by the root systems of trees, the variety of leaves and fronds, the different types of bark, the flowers and petals, even the thickly packed dead vegetation that made the ground spongy as we walked on it.

"Whence is it that Nature doth nothing in vain," asked Sir Isaac Newton, "and whence arises all that Order and Beauty which we see in the World?" Perhaps, if we could only understand it, even the Ebola virus was not in vain, and was a part of that order and beauty.

To call Ebola virulent is redundant, since presumably every virus is by its nature virulent; but of all the strange and savage diseases that have emerged from the African forests in the last half of the twentieth century it is the most horrifying. Not long before, in the Democratic Republic of Congo, a man had found a dead monkey in the forest near his home, and had cooked it carelessly before eating it. Within a few days he had started exhibiting the disgusting symptoms of the disease, hemorrhaging from every orifice, and was soon dead. Thirteen of his relatives, obliged by tribal custom to prepare his body for burial in a particular fashion, all died of the disease as well. It isn't particularly easy to catch Ebola unless you come into direct contact with the body fluids of someone who is already suffering from it; but in the Tai forest, where the monkeys had been dying of the disease, it was strange how conscious I became of every little cut and nick on my hands, legs, or face.

No one yet knew which species of animal carried the disease and passed it on, but the Tai forest was small enough for the scientists to be able to track down the link. Even so, it was a huge enterprise, involving the capture and killing of thousands of different animals for study: a hundred examples of each of the dozens upon dozens of different species here.

Our guides stopped under an enormous tree, a hundred or more feet high, with ridged roots the height of a low wall above the ground snaking out on every side. Close by was another, with roots like rocket fins that lifted up the bole of the tree so it did not touch the ground at any point. Long lianas hung down from the forest canopy, ready for the swinging of a Tarzan.

Up the side of the biggest tree of all was a steep wooden ladder, which led up to a platform twenty feet or more above the forest floor. Here the men who had brought us set about rigging up nets to catch the

bats that flew through the forest at dusk; these were the most likely carriers of the virus. But since there were forty-six different types of bat in
Tai, that meant trapping nearly five thousand individuals altogether.

Somehow, probably via the bats' urine and feces, the virus was being
passed on to the monkeys. Hunters in the neighboring villages would
come into the forest to shoot them, since monkeys are a delicacy in the
area, and sometimes they would pick up the body of a dead one in order
to eat it or sell it for meat. In this way the virus had passed to humans.
And although each outbreak of Ebola involves a very limited number of
people, the possibility always exists that it might mutate and link up
with, say, an influenza virus—perhaps something like the one that killed
more than twenty million people at the end of the First World War. The
consequences would be unimaginable.

Sounds travel well in the forest. We could hear a pack of black-and-
white monkeys crashing through the trees a long way off, and hurried
to film them. It was while the cameraman was trying to catch a glimpse
of them, eighty or a hundred feet above in the forest canopy, that he and
Lucien, the scientific assistant who was acting as our guide, smelled the
unmistakable stench of death close by. They followed it, and found the
body of a monkey lying on the thick, leafy forest floor. It had been there
for around five days, and had so many white maggots on it that it seemed
to seethe and move.

Lucien called his helpers excitedly. Each time they discovered a
monkey's body there was a good chance it had died of Ebola, and that
meant more evidence of the transmission of the disease. With great caution they put on white masks and thin hospital rubber gloves. Lucien
knelt down and picked up part of the body. It crumbled in his hand. He
dropped its tail, legs and ribcage into a specially sealable plastic bag, and
then, like a trophy-collector, held up the monkey's head. The surrounding matter came away, and the grinning skull of the animal shone
out, clean and white: the very face of Ebola.

Being on the road in Iran is like driving down Highway 1 in California on
drugs. All the basic elements are there, but they are somehow weirdly distorted, and the colors are all brighter and more interesting. The driving is

lunatic, the lane discipline is abysmal, yet everyone stops at the toll booths, you always see at least one car wreck, and you eat terrible things at roadside cafés: not totally dissimilar, therefore.

I was in an elderly Land Rover with the head of the British Institute of Persian Studies, who used it for traveling around Iran inspecting such archaeological digs as had not been interrupted by the war and the revolution. Now, though, we were on our way to join a camping expedition in Alamut: the Valley of the Assassins. Two of the best travel books in English had enhanced my enthusiasm for the trip: Freya Stark's *The Valleys of the Assassins*, of course, and Robert Byron's *Road to Oxiana*. The war with Iraq was at its height, the Islamic revolution was still crushing its victims, and life wasn't easy. All the same, the invitation was too good to miss.

We had already broken our journey at Karaj, a dormitory town for commuters to Tehran, and bought some large, soft peaches, some hard pears, and a fine melon, which we washed with the hose provided. After the food restrictions of wartime Tehran it seemed superb. Now we stopped at Qazvin, once famous for its grapes, its wine and its homosexuality.

Since we were heading on as fast as possible, we didn't have much time to investigate, but all we could see of this trio of specialties were the grapes: thick and butter yellow, full of pips and rich flavor. Robert Byron had liked the local wine so much, fifty years earlier, that he bought the entire stock of the local hotel. Now, seven years into the revolution of the ayatollahs, it wasn't even a good idea to ask for any; and the penalties for making alcohol had frightened off all but the most determined bootleggers. Everything else seemed easily available: fruit, dairy products, meat. The shop where we stopped had a wide range: Japanese tuna, Soviet candles, smuggled American mayonnaise, and "Shark" razor blades, which Iranians say have shed more blood than all the sharks in the Persian Gulf put together. We bought our supplies for the trip, drank some white grape juice, and headed off.

The sun had gone down by the time we found the sign that said To Alamut. We were to meet up with some friends, mostly foreign diplomats, who had left Tehran ahead of us and had probably set up camp already. The trouble was, we hadn't agreed on the exact place. We couldn't miss it, they'd said, which is always an indication that you will. As it turned out, the Valley of the Assassins was not a single valley at all, but an entire range of vales between hills, some of which the Assassins had fortified. I should have paid more attention to Freya Stark's title, and realized that a woman as precise about her words as she was would not have put "Valleys" in the plural if there was only one of them.

It grew dark, and we bucketed noisily up and down these hills and vales. Sometimes we would see a light in the surrounding blackness and follow it, only to find that it was an oil lamp in the window of an isolated farmhouse. Otherwise nothing except darkness and silence. Occasionally we stopped and got out and shouted, but only the echoes came back to us. Yet we did find them in the end: a small, civilized little encampment in a fold in the hills, with food cooking encouragingly on a fire and genuine, and quite decent, wine to drink.

I lay out in the clear, thin, warm mountain air that night, watching the shooting stars stream across the sky as the earth entered the asteroid belt. The night was so silent it beat in my ears. In the morning I turned out my sleeping bag and a little greenish yellow scorpion ran up toward my hand, carrying its sting like a streetfighter with a knife. We must have spent the night together. I slipped a glass over it and showed it to the others. At first I thought I ought to kill it, but my night under the stars had altered my mind about such things. I took it over to the edge of the hill we had camped on, and dropped it out of the glass. It scuttled angrily away into the rocks.

In the hard air of the morning we could see the hills camouflaged with thornbushes, which we had toiled around in the Land Rover the previous night. They were crossed by roads of white gravel like healed scars, and where the Shahrud River ran, there were startling patches of bright green rice paddies. Up in the hills the dead bushes looked like the bleached skeletons of small animals, and crickets with blue or scarlet underwings burst suddenly out of them, flying awkwardly and without much aim. The air smelled clean. It was starting to be very hot. The closer we got to the Shahrud, the more black dragonflies we saw, buzzing around us like military helicopters on a mission. Of the castles of the Assassins, which we had come here to visit, there was no sign whatsoever.

Europe first heard about the Islamic sect called the Isma'ilis, nicknamed the Assassins, from the Crusaders. Nowadays it is an ultra-respectable religious group whose leader is the Aga Khan and whose cultural center stands opposite the Victoria and Albert Museum in South Kensington in London, and it is hard to think that it might ever have been connected in the popular minds with drugs and murder. Yet it was so. Their first important European victim was Conrad of Montferrat, king of the Latin kingdom of Jerusalem, who was murdered by a lone Isma'ili in 1192. The popular explanation for the fanatical determination and courage of these killers was that their leader sent them out drugged with hashish. They were *hashishi yun*, hence "assassins," which goes to show that the tabloid newspaper instinct has always been with us.

By the 1340s the word *assassino* was in common use in Italy to mean "murderer." It spread to France and eventually—much later, of course—to England. Like most tabloid terms, it was misplaced: the nickname was specifically attached to the Syrian branch of the Isma'ili sect, rather than to the Persian branch, which was based at Alamut and carried out the first murders.

Alamut's founder was Hasan-i Sabbah, who was born in the middle of the eleventh century in what is now Iran—either in the holy city of Qom or, more probably, Reyy, outside modern Tehran. The legend is that he went to school in Nishapur with the poet and mathematician Omar Khayyam and the future statesman Nizam al-Mulk. The three of them made a pact that whoever succeeded in life first should help the others get on in their careers. Nizam al-Mulk went to work for the Seljuk sultan whose empire included Persia, and quickly became one of the best and most famous politicians of his age. He kept his promise to the other two, by ensuring that Khayyam would have the money to study and write and by giving Hasan-i Sabbah a job in the Seljuk administration.

But Hasan-i Sabbah soon came to feel that his abilities had not been properly recognized. He plotted against the Seljuks, and then took to the mountains around Alamut, where he and his followers terrorized the regime and eventually murdered his former school friend and benefactor.

It's a great story, but it has the distinct drawback of not being true. Nizam al-Mulk was a good thirty years older than Omar Khayyam or Hasan-i Sabbah, and since they came from completely different areas it isn't likely that they went to school together. Nor, in all probability, did they even meet. But it is clear that Hasan-i Sabbah became embittered by working for the Seljuk sultanate. He joined the Isma'ili sect, which was then in opposition not just to the Sunn'i and Shi'a branches of Islam, but also to the Seljuks themselves.

In 1090 he ordered his followers to infiltrate themselves into the castle on an inaccessible ridge of rock at Alamut, six thousand feet above sea level, and then he made the owner an offer he couldn't refuse: a huge amount of gold if he would sell, death if he wouldn't. The owner took the money and ran. Hasan-i Sabbah then made Alamut into an impregnable fortress with a superb library: the best, people said, in the world. There he turned his sixty or so followers into a thoroughly disciplined and highly motivated terrorist organization; and in 1092, sensing that at last they were ready for the task he wished to set them, he gathered them together and asked for a volunteer to murder Nizam al-Mulk, the Seljuk vizier.

One man, Bu Tahir Arrani, placed his hand on his heart to show that he was willing to accept the task. Not long afterward, as Nizam al-Mulk was being carried in a litter to the tent of his wives at Sahna, Arrani approached him in disguise and stabbed him to death. When the news was brought to Hasan-i Sabbah in his library at Alamut he said, "The killing of this devil is the beginning of bliss."

It was certainly the beginning of a long reign of terror. Hasan-i Sabbah never again left his mountaintop at Alamut. He sent out his men to murder political leaders and buy books for his library, and he spent the remaining thirty-three years of his life in study and prayer, becoming popularly known as the Old Man of the Mountains.

Alamut is a long ridge of rock, and its sides slope down sharply to a single stream in the valley far below. From a distance it is hard to spot even the outline of the castle now. In 1256 the Mongol army approached across the plain—it was said you could smell them a mile away—and under the ferocious Hulagu Khan, who had already destroyed many of the cities of Persia and would go on to raze Baghdad to the ground, wiped out the impregnable fortress utterly. As for the greatest library in the world, that was largely reduced to ashes. The Mongols didn't hold with reading.

They must, however, have been fit. The slope that led up to Alamut, five hundred feet or more above us, was extremely steep: so much so that with my leather-soled shoes I had to cling on to clumps of grass and heather in order to make my way up. As I hauled myself wearily up the final slope, well behind all my companions, I came across a cave in which three Iranians were resting from the heat.

"*Engilisi?*"

I agreed that this was a possibility.

"*Marg bar Thatcher,*" he said conversationally; death to Thatcher.

Well, of course, I understood how he felt, but I felt obliged to tick him off.

"*Shoma biadab,*" I answered, which is ungrammatical Persian for "You're being rude."

The poor man was deeply embarrassed. Rudeness is not usually an Iranian failing; on the contrary, they have a tendency to be infuriatingly and endlessly polite. I suppose he thought it was a friendly gesture: the only thing you could possibly say to a visiting Brit. He placed his hand over his heart much as Bu Tahir Arrani must have done on this same rock nine centuries earlier and bowed speechlessly. I was in such a good mood at having stopped clambering up a virtual wall of scrub and grass, and at having remembered the word *biadab*, that any momentary irritation had already passed. We all smiled, shook hands and said goodbye, and the three of them ran suicidally down the slope I had just climbed.

I shall never forget the extraordinary view. The slicks of desert, the violent green of the rice paddies, the distant mountains, the rivers in their courses—it was like being taken up on a pinnacle of the Temple and shown all the kingdoms of the world. Of the Assassins' castle itself, almost nothing was left except a few steps, some low walls, a path or two, and a couple of water cisterns cut deep into the rock. It was impossible to imagine where the Old Man of the Mountains had had his library, from which he could look out at this superb view.

Perhaps some of the books survived after all. The Mongols were too canny to make a frontal attack on Alamut. They just camped around the base of the rock and offered to allow the defenders to leave with all their belongings if they surrendered. They did; perhaps the smell was enough for them.

We climbed down the slope again, as alarming as climbing up it in the first place: I could see why the Old Man of the Mountains had never left Alamut. At the base of the rock we bathed our feet in the streams, and found that the children of the village had smashed the window of one of our vehicles. Now they picked up stones to throw at us, but we shouted at them and they ran away.

We drove away with an escort of running children, joking and laughing and trying to jump on the back of the Land Rovers. But when I produced my camera and started taking pictures of them, they covered their faces and ran off, howling with fear. Then we picked up speed, and the dust hid the children, and the village, and the Rock of Alamut, and we became small objects moving across the view that the Old Man of the Mountains had seen every day from his incomparable library.

It was the summer of 1991. The Gulf War was over, and Saddam Hussein still seemed like a beaten man. Those of us with a sanguine turn of mind hoped he would fall within a few weeks or months. He would have fallen earlier if the Americans and British had given their support to the Kurds and Shi'ites who had risen up against Saddam at the end of the war and tried to overthrow him.

But the Americans believed that without a strong man like Saddam, Iraq would fall into its three component parts: the Kurdish north, the Sunni center and the Shi'ite south. This, they thought, would make their enemy Iran even stronger, because Iran would swallow up southern Iraq and weaken their friend Turkey, since the Kurds there would make common cause with the Iraqi Kurds. When Americans try to think in geopolitical terms they usually get it wrong. They certainly got it wrong this time.

We were bashing along a road in northern Iraq in the hot sunshine. The dust caked my eyes, and I could taste its iron earthiness between my lips. The driver, a Kurd with a complexion that looked as though borer worms had been at his face and an old rag that might once have been red and green tied around his head, seemed to be singing. Perhaps he was groaning; the objective difference was marginal. Our car, an elderly taxi that had lost most of the things that once made it a Mercedes, hit a bump in the dirt road and shot up into the air. Then it came down again, hard. My head connected with the back of the seat in front.

"Look, for fuck's sake!" I shouted.

It looks stupid on paper, and it didn't sound any more intelligent when I said it. I felt slightly better, all the same.

"What to do?" asked the driver with the worm-eaten face, looking around at me wolfishly.

His teeth, I noticed, were a remarkable yellow, like very old ivory. He had a point. We were in a hurry, the road was awful, his car was old and not very good; which part of the syllogism did I want to change?

"Well, just try and be a bit more careful," I muttered, as though that would solve anything.

Maybe, I thought, I should be a little more emollient. The driver spoke English moderately well; and anyway, people right across the globe nowadays recognize words like "fuck" even if they speak no other English, and resent it; one of the many things Hollywood has done to make our world a better place.

The producer, a charming and intelligent man who looked like a film director's idea of an English empire builder, smiled at me soothingly. I could guess what he was thinking: *Time is running out for this film, I have taken an immense risk on setting out on this journey, the blame will be entirely mine if it goes wrong, and all this idiot can do is complain that he isn't comfortable.*

I didn't like the discomfort, it was true. My knees were up against my chin, and my feet were resting on some of the camera gear; the rest of it was with the camera crew in the other broken-down Mercedes following a half mile or so behind us. We were making a film about how the Americans and the British had let Saddam off the hook. By that stage it wasn't possible to get into any of the areas that were controlled from Baghdad: I was persona non grata there, as a result of various things I had written for the British newspapers about my experiences before and during the war. There was, in particular, an article where I suggested that the best thing would be for some senior army figure to put Saddam out of everyone else's misery. This hadn't apparently gone down all that well with some of Saddam's more loyal officials.

But it was still possible to get from southern Turkey into northern Iraq, which was no longer under Saddam's control. That's why we were here. The Turks didn't like people doing this kind of thing, so we had to slip past them. There were also problems about trusting oneself to the locals; a few weeks earlier one of the cameramen who worked with me when the bombing of Baghdad started, Nick della Casa, had been murdered somewhere near here, together with his wife, Rosanna, and her brother Charles Maxwell, by a guide they had hired. Another reason, perhaps, not to upset the worm-eaten one too much.

The producer and I had decided that we had to film inside Iraq, but we didn't know what we would find or even where we would find it. It was a complete shot in the dark. Someone had told us Saddam's men had committed atrocities at the town of Suleimaniyeh, and that's where we were heading. It was only a hundred kilometers away, but on roads as bad as this a hundred kilometers was a very long journey indeed. I looked out at the brooding Zagros Mountains, which ran parallel to the road on our left; tens of thousands of refugees had crossed them in terrible conditions a few months earlier. It was there that an exhausted Kurdish woman had shouted to a BBC correspondent the bitter, accusing words that had gone around the world:

"Five million people are in this coldness and this rain. Who is responsible for this? Our house is destroyed. Some of us, we don't know where they are. . . . Mr. George Bush is responsible for all this. He could destroy Saddam and his army but he don't try. . . .

"Kuwait is one million people. He do all this war for one million people. We are five million. Saddam Hussein bombing, helicopters destroy us. They saw this. They did nothing. Why? We are human, like you. *Why?*"

The question still hung over the landscape.

The summer seemed permanent, fixed on the sweeping country like a brilliant lacquer; unthinkable that the brown grass could turn green with rain, that the leaves could fall from the trees, that snow could damp down this light brown dust. The road stretched ahead, a yellow rutted strip in the surrounding colorless, hot landscape.

Sometimes we would pass a small, typically Mesopotamian house, built out of concrete or the gray-brown mud that gave the landscape its color, and surrounded by bright green thornbushes by way of a hedge. Chickens would scatter, half-naked children would peer at us, a woman hanging washing on the line would turn to look at us. Often, as we neared Suleimaniyeh, there would be no chickens and no inhabitants and the houses would be smashed and looted. Each time we passed a house like this the driver would shake his turbaned head.

"Saddam," he would say, and add what sounded like a curse in the Kurdish language. "Kurds not stay together."

He was right there. The various Kurdish movements were always linking up with one another and then going behind one another's backs to do a deal with Saddam. The last time I had been allowed back to Baghdad, I had been eating a frugal meal in the restaurant of the Al-Rashid Hotel when the Kurdish leader Massoud Barzani had come in with his heavily armed entourage to discuss their latest agreement with Saddam. Barzani was extremely nervous; not only is it a dangerous thing to accept the hospitality of someone with as bad a reputation as Saddam, but he had aroused the particular hatred of his Kurdish rivals who thought he was betraying them.

The staff in the restaurant, demoralized and despairing like everyone else in Baghdad at the time, were nervous about having to look after such an obvious target. One of them, a tall, cadaverous waiter I knew and liked, came out of the kitchen with a brass coffee pot and a dozen little cups on it. I watched him: it was plain how frightened he was of all these men with their guns on the table. Somehow, on the long walk to their table, his foot caught on something and he dropped the tray. It sounded like a hand grenade going off.

The security men around Barzani threw him to the ground and waved their guns about wildly. Sitting not far away, I put my head on the table and waited for the shooting to start.

It didn't. The waiter lay motionless, spreadeagled on the floor in his grubby white jacket, the pool of coffee gradually spreading until it reached his sleeve and seeping into the material and all along his arm. Then one of the Kurdish bodyguards barked something, and put his gun away. Barzani picked himself up, trying to look dignified, and I raised my head. Everyone had taken his place at the table again before the poor waiter felt it was safe to do something about the spilled coffee.

Now, as we bumped and jerked our way along in the shadow of the Zagros Mountains, I saw some thin, drooping, colorless weeds that looked oddly familiar by the side of the road. It was some time before I realized that they were wild oats. The wind had sown them here. It had also sown wild wheat and wild barley. Sometimes the plants would spread out, feeble and skimpy, over wide stretches of open land; sometimes they would simply line the roadside, where the passing cars had thrown the seeds. A quarter of the size, yield and color of arable crops, they were nevertheless the ancestors of the crops that are grown around the world. At some unthinkably distant time in human history someone must have thought that the wild wheat, barley and oats might be edible, and after that, perhaps thousands of years later, someone else tried growing them for harvest.

This dull, empty landscape with its brooding mountains had once been the hinterland of the Babylonian civilization, which in about 500 B.C. invented the concept of the zodiac, the belt around the earth that contained the sun, moon and planets. This division of the sky led the Babylonians to divide it into 360 parts, or degrees. The Babylonians also invented seven-day periods that were associated with phases of the moon. Each of these seven days ended in an "evil day," when particular taboos were required to propitiate the gods, and there was a full-moon day called *shabbatum*.

The Jews who were held captive in Babylon took on many of these ideas, and particularly the need for reserving one day a week for special prayers; they called it *shabat*, the Sabbath. It was a curious thought that there might be a faint connection between the wild plants beside the road and the habit of closing shops throughout the Western world on Sundays.

It took us six hours to reach Suleimaniyeh. On the outskirts of the town was a tall, conical hill: the remains of a *ziggurat*, an ancient Babylonian temple like the Tower of Babel. We climbed it, and filmed from its summit, fifty or more feet above ground-level. Below us lay an extraordinary sight: a sizeable town in which every single structure, right down to the sheds and outside lavatories, had been bulldozed down by Saddam's soldiers. The taller buildings had been neatly folded over by high explosive. Most of the houses were single-story, and the flat roofs had folded in the middle and fallen into the rooms below.

There were rubble and dust everywhere; and yet the town was still fully inhabited. In the wealthier areas people parked their cars in front of the ruins of their houses and lived in tents outside. Poor people had to live, crouched down, inside what remained of their houses. Shopkeepers traded from stalls in front of their old, destroyed premises. Children scrambled over the wreckage and played. It was a living, active, busy town that had undergone extreme punishment. Not many people had been killed, but the destruction was total.

"Saddam's men destroyed everything," one elderly trader told us, "because he knew we wanted independence."

None of it came as any surprise to me. Three years earlier, in the summer of 1988, I had been taken by the Iranian army to another Kurdish town, Halabjeh, to see how Saddam treated people who were disloyal to him. Toward the end of the Iran-Iraq War, the Iranians had staged an unexpected attack on northern Iraq, and the people of Halabjeh had welcomed the invading troops with open arms. A day or so later planes from Saddam's air force flew overhead and bombed them with poison gas.

I had wandered through the ruins of Halabjeh, looking at the bodies of people who had died the horrible, slow death of nerve gas or the mercifully quick one of cyanide. In one house a cyanide bomb had penetrated the room where a family of six had been eating their meal. The gas worked so fast that one of the older men was lying on the table, a piece of half-eaten bread still in his mouth. Others had died in the act of speaking to one another. Out in the streets a mother lay beside the bodies of three children: all victims of nerve gas. They were twisted in their cruel death agony, strangled as it were from within by the collapse of their breathing functions; the woman had been trying to shield them from the fumes of the nerve gas. Not far away was a truck with the bodies of twenty or more people on it. From their positions it was clear they had been trying to scramble aboard. Presumably they had survived the first gas attacks and were trying to escape when Saddam's planes came back.

What had happened in Suleimaniyeh was less savage than that. And yet to go from house to house, ordering the people out and tossing hand grenades inside, was savagery enough. While our camera crew wandered round filming the results, I went in search of someone who could explain to me what it meant in practical, human terms. I was walking through some back streets when I looked over a wall and saw a small but beautifully kept garden: a rare thing in the workaday world of a provincial Mesopotamian town.

The door hung loose on its hinges, and I pushed it open. The house had collapsed, of course, but the soldiers had lifted off a large section of the roof and thrown it onto the little patch of well-tended grass in the middle of the garden. Rosebushes, a dozen of them, had been planted around the edges of the lawn. Most of them had been broken down or snapped off. One part of the house, no larger than a small room, had been crudely repaired, and this was where the inhabitants now lived. As the gate swung shut behind me a woman in her forties emerged, smoothing down her long dark blue dress. How, I thought to myself for the twentieth time that afternoon, do people who live in this kind of squalor manage to keep themselves so clean and tidy?

She came toward me with a smile. I explained who I was, and although a visitor from the BBC must have been about as unexpected in Suleimaniyeh as an Inuit, she acknowledged me without surprise. She even spoke a little English.

"I sorry for all these . . . confusion. You like tea?"

I would, I said, like tea very much. Behind her, two younger women, beautiful in the rich, dark way of Iraqi Kurds, emerged and smiled shyly. One of them began to heat some water on a stove. What had happened here, I asked, and why was the section of roof lying on the garden?

One of the daughters brought over the tea. It was strong and heavily sweetened. We sat down on little folding chairs, as though it was a picnic, and this woman with her fine, strong features answered my questions while her two beautiful daughters, their heads down, glanced at me through their eyelashes and smiled. It was as charming a scene as any male could conjure up for himself.

The soldiers had come there, the woman explained, and had destroyed her house like all the others. She had been afraid they would rape her and her daughters—it was a difficult subject for her to talk about—but the officer in charge had said they had no time to wait for that. He had looked at the garden and ordered his men to throw the section of roof onto it and to destroy the rose bushes.

"Why?"

She spoke indistinctly, and turned her face away from me. Perhaps it was because her garden was a statement of independence; or maybe just because it was beautiful and rare. I offered to clear it for her, but she said some of her relatives would be coming soon to help. Her husband had been the original gardener here, but he had been hanged a year or so before; the Iraqis wanted to make up the numbers for a public execution. She and her daughters had kept the garden in his memory.

Not every rosebush had been destroyed. One had a single dark red rosebud on it, the color of her daughters' lips. She snipped it off with her fingers and handed it to me.

"Please think of us."

I have kept it ever since.

4
Villains

*Mr. Kurtz lacked restraint in the gratification of his various lusts.
. . . There was something wanting in him—some small matter
which, when the pressing need arose, could not be found under his
magnificent eloquence. Whether he knew of this deficiency himself
I can't say. I think the knowledge came to him at last—only at the
very last. But the wilderness had found him out early, and had
taken on him a terrible vengeance for the fantastic invasion.*
—JOSEPH CONRAD, *Heart of Darkness,* 1902

I wrote earlier of hotels that become press centers; but there is a particular type of news story which takes place entirely in hotels. The journalists are staying there, and so, often, are the main participants. All the
twists and turns take place in the hotel's public rooms. Major develop-
ments take place as a result of chance meetings in corridors and lobbies.
The staff become strangely complicit in the whole affair, tipping you off
about the movements of the people you are trying to corner and the
activities of your rivals.

I usually prefer a more active, roaming kind of journalism, but there
is nevertheless a curious attraction about something as neat and self-
contained as the big hotel story. Oddly enough, in my career the main
examples have often been associated with wars: in Kinshasa during the
mercenary campaign in Angola, in Baghdad during the Gulf War, in
Belgrade during the bombing campaign of 1999.

As a result, some odd relationships are engendered. In Kinshasa it
quite often happened that I would have my meals or travel in lifts beside
people who had threatened to kill me. We would nod curtly to one

another, look pointedly away, and pretend that everything was entirely normal. I remember saying "Have a nice evening" to one particularly unpleasant character, but that was just bravado. In Baghdad I got onto weirdly good terms with the spooks whose job it was to keep an eye on me and my colleagues, making sure with a kind of ersatz courtesy that they knew whenever I was leaving the hotel; though only, of course, when it didn't matter if they followed me.

It is familiarity that has this strange effect, of course—that, and the fact that being in a hotel makes you slip into a guestlike pattern of behavior. Screaming, shouting, making threats, or begging for mercy are not things you do in a hotel lobby, so you don't do them even when there is every reason to. Like the Graham Greene character who knows he is going to be stabbed during a séance but cannot somehow break the convention that obliges him to carry on holding hands with the people on either side of him, you nod politely to the person you are trying to escape from, and dodge round the nearest pillar as quickly as you can. A hotel plays something of the function of the medieval notion of sanctuary: if you perform the correct rituals, then you are given a measure of protection. It is, I suppose, the power of convention. Don't knock it: it can save your life.

Ever since I first became aware of him, I had tried to corner the Serbian warlord Arkan and persuade him to let me interview him. It was difficult, and one of the hardest things about it was that I couldn't find anyone who dared to act as a go-between to fix it up. Justifiably, Arkan had a very bad reputation indeed. As a result of the operations his followers, the Tigers, carried out in Croatia and Bosnia, he was indicted by the War Crimes Tribunal at The Hague in early 1999. There was obviously a degree of political calculation about this, not so much by the Tribunal as by the British and American governments that handed over secret intelligence about Arkan's responsibility for massacres at precisely the time when they were targeting Serbia. But there was nothing innocent about Arkan, even if not everything against him had yet been proven.

In 1992, just as I was leaving Sarajevo for the Croatian frontier, a friend of mine handed me an Arkan badge as a joke. I put it absentmindedly in my pocket, and forgot about it until I was going through the metal detector at Zagreb airport. The buzzer sounded, and I emptied the contents of my pockets into a plastic tray. It took me a long time to talk my way out of that, once the security guards had spotted Arkan's curiously chubby, angelic features. I thought at one stage they were going to shoot me then and there.

The years went by, and apart from an unsuccessful attempt to contact Arkan through the priest who married him to a famously beautiful Serbian rock star, I let the idea of an interview slide. (This priest was only Orthodox in terms of religion; in every other way he was barkingly eccentric. We were invited round to his house in Belgrade, which stank of cats. He served us tea, talking with great affection of Arkan, and called his wife to join us. When she came in, she was wearing a ludicrous little-girl blonde wig, and carried a large, resentful and smelly black-and-white tomcat. It was clear why the cat was resentful: she had painted large roundels of rouge on its white cheeks.)

And then in March 1999, I found myself back in the Hyatt Hotel in Belgrade, waiting for the NATO bombing campaign in Kosovo and Serbia to start: the hotel emptied out, the corridors, which had been full of journalists hurrying around with equipment and suitcases, became silent, and the staff were too nervous of the coming onslaught to pay much attention to the handful of guests who remained.

Arkan spent most of each night in the hotel. It took me some time to realize that this was not solely in order to terrorize the few remaining journalists; it was because the Hyatt was the only place left in Belgrade under the bombs where the electricity supply was assured, and where the management was prepared to serve him drinks in the early hours of the morning.

He would turn up in his black four-wheel drive with blacked-out windows, driving fast and noisily up the ramp of the hotel and followed by another vehicle filled with security men and women. Parking carefully in the no-parking zone in front of the main entrance, he would jump down, help his sensationally attractive wife out, and go inside. The hotel staff would bow and scrape before him—most of them, at any rate. Arkan was not the kind of man you annoyed in Milošević's Belgrade.

A few of his men would hang around all evening by the vehicles.

Others would take up positions in the lobby. At the entrance to the coffee lounge a woman dressed in black would usually stand on guard, walkie-talkie in hand. She too was distinctly attractive, but when I tried to make eye contact with her it was like making eye contact with a bust of Lenin.

Inside the coffee lounge, meanwhile, Arkan would be holding court. The lounge closed at 11 and he rarely arrived before half past, but the hotel put on extra staff to look after him. He would always be surrounded by grinning, obsequious characters from Belgrade's political and business life, laughing earnestly at his jokes and nodding at his statements. He favored gangster chic—dark suits, white shirts and carefully selected silk ties. After a while, when the foreign journalists returned to Belgrade and the hotel began to fill up again, he would arrive in the evenings disconcertingly prepared in case someone wanted to do a television interview with him, the pancake makeup on his face as brown and unconvincing as an artificial tan.

Early on, when the man from CNN and I were almost the only television people in the hotel, he agreed to give his first interviews. Thinking (wrongly, of course) that CNN had a bigger audience and was more influential than the BBC, he spoke to them first. I turned up at the TV station in order to fix a time for our interview.

"What are you doing, hanging out with the McDonald's of television like this?"

I didn't just say it to irritate the CNN correspondent; I wanted to make it clear to Arkan that I would never defer to him, and that I wasn't afraid of him either. It wasn't true. Knowing what he could do, I was very frightened of him indeed; but it seemed to me to be bad for business to show it. He agreed to be interviewed the following afternoon, and would only speak on condition that the interview was broadcast live. That caused a good deal of difficulty for the BBC, and plenty of backbiting from the less loyal element at home.

I had a very narrow tightrope to walk. On the one hand, I wouldn't dream of giving an indicted war criminal an easy ride. On the other, his temper was famous. What I needed to do was satisfy the BBC's audience that the right questions were being put in a properly tough manner to

Arkan, and at the same time be able to keep on reasonably good terms with him. It seemed likely that at some stage during the NATO bombing we might have trouble from the even more dangerous set of thugs in Belgrade loyal to Arkan's enemy Vojislav Šešlj, whose party had joined the coalition run by President Milosevic. Šešlj had a lot of power, and he loathed the BBC. If anyone came to the hotel to take us away or murder us, it would be Šešlj's men, not Arkan's. In the looking-glass world of Belgrade, Arkan almost counted as one of the good guys.

These were distinctions that weren't obvious in London; why should they be? But there was a certain amount of disagreement about whether we should or shouldn't interview a man with Arkan's record.

"We wouldn't, after all, have interviewed Heinrich Himmler about the Holocaust," one wiseacre complained.

Of course we would have interviewed Heinrich Himmler if we had had the chance, and Adolf Hitler too—and Joseph Stalin for good measure. We would have put the proper, tough questions to all of them, and broadcast their answers. Our kind of journalism is about placing the facts in front of people and allowing them to decide what they think. It isn't to be the cheerleaders for our side; there are enough of those already.

Arkan wasn't in the Heinrich Himmler league, though given the right circumstances he might have been. All the same, I spent much of the previous night trying to work out how I could give him a tough interview and yet not provoke him too much. At around 4 A.M. I came up with the answer. Unusually, it still looked good in the morning.

A few hours later Arkan and I sat side by side in the Belgrade TV studio. It was swelteringly hot. There was an air raid of sorts going on at the time, and power for unnecessary things like air conditioning was heavily rationed. Arkan and I sweated away, but it showed more on him because of his makeup.

The countdown from London sounded in my head, and I introduced him by his proper name, Zeljko Ražnatović.

"May I call you Arkan? It's easier on the tongue," I said; and for a week or so afterward "May I call you Arkan?" became a slightly mocking catchphrase among the staff of The Nine O'Clock News.

Then I produced the line I had worked out in the early hours of the morning.

"I can do one of two things. I can either ask you easy questions, which won't upset you, or I can ask the hard ones. Which shall it be?"

He twitched his shoulders in an I-can-take-anything-you-throw-at-me kind of way, and said, "The hard ones," as I knew he would. From that moment on I would be able to square the circle.

I asked him about the war crimes for which he had been indicted. For a time he stayed calm, reproducing the answers he had worked out and given on various occasions before.

"Any women and children who died were killed by accident. As for the Croat and Muslim men we killed, they died in a fair battle. War isn't nice, you know. But they were legitimate targets that we killed, and only legitimate targets."

I pressed him, and he didn't like that. Sitting beside him, I could see his neck swelling and the veins standing out on his forehead. He started to shout. Slightly awkward, I thought to myself, and for a time I felt I'd blown it. Then, somehow, having talked himself up into a rage, Arkan talked himself down again. The neck, the veins and the voice all began to subside of their own accord; I didn't even have to throw him a few tame questions to calm him.

His English remained pretty good throughout, and by the time I cut him off he was enjoying himself. I felt pleased: I'd asked him far harder and more difficult questions than the CNN man had the previous day.

As we walked down the corridor afterward I broached the subject of the threat from Šešlj and his men.

"The BBC will have no problems here," he said. "Believe me."

I did.

Arkan was a strange man, capable of the most violent rage, and yet in other ways clever and highly rational. He had escaped from prison in Sweden, and had spent a lot of time in most of the main Western countries, involved in smuggling, gambling and other illegal things. Nevertheless he saw himself as a kind of medieval knight, called in to save his people from destruction. He used violence openly, yet he managed to convince himself that his methods were chivalrous. No matter how many times I put it to him that the women and children who had died had been murdered savagely by his followers, he denied it. The mental wall separating his self-image from any wrongdoing was high and impenetrable: he was totally self-convinced.

Arkan more or less invented the concept of ethnic cleansing, and many innocent people died when he and his Tigers passed through. But whereas Šešlj's men carried out their disgusting atrocities and slipped away, Arkan was mainly a showman. He couldn't resist a camera. He wanted everyone to know he was a big figure, and so when the massacres and the ethnic cleansing happened it was Arkan who gave the television interviews. Others, with worse records and names that were harder for Westerners to remember, kept their heads down, did their looting and murdering, and disappeared from the public record.

And so it came about afterward that the man I had once tried hard to track down now greeted me in the lobby of my hotel every night when I came back from filming or doing some live broadcast. We would shake hands, though I would have preferred to avoid it. It was hard to resist his warmth altogether, though I always kept some element of mockery in my relationship with him in order to maintain a clear moral distance from him.

I am trying to be honest about this, because the easy, politically correct thing to do would be to say how much I loathed him; and there will be plenty of people whose acquaintance with serial murderers is limited to the cinema and the television screen who will no doubt feel I should have spat in his face. Instead, I fell back on humor. I took to saying, "Hello, Arkan— good day's ethnic cleansing?" when I saw him: partly to amuse and impress my friends, but partly to show myself, and him, that I knew precisely who and what he was.

When I fell and ruptured the tendons of my left quadriceps, and had to undergo a difficult and painful operation in a Belgrade hospital, Arkan was full of sympathy; and when I left the hospital and was installed in the hotel again, he showed an interest in my condition, which was unwanted from my side, yet which I found somehow touching. The last time I saw him was the night before I left for the Hungarian border, having been thrown out of Serbia for saying the wrong things about

President Milosevic. Arkan told me he had rung the specialist who carried out the operation to find out what the prognosis was.

"You're going to be all right," he told me, gripping my hand with both of his.

I could imagine how nervous the poor specialist must have felt, with one of the most dangerous gangsters in Serbia on the other end of the line, asking him to give assurances about my condition. But I shook Arkan's hand with some warmth, if only to forestall the possibility of an affectionate bear hug, and said my goodbyes to him.

Within seven months he was dead, shot outside the InterContinental Hotel just opposite the Hyatt. He had shifted his unwanted custom there after the bombing finished. When I stayed at the InterContinental soon afterward you could still see one of the bullet holes in the wall behind the reception desk, and they would show you a key holder that had been hit by a bullet. Somewhere at the back of the lobby was a leather armchair that had been stained with blood—either Arkan's or that of the two men with him when he died. The killer was an off-duty cop, but it was unclear who'd hired him.

I feel no great sympathy for a man who had been responsible for so much death and suffering. Arkan was a murderer, a crook and a swaggerer; but I would have preferred to see him jailed than murdered.

My abiding memory of him in the Hyatt Hotel came not from anything I saw myself but from a word-picture drawn by my friend and colleague in Belgrade, Mike Williams. One evening Mike went down to the bar in the hotel to watch the football match between Manchester United and Bayern Munich. Arkan, who owned a soccer team in Belgrade, was passionate about Bayern Munich. He sat there in deepening gloom as it became clear that Manchester United were going to win. His guards had long since stopped watching the screen, and were watching the guests instead. Arkan, of course, was holding the remote control for the television; the Arkans of this world always do. Ten minutes or so before the match was due to end, he decided Bayern Munich was going to lose and flicked moodily to CNN.

Some young woman was asking brightly, "So what are the chances of getting Arkan and other indicted war criminals sent to The Hague for trial?"

We expect to know evil when we see it in people, just as we expect to know goodness. It should show itself, we think, in some kind of aberrant looks or behavior. And yet it isn't like that, somehow. Wickedness can flicker briefly across someone's life and leave no obvious mark whatsoever. If I hadn't known what Arkan had done, I would have taken him for a small-time hood; which is, of course, precisely what he was—a small-time hood who, thanks to the circumstances he found himself in, was guilty of the deaths of many innocent people.

Weakness can lead to worse things than outright willful evil. So, sometimes, can simple efficiency, misdirected. This chapter contains cases to illustrate these points: an international organization that allowed millions to die because it couldn't quite summon up the courage to say anything about it, a man whose brainwave has brought more chaos and death to the world than just about anyone else. They are ranged alongside people who are more conventionally evil: kidnappers, torturers, murderers. I have added the case of a man who preyed on the weakness and misfortunes of others in the most despicable fashion, and who may yet have done more good than bad as a result.

In other words, these things are not as clear-cut as one might imagine. One of the most evil people I have come across—I cannot say met, since I only observed the traces of her wickedness—was clearly a loving mother, a committed Christian, and a conscientious teacher. She ran a school in Kigali, the Rwandan capital, and when the outburst of almost inexplicable race violence welled up there in 1994 between Hutus and Tutsis, she led a large gang of killers to the houses of Tutsi families whose addresses she knew because their children attended her school. In her house, alongside the school, we found a blackboard with directions for the killers: where they were to go, the weapons they were to take, how precisely they were to use them—stabbing, maiming, murdering. And in one of the rooms I found photographs of her with her own children on her knee, and others of her affectionately posing with some of the children she taught, and attending their First Communions.

These things are not at all simple. The pathology of wrongdoing is far more widespread and reaches far deeper than most of us would prefer to think. If the controls are lifted, people can be capable of crimes that under other circumstances they would themselves be the first to be horrified by.

In the past, people used to be free in quoting Hannah Arendt's phrase about the banality of evil. But perhaps evil isn't banal so much as widely latent; all it takes to summon it up is a political and social breakdown of the kind the twentieth century taught us was all too easy.

I once sat through the trial of a man for theft and the resulting amputation of his right hand. It was the single most shocking experience of my life: worse than seeing a trio of murderers hanged, worse than watching people die in gunfire or shellfire. What made it so horrific was the calmness and silence of it all.

The trial took place in Mogadishu, the Somalian capital. It was very brief, and the accused man didn't deny the charges. Anyway, he had been caught with the stolen goods on him. When it ended, the judge, a Sunni cleric in the whitest of robes, proclaimed the sentence so easily and conversationally that I assumed it was just another stage of the trial, until his words were translated for me. The accused man had been expecting the sentence. Immediately, he rolled back the sleeve of his grubby robe and stood there, his arm bare, with stoic dignity.

There was no ceremony. The executioner, a thin, staid little man with glasses who doubled as the clerk of the court, reached into a wooden box and pulled out a large kitchen knife, then walked over to the thief, swiftly tied a tourniquet round his arm and took hold of his hand. With the deftness of considerable experience he worked the knife between the bones of the wrist, and the hand came away in his in less than a second.

The thief kept his eyes on the wall behind the judge the whole time, and made no sound. The involuntary intake of breath I gave was the only noise in the room. Then the thief's wife took him away, with as little emotion as he himself had shown. The hand was thrown out onto the dusty ground outside the court, close to a pair of feet that had been amputated earlier and that stood together, like a pair of brown shoes in the dust.

There is, in Islamic society, a clear dissociation between unbearable suffering and the agents who inflict it. Once, driving through one of the northern suburbs of Tehran, I noticed a large portrait of Ayatollah Khomeini on the wall of a building, with several uniformed Revolutionary Guards sitting on a bench in front of it. I told the driver to stop, and asked the cameraman to get a shot of them, with me standing in front of them. I wanted the picture for the cover of a book I was writing about Iran.

They were very polite. They asked us to forgive them for refusing, but pointed out that the portrait was flaking and said it might be disrespectful if we showed it. I countered that argument, only for another to be produced: we would need the permission of the commanding officer. Soon afterward he emerged: a gentle, unworldly, smiling man, who explained to me that it would not be possible. I argued some more. He grew more and more embarrassed, and smiled harder, and still said no. Why not, I asked?

"Because this is a special place."

A kind of prison, it emerged. But what kind of prison?

"A prison where we—we ask people questions."

"You mean it's an interrogation center?"

That was exactly what he meant; and at that moment a vanload of new prisoners arrived. They looked understandably frightened, and their hands were tied. They were on their way to be tortured, and they knew it.

There was obviously no question of getting any pictures of this place. The commanding officer shook my hand with the greatest warmth, and placed his hand over his heart as a sign of affection and respect. He looked even pleasanter, and even more unworldly. Then he went back indoors, to the job of ordering the electrodes to be attached to the new arrivals.

Was he evil? Only in the effects of what he did; there seemed to be nothing intrinsically bad about him, from the little I saw of the man. It wasn't that he was merely obeying orders; he agreed with his orders, and he put them into practice as conscientiously as any SS guard.

Yet there are degrees in these things; and the lowest degree I have come across in this line was represented by a man named Raúl Vilariño, a naval petty officer who had worked for the Argentine military death squads during the so-called Dirty War of 1976–82. Thousands of people, mostly young, well-educated and liberal or left-wing, disappeared—kidnapped by the death squads, routinely tortured, and then murdered, often by being dropped out of military planes over the Atlantic Ocean. The military who seized power in the coup of 1976 thought that by these means they could stamp out terrorism and those who supported it.

I first heard of Vilariño through a Buenos Aires news magazine, which he had contacted in order to make a clean breast of the things he had done. When I saw him, I was appalled by his appearance: his big, coarse features surmounted by thick, oily hair, his eyes bulbous and staring. He was in his late thirties, but looked at least ten years older. One of the main architects of the terror in Argentina, Admiral Emilio Massera, a member of the junta that seized power in March 1976, had spotted Vilariño a few years earlier, and had earmarked him for "special duties." He worked with a small group of others at ESMA, the Argentine Navy's engineering school. It became one of the main torture and execution centers, and Vilariño was one of its most important operatives.

Yet there is something in all of us that prefers to block out the worst of our realities. Vilariño's account of his activities always seemed to end when he delivered one of his kidnap victims to ESMA, a place where unthinkably dreadful things happened, and where virtually every one of the prisoners was later murdered. According to Vilariño, he played no part in the actual process of torture, though he knew all the names of the torturers and could even describe their hours and conditions of work. But even though he was making a confession, he always seemed to disappear from the scene at the key moment in his narrative.

As the disappearances continued, any suggestion of strategy or purpose behind the kidnappings began to disappear. The targets were no longer specified left-wingers; often they were simply picked up by mistake, sometimes because they had the same names as real suspects. Increasingly, they were just taken because they caught the kidnappers' eye, and the process became increasingly depraved.

One day the most infamous of the kidnappers, Captain Alfredo Astiz, brought in a woman in an advanced state of pregnancy together with her little daughter of six or seven. Vilariño said the little girl was frightened and upset, and that he played with her for a while until she and her mother were taken away. At that point, he said, he was sent out on a mission. When he came back he found them both suffering from serious injuries. He tried to ensure that they received proper medical help, but they were taken away and never heard of again.

There were various other stories of this kind, in which Vilariño always seemed to want to help the victims, yet somehow was never on hand when it mattered. One of his closest friends and associates committed suicide, leaving a note that said he could not continue doing the job any longer. Vilariño did continue, but he always maintained that his group, the original detail, would never have done the kinds of things he witnessed later. It is a terrible story, and Vilariño was a terrible man, his haunted eyes looking at you as though they were seeing something altogether different, and his handshake painfully strong and yet distinctly damp. Afterward I badly wanted to wash my hands, and when I had done it I could still feel the pressure of his fingers and the dampness of his palm. I never, I think, came across a more wicked person; and yet even he wanted to think well of himself, and doctored his account of things to ensure that he could.

"This harsh and magnificent landscape," Lord Curzon called it, "with its harsh and magnificent people." The nineteenth-century British traveler and twentieth-century British statesman loved Afghanistan, as so many British travelers have before and since. In those days he was still a young man, far less pompous than he later became. Knowing the enjoyment the people of central Asia take in a splendid appearance, he went to a theatrical costumier before leaving London and hired all sorts of meretricious but impressive-looking orders and medals to wear when he went to visit the king of Afghanistan. They produced a sensation.

Like Curzon, I am haunted by that landscape, and am always impatient to go back to Afghanistan to see it again: even at the age of fifty-eight, even at the cost of all the physical discomfort and danger that is likely to be involved. There is something about the look of the mountains and the clear, thin air that make you feel somehow stronger and more effective and, I would say if such things were not so desperately unfashionable nowadays, more of a man.

I first saw Afghanistan's hills of amethyst and plains of amber in January 1980, at the time of the Soviet invasion. But I saw them only at a distance, from the Pakistani side of the border at Torkham. Nine years later, in February 1989, I crossed the border at last to report on the Soviet withdrawal. Soon afterward I found myself trekking across it to Kabul disguised as an Afghan but absent-mindedly carrying a bag from Heffer's bookshop in Cambridge. Then I went back in the early summer of 1989 to finish off the documentary we were making.

It was hot, and the distant hills shimmered. We had driven up from Pakistan through the Khyber Pass, past the headquarters of the Khyber Rifles.

We drove along the relatively well-maintained road from the Pass to Jalallabad. It was there on the city walls in 1841 that the British watchers had seen a single rider, Surgeon Brydon, slowly making his way toward them from the direction of Kabul, and had realized slowly that he was the sole survivor of the disaster that had befallen the British army there. Scarcely anything had changed since those days: the buildings of dried mud-brick, the turbans and long robes of the occasional passerby, the hunters with their long *jezails* or muskets, often made at the Tower of London armory in the early nineteenth century and adapted infinitesimally over the years to make them superbly effective for the shooting of game.

We were, quite literally, looking for trouble. Jalallabad was in the hands of forces loyal to the Communist system, and was under sporadic attack from the various mujaheddin groups that controlled the countryside. Our aim was to record a piece to camera, tying our documentary together, in a place where there was fighting.

Eventually we heard it: the sullen boom of artillery, the lighter crash of mortars. We drove on, and found a group of mujaheddin in a meadow beside the road, firing randomly at the town. In the long and depressing tradition of warfare in Afghanistan, they had little interest in what they were hitting: It could have been the military headquarters or it could have been the local maternity hospital. As long as it was in Jalallabad they didn't care.

Nor did they seem to understand the fundamental value of the mortar, which is that you can move it around and so avoid the danger that the enemy will spot you, get your range, and fire back. This mortar was fixed, stationary; the meadow was a comfortable and easy place to fire from, and the mujaheddin were settled in there.

They were pleasant enough to us, and welcomed the diversion we provided. At that stage in the war the different mujaheddin organizations were more united, and here as elsewhere various groups were working together: the more moderate Jamiat-e-Islami side by side with the fiercely fundamentalist Hezb-e-Islami. It was impossible to tell the difference between them: they all wore green turbans and *shalwar kameez,* and they all had AK-47s. Everyone in Afghanistan who considered himself to be a man carried an AK-47.

For a while we filmed them as they fired off their mortar rounds, cheering every time a cloud of gray smoke went up over their latest hit. I got ready to do my piece to camera while the firing went on behind me.

It was then that the figure in white appeared. He was clearly an Arab, not an Indo-European like the Afghans around us. His robes were spotless, and his beard sensational. He appeared to be in his middle twenties, though it was hard to be certain. His AK-47 was slung over one shoulder, and he had a nasty-looking knife stuck in his belt. His calf-length boots looked expensive.

I had a good view of them, because he jumped up on a wall beside me and started haranguing the mujaheddin, pointing to us and getting very excited.

"Problem," said our translator. "He wants them kill you."

You, you notice. It was like the ancient joke about Tonto and the Lone Ranger.

There were four of *us,* the cameraman, sound recordist, producer, and me. The mujaheddin numbered around eighteen.

The harangue went on for some time, but with a certain relief I could see the man in white wasn't getting anywhere. The audience listened carefully, and considered the merits of the case judiciously. But in the end they voted along party lines: the extreme Hezb-e men in favor of the proposition, the moderate Jamiat men against. It was a good job we had chosen this particular mujaheddin post; there was another a few hundred yards up the road where the proportions were reversed, and Hezb-e had a majority.

The Arab could, I suppose, have used his AK-47 on us, but the Jamiat group, with that sense of hospitality you always get in Muslim communities, had decided that we were their guests and that they were therefore obliged to protect us as long as we stayed with them. If he killed any of us, the rules of the game would have obliged them to kill him. Very comforting.

Anyway, once that was settled we went back to recording my piece to camera. I had to kneel down so the cameraman could see the mortar firing behind me, and what with the ache in my knees and the loud explosions as each round went off, I suppose I rather took my eye off the man in white. After a while, though, I became aware of another haranguing, a little farther off. He was shouting at the driver of an ammunition truck.

"Says, come and run over infidel," our friend translated, meaning me in particular. "Says, he give five hundred dollars to do it."

It wasn't much, and I felt obscurely annoyed at being priced so moderately. It certainly wasn't enough for the driver, who shook his head and laughed, and drove off in the direction of the road.

The figure in white ran off toward one of the archways under the road where the mujaheddin slept, and we followed him over there, intrigued. We found him lying full length on a camp bed, weeping and beating his fists on the pillow out of frustration at not being able to kill us. I almost felt like comforting him, but resisted, of course. We moved on quite soon after that: the tears wouldn't last forever, and even five hundred dollars was a reasonable amount of money.

I never forgot his eyes, or his beard: setting one's prejudices aside, he was a splendid-looking character. We assumed he was a Wahabi, a member of the extreme Saudi Arabian fundamentalist sect that had become heavily involved in the war in Afghanistan. I had seen another member of the sect a few months earlier, as I queued up at a completely redundant Pakistani border post to show my passport before crossing into Afghanistan.

Distinctly less impressive-looking, he had hissed at me, "If I see you across the border in Afghanistan I will kill you."

Fortunately he hadn't seen me once we crossed the border; I was going too fast.

Nine years later I saw the face of the man in white again. The American press was full of excitable claptrap about Islamic fundamentalism, and a Saudi millionaire had suddenly become Washington's Public Enemy Number 1: Osama bin Laden. There he was in the newspaper photograph. The beard was a little grayer than when I had seen him standing on the wall lecturing the mujaheddin on their Islamic duty to butcher us, but the eyes still held that crazy, handsome glitter: the Desert Sheikh meets Hannibal Lecter.

Not long afterward I sent him a message through a particularly good channel in Pakistan, asking him to record an interview with me. I received an answer a week or so later. The fundamentalist Taliban who now controlled most of Afghanistan were unwilling to allow him to speak in public, but if he were able to speak to anyone from the Western media, I would be the first. He himself wanted to do it, the message said, and in particular he wanted to speak to the BBC because its voice was heard everywhere.

Times change, and we change with them. This was Osama bin Laden's version of becoming mellower as he grew older. Now the genuine fanatic who once wept because he couldn't kill an infidel wanted to talk to the infidel in order to demonstrate that he was still fanatical.

It didn't happen, all the same.

Izhevsk is the kind of place any right-minded person would want to get out of from the moment they understood anything at all about the world. A thousand miles of flatness separate it from Moscow, and it is an ugly, boring, dusty little town with a few factories, a railway station, an Intourist hotel, and a main square with a statue of Lenin in it. Maybe the statue of Lenin has gone now; I'm not interested enough to want to go back there and find out.

There is only one thing that distinguishes Izhevsk from every other small Gogolesque city in Russia: from here has come the world's great Equalizer, the potential to make every bandit and terrorist and ragged volunteer a match for the best soldiers and policemen in the world. One of Izhevsk's dreary factories turns out the *Avtomat Kalashnikova,* first produced in 1947. We know it as the AK-47, and during the second half of the twentieth century it killed more good men and women than any other gun in existence. In its time the AK has convulsed entire nations: Gambia, Sierra Leone, Congo, Somalia, Sudan, Afghanistan, Tajikistan, Georgia, Bosnia, Lebanon.

I went to Izhevsk in the summer of 1988, because Mikhail Gorbachev was paying a visit there: *perestroika* and *glasnost* still meant something. It was hot, and pollen from the lime trees filled the air like snow. The local Party boss shook the great man's hand and beamed for the photographers. As Westerners, we were there on sufferance: ten years before, if I had asked to film in Izhevsk, I would have laid myself open to accusations of industrial espionage. Now things had changed.

The security men were thick around Gorbachev, brutally pushing everyone out of the way if they came too near. One man, however, hovered by his elbow the whole time, and Gorbachev inclined his head to listen to him. He was short and stocky, and wore an open-necked shirt with short sleeves, a pair of slacks and plastic sandals. Mikhail Kalashnikov was the reason Gorbachev was in town. If it had not been for him, Izhevsk would have continued turning out second-rate guns, as it had done since Catherine the Great's time.

It was only after Gorbachev had left, taking his security men with him, that I had a chance to talk to Kalashnikov. I tapped him on the arm as he finished waving goodbye. He was a very modest man, with the flat, open features of the Russian hinterland. Could I, I asked, put a few questions to him? He smiled shyly, as though he would rather be somewhere else, and then he nodded.

I asked him first how he had come to invent the AK-47. It was clearly a story he had told many times before.

"You see, I was a sergeant in the Great Patriotic War, and my tank was hit by a shell. I had injuries all over my body. So I spent a long time in hospital. And in the beds all round me were other soldiers, and they were always complaining about the same thing: the equipment they had was not as good as the weapons the Germans had.

"In particular our rifles. They jammed very quickly, and they were difficult to take apart. It needed a long time to unjam them, and a lot of our men were killed as a result. As I lay there in my bed I thought that I would invent a rifle which was simpler and better than the ones we had. I had always been interested in guns, and I was good with my hands.

"And so, even before the war was over, I began to work on it. I made each part stronger than before, and cut down the number of parts. I wanted to make a rifle you could take apart even if you were injured or couldn't see properly. And in the end I came up with the *Avtomat Kalashnikova.*

"It wasn't easy, and I had problems persuading the authorities to accept my prototype. But once they tried it, there were no more problems."

The AK-47 is the simplest of weapons. I have seen a fourteen-year-old strip one down in Afghanistan, oil it, clean it and reassemble it in a matter of a few minutes. Because the aim is simplicity, it has fewer parts that can go wrong. It is not as accurate as other weapons, but it has a ferocious rate of fire. And it is the ultimate status symbol, more than a half century after its invention.

In warfare in the Third World, no one prefers a complex American or German automatic weapon. Afghans still trade in their foreign-made guns in exchange for Russian AK-47s; Chinese-made ones are well thought of, though they are not as highly prized as the Izhevsk models. Even a Pakistani-made version has a certain value. It has been estimated that 80 million AK-47s have been made, and that the majority of them are still in use. The Kalashnikov is the very symbol of terrorism and resistance.

"There must be times when you reflect on all the misery that your invention has caused the world."

His answer was as well rehearsed as Arkan's about atrocities.

"Of course I am sorry that anyone should blame the AK-47 for anything. But you see I am very proud of what I have achieved with this weapon. People say it is the best in the world; and it is not my fault, or the AK's fault, if it is used in the wrong way. Terrorists use it, I know. People often tell me that. But the people who should be criticized are those who allow them to be used."

"You mean your own government, which exports them?"

Kalashnikov was too embarrassed by the question to answer.

At this time, he was seventy, yet he continued to work at the weapons factory that produced his brainchild, the world's best assault rifle. He had earned scarcely anything from the enormous international sales of the AK-47; his way, perhaps, of avoiding the guilt. He had an ordinary flat in Izhevsk, with one separate bedroom and a sitting room that served as another bedroom at night. He drove a Lada car, and he had a small dacha in the countryside outside the city.

His modesty was admirable; and yet in terms of the effects of what he had done—the number of people killed and the amount of misery caused—I have never met anyone worse in my life. He might merely have been in charge of designing the machinery; but it was the machinery, in its extraordinary efficiency, that did the damage. Andrei Sakharov, having been the father of the Soviet Union's nuclear weapons, became the country's leading political dissident. Mikhail Kalashnikov, one of the few ordinary Russians whose name is known in every country in the world, felt no remorse, and later went into politics on his own account. Perhaps it doesn't matter: His remorse would not have saved a single life. But the basic point is that you do not have to be evil to do evil. In an industrial and post-industrial world, it is sometimes enough merely to be efficient.

For the first time in weeks I woke up to silence: or, at least, to the silence of the guns. In its place there were other noises: the noises of a city beginning its day. The siege of Sarajevo was suspended for a couple of days, thanks to the UN. The Bosnian Serb artillery on the mountaintops surrounding us had gone quiet, and people were able to venture out of their shelters into the morning sunshine.

My camera crew and I went out with them, driving along in our clumsy armor-plated Land Rover. Two hours of peace, and the café owners had put out chairs and tables in the sun. Already customers were sitting down and enjoying themselves in safety for the first time in months. As for us, we felt completely liberated. We knew, as the people around us did, that it wasn't going to last. The Bosnian Serbs would always claim that the Bosnian government forces had broken the truce and would start firing again; and anyway the Bosnian government wasn't enthusiastic about truces. Its main hope was to drag the United States into the war on its side, which meant impressing American television viewers with the sufferings of the people of Sarajevo. So both sides had a vested interest in making the ordinary people suffer; that's the Balkans for you.

The siege of Sarajevo by the Bosnian Serbs was the worst crime I have ever witnessed, but that doesn't make the Bosnian government entirely guiltless. I liked several members of the Bosnian government as individuals, and detested the loathsome General Ratko Mladić who organized the siege and the ludicrous fanatic Radovan Karadžić who had instigated it. But the only side I really sympathized with in this entire miserable war was the side that was totally unrepresented by any of the politicians: the ordinary inhabitants of the city.

There was no suffering this morning. You could see the enjoyment on the drawn faces of the people as they turned them to the sunlight. It was cold and there was snow on the ground, but it covered the heaps of rubble from the shelling and there was something bracing and hopeful in the air, which made you feel that in spite of everything— the food shortages, the lack of power, the anxiety about water supplies, the war damage, the uncertain duration of the truce—life was worth living.

We filmed for a while, then sat down at a little outside café that had sprung up out of a previously shuttered and war-damaged house and drank tiny cups of bitter coffee with some kind of ersatz sweetener. It tasted extraordinarily good in the sharp air. Then I saw her: a young woman in her late twenties, wearing a widow's black cloak and holding hands with her two little sons. There was a look of ineffable sadness on her beautiful face. In the devastation of Sarajevo, on this bright wintry morning, she looked like the personification of the city.

We invited her to sit down with her children and have a cup of coffee. There was a listlessness about the way she agreed, which showed that she felt nothing in life had much meaning. She even spoke good English. Her name was Yasmina, she said, and her husband had been killed on Mount Zuć—she pointed to it, across on the outskirts of the city—six weeks earlier. Now she had nothing left but her two boys. No,

she didn't object to being interviewed: why should she? What she meant
was that she didn't care whether she lived or died.

"The Bosnian Serbs have agreed this truce, and it seems to be holding. You must be relieved to be able to come out into the sunshine in
safety?"

Yes, she said, though it was obvious she didn't care.

"And what are you hoping for now?"

It was a tabloid newspaper question, but one that might just possibly
bring some more active response.

Her face took on a sudden life, and she looked at me as though she
had noticed me for the first time.

"I hope that those who have killed my husband and made me suffer
will suffer ten times as much as I have. I hope they and their mothers and
their wives and their children will suffer forever."

The cameraman looked at the translator, and I looked away. This
naked intensity of emotion was something none of us could cope with,
like a sudden surge of power down an electrical cable. I thanked her, and
said goodbye.

"I can't somehow see you using that," said the cameraman, as we
looked for someone else to interview.

It was more than a week later before I heard from Yasmina again.
The truce had broken down, and the shelling had resumed, though
some of the phones seemed to be working. Immediately when I heard
that empty, flat voice at the other end of the line, I knew whose it was.

"Please, I need some help. Can I come and speak to you?"

She arrived at the hotel half an hour later, climbing as we all had to,
through one of the windows that had been blown out by the shelling. It
was dark and freezing cold in the vast lobby, and not altogether safe. But
my room was almost unbearably cold, and our office, though heated by
our generator, was full of people drinking whisky. Besides, she sounded
as though she wanted to speak to me in private.

We settled down on one of the garish sofas in the lobby. The gloom
was so intense that I could only just make out her lovely features.

I was, she said, the only person she could think of to ask for advice; she
didn't know any other Westerners, and this was a matter only a Westerner

could help her with. It was clear then why she had come to see me: she wanted to get out of Sarajevo. People constantly begged the foreign journalists in Sarajevo to help them escape. Once or twice it had even worked.

It was one of the most disgraceful features of the siege of Sarajevo that the United Nations forces, which were supposedly in the city to help the inhabitants, actually policed the siege for the Bosnian Serbs. The UN controlled the airport, and refused to allow any of the inhabitants to leave the city unless they were employed by the media; in which case it was ludicrously easy for them to catch a plane and reach the outside world. UN planes would take off each day when the shelling allowed, taking soldiers, UN employees and journalists; and yet the UN would not take the sick, the badly injured or the desperate out of the city. If they had, the argument went, they would be siding with the Bosnian government and the Bosnian Serbs would regard the UN as combatants.

I could see the Lewis Carroll logic, but it seemed intolerable to me that the UN should ignore so much suffering; and I had done my part, as many journalists did, to help one or two deserving cases leave. If I had done more, I would have felt rather better with myself.

But why should this woman, who plainly didn't care if she lived or died, want to escape?

"My children," she said. There was a short silence. "And I cannot bear to be here, where I used to be with him. It is a worse torture than anything you can understand. Everywhere I go, he is there. I have no peace. I don't care for myself what risks I run, but I cannot take the children out through the tunnel. I must go by plane. That was what my husband told me. He said, If they kill me you must get out of here with the children. I promised him."

The tunnel was certainly an escape route, but it had particular dangers. There was another: running across the airport in the darkness. But, to their great discredit, the UN soldiers would catch escapers and turn them back. People did escape that way, but only the young and fit.

"I don't see how I could help your children get out."

"Oh, that's all arranged. I know how to do it. I just need someone's advice on whether it's safe."

"Safe?"

It seemed a strange concept, under these circumstances. From time to time the journalists who were the only inhabitants of the Holiday Inn would come through the lobby and see us talking there, our breath curling up above us in the freezing atmosphere. Sometimes, too, there would be a distant explosion as the filthy war ground on, taking its daily toll of the innocent.

"I mean, will it work? I don't care what I have to do, but I'll go mad if I stay here any more."

"It can't work, with your children."

"Oh yes, it can. He's promised me."

"Who has?"

And then it came out. In the UN headquarters there was a fairly senior figure who, in exchange for money, was in a position to get the necessary papers and permissions. She said his name; I even knew him slightly.

"You've seen him?"

She nodded, without looking at me.

"And he told you he would get the children out?"

She nodded again.

"I've heard that he does get people out," I said. "It's quite easy, if you've got the papers. I just never heard that he could get children out."

"If I pay him enough, he will."

"And you've got the money?"

"It's not just money."

I began to see what the price might be. I'd heard the rumors.

"I must sleep with him. And pay three thousand Deutschmarks each."

"And you're prepared to do this?"

"What do I care?"

I could see that sleeping with a venal UN official would mean nothing more to her than sitting here in the cold lobby of the hotel, talking. But it enraged me that he should take advantage of her pain like this.

"All that worries me is, will he do what he promises?"

"I'll go and see him," I said.

"Be careful."

She wasn't worrying about my safety.

At the old telecommunications building where the United Nations had set up its headquarters, security was in the hands of the French Foreign Legion. I drove around in the BBC Land Rover, willing it up the steep, icy slope and letting it run into a natural parking place near a line of the strangely designed armored personnel carriers the French drove about in. A *légionnaire* stood in the entrance to the security checkpoint, his blue helmet on the back of his head, his front teeth missing, his hands in the armholes of his flak jacket.

"How're ya doin'?"

No point in speaking French to him. He was from somewhere outside Belfast: County Down, I should guess. I didn't ask; with *légionnaires* it was bad form. I showed him my UN accreditation and he gave me the lightest of security checks. I wandered through. There was some shooting going on at the Jewish cemetery up on the hill above the PTT building, but nothing to worry anyone here. Not enough *did* worry the UN, it seemed to me. There was another checkpoint inside, where they were a little stricter. I wasn't carrying anything of interest to them anyway.

I knew the office the UN man worked in. It was, as always, full of people hanging around waiting for something: the worst and most inquisitive of audiences. We couldn't talk about anything so private here.

"Hi," I said, trying to sound as though I liked him.

"Hi."

Although I knew him, I doubt if he knew me. He was offhand, as though I was the last person he was interested in meeting. Probably I was.

"I've come to see you about Yasmina," I said quietly.

He steered me into a side office.

"She told you about our . . . arrangement?" At the thought of it, his eyes seemed to twinkle. He gave me an all-lads-together grin, self-deprecating yet proud of himself. I felt like grabbing him by the throat, but I resisted. "She's very beautiful, no?"

I knew exactly then who he reminded me of, not physically in any way, but morally: the police chief in *Casablanca,* played by Claude Rains, who lets people out of Vichy-controlled Morocco if their wives sleep with him.

Policeman: Excuse me, Captain; another visa problem has come up.

Claude Rains [going to the mirror and adjusting his tie]: Show her in.

I suppose I should have told him that what he was doing was beneath contempt, but it would have sounded pompous, and anyway he might have changed his mind about helping her to leave.

"She just wants to be certain that you'll help her."

"Of course I'll help her. Wouldn't you?"

"Because I'll know if you don't."

The officer laughed. "You don't have to worry. She will be safe. She and the children will all go."

He might have been despicable, but at least he ensured that some people could leave the city. Even if he was only in it for sex and money, he was doing what the UN itself should have been doing: breaking the siege. His colleagues were catching people who tried to escape and returning them to this hell. It was at that point that I decided finally not to mention this subject to anyone, or broadcast or write about it until the siege was over. The man was doing the right thing: it was just the price that was wrong.

I saw Yasmina very briefly on the day she left Sarajevo. I wasn't even certain whether we met by accident, or she had come to say goodbye. Did you sleep with him, I wanted to ask, but the beautiful empty eyes turned slowly to meet mine and I lacked the courage.

Why did I want to know, anyway?

"I hope everything goes well with you and the boys," I said, for the want of anything better to say.

She shook my hand and echoed, *"'Well?'"*

I have never been able to forget the utter despair with which she said that word.

You do not have to do anything positive to help the cause of evil; it is often enough to do nothing at all. This is the story of a group of decent, benevolent men and women who could have done something about the greatest evil of the twentieth century and decided not to.

I came across the case in 1997, when I was making a series of television documentaries about the International Committee of the Red Cross. The experience left me with little except dislike for the ICRC, though I came to have a great deal of respect for many of the delegates who worked in the field.

Altogether we filmed in four continents. Sometimes, as when we drove up into the mountains near the city of Bucaramanga in Colombia and filmed an ICRC delegate making contact with a group of left-wing guerrillas who had kidnapped a businessman and were holding him there, I was deeply impressed by the work the ICRC was doing. The businessman was later released as a result.

But as an institution, the International Committee of the Red Cross has never managed to shake off the effects of what it failed to do during the Second World War. In recent years its president, a stout and rather pompous character named Dr. Cornelio Sommaruga, has spent a good deal of time touring the world apologizing for his organization's wartime record. These apologies, in the nature of things, are never quite enough to satisfy those who feel that the ICRC, through its feebleness and lack of moral courage, betrayed them and their relations.

"I am convinced my predecessors could have done more, could have been more active," he says.

That is pretty much the extent of the apology. Big institutions, and they don't come much bigger than the ICRC, have a rooted dislike of admitting that they might have been wrong.

Nevertheless, in 1997, the ICRC had become sufficiently disturbed about its reputation to allow the BBC to have unprecedented and exclusive access to its operations around the world, and to inspect its archives. As it happens—and this, too, seemed rather typical of the ICRC—it also promised much the same thing at the same time to the writer Caroline Moorhead, who is a good friend and colleague of mine. The moment when she and the documentary's producers realized that we had both been promised the same exclusive was an interesting one, but we agreed to co-exist on our projects, and all turned out well. Her book, *Dunant's Dream,* was published at the same time as our documentaries were broadcast.

The ICRC's basic problem during the Second World War was that it was a wholly Swiss organization, and the government of Switzerland was represented on it. So although it had great international responsibilities, and was the only organization capable of overseeing the interests of the wounded and the prisoners of war on all sides, it was also an unofficial arm of the Swiss government. And the moment came when it was forced to choose between its humanitarian obligations and its Swissness. It chose Swissness.

The ICRC had other problems. The most energetic and effective figure on the Committee was Dr. Carl Burckhardt, who later in the war became the ICRC's president. Burckhardt was a Swiss–German; and that seems to have given his sympathies a marked pro-German tilt. Like many people of his class and time, Burckhardt was terrified by Communism, and saw Nazi Germany as Europe's bastion against the Soviet Union.

In 1935 he visited several German concentration camps on behalf of the ICRC and found them "hard but correct." One of these camps was Dachau. His aim in going there was not so much concern for the inhabitants as the desire to demonstrate that the ICRC had the right and the ability to visit the camps. Once the war had begun and people began to die in large numbers in the camps, this was a right that Burckhardt showed no interest in asserting again.

In 1936 he went back to Germany, where he met the Nazi leadership and was enchanted with them. In the ICRC archives we found the letter he wrote to Adolf Hitler on his return to Geneva. It ended:

> *What especially and permanently impressed itself upon me was the spirit of co-operation which informed everything. It opened a whole new vista and understanding for me.*
>
> *Your deeply devoted, deeply grateful and deeply respectful,*
> *Carl Burckhardt*

This, then, was one of the key figures whose intervention would soon be required if the victims of the concentration camps were to be saved—those camps that he had found "hard but correct."

From 1941 onward, as the deportations began and the cattle trucks made their long journeys across the face of Europe, the ICRC archives are full of emotional letters from individuals and national Red Cross committees:

My brother has been deported from Romania. Is it possible to find any news of him?

We have desperately anxious relatives here in England enquiring about their family members in Occupied Europe. Please help us.

My committee has received disquieting news that hundreds of Jews, particularly old people, are being deported from this country.

There were heartbreaking scenes in Budapest Station: pregnant women collapsed during the transportation, children separated from their parents screamed and wept from fear and shock.

Thousands of Jews headed for the safety of Switzerland, only to find that it had closed its borders to them.

On the third floor of an anonymous office block in the center of Geneva is the headquarters of the World Jewish Congress. It was in these rooms in 1942 that Gerhard Riegner, who still works there, first heard that someone had arrived from Berlin with a disturbing message. Riegner, a short, plump man now in his eighties, sun-tanned and prosperous-looking with a hoarse, harsh voice, still refuses to name the man in question, but he was an important German industrialist who had recently met Himmler, Heydrich, Eichmann and other participants at the Wannsee Conference, which decided the fate of the Jews. Realizing the scale of the task they had undertaken—the entire elimination of Jews, Gypsies and other races—the Nazi leaders called in professional help: the leaders of German industry.

This man had listened in horror to the instructions he was given. He did not feel able to refuse, but at the first opportunity he took the dangerous step of leaving Germany and going to Switzerland. He sought out Riegner, and told him what was going to happen. There was, he said, still a little time: the extermination camps would not be operational until September or October 1942. Perhaps an international appeal could be launched?

The news tortured Gerhard Riegner.

"These were the most terrible years of my life. Here there was beauty, sunshine, Mont Blanc, the Lake—and a few miles from here, Hell started."

He made urgent contact with the British and American embassies, but the diplomats there refused to believe him. His only hope was the International Committee of the Red Cross. He had carefully cultivated several of the Committee members in the past few years, and now he went to see each of them in turn, impressing on them the urgent need to do something to forestall the German plan.

There were twelve members of the Committee. All those he spoke to were deeply shocked by his news, and fully in favor of launching an appeal to the world on behalf of the millions who had been sentenced to death. But the weeks slipped by, and it was only after pressure had been brought on the Committee's president that he agreed to call a special session to discuss the issue.

It was held at the Metropole Hotel on Wednesday, 14 October 1942. Across the border in Germany and farther off in Poland, Czechoslovakia and Ukraine, the extermination camps were already coming into operation. A preliminary sounding of the twelve members of the Committee had shown that nine were in favor of making an appeal on behalf of the civilians who were imprisoned and facing death. It seemed like a certainty.

Already, though, the revisionists had been at work. The appeal would not be made to the Germans only, demanding that they should stop the genocide of the Jews and others. Instead, it was a watered-down, generalized exhortation to all the belligerent countries to respect the rights and lives of civilians. Even so, the reason for the appeal would have leaked out, and the exercise might have done some good.

One of the Committee's twelve members had never attended a meeting before. This was Philippe Etter, a government minister who was now, according to the devolved constitution of Switzerland, acting president of the country. Etter was a curious-looking man, his ears oddly cocked back on either side of an entirely bald head. Above his habitual starched wing collar, this made it look like a large brown egg on a plate.

The meeting began at 2:30 in the afternoon, and the appeal was the only item on the agenda. The dry minutes, typed in French, took on a remarkable drama as I read them in the ICRC archive room. They showed that member after member argued in favor of making a public statement, especially the four women on the Committee. Mme. Frick-Cramer, for instance:

> *The Committee simply cannot keep silent in the face of the worsening methods of war and the extension of hostilities to the civilian population. If we keep quiet, we could risk the very existence of the Committee after the War.*

Other speakers agreed, until there were only two who had not given their opinion. The first was Carl Burckhardt. He took issue irritably with someone who had said that making an appeal like this was a courageous act. He couldn't see why it was so courageous. To him, it simply risked annoying the belligerent nations; by which he meant the Germans. He advised strongly against doing it.

Last of all came Philippe Etter, who was speaking with the full weight of the Swiss government. He was much more emollient than Burckhardt. He found the initiative truly noble—but he just had one or two slight hesitations about it. Firstly, he reminded them, the central principle of the International Red Cross was that they should be impartial, as between different belligerent countries; but since it was only Germany and not the Allies who were deliberately waging war on civilians, how could they possibly be impartial? The appeal was clearly directed at one side. It would negate everything the International Red Cross stood for if they issued this appeal, and it might destroy all the good they had done. Finally, there was the practical danger to the Swiss nation. Who knew? The Germans might be so angered by this one-sided appeal that they would invade Switzerland itself.

All around the table the arguments for humanity and nobility collapsed: Switzerland itself could be in danger.

Just before 5:00 it was put to the vote. Which members wished to send this general appeal? The minutes record the result in their tidy typewritten letters:

> *No Members of the Committee were in favour of this.*

So the organization as a whole decided to do nothing. It would continue to help prisoners of war, but it would interpret its statutes strictly and concentrate only on combatants. In this war against civilians, the civilians were on their own.

One of the key figures in our documentary was an elderly man named Maurice Rossel, who had been a delegate of the ICRC in Berlin for much of the war, and had managed to get into several concentration camps. To me he sounded rather engaging. He lived for six months of the year on his own in the Swiss mountains, studying philosophy and collecting old farm implements which he restored and displayed in a barn behind his cottage. Then, when the days grew shorter and autumn came, Rossel would return to his wife and their house in the nearby town. He had never spoken publicly about his wartime experiences. For our documentary, though, he was prepared to go on camera and answer questions.

The cottage was charming. Cows grazed in the field beside it, their bells tinkling faintly. A rabbit ran across the open ground. Bees fumbled in the phloxes and hollyhocks in front of the door. A sundial was set on the wall; "Lente Hora, Celeriter Anni," it said in the usual complaint of the elderly: The hours go slowly, the years fast.

"I delight in speaking with old men, as living histories," the seventeenth-century antiquary and gossip John Aubrey wrote, and I share his feeling. I was looking forward to meeting an old man who had seen so much and now lived the idyllic life of the philosopher.

"You're late," complained the philosopher when we arrived.

He was in his late eighties, with the almost feminine softening of the features which some old men develop. He must have been good-looking once, I thought, with those liquid dark brown eyes and the self-consciously attractive Maurice Chevalier twinkle in them. For the time being, though, he was annoyed with us. We were too many in number, too slow, too intrusive, and I was too big and not articulate enough in French for him. He spoke to me in the deliberate, precise way you speak to children. And although he had never been interviewed before, everything he said sounded carefully rehearsed.

"I was chosen to be a delegate in Berlin. I packed a little suitcase and left for Basle, where I took the express and arrived in Berlin. Training and instruction? None. Quite simply none."

At first I thought I rather liked him. He sounded like a rebel, and he criticized the ICRC leadership as being too pro-German. And yet there was always something faintly defensive about what he said, as though he were preparing his defenses at this stage for something that might come up later in our interview. What that something might be, I didn't know.

"The ICRC had no right whatever to inspect or criticize or transmit information about civilian internees. Only people covered by the Geneva Convention: that is, military people."

"But you had great freedom of operation in Berlin, because Geneva was a long way away and communication was so difficult. You could do whatever you wanted. You could, for instance, have condemned the terrible things you must have seen when you went to these concentration camps."

A look of intense irritation crossed his face.

"It was extremely difficult to put in jeopardy an organization which is responsible for the lives of so many men—six million prisoners of war, to be exact. Would you want to put that at risk just to kick up a fuss and say something which the Allied governments already knew?"

I recognized the tone. It was that combination of officious timidity and defensiveness that I had encountered time and again in dealing with the ICRC—the retreat behind the rules.

Rossel described how, in order to get to the concentration camps, he would go out to the nightclubs of Berlin and Vienna with senior SS officers and bribe them to give him the necessary passes. They particularly wanted nylon stockings to give to their mistresses, and Camel cigarettes for themselves.

The thought that this strange, half-feminine old man might once have sat in nightclubs with senior SS officers drinking champagne and ogling the cabaret was a curious one. But why did he want to go to see the camps, given that the International Red Cross was not prepared to perform any useful protective function for the prisoners, and he himself had made it clear it was his own initiative?

I didn't put the question clearly enough, and he didn't answer it anyway. Later I wondered if it was just in order to say he'd done it—a kind of war tourism, a professional curiosity. It seemed not to be from any humanitarian motive, since he scarcely spoke about the condition of the prisoners. At Auschwitz he got no farther than the *Oberstürm-bannführer's* office.

"Weren't you tempted to ask him what was really going on in the shower blocks at the camp?"

"Can you really envisage putting those questions to a chap you know won't reply, who will simply make fun of you? It'd be the end of the conversation, wouldn't it? Oh yes, I can really imagine it: 'Excuse me, *Oberstürmbannführer,* how many thousands of people are you gassing in your showers every week, every month?' You can imagine how well that would go down. Don't forget, I had to get out of there alive. It wasn't guaranteed."

But why did he have to get out of there alive? What was so important about going to these places where terrible things were happening, *if he did nothing about them?* What was so important about living, if he could bring no help to the dying?

We moved on to the question of his visit to the concentration camp at Theresienstadt, in Czechoslovakia. He was edgy and irritable now, and I was coming to dislike him intensely.

For some obscure reason the SS decided late in 1943 to turn Theresienstadt into a showplace. It seems almost insane; the concentration camps and their horrors were something to be hidden rather than boasted about, and who anyway would believe that they were really like holiday camps?

Maurice Rossel and the ICRC did; or at least they pretended they did. The invitation to visit Theresienstadt eventually came in June 1944, after the SS had spent months easing the pressure on the hideously overcrowded camp by sending eighteen thousand prisoners to the extermination camps earlier than scheduled, and fattening up those who remained. The SS were going to make a film about the place as well.

In Israel we interviewed two women in their early seventies who had been friends in Theresienstadt and had stayed together ever since. Now they live on a kibbutz in Israel and run a small museum about the camp.

Even their names are almost the same: Alisah Schiller and Alisa Shek. One is thin and gray-haired, the other is well-built and blonde. They bicker and correct each other, like all couples who have stayed together for a long time, but their friendship has endured through everything, including the extermination of all their relatives. They were both fifteen in 1944.

"We were told there was a commission coming from the Red Cross," says Alisa Shek, "and that the camp must look spick-and-span. People started to sow grass on the big square where the soldiers had exercised. They had to scrub the streets and paint the façades of the houses where the commission would go."

The SS imposed the strictest limitations on Maurice Rossel. They forbade him to speak privately to the prisoners, and they accompanied him everywhere and at all times while he was in the camp. So why, I asked him, did he agree to go? There was no answer: just a shrug of the shoulders and a projection of the lower lip.

Rossel insisted that it was a terrible experience for him. He was shown the prisoners sitting reading in the sunshine, or listening to the orchestra which played classical music, or eating good meals.

"It was horrifying: a Kafkaesque drama which you had to live through to understand. To be there, as in a piece of theater, when you knew that was all it was. It was a farce. And to know they were condemned to death!"

But he didn't put any of this in his report to Geneva. Instead, he described the camp precisely as the SS showed it to him.

"Some people probably thought the Red Cross would see through the whole bluff, but they were mistaken," Alisa Shek says.

"I'm not so sure," interjects her friend, Alisah Schiller. "I'm not sure they didn't see through it."

"I'm sure they didn't, because of the report we read afterward. They said it was much better than they'd thought it would be, conditions were good."

"Yes, but I think there were political reasons too, not only that they—"

"And it's the lack of imagination of the Swiss."

"Ah, yes."

The two elderly ladies carry on this way for a long time as they sit in the Israeli sunlight, disagreeing companionably. They must have had the same argument dozens of times before.

As for Rossel, he comes out of the whole episode very badly. It was one thing to meet the commandant of Auschwitz face to face and not challenge him about the thousands of daily murders. But to play the dupe at Theresienstadt seems somehow worse than playing the coward at Auschwitz.

"Why didn't you include these details in your report?"

"I knew my report would be sent to Geneva by the diplomatic bag. I knew therefore that the Gestapo would have it in twenty-four hours, and I would soon have to be making requests of them again."

Those pointless requests, to allow him to be a tourist at yet another place of mass murder.

"And I didn't want to get the ICRC into trouble."

"You couldn't go to Geneva and make your report face to face?"

"It was possible but difficult. I made the journey only twice. It wasn't a piece of cake."

At the time, Alisa and Alisah, the fifteen-year-olds, thought that at least the transport of prisoners from Theresienstadt to the death camps would stop as a result of Rossel's visit. But that was in June, and by September nearly thirty thousand people had been put in the cattle trucks for Auschwitz. He achieved nothing by going there, except to play the game as the SS wanted.

"Can you be proud of what you did?"

"I'm not ashamed. I could say I made mistakes back then. Of course I've been useless at times. I'm just a mediocre person."

I didn't believe he thought this for a moment. I felt constrained by his age from following the line of questioning too heavily, but I couldn't let it peter out altogether.

"In the night, isn't there sometimes a voice in your head that says, 'If only I'd told the Commandant at Auschwitz that what he was doing was horrendous'?"

"That's never happened, and it wouldn't occur to me because these people were proud of their work. They were convinced they were purifying Europe. They were proud of what they did, not ashamed of it.

"Either you get that into your head or you haven't understood anything. You know nothing about the ways of the SS. Nothing."

By now the sly wit has vanished, and been replaced by anger.

"You are naïve, really naïve. But it will pass. You will see. Innocence doesn't last long."

At last we came to an end. I found it hard to speak to him as we packed up the camera gear and the lights: not because I was annoyed at being called naïve, but because I was embarrassed by his cowardice and lack of self-understanding. The question I should have asked him was the question I wanted to ask again and again of the ICRC itself: if it couldn't do any good, what on earth was the purpose of its existence?

Maurice Rossel, the man who failed to tell the world about the concentration camps, waved us goodbye as we left with a sweeping gesture of his arm, as though he were sweeping us out of his life for good. He would never, he said, speak about these things in public again.

But when he sat in his cottage looking out over the sunny meadows and laid his philosophy book aside, what were the images that came to his head? The doomed orchestra playing to the doomed audience? The specially fed children playing in the sandpit? The SS men saying please and excuse me to their victims? Or the truckloads of skeletal wretches who had hoped that his visit would save them from the death camps?

How could anyone live with that much failure to stand up and say what was really happening?

5
Icons

Whenever I answer questions at conferences or dinners or public lectures, the same subjects always come up. In Internet jargon they would be known as FAQs: frequently asked questions. In my case they should be AIAQs—almost invariably asked questions. Which is your favorite country, who is the most impressive person you have met, and have you ever feared for your life?

My answers vary, depending on mood, digestion and the general receptivity of the audience. The one about fearing for my life seems to be predicated on the idea that nothing particularly dangerous happens to anyone nowadays, so it can hardly have happened to me; in fact I am always fearing for my life, usually unnecessarily. As for the others, they are just a way of getting me to talk about places and people. Depending on my mood, my favorite country can be Iran or Afghanistan or anywhere in central Asia or Latin America: somewhere that will take people by surprise. The real answer—France—would shortchange an audience looking for exoticism.

The AIAQ about the most impressive person I have met is altogether different. I have, of course, met dozens of people who have impressed me. Audiences like it if you answer "Nelson Mandela," because he is the person who has made the most impact on them of a moral nature in the modern world. He is as wonderful, charming and unpretentious a person as you could hope to come across. His forgiveness, his love of his fellow man, his breadth of vision are qualities that have enriched the entire world. And yet when he became president of South Africa he turned a blind eye to all sorts of corruption and nastiness going on inside his party, the African National Congress, merely because it *was* his party. He isn't, in other words, perfect; and people often seem to have a problem with that.

I write this, not to pull a great man down, but to make the point that hero worship of the Victorian, Thomas Carlyle variety is self-deceiving. If someone as magnificent as Nelson Mandela can be less than admirable in some respects, what hope is there for an ordinary mortal who is just trying to get by in life—especially political life? The best we can do, it seems to me, is to honor the moments when someone behaves well, and try not to be surprised when they don't.

And so, after decades of watching and interviewing people at the hero level, I have come to be grateful for much less: for glimpses of an underlying decency and humanity, for moments of courage and quick-wittedness in the face of fear and disaster, for the instinct to say or do the right and proper thing when it is inopportune or dangerous.

Some people who did the right thing when it mattered will appear in these pages. So will others who were not necessarily heroic, but who stand out in the memory as shining lights of attractiveness and fascination. Sadly, many of them are now only memories.

Close to our old flat in London, there was a very expensive restaurant called La Tante Claire. The staff treated you as though they were doing you a major personal favor by allowing you to hand them large amounts of your money, and the only time Dee and I ever went there, as the guests of our friend Jan Serfontein, we both had duck and were up all night with food poisoning. I decided to write about the experience for the *Spectator*, but the editor warned me to be careful because the owner was suspected of being litigious. I thought about it, and finally remembered a line from an old W. C. Fields film: "I ain't sayin' this steak is tough, I'm just sayin' I ain't seen that old horse around lately." I wasn't saying the duck had poisoned me, I wrote; I was just saying I wouldn't ever go back to La Tante Claire. I had quite a few letters of congratulation after that, including one from Sir Alec Guinness. "Their pretension is intolerable," he wrote. "I will never darken their door again."

They had some reason to be pretentious, though. For a time, it was one of the most fashionable places in London. On two different occasions, when I walked past, I saw Diana, Princess of Wales, having lunch at one of the tables with some friends. This was interesting, because the table in question was the only one in the restaurant that could be seen by passersby in the street. Diana had deliberately chosen it in order to be seen.

Royal reporting isn't my thing, and like a great many people I thought the hounding of Diana by the tabloid press was one of the most disgusting spectacles of modern times. And yet the defense the tabloids put forward—that she sought out the publicity—was certainly true; though it would be more accurate to say that she craved attention, not the destructive and unjustifiable prying which the tabloids went in for.

Their money lured her friends and associates (and the unspeakable people such as those who recorded her private telephone conversations and those of her husband) into betraying her. Diana was not a saint; hers was a complicated and quite fragile personality, which could not stand the strain of so much savage interference. The way the tabloids smacked their lips over the most intimate details of her personal life shamed our entire society; and sometimes journalists seemed to be the only people who did not understand this.

I first met Diana in 1989, at a state banquet at Buckingham Palace for the president of Nigeria. It was a superb occasion, and when the lights went down and a lone piper strode along the corridor leading to the hall, accompanying the waiters in full livery who were bringing in the pudding, there was an audible and delighted intake of breath all around me. They do things the old-fashioned way at Buckingham Palace. After dinner, the ordinary guests stood around in one drawing room drinking coffee, while the royal family and the guests of honor stood in the adjoining one. There was no physical barrier between the two rooms, yet no one crossed the *cordon sanitaire* without invitation.

I had just come back from a fairly high profile trip to Ceauşescu's Romania, where I had been arrested several times. One of the royal dukes wanted to talk about all this, and once across the magic line I stayed there, chatting to other people as well. When the conversation finally ran out I stood slightly irresolute and wondering whether I should leave. Then a low, half-familiar voice spoke behind me.

"I've been looking forward all night to meeting you."

The words carried an extraordinary attraction. I turned and saw Diana standing there in a low-cut white dress with diamonds around her neck and in her hair. I was of course mesmerized; I suppose that was the point of the whole thing. It didn't matter to me that she must have used the same line hundreds of times before, and probably several times that evening.

We talked for half an hour, while the waiters went around with trays of superb brandy. I didn't need the brandy. Did she mind, I asked, if I didn't call her "Your Royal Highness"? She didn't. She told me about her life, and about the way the tabloids made her life a misery.

"If you ever need any help in that department," I said, "just let me know."

I didn't know exactly what I meant by that, but I was definitely in knight-errant mood.

"Thank you," she said. "I won't forget it."

We were interrupted by the Duchess of York, who came bouncing up, red-haired and full of gossip. I was faintly annoyed at the interruption, but after the general starchiness of the evening there was something mildly refreshing about her approach. Until, that is, the Queen went past and said something I didn't catch, and the Duchess of York put her tongue out at her back. Maybe I was too conventional and easily shocked, but Diana looked quickly at me, frowning. The Duchess of York giggled and bounced off.

Not long afterward the Prince of Wales came over, and after a few more words they walked away together.

"It was wonderful to meet you," Diana murmured.

There are few things more susceptible than the heart of a man in early middle age, and I was completely bowled over. Plenty of others must have had precisely the same experience. It was too late to find a taxi, and I walked home to South Kensington in my rented white tie and tails without noticing the cold, the distance or the stares of occasional passersby.

My unspecific offer of help was never, of course, called in. I saw her twice at a distance, driving along High Street Kensington to her favorite cinema; twice as I passed the window of La Tante Claire; and once at a dinner party that Dee and I went to, not long before her death, where we spoke only briefly. By that stage her marriage had long since collapsed, and there were endless rumors about her private life. She looked quite sensational, tucking her long legs under her on the sofa in a way no one could fail to notice.

Early in the morning on Sunday, 31 August 1997, Dee and I were woken at our home in Dublin by a friend calling from Australia. Diana had been badly injured in a car crash in Paris, he said. I ran to the television set in the next room: by now the confirmation had come through that she was dead. It was devastating. I rang the BBC; they wanted me to come to London at once. We had moved to Ireland a few months before, and I had promised my boss that if ever I were wanted I could be at Television Centre within four hours. This was the first big test.

We drove to the airport without taking the time to ring ahead and make a reservation, and we were still too shocked to say much to each other. The significance of the date hadn't occurred to me until I saw the crowd that had gathered outside the airport entrance: it was the last day of the summer holidays, and we had to queue up to get inside the airport building. All the flights to cities in Britain were fully booked. It wasn't even possible to get a seat on a plane to Paris or Amsterdam or Brussels.

In the end, by paying more, we got ourselves onto the head of the waiting list.

"You'd be first," said a charming woman from Aer Lingus, "because we know why you've got to get back, and we're really, really sorry about that. But there's a gentleman from England whose wife is having a heart and lung transplant today, and we thought you'd understand if we let him go first in the list."

I did understand, though it made me even more nervous. In the end there were enough seats for all three of us.

"Hello, John," said the man ahead of us in the queue. "Amazing story, eh? Oh, by the way, I'm from the *Daily* ———."

It was one of the leading tabloids. I understood now what had happened.

"Hope all goes well with your wife's heart transplant," I said, with heavy irony.

"Oh, that."

He laughed, pleased with his stratagem.

I thought of saying this was the kind of reason that brought the amazing story about, but decided against it. Why bother?

That evening I wrote the obituary on Diana for the main television news. I tried not to be sentimental about it: the pictures of a vulnerable, wounded young woman trying to rebuild her life, and the knowledge of where it had all ended, supplied all the emotion that was required. No need for words like "tragic" or "shocking"; everyone watching could supply them for themselves. And of course the tabloids were full of that kind of thing. For them, it was an amazing story.

Soon, though, it was becoming obvious that something strange was starting to happen in British society as a result of the death. The royal family had stayed at Balmoral, and the two princes, William and Harry, had gone to church on the morning after the accident in Paris, with what feelings one can only try to imagine. This was the way the British of all classes once behaved at times of great emotional strain, but by the end of the century only the upper class still did so.

The rest of society wanted to see grief, and felt robbed and let down if they did not. They expected the royal family to take the lead in the nation's mourning, forgetting how much of a trial Diana had been to her former husband and his relations, and how much criticism she had received from Buckingham Palace herself.

By Tuesday, queues were starting to form in the Mall, as people went to pay their respects to Diana in the only way open to them: by signing a book of condolence. I thought we should take this manifestation of the public mood seriously, and volunteered to go down to film the queues and talk to the people in them.

It was clear, the more I listened, that complex emotions were coming to the surface. They were not just unhappy at the princess's death; they did not merely feel, as I did, that something of beauty and glamour had been taken away from us. They were angry. They believed that the Palace had betrayed her. For these people she had represented the new mood of British society—softer, gentler, more concerned—whereas the Palace represented the older ways: more judgmental, stricter, more in control of its emotions.

Many of the people in the queues were natural royalists, who simply wanted the Queen and her family to understand the feelings they themselves were experiencing and show that to some extent they shared them. But there was another and even more significant element: those from the more vulnerable sections of society. I quickly realized from walking up and down the queues, talking to the people there, that there was a high percentage who were divorced, or out of work, or who belonged to an ethnic minority.

There was an overwhelming sense among these people that Diana too had been discriminated against; that somehow she belonged on their side of the social divide, ranged with them against the successful and hard-nosed and wealthy—the people who showed no emotion because they felt none.

Probably none of it was true for a moment. The royal family, though most of them may well have been infuriated in the past by aspects of Diana's behavior, seemed to be as shocked and bereaved as everyone else. But there was that twofold, invisible barrier, much like the barrier that kept the ordinary guests at Palace banquets from mingling with the members of the royal family unless invited: the culture of the stiff upper lip, which most of the rest of society had come to find inexplicable and unnatural, and the immobility that an outdated court ceremonial had helped to create. A court where it is still frowned on to speak until you have been spoken to, where bowing and curtsying are still pretty much mandatory, has closer links with the Victorian world than our own.

"They're so cold," one Asian woman said as she stood in the warm afternoon sun. "They don't seem to care what ordinary people feel about it all."

A young white man beside her nodded. "They should come down here and see us standing here."

Others were fiercely outspoken about the tabloid press.

"They're the ones that killed her. They never left her alone, all her life. I told my husband I wouldn't ever read a newspaper again, I'm so angry about them."

Over the next couple of days all these feelings intensified. Once a small group of women warned a photographer from one of the tabloids that they would smash his camera if he took a shot of them, and he moved away. But it was the Queen and her family who came in for the main criticism.

"They should be down here, where she is."

The speaker pointed with his head to the Chapel Royal, where the princess's body was still lying.

By this time the tabloids themselves had thrown their weight behind this kind of opinion, campaigning for the flag on Buckingham Palace to be flown at half mast, and claiming victory when a Union Jack was raised on the flagpole for the first time in Palace history, and finally came to rest halfway down it. They seemed to be trying to ingratiate themselves with the people who believed that they had been partly responsible for Diana's death.

Much later than they should have, the royal family returned to London. The kinds of things the crowds in the Mall wanted were starting to happen.

And by now there was another focus for people's emotion: the heaping up of flowers at the gates of Kensington Palace. The road alongside was thronged with people carrying bunches of flowers. The florists' shops had to restock several times a day, and they were careful not to overcharge. Eventually the sea of flowers was great enough to be clearly visible from the planes coming in to land at Heathrow, and some pilots claimed that the sun reflected from so much cellophane blinded them. The whole thing was threatening to get out of hand. The crowds were growing, the public emotion was stronger than ever.

It was a kind of hysteria, of course, and it grew by emulation. The more the television news bulletins showed what was happening, the more people wanted to come and express their own feelings and leave their flowers. There was something increasingly disturbing about it all, and the messages on the bunches of flowers, like inscriptions at the shrine of a saint, often seemed to hint at inner pathologies that had become focused on Diana.

"God bless you, my darling. You understood, but they couldn't understand you."

"Never to be forgotten in our lives."

"You will live on for me through all eternity."

"I always felt you knew what I was going through. Just as I knew what you were going through."

Hysteria is infectious, and many of us who did not want to leave flowers or a message there felt the emotional pull of it all.

The funeral the following Saturday brought all the different strands together. I was asked by the *Sunday Telegraph* to write their news story about it, and was given a ticket to the press seats in Westminster Abbey. It would probably have been more sensible to have watched the entire proceedings on television, because I would have seen the coffin carried through the streets accompanied on foot by the Prince of Wales, his father, Earl Spencer, and Diana's two sons: one of the most moving sights in modern British history. I could have seen the Queen, who by tradition bows to no one, incline her head as the coffin passed Buckingham Palace: another gesture of change in the semiotics of royal behavior. But I had decided that seeing everything secondhand would be no real substitute for seeing one important thing for myself.

I made an early start. The morning was beautiful, with the sun slanting down between the buildings and the empty streets silent and clean. I asked the driver to stop at a garage near the Abbey, and I went in to get some paper handkerchiefs; I knew they would be needed. All the garage had was a large box of industrial-sized tissues, but I took them just the same.

The crowds were already building up outside the Abbey, and vast television screens had been erected in the nearby parks so that people could watch what was happening. A queue of invited guests had formed at the gate that led to the Abbey's north door. There were various people in it whom I knew, including the comedy actress Ruby Wax, who had been a friend of Diana's. I talked to her for a while in a muted kind of way, then took my place at the end of the queue. Behind me was an elegant woman in a black suit and stunning hat, who turned out to be the editor of one of the leading fashion magazines.

It seemed a long wait, in the early morning sun. No one laughed or spoke too loudly. A couple in late middle age, well turned out, deeply tanned and of a matching shortness, came up with apologetic grins on their faces and got into conversation with the man directly in front of me. It was plain he didn't know them, but they started talking animatedly about some resort I hadn't heard of, and he seemed to go along with it. Soon they were chatting and laughing with him, instant old friends. It was the only loud conversation in the entire queue. Finally they looked around at me with another set of apologetic smiles, and pushed their way into the queue alongside him.

"Who are the tiny twosome?" I asked the elegant woman beside me.

"Ralph Lauren and his wife."

It occurred to me that she might not want me to speak too loudly, in case I offended them and they withdrew their advertising from her magazine. Inside the Abbey at last, the editor and I worked our way toward the front, as determined to get a good view as the Laurens were to be there at all. We finally found seats beside Gladstone's statue, a few yards from the high altar, among the court officials from Buckingham Palace: older men and women, correctly dressed and correctly behaved, determined to show a becoming reserve. These, of course, were the people whom Princess Diana had identified as her enemies; perhaps in order to avoid looking any closer at the family into which she had married.

There was silence everywhere in the Abbey, and then a sound I shall never forget: the quiet, determined squealing of rubber-soled boots on the floor-tiles of the Abbey, as six bareheaded Guardsmen carried Diana's coffin down the aisle and up the steps before the altar. With the sound came the scent of the lilies that lay on the flag-wrapped coffin, flooding the chancel like the memory of the beautiful, flawed woman whose body lay inside it. It still seemed impossible that so much ardor and elegance could have been taken out of the world.

The service began. Unlike most of the funerals that had taken place here, there could be no sense of thanksgiving for a life well spent, of achievement and honor and long service. Diana's life had been a battle-field, and she had died a pointless death, killed by the pursuit of the media, the vulgar desire of a rich man and his son to own her like a tro-phy, and the misjudgment of a drunken driver.

Beside me, the courtiers stiffened: Elton John was going to play the song that had echoed through the entire week, "Candle in the Wind." It was the first major concession to the feelings of the crowd outside, the first real departure from the traditions of a state funeral. "Extraordinary how potent cheap music is," says someone dismissively in one of Noel Coward's plays, and although the song characterized the entire show-business ethos of Diana's later life, it was indeed potent; though why Elton John should merely have recycled an old song about Marilyn Monroe and not have written something new was never explained.

Now the piano rang shrill and sharp through the Abbey, and the words, which almost everyone in the world seemed to know by now filled the place. I looked covertly to my left; one of the older courtiers, a haughty-looking man in formal clothes, had tears running down his cheeks. In a sudden access of fellow-feeling, for tears were running down my own, I passed the box of paper handkerchiefs down the line. Several members of the group took one as the box went by.

Earl Spencer spoke from the pulpit. I had met him once or twice in the past, when he was starting a career in television with one of the American networks: a pleasant, unaffected young man, eager to please. Now, ten years on, he had thickened and broadened and matured. His words had real power, and the combination of passion and firm self-control was precisely what the British had wanted. Self-control alone might have been enough in the past; now they required emotion as well.

His address had the power of a Shakespearean funeral oration. It was full of open fury against the tabloids and hidden resentment against the royal family, which had taken Diana in and later turned against her because in private she had too many problems while in public she was too much of a star. Somewhere, too, was the sense that the Spencers had been the companions of kings in England when the Windsors were merely German princelings. It was angry, uncomfortable and necessary. I do not think I have ever heard a better speech.

It caught exactly the mood of the vast crowds outside the Abbey. When it was finished there was a faint rustling sound, which grew louder and louder until it swept in through the open west doors of the Abbey itself: the applause of the people in the parks and the streets, who had heard Earl Spencer on television. Inside, most of the invited guests took up the applause, row by row, until it reached the front line of seats where the Queen and her family sat, dressed in the deepest black. They did not applaud, and neither did the courtiers.

I listened to the sound of clapping and smelled the scent of the lilies and looked at the flag-draped coffin in front of the high altar, and thought how empty even the lives of people like me who didn't really know her were going to seem. I don't think I have ever passed Kensington Palace since, or driven down Kensington High Street, without thinking of the glamour that went out of London with her.

One of the bravest men I ever met was a former mayor of a nasty little town carved out of the Peruvian jungle: a drug town dominated by a psychopath who was in command of the local army base. It wasn't the kind of place where you would want to make a stand for any kind of principle. There would be no one to back you up, no one even to tell the outside world that your body had been found floating in the river, weighted down by stones.

The town, in the heart of the Huallaga Valley, the main coca-growing area of Peru, was called Tocache; the ex-mayor was Luis Zambrano. He was in his thirties, a teacher by profession, neatly turned out and slightly built. You probably wouldn't notice him in a crowd, unless you spotted the hint of determination that showed in the set of his mouth and chin.

The local army commander, who had the power of life and death over the people of Tocache, was deeply involved in the coca trade. Zambrano found this out, and insisted on telling the radio station that covered the Huallaga Valley. Nervously, the station broadcast the interview he insisted that they should record with him. Soon afterward Zambrano's house was firebombed, and he and his family were lucky to escape with their lives. He was expecting the arsonists back at any time.

I happened to come to Peru soon afterward with a television team, in order to make a film about the drug trade. We contacted Zambrano, and he agreed to be interviewed. Revealing the truth about what was going on in Tocache had been dangerous enough the first time; to repeat it now must have seemed almost suicidal.

We had been flying from town to town along the Huallaga Valley in a small chartered aircraft, keeping on the move all the time and never letting anyone know where we would be spending the night. That way, we reasoned, we could avoid a visit from the local death squads. We certainly weren't going to spend the night in Tocache. Our pilot, who may have been involved in the drug trade himself from time to time, warned us that we would have to take off no later than four thirty. It seemed like a tall order.

We landed at ten thirty in the morning. The airstrip was well maintained, and there were a half dozen small planes parked beside it. In a tiny piss-poor place like Tocache, that showed it was an important drug route, and that the army was heavily involved in the trade. The soldiers who were sitting around guarding the place were hostile. We were all distinctly nervous. In the intense heat we were sweating heavily by the time we reached the army tents that acted as the airport terminal. A soldier with "NAZI" written on the stock of his rifle questioned us a little, then pointed out where we could hire a couple of broken-down taxis.

A Landcruiser painted a familiar shade of light blue was parked nearby, and our Peruvian fixer went over to talk to the two men in it. They worked for the UN anti-drug program, but they were far too scared to help us. They were even too scared to talk to her, and eventually wound up the window and sat there, ignoring her.

There was a faint buzzing sound in the distance, like a wasp caught in a jam jar. A cloud of dust appeared at the end of the road: a man was heading toward us on a motor scooter. It was Luis Zambrano, who had promised to lead us back to the place where he was now living. We climbed into our ramshackle taxis and followed him.

The house was small, painted gray, and had bars on the windows. It looked uninhabited. There was scarcely any furniture in the room inside: The Zambranos had lost virtually everything they possessed when their own house was burned.

We got out and looked at each other. Zambrano's white shirt was well ironed, his moustache was carefully trimmed, there were neat creases in his trousers. He looked very small and slight as he lowered himself into his borrowed armchair. But I could see at once that he had a real presence. This was not the kind of man you would want to suggest some cheap scam to; you would be too nervous of the firmness and honesty of his response.

When we had set up the camera, he started to tell us his story. He had been elected sub-prefect, or mayor, of Tocache a couple of years before in 1990, promising to clean up the town and stop the drug trade. Directly he took office he found he was expected to attend a monthly meeting with the local army commander, Comandante Alfonso, plus the police commander and the chief prosecutor.

At these meetings the main subject to be decided was which group of drug runners should be used, and how much it should have to pay the men around the table. The division of the spoils was clear: the other three received $5,000 each, but since the mayor had no power to interfere with the flights he received only $200. There were at least seven flights a week from Tocache. Zambrano told the others he wasn't interested in taking his share. They laughed, and divided up the extra $200 among them.

For the army, there was a huge fortune to be made from the drug trade. Alfonso couldn't keep all the money for himself; he had to pay off his junior officers, and he also had to keep his seniors in the regional and national army headquarters sweet. But it was essential for the army to be able to demonstrate to the government in Lima that there was a continuing threat from the local Maoist guerrillas, the Shining Path (who also took a share of the drug money). As a result the army base in Tocache had to be kept at full strength.

Murders were frequent; as far as the authorities in Lima were concerned, they were the work of the Shining Path. In fact the army had taken to killing people on commission—for unpaid debts, for adultery, for any reason or for no reason at all. The bodies would be washed up along the banks of the Huallaga River. They were usually weighted down by stones that had been painted white: the kind of stones you found at the army base. The army didn't mind everyone knowing they were behind the killings. They were the only power in Tocache.

Zambrano explained all these things lucidly, without pulling any punches. I asked him if it wasn't dangerous for him to speak out.

"Perhaps it will be; I don't know. All I know is that it is my duty to say these things. No one else will do it if I don't. This is a town where everyone is scared. I'm scared too, I don't deny it. But you cannot always live on your knees, afraid of what may happen. That is no way for a free man to live."

His wife, Daisy, was sitting listening to him. She was about his age, and her face showed the strain she was suffering; but she still gave him her full support. Now their three young children came in, wearing their crisply ironed school uniforms: two girls of ten and eight, and a boy of six. As they stood there, Zambrano told them that they must on no account let anyone know at school that a television crew had been in the house.

"Otherwise Daddy could be in trouble. All right?"

The three children nodded solemnly, their eyes on his face.

"Now hold each other's hands."

They filed out in silence, and the door creaked shut behind them.

After that we went round to the army base to confront Comandante Alfonso. Zambrano knew what we were planning to do, but asked us not to say that we had interviewed him; he was planning to leave town for a few days, in case of reprisals. We talked our way into Alfonso's office, and sat down in front of him. He was an extremely tough character, with that occasional savage wit of the far right-winger. I told him in the clearest terms that everything that happened in Tocache now would be known around the world—meaning that if he took any action against us, or Zambrano, or anyone else we might have filmed, he would be in trouble. He must have known that our arrival in Tocache would cause him difficulties anyway. There was a distinctly awkward moment when he realized that we were secretly filming him, but we got away at last. He offered to put us up for the night at the army base but we refused. We even reached the airstrip by 4:30.

As for Zambrano, he did not suffer for speaking to us. The interview he gave us was seen in many countries, including Peru itself, and this gave him a considerable measure of protection. He stayed in Tocache for a while, and then moved to Lima.

The one who really suffered, satisfyingly enough, was Comandante Alfonso. He was shifted from Tocache, which had been such a gold mine to him, and was transferred to a base in the obscure jungle province of Apurimac. That was the last that was heard of him.

> No spring, nor summer hath such grace,
> As I have seen in one autumnal face.

I never had the courage to quote John Donne to Martha Gellhorn. She would have been annoyed, yet I suspect privately flattered. She did not like being old, although she spoke sometimes of her "golden seventies," which for her were years of reflection as well as of remarkable travel. They were also the years when her books were republished, when she was honored as she had not been for decades, and when a new generation of reporters, male and female, discovered and admired her.

"Whatever value is there in living to be eighty-eight?" she asked, curled up in her chair with a glass of Famous Grouse at her side and a cigarette in her long fingers.

"The value of seeing things through—seeing what happens at the end of the story," I said "things like Communism, or Reagan."

She snorted. "Seeing is precisely what I can't do, darling. I'm blind and lame."

She was neither, of course. She certainly had difficulty in reading in her last years, thanks to a careless eye surgeon who had made a mistake during a cataract operation, but she was perfectly capable until the very end of noticing that I looked tired, or had caught the sun, or was sweating because I was late and had run most of the way to her flat.

Nor was she lame; she merely had problems in getting around as fast and enthusiastically as she had throughout the rest of her life. But her impatient, essentially young spirit was deeply frustrated at all the obstacles that old age left lying around everywhere for her. She wanted to hop onto a chair and pick out a book from the top shelf and read it; or to run out and catch a cab to the airport and fly somewhere on a whim; the old woman sitting here curled up with a glass of Scotch was merely an encumbrance to this younger self.

"Age is such a drag," she said. "It gets in the way of everything. Just like eating gets in the way of my drinking."

I met her far too late in life. It was 1991, the year of the Gulf War, and the man who had been my publisher was organizing that year's Cheltenham Literary Festival. Richard Cohen was himself an interesting figure, a dashing Olympic-level fencer who edited the novels of Jeffrey Archer, set up his own publishing company, and eventually delivered the coup de grâce to Archer's political career by revealing that Archer had tried to persuade him to change his testimony in the *Daily Star* libel trial. At Cheltenham he set up a debate on war reporting, and invited me to be a panelist, together with Max Hastings, the editor of the conservative *Daily Telegraph,* and Philip Knightley, the author of a seminal work on war correspondents. He had, he said, also managed to persuade Martha Gellhorn to be there.

"But she must be around a hundred and fifty," I said, with the dangerous arrogance of middle age.

"You see if you think that when you see her," Cohen answered.

Martha was dressed up for the occasion, in a dark green coat with an expensive-looking fake fur collar and black slacks. Her hair was blonde, and her makeup was perfect. From where I was sitting alongside her she could have been sixty; from where the audience sat she must have looked about my age.

And she was sharp. She didn't like Philip Knightley because he had questioned the authenticity of the famous photograph by Robert Capa of the moment of death of a soldier in the Spanish Civil War. Capa, she told me much later, when we were on close terms, would have been her lover in Italy during the Second World War if she'd wanted him to be, and she was always devoted to his memory. Max Hastings she didn't like because he was a Tory.

She didn't take to me either. She clearly thought I was a boring establishment figure, reporting from safe places while real reporters like her wandered the battlefields of the world, unprotected by big organizations, and ignoring the official handouts which are so often the basis of news reporting; "official drivel," she called them. She was probably right.

Martha snorted sardonically a good deal while the rest of us were speaking, pulling on the inevitable cigarette, and then launched into a sharp critique of recent war reporting, excluding only John Pilger, the left-wing writer who was always a particular favorite of hers. I was sorry to feel that she had dismissed all of us on the panel so comprehensively, because I saw she was a serious character, a writer as engaged with the present as any of us. She was a lifelong radical, who had been everywhere and seen everything and yet had never lost the sense that things should be better than they were, and that there was no real excuse why they should not be.

By this stage I had locked horns with Max Hastings. Audiences enjoy a little aggro, and although I had always liked Max I was prepared to give them their money's worth.

"War correspondents—" he began.

"I'm really sick of this whole expression 'war correspondents,'" I broke in, quite unfairly.

Then I started raving on about how journalists were just journalists, and that by calling themselves war correspondents they were congratulating themselves on something that ought to be a matter of sadness and shame. It wasn't merely said for effect: I have genuinely come to detest anyone who regards war as glamorous or enjoyable. There are plenty of them around, whether in Bosnia or Chechnya or the Gulf. They tend to wear colored scarves around their necks and tuck their trousers into their boots, and the suffering of the people around them means a great deal less to them than the figure they cut.

"For the first time," Martha's cultured East Coast drawl broke in, "someone here is speaking some sense. Wars are frightful, wicked things, and anyone who wants to specialize in reporting them is either a charlatan or else lacks any scintilla of humanity."

The audience applauded her mightily, and poor Max Hastings, unfairly caricatured by us both as some kind of affected yet blood-thirsty *poseur*, lapsed into silence.

"I like you," Martha said to me afterward. "You were quite right back there. No one but a self-regarding dolt would call himself a war correspondent. The only point in reporting on a war is to look at ordinary people in terrible situations. You must come around for a drink when you're in London."

She had settled there in 1960, after living in Cuba, Mexico, Kenya, and various other places during the previous fifteen years. She had never entirely felt at ease anywhere since the end of the Second World War, but her cottage in Wales and her flat on the top two floors of No. 72 Cadogan Square were where she had decided to make her life for good. In the 1930s she had disliked Britain, feeling that it was too stodgy and self-satisfied; but her view of it changed during the War, as she saw how its people responded to adversity.

"I come from what they used to call good stock," she said once, and indeed she did.

Her father, George, was a leading gynecologist in St Louis; Edna, her mother, was a graduate of Bryn Mawr College. They were wealthy and liberal, great supporters of women's suffrage, and Martha (who was born in 1908) and her three brothers were brought up in a happy and stimulating environment. The three brothers were all trained in the liberal professions, and Alfred, younger than she and every bit as energetic and radical, was still in charge of the New York public health system in his mid-80s.

Martha followed her mother to Bryn Mawr. She left early without graduating, went in for a little journalism, and traveled to Europe. She told me how she had joined a delegation of French students on a trip to Berlin, where they were invited to lunch by Baldur von Schirach, the head of the Hitler Youth.

"He was of course disgusting; that goes without saying. But I endured it for the sake of the experience. It was only when his servant spilled his coffee and the brute hit him that I couldn't stand it any longer. I walked right out of the house, there and then."

In 1935, back in America, Martha began traveling around the country interviewing unemployed people for a book she called *The Trouble I've Seen*. It caused a sensation, not least because it was written by a woman of twenty-seven who was beautiful and well-educated. The book shows remarkable powers of observation, and an unshockable pity. She not only sympathized with the people she met, she entered their lives and understood them. Her war reporting has a sparse strength and a superb ability to turn what she sees into clear expression; but *The Trouble I've Seen* still has such power that it is hard to read with equanimity.

At Christmas 1936, some months after the death of her father, Martha suggested that her mother and her brother Alfred should go with her to Florida for some sunshine. In Miami Alfred noticed a bus with Key West marked on its destination board. They had never heard of the place but thought it sounded intriguing, so they caught the bus. When they got there, Edna Gellhorn spotted another interesting name: a bar called Sloppy Joe's. They went in. Shortly afterward Ernest Hemingway came swaggering into the bar and spotted Martha immediately. They must altogether have made an attractive group: Edna herself was a striking-looking woman.

Martha knew exactly who he was. He struck up a conversation with Alfred and Edna, but it was Martha he kept looking at, with her shorts and her long blonde hair; and when the others left Florida a few days later Martha stayed on, to the annoyance of Hemingway's second wife, Pauline, who was in Key West with him. When Martha left a couple of weeks later, Hemingway followed her and caught up with her the following day. They agreed to go to Spain together to report on the Civil War.

In Madrid Martha soon saw a side of Hemingway that she would eventually come to loathe. Even before they became lovers he would lock her bedroom door from the outside to prevent anyone from getting in, and when the hotel came under shellfire she was trapped inside. Soon Hemingway was telling everybody that she was the bravest woman he had ever known—braver, he said, than he was himself. There, at least, he was right.

Sixty years later, she still remembered the attraction he had had for her.

"He made me laugh. In those days he was fun. I could forgive every-thing else about him."

All her life she preferred men who were content to remain her friends to those who were determined to be her lovers; the sexual side of any relationship was less important to her than the companionship, she said. But in those heightened circumstances his love of what she always called *La Causa,* the Spanish cause, was another important ele-ment in his attraction for her. So, too, must have been his ability as a writer. His drinking, his ferocious temper, his violence—these problems were present from the start, but were less obvious then.

When I knew her, she always referred to marriage with Hemingway as 'a life-darkening experience.' It was a phrase she had honed carefully.

"He was fine until we married. Then, right from the very start, the fun left him. He became terrible. It was the act of possession that trig-gered it."

There was also the submerged rivalry between two writers. Martha described how, when they lived in Cuba, they were both working on books and would write in silence, ignoring each other's presence. The success of Martha's novel *Liana* was something Hemingway acknowl-edged; in a letter to his mother he said he thought Martha was a better writer than he was. But he cannot have enjoyed it.

He was savagely competitive. In *A Moveable Feast,* he destroyed Scott Fitzgerald's character once and for all, presenting him as a drunk and a weakling; and this was largely because their names were so often linked and Hemingway was determined to dominate the partnership. Reread-ing the book, I found that Hemingway had shown another writer, the adventurous and freehanded Ford Madox Ford, as a ludicrous, pompous, stuffy old buffer. Why, I asked Martha?

"Oh, that's clear enough. Ford gave him his first chance—published him, lent him money, praised him. Ernest had to get back at him after that. He couldn't bear the idea that he had once been dependent on somebody."

And yet she and Hemingway seemed happy enough at first. Eleanor Roosevelt had become a close friend of hers, in spite of the disparity between their ages, as a result of reading *The Trouble I've Seen*. Now, even though there were problems over Hemingway's divorce from Pauline and he and Martha were still not married, the conventionally moral Eleanor Roosevelt managed to persuade her husband to let the couple live together in a cottage on the White House grounds. They would often dine *à quatre*.

Years later, when John F. Kennedy was elected president, Martha was invited to his inauguration ball. She could not think why, since she knew nobody there. Suddenly there was a movement in the room, and Kennedy himself, accompanied by a crowd of others, headed over to the corner where she was standing alone. Martha wondered if he were going to offer her a job, but instead he wanted to ask her a question.

"You lived on the White House grounds; how did FDR get out at night to . . . you know?"

Martha, deeply relieved at not having to reject some embarrassing offer of a job in the new administration, told him about the little gate manned by bribable guards that Roosevelt had used. Kennedy seemed deeply relieved.

"You may just have saved my life," he said.

By the time Martha left for Europe to report on the Second World War, her relationship with Hemingway was on the slide. He was often drunk, and may also have been violent, though Martha was too discreet to tell me that. She came from a class and a generation that did not talk openly about these things. Time and again she wrote to Hemingway, urging him to come to Europe. She was contemptuous of the lazy, safe life he was continuing to live in the United States and Cuba. The tide of the war had long turned by the time he finally bestirred himself to make the trip.

The hotel from which the international press covered the British end of the war was the Dorchester, and Hemingway insisted to the management that he must have a safe room there. He found one on the protected side of the hotel, on the second floor. A wealthy elderly lady was living in it already, but Hemingway demanded that the hotel management get rid of her. Martha, demonstrating her dislike for him and her contempt for what he had done, moved up to the exposed top floor, where *Collier's* magazine, whose roving correspondent Martha was, now rented a permanent room for her. She would come back after weeks away in Italy or Normandy and stumble into the room, only to find that someone from the Free French or the Free Poles had borrowed it to spend the night with his girlfriend. Martha would have to find somewhere else to go, and come back the next morning.

Many of the wealthier inhabitants of Mayfair had also moved into the Dorchester because they had to close up their own houses for want of servants. The Hon. John Gilbey was the head fire-warden, and the family firm provided him with his own non-rationed supply of gin. There would be parties on the roof so that Emerald Cunard and other stars of London social life, fueled with Gilbey's gin, could watch the bombing. It was from there that Martha watched the first V–1 missile to hit London fly eerily along the line of Park Lane and crash into the much less select Cumberland Hotel at Marble Arch, a couple of hundred yards away.

The smaller news organizations could only have one accredited frontline correspondent in each theater of war. Hemingway, knowing this, approached *Collier's* and offered to write for them about the war in Europe. This meant that Martha would automatically lose her accreditation, with its honorary rank of captain; but she wandered around the front lines of Europe without it for the rest of the war, finding that her looks and courage and intelligence were enough to get her accepted everywhere.

"With all those soldiers about, you must have had some problems, surely?"

"Never. Maybe things were a little different then; there was more idealism, I suppose, and people still understood the concept of behaving like gentlemen. But I never had a single night's difficulty."

Because Hemingway was now *Collier's* accredited correspondent, he was taken secretly to a staging area before the D–Day invasion and watched the landings from an attack transport off the Normandy coast. The first Martha heard about it was at a briefing given some hours after the landings had actually begun.

She immediately left for the coast and managed to smuggle herself onto an unarmed hospital ship that was leaving the following dawn. The nurses on board adopted her, and hid her in a lavatory when the security men searched the ship. Getting to the Normandy coast was an extremely dangerous business: The hospital ship had to make its way through a mined channel under heavy shellfire. On the night of 7 June, Martha slipped ashore with the stretcher bearers, and stood on the soil of Europe only forty hours after the first landings, the first American journalist to do so.

Hemingway, who had had to watch the landings from his transport ship, went into a frenzy of anger. He demanded that *Collier's* should bury Martha's story at the back of the magazine, and for the rest of his life he insisted that she must have lied about going ashore since she hadn't had the necessary accreditation. In fact the American authorities arrested her on her return to England for being on the hospital ship without permission, and put her into a camp for American nurses. That night Martha climbed over the wire and made her way to a military airfield, where she told a pilot that she was desperate to see her fiancé, who was based in Italy. The pilot let her stow away on his aircraft.

That was the end of her marriage to Hemingway. Martha had nothing but dislike for him now, and he had begun an affair with someone else anyway. Martha was the only one of his wives to have left him; he never forgave her for it. Throughout the rest of his life he reserved some of his worst spite for her.

In the summer of 1997, less than a year before she died, she told me she was going back to her cottage in Wales to sort out some correspondence. She had lived there for most of the 1980s with a couple of cats, swimming every day in the single-lane pool she had installed in the garden.

I noticed the note of finality in her voice. What correspondence, I asked?

"I'm going to burn everything Ernest sent me."

I tried my hardest to dissuade her, but it was quite impossible. When she got back, I went around and saw her again. Had she, I asked, really burned everything?

"Everything. It made me feel a lot better."

I remembered seeing a letter signed by Hemingway for sale in New York for $5,000.

"How many did you burn?"

"Oh, I've really no idea. Dozens, maybe more. He used to write such a lot."

The life-darkening experience had finally been dealt with. She was putting the last part of her life in order, and getting ready for the end.

It was a great sadness to me that I hadn't known Martha when she was a little younger. When after her death a friend of mine, the novelist Nicholas Shakespeare, quoted some of her letters to him in a charming article he wrote, I was consumed with jealousy. "Sweet Shakespeare," one of them began. By the time I first met her, her eyesight was going and she no longer wrote letters.

Yet she remained magnificent to the end, heading off abruptly to Egypt or anywhere else hot in order to snorkel. I even joined her for a day at her hotel in Ras Mohammed, on the Red Sea. When she was eighty-seven she traveled to Rio and reported on the fate of the street children who were being murdered by the police at the request of shopkeepers. It was precisely the kind of subject that Martha relished: difficult, dangerous and morally clear cut. She was unhappy with the long article she wrote about it, although it seemed to me to be excellent. I would have been very pleased with myself if I had been able to write anything so crisp and clear.

Going to see her was a pleasure I hoarded up in advance. She didn't always like the wives and girlfriends of her disciples, but she became very fond of Dee. She even came with us to dinner at the Dorchester; the first time, she said, that she had been back there since 1945.

Martha had known so many people in her life: Picasso, George Orwell, Greta Garbo, Diana Cooper, Duff Cooper, Chiang Kai-shek, Chou En-lai. If you worked hard you could even get her to talk about them. I relished everything about my visits to her: the way she would say "Come up, darling!" over the intercom, the heavy front door, the small, varnished, unsteady lift, the open door of her flat. I would kiss her, and see her bright, unlined face looking enthusiastically yet never quite uncritically up at me, and I would accept the first Famous Grouse of the evening.

"Now," she would say, pushing a bowl of crisps or nuts toward me, "tell me everything about it."

"It" might be the Congo, or the Amazon, or Afghanistan; it fueled her own imagination and her own extraordinarily wide-ranging memories, and she would ask the kinds of questions that showed she was there in spirit. Although she did plenty of traveling for herself still, I felt that in my adventures she relived her own.

"Tell me again about the Taliban," she would say.

She loved the idea of bearded, turbaned warriors with Kalashnikovs who put on eye makeup and gold high-heeled sandals and painted their toenails red.

But it was always better and more interesting to listen to her stories.

"No one cares about that sort of thing any more," she would say; but I could see it gave her pleasure.

Each time I went to see her I would determine not to drink so much whisky that I would forget what she had told me. Each time I succumbed, and duly forgot. Perhaps that was her intention.

Her own papers have been lodged with an American university, and cannot be opened to the public until twenty years after her death.

"By that time everybody alive will have forgotten that I ever lived." Inconceivable.

Sometimes, when I was writing a book, Martha would ask me to read a passage to her. She was a tough critic.

"I have to be able to feel it. I need to see the color of the walls, and what the people are wearing, and the view out of the window. You aren't giving me enough of that."

I despaired of ever matching that powerful, reserved, perceptive tone of hers, which was so like the rhythm of her speech that even now that she is dead I only have to read a couple of lines out loud to hear her voice in the room. She was the clearest-headed of observers. "I gave up trying to think or judge," she wrote about the Second World War, "and turned myself into a walking tape recorder with eyes." She went to Dachau shortly after its liberation:

I have not talked about how it was the day the American Army arrived, though the prisoners told me. In their joy to be free, and longing to see their friends who had come at last, many prisoners rushed to the fence and died electrocuted. There were those who died cheering, because that effort of happiness was more than their bodies could endure. There were those who died because now they had food, and they ate before they could be stopped, and it killed them. I do not know words to describe the men who have survived this horror for years, three years, five years, ten years, and whose minds are as clear and unafraid as the day they entered.

Dachau, you recall, was one of the camps that Hitler's "deeply devoted, deeply grateful and deeply respectful" Dr. Carl Burckhardt, who became president of the International Committee of the Red Cross, had visited in 1935 and pronounced "hard but correct."

Whether writing about bugs in a Depression-era house (*The Trouble I've Seen,* 1936), or taking a plane into German-occupied Prague (*A Stricken Field,* 1940) or attending open day at an African leper colony (*Travels with Myself and Another,* 1978) Martha was always wonderfully fresh and funny and sharp. She was, she said, a journalist first and a writer second, and a woman only third. She became something of a hero to the feminists, but that irritated her: "As though somehow we're a different species from men."

She had been ill for some time with cancer, but she always insisted to me that it was an ulcer. I believed her, because I wanted to. Her eyesight was fading quite fast, and her recent travels had been a disappointment. In Corsica, where she had gone snorkeling a few months earlier, she had been mugged. For a free spirit like hers, the options were becoming too restricted.

She had, the last time Dee and I saw her, stopped taking whatever tablets it was that she had relied on, and said she felt easier as a result. I looked at her very carefully, but could see no signs of anything different: no obvious pain, no anxiety. Somehow or other Dee and I had managed to get our previous appointment with her wrong, and Martha had got up from her bed to make us dinner and we had not appeared. I felt terrible, and apologized grovelingly in letters and with flowers. Her annoyance quickly passed.

Her brother Alfred was there, leaning over her chair, and the two of them made a superb picture of elderly elegance. I knew something was going on, but I couldn't work out exactly what. Suitably, since she was one of the great travelers of the twentieth century, we used the language of travel.

"Don't go away," I said quietly to her at last over my glass of Famous Grouse, with a sudden sense of urgency and alarm.

"Darling," she said in that lovely upper-class American voice of hers, "I'm not staying around forever."

Three days later she died in her sleep. She was, her son said, smiling.

6
Dictators

Two Soviet jokes:
1st prisoner: What are you in for?
2nd prisoner: I said something nasty about Comrade Popov in 1937. And you?
1st prisoner: I said something nice about Comrade Popov in 1938.
2nd prisoner: And what about you, comrade?
3rd prisoner: I am Comrade Popov.

Q: When Mayakovsky committed suicide in 1930, what were his last words?
A: "Don't shoot, comrades."

There was a lurch, and I came awake. For a moment I couldn't think where I was. There was a strange smell, and I seemed to be trapped. Then I knew. I was jammed into an unreasonably small bunk on a passenger ship from Malta to Libya, and the smell was fuel oil mixed with coffee. Breakfast was being served.

A partly fried egg with a dot of blood in the yolk looked up from my plate.

"Somehow," I said to Bob Prabhu, my cameraman, "I don't feel hungry anymore."

We went on deck. The Libyan coast lay like a green-and-brown stripe along the horizon, and the early sun was cheerful and warming.

"Good morning, Mr. Simpson," said a man in a tweed sports jacket. He was, it turned out, a doctor from somewhere in Yorkshire, and he was paying a visit to his parents back in Libya.

Other passengers gathered around. I have noticed that the most ardent viewers of BBC news programs in Britain are those who have settled there from other countries; perhaps they are always hoping to see some news from home. These men were gloomy about Libya. The UN sanctions that had been imposed as a result of the Lockerbie bombing had had a serious effect on the entire country. It was 2000, and you couldn't even fly there because of the UN sanctions against Libya: hence our sea-crossing from Malta.

"So why are you coming to Tripoli?"

I explained that Colonel Gadhafi had offered us an interview.

"Maybe he's going to tell you that he'll let those Lockerbie fellows go."

Having interviewed Gadhafi before, I doubted it. That time, everyone had expected him to make some big statement about cutting his support for terrorist groups; instead he had explained to me in some detail the intricate constitutional workings of the Socialist People's Libyan Arab Jamahuriyah. There had been another problem too: he had spoken an English so heavily accented it was impossible to understand.

"Maybe he's been taking lessons," Bob said optimistically. He always looks on the bright side of life.

Onshore we were met by a government official, and no one examined our bags. This was good, since I had brought a bottle of Laphroaig with me, forgetting that Libya was a dry country with unpleasant penalties for those caught carrying alcohol. The bottle clinked audibly as I put my suitcase down.

Outside the Customs post, everything had changed. Tripoli was poorer and quieter, and yet there were far more shops. Colonel Gadhafi's attempt long before to close down private commerce and replace it with monster state supermarkets had been such a dreadful mistake that he had been forced to give up the whole idea. We checked into a vast, empty hotel with tiny beds, dirty carpets, taps that came off in your hands, and a dining room that always seemed to be empty.

"If it's anything like last time, we could be here for days before we get the interview," I said gloomily as Bob and I chewed some unidentifiable meat in the restaurant.

But it wasn't anything like last time. Gadhafi seemed enthusiastic to see us, and we were told to be ready by the day after next. We visited the Roman museum in Green Square in the heart of the old city, and were arrested by the security police because Bob took a photograph of some statuary. In Libya it is always the security police who are called when anyone has a problem with foreigners. Within about a minute of hearing that we were in Tripoli to interview Gadhafi, though, they ushered us out in the sunshine of Green Square again. In Libya it's not who you are that counts, it's who you're interviewing.

The following afternoon a large black limousine arrived and we were helped into it. We headed out of Tripoli toward the surrounding desert.

"Where exactly are we going?"

"To see the Leader."

"Sure, but where?"

"Ah, nobody can say."

So that was clear.

We drove through the dusty outer suburbs, where little green flags fluttered in the sharp wind, mudbrick took over from concrete, and donkeys and camels stood outside the houses instead of cars. The desert proper had scarcely begun when we reached a vast military compound. Seeing an official car, the men lounging at the gate made a special fuss about asking for our passes, searching the boot, and checking our license plates.

The army base was big, and most of it was just desert. We rattled along the track, and as the sun began to decline over the horizon we finally saw Gadhafi's tent. It looked exactly as I had remembered it: the size of a tennis court, and panelled in green, red and white canvas. Inside, the ground was covered with expensive carpets.

"Fantastic," I said.

But we didn't stop there. Instead, we were driven over to a large vehicle like an American Winnebago. We followed our guide up the steps, ducked our heads, and found ourselves in a tiny room, just large enough for four people. There were no windows.

"For interview," said our guide proudly.

"If we survive half an hour in this," I said, "the pictures won't be worth broadcasting. This is useless."

"Completely," said Bob, shaking his head.

The guide's face fell. He was a nice fellow, and easily hurt.

"The only place to do it is the tent," said Bob.

"But I don't think—"

Something about Bob's expression made him head down the steps quickly.

The tent was much as I had remembered it: roomy, pleasant, but dappled with strange colors. Bob was certain that wouldn't matter; the background of red and green panels would explain the odd coloring to the viewer. I felt that the entire experience was so weird that the viewer would be inclined to accept anything anyway.

He labored away in the afternoon heat, setting up his lights, unraveling his microphone cables, testing the camera. It was hard work on his own. I paced up and down, trying out questions. This would be a difficult interview to structure; interviews with Gadhafi always were.

Bob was still not quite finished when the neatly suited officials who had been sitting around watching stood up and walked over to the entrance.

"He's coming, Bob," I said warningly.

We needed some good opening shots of him walking in.

And then I saw him.

"You'll never guess what he's wearing," I whispered. Bob was already taking his camera off the tripod.

At a distance of twenty yards, as Gadhafi approached the tent, it wasn't so much the Hawaiian shirt that seized the attention; he had been wearing them ever since he had fallen under the spell of Nelson Mandela. It was the hat, an elderly straw number. Gadhafi had it on sideways, and I could even see the three little brass-rimmed ventilation holes over his forehead.

He was also on crutches. A year before he had suffered some mysterious accident, which the conspiracy-minded insisted was an assassination attempt. Gadhafi himself insisted he had fallen over and hurt his leg while playing football with some boys. Later, when I too fell over, rupturing the tendons in my left knee and hobbling about on crutches and walking sticks for a year afterward, I was more inclined to believe him.

Surely, I thought, one of his officials will have a quiet word and make him take the hat off, on the grounds that it makes him look barking mad. But no, they just smiled ingratiatingly and let him walk into the tent like that.

Everyone knew that Gadhafi marched to a different drummer. "That madman," President Sadat of Egypt used to call him. But he wasn't a savage Stalinist despot like Saddam Hussein of Iraq, nor a brutal autocrat like Hafez al-Assad of Syria, and certainly not a grand luxurious *roi fainéant* like the royalty of the Gulf. Strictly speaking, he didn't govern at all, since all power in Libya was notionally vested in the Committees, which were supposed to govern every level of life, from top to bottom. "Committees Everywhere!" was the depressing slogan that faced you in the arrivals hall at Tripoli airport in the days when the planes were allowed to fly; it sounded like local government hell.

In practice, of course, his people ran everything. Gadhafi had a particularly nasty secret police organization, and no one in that vast, underpopulated country did anything that the state didn't like; except perhaps the black marketeers and criminals, of whom there were a certain amount. People disappeared or were tortured, and murdered secretly abroad; yet Gadhafi in his later years presided benignly over everything, pretending not to know precisely what was going on. Pretending not to be in power.

That, at any rate, is what I had always believed. I had found Gadhafi an engaging if oddball character in the past and felt a kind of sympathy for him now. Yet it seemed strange that none of the intelligent, Westernized characters around him would dare to suggest that he take his silly hat off for our interview. Was it because their own power and influence depended on keeping him sweet? Were they just courtiers, who were ruled by his whim as much as the rest of the country was? Was he just playing at being an eccentric?

I didn't think so then, and I don't think so now. Shortly before Bob and I arrived in Libya, I had been asked by a London newspaper to review a book of short stories which Gadhafi had written. It was an extraordinary collection: not really stories so much as homilies and parables. But the strangest thing about it was the general air of fatigue and gloom that enveloped every page. It was called *Escape to Hell*, and even with big type, small format and a long and unnecessarily respectful introduction by my old sparring partner Pierre Salinger (once upon a time press spokesman to President Kennedy, and now an increasingly eccentric figure himself) it made less than two hundred pages.

Perhaps the most extraordinary passage in this extraordinary book seemed to show that he was sick of governing his country:

> [W]hat can I—a poor bedouin—hope for in a modern city of insanity? People snap at me whenever they see me: build us a better house! Get us a better telephone line! Build us a road upon the sea! Make a public park for us! Catch oceans of fish for us! Write down a magic spell to protect us! Officiate at our wedding! Kill this dog, and buy us a cat! A poor, lost bedouin, without even a birth certificate, with his staff upon his shoulder. A bedouin, who will not stop for a red light, nor be afraid when a policeman takes hold of him . . .
>
> I feel that the masses, who would not even show mercy to their saviour, follow me around, burning me with their gaze. Even when they are applauding me, it feels like they are pricking me. I am an illiterate bedouin, who does not even know about painting houses or sewage systems . . .

Time, you might think, for his next injection. But no matter how depressed most politicians get from to time, they usually have someone on hand to stop them sending this kind of thing to the publisher. Not Gadhafi.

And now he was sitting opposite me, the bush of dark hair thinning and graying, the crevasses on either side of his nose and mouth deepening as he smiled, fussing over the arrangement of his crutches and his clothes, and keeping his hat still jammed sideways on his head. He looks, I thought, like Joe E. Brown in *Some Like It Hot*.

Then he turned his head so that the front of his hat was pointing at me, snapped his fingers, and one of the aides came over carrying a horsehair fly-whisk.

The flies were indeed a nuisance in the tent, but they were too small for the viewer to see; so when Gadhafi lashed around himself with the whisk it looked as though he were whipping himself in a pious frenzy. Maybe I should have advised him to put up with the flies, to take the hat off, to change the shirt. It wasn't that I didn't dare to do it; I have done many more difficult things in my time. It was simply that these were the outward and visible signs of an inward eccentricity that was central to the character of the man. I didn't want him to change a thing.

I still didn't know if he had a purpose in giving this interview. I questioned him on all the obvious subjects, but he was scarcely forthcoming about any of them: Lockerbie, internal politics, the attempts to assassinate him (including, a defector from MI5 had recently said, a plot hatched up with the knowledge of the British Secret Intelligence Service).

He answered all these questions absently, smiling occasionally as though he had been reminded of something particularly absurd, and whipping himself with his fly-whisk. Bob Prabhu crouched over the camera, sweating in the heat. He had been right: Gadhafi had been taking English lessons. Sometimes he lapsed into Arabic, but when I urged him to repeat what he had said in English he would always do it, smiling indulgently as though I had asked him for some rather ludicrous favor.

I was starting to run out of questions, and perhaps he realized it. As I began another one he broke in.

"I have something to say. If the two men the English government say were guilty of the Lockerbie bombing are guilty, then there is no reason why they should not be tried for it. We think they were not guilty. But there is no reason for them to stay. They can go. They want to go."

That's convenient, I thought; but I knew now why we had been invited to interview the Leader. This was the move that would unblock the entire issue of sanctions. Gadhafi had cut the two Lockerbie suspects loose, after all the reassuring things he had said to them in the past about protecting them from the callous inequities of the British legal system. Bob and I didn't merely have an interesting collector's item on our hands, we had a sizeable scoop.

That evening, as I began to write my account of the interview, Bob knocked on my door. I know him well, and love him dearly, and could see that something was up.

"There's something funny about the interview," he said. He'd been watching it on the portable monitor in his room.

Oh Christ, I thought, he means there's tape damage, or electronic interference. I remembered an interview I once did in a military base in

Iraq, which was so crackling with electronic gadgets of different kinds that the material we shot was unusable.

"Nothing like that," Bob said. "Gadhafi was making noises, that's all."

"Whatever are you on about? What kind of noises?"

"Kind of personal ones." He looked away.

As I say, I know Bob. He is a very modest man, especially where bodily functions are concerned.

"What, stomach rumblings?"

Borborygmi can be a nuisance in a television interview.

"No, worse than that."

"What, farting?"

Now I'd embarrassed him. He nodded, wordlessly.

"Look, that's absolutely stupid, Bob. I was sitting opposite him. If he'd been farting I'd have heard it. You're imagining it."

"Well, listen to the tape."

I listened. There was absolutely no doubt about it. The personal microphone which Bob had pinned on Gadhafi had picked it up very clearly, though I hadn't noticed it at the time. The wind passage lasted for about ten minutes of our half-hour interview. Gadhafi would rise up a little in his seat, the thunder would roll for fifteen or twenty seconds at a time, and then he would sink back into his seat with a pleased expression on his face. It may have happened to me before without my knowledge, but never, I think, in so concentrated and elaborate a fashion.

We ran the interview in truncated form on the *Nine O'Clock News,* and in full on *Simpson's World.* The wind-breaking was audible in both versions, but I thought it best not to draw attention to it. To be honest, I couldn't think how to express it in my script. With the *Sunday Telegraph,* though, I felt I could let rip: "During part of our interview, Col. Gadhafi broke wind audibly and at length."

The foreign editor, a particular friend of mine named Con Coughlin, headlined the article "Warm Wind of Compromise Blows From Gadhafi."

Bob and I left Libya the following day, after a trip to the spectacular ruins of Sabratha, one of the two Roman sites that, together with Leptis Magna and what is now itself called Tripoli, made up Tripolitania, the three cities of the Libyan coast. We had come to know our driver quite well, and we decided to get him to take us across the border to Tunisia rather than face the long sea-crossing back to Malta.

The journey was tedious, and it was dark when we reached the border. There was no government official to shepherd us through this time. As we lugged our cases into the Customs Hall, large, echoing and full of flies and dirty scraps of paper, I suddenly remembered the bottle of Laphroaig. I hadn't even opened it. The Customs man won't look properly, I told myself.

But he did. He delved down through my dirty clothes and found it, neatly packaged between the pair of black shoes I had worn for the interview. He pulled it out by the neck. I looked at him properly for the first time: he was big and fat, his uniform had not been cleaned for months, and he was extremely angry.

"Oh God," groaned the driver beside me. "One litre, one year. One litre, one year."

I felt a strange, Gadhafi-like calm.

"Are you going to give me a year for that? Surely not."

He made an angry muttering sound, and thought about it. It seemed to take him a long time: Maybe he was reflecting on all the forms he would have to fill if he made a case out of this. Then he threw the bottle carelessly back into the case and closed the lid.

"*Y'alla,*" he said, with what sounded like a certain contempt. "Go."

As we drove across the border into Tunisia the driver's despair turned to delight.

"One litre," he would shout, and Bob and I would reply dutifully, "One year."

This went on for some time. He was still laughing and saying "One litre" when we said goodbye to him and transferred our gear to a Tunisian taxi.

"Take us to the best hotel in town," I told the new driver grandly; after all our privations and problems I felt we deserved it.

He drove us through the belt of small boarding houses and private hotels and on into the more expensive part of town. The hotels became bigger and grander, until they reached the full five-star level. Then, mysteriously, we were back in the boarding-house zone again.

"I said the best hotel."

"Sir, yes, no problem. Best hotel."

We drove a little farther. The road surface wasn't so good now, and the street lights were farther apart. Suddenly he turned to the right and stopped. Bob and I peered out at an ordinary, rundown house, scarcely bigger than a bungalow.

'THE BEST HOTEL,' said the board over the gate.

I pressed the doorbell twice and then once again more briefly. That was what we had been told to do.

"I'm not absolutely sure this is right," said the languid voice beside me.

I was no more certain than my cameraman was. His name was Rory Peck, and he was the owner of the languid voice. And then the door opened, and both of us could see it was exactly right. The face that peered suspiciously out at us was thin and dark and nervous: a black marketeer's face. The first thing it did was to check whether there was anyone behind us. Then it raised a single eyebrow.

Rory explained in his halting Russian, half genuine and half invented, who we were and what we wanted. The face said nothing, but I had the impression that we were expected. The door opened a little wider.

It was a miserable place, in a huge decaying block on the outskirts of Moscow. One of the two rooms was filled almost to capacity with cardboard boxes from Korea. The inlaid wooden floor was coming slowly to pieces thanks to the damp, and there was a nasty smell. The passageway was dark, but he didn't turn on any lights.

The black marketeer slept in the other room. Against the wall were propped a few objects under blankets and dirty sheets.

"Painting," said the black marketeer tersely, and pulled the coverings away. As we stood in the next room he pulled out a gigantic canvas, wheezing, and lugged it out into the passage where we were waiting.

While Rory looked at the large painting, I went into the bedroom and examined a couple of others. The first was a large unframed canvas showing Stalin walking the battlements of the Kremlin with Marshal Voroshilov, his talentless, toadying sidekick from the days immediately before the German invasion of Russia in 1941. The other was a scene from a revolutionary political meeting with Lenin haranguing a crowd of sailors. Both subjects were, of course, shot through with irony. Stalin never showed himself anywhere that he could be seen by ordinary people, and soon after the Bolshevik seizure of power the sailors from Kronstadt who had helped it along staged a rebellion against him and were destroyed.

It was 1990, and the whole Soviet system was only a year away from collapse. Yet even at this late stage, the concept that you could buy something from a freelance dealer was something the authorities could still not easily accept. By offering dollars to a Soviet citizen, even in exchange for Soviet paintings, we ourselves were not committing an offense; but the Soviet citizen was, by accepting the money. If we had been caught, it would have been confiscated, and we would have been given an official warning. Yet the police, badly paid and demoralized, would not have interfered with us even if the law on this kind of thing had been clear. The black marketeer's nervousness was merely the result of years of conditioning.

I took the Stalin, the Lenin and an official portrait of Molotov, which made the dreadful old crook ("Every time I shake his hand, I remember the thousands of people he's killed," Ernest Bevin used to say) look rather avuncular. They cost me, as I remember, thirty dollars apiece.

Rory bought the big canvas in the passage. It was a rather good painting from the early 1920s of the assault on the Winter Palace. Its ferocity and valor were completely fictitious, since the Palace was merely defended by a brigade of (by that point) mostly hysterical women, and a bunch of scared, untrained teenaged boys. Far from charging across the square under fire, as shown in Rory's painting, the attackers lined up meekly at the kitchen door, which someone had left open, and there was no serious resistance. But that's the great pleasure of political art: it's as full of meaning and seriousness as a detergent advertisement.

Dictator kitsch, as an artistic genre, is superbly, satisfyingly pompous and self-deceptive as well as being utterly inartistic: the equivalent of those society portraits you see in the back pages of expensive magazines, where all the sitters are beautiful, all the wrinkles have been ironed away and all the necks are smooth. Time and reality have been airbrushed out.

Dictators like to believe that they are young and handsome, just as they like to believe their people love them.

At the rallies staged in the center of Bucharest for President Nicolae Ceauşescu of Romania, the dictator's dictator, one in every twelve participants was given a placard to hold up, with the great man's face on it. Not the bad-tempered, increasingly haggard face of the late 1980s, but the young, dark-haired, thrusting face like a soccer star from twenty years before.

At that stage, briefly, the man had been genuinely popular because he stood up to the Russians when they invaded Romania's neighbor, Czechoslovakia, in 1968. Within seven or eight years the popularity had evaporated completely, and the difference had to be made up by his public relations men. They created wonderful epithets for him, which the newspapers obediently printed and grovelers repeated during the interminable speeches that were made wherever he went: The Flag of Our National Pride, Our Prince Charming, The Polyvalent Genius, Our Secular God, The New Morning Star.

Ceauşescu art was the visual equivalent of all this groveling. During the revolution a brave museum curator went around gathering up all the examples he could find: not a safe thing to do at a time when people had switched from a dull acceptance of Ceauşescu to a violent loathing for every symbol of his rule. Anyone showing an interest in conserving this frightful stuff could easily have been accused of pro-Ceauşescu tendencies and might have been lynched. The curator, a clear-sighted and intelligent man, explained that these pictures were an important part of modern Romanian history, and would one day be required when the country was capable of examining its past rationally. He showed me his collection, though he wouldn't allow my cameraman to film it lest the mob came around and burned them all. If he hadn't been so high-minded, I would have offered him a hundred dollars for anything in the collection.

To the connoisseur of dictator kitsch, the paintings were superb: Ceauşescu as a preternaturally handsome young man, defying some down-at-heel landlord; Ceauşescu as an aspiring Party hack addressing a rally of happy workers; Ceauşescu and his witchlike wife, Elena, opening a vast, environmentally destructive hydroelectric project on the Danube;

Ceauşescu standing in a crowd of workers and peasants (something he never really did, of course) and laying his hand on the head of a thinly clad young boy in faintly pederastic fashion as he gently explains his theory of Building Up the Multilaterally Developed Socialist Society to his rapt audience. As with Nazi and some Soviet art, there was the frequent whiff of sexual irregularity about Ceauşescu art.

It is the shamelessness of dictator kitsch that is so attractive—the idea, which both the artist and the commissioning official know to be utterly false, that the president is a man of the people who shares the conditions of their life and is respected and loved by them. Perhaps the Great Man believes it; perhaps he is merely watching out for any sign that the people around him *don't* believe it. The portraits of dictators are on display, not simply to convince the people that they really love him (whatever they might think), but as a pledge of loyalty by the system. Dictators are rarely men of much imagination: they like to see hard evidence that the system is presenting them as they want to be presented.

Saddam Hussein's art was, if anything, worse and madder than Ceauşescu's. Every public building in every city, town and village in Iraq had its huge official portrait of the appalling barbarian, always smiling and often extending his right arm in greeting, a trademark gesture which many Iraqis privately found infuriating. In a country of ethnic and religious diversity, he presented himself as the sole unifying figure (President George Bush unwisely bought this line in 1991, and decided not to allow Saddam's overthrow); as a result his portraits showed him wearing Kurdish costume, worshipping at Christian, Sunni and Shi'ite shrines, or crowned with an Arab *k'fir* and wearing white robes.

I had two particular favorites: in one he sported a green eyeshade and carried a tennis racket; in the other he wore a university gown and had a mortarboard on his head, while holding a set of scales in his right hand and a sword in his left. This was displayed outside the law faculty building at Baghdad University, just in case any of the students there forgot who the fount of all justice was in Iraq. The sword was a particularly good touch.

I was banned from Iraq for the lifetime of the Saddam Hussein regime (or of the man himself, which was not quite the same thing), and could no longer trawl the shops and bazaars of Baghdad for Saddam watches, clocks, scarves, ties, shirts, lapel badges and so on. In the five months I spent there before, during and after the Gulf crisis of 1990–91 I showed an interest in these things, which the authorities regarded as unhealthy. They forbade me, for instance, to film the sixty-foot ceremonial arches composed of human arms holding crossed scimitars (the arms were modeled on Saddam's own, and were of course made by a British foundry), because they knew I was inclined to make fun of them.

This particular monument had a special brutality to it. In the roadway beneath the arched arms the architect had set, on Saddam's particular instructions, hundreds of Iranian helmets from the Iran-Iraq War. Whenever Saddam celebrated a military triumph—which was often, of course—he would drive between the two arches, his arm extended in his emperor-like gesture, passing over the helmets of his enemies like a Mongol chieftain driving his chariot over a hill of skulls. Each of the Iranian helmets had a bullet or shrapnel hole in it, to add to the gruesome effect; though I became a little more skeptical about the genuineness of the Iraqi show after I discovered that a friend of mine used to collect abandoned Russian helmets in Afghanistan, fire a round from an AK-47 through them and smear the inside with chicken blood in order to sell them to American collectors.

What was not in question was the bad taste of a man who wanted to drive over soldiers' helmets, under an arch modeled on his own arms. You have to have a certain cast of mind for that kind of thing: apart from anything else, it requires a major sense-of-humor bypass. This is another feature common to most dictators: they do not altogether see the funny side of themselves and what they are doing. Hitler's courtiers first tried to hide from him the fact that Charlie Chaplin had taken him off in *The Great Dictator,* and then ascribed it to the international Jewish conspiracy.

There are many fewer dictators around nowadays; the international climate no longer favors autocracy, and the World Bank and the International Monetary Fund disapprove. Like some large mammal with a valuable coat, the dictator's very existence is in question. Robert Mugabe of Zimbabwe, a man I have met and interviewed several times over the past twenty years, turned himself into one and mobilized an army of thugs ("war veterans") to do his dirty work. Yet one day soon he will pack up and leave office. Dictators are not what they used to be.

Not even the U.S. State Department defends them any more, even though it once set so many of them up. The British and French governments, who have always been able to swallow almost any appalling behavior if they thought it would earn them a pound or two, are finding that the field of opportunity has diminished drastically. Only the Israelis habitually send advisers and sell weapons to regimes that others prefer to avoid.

Perhaps, instead of waiting to applaud when their people chase tyrants from office and kill them or put them on trial, we should tempt the few remaining dictators to go early by offering them a place in a theme park where they can stage mock executions, hold triumphant march pasts, invest their money in imaginary Swiss and Luxembourgeois accounts, and decorate the streets and buildings with their own gigantic portraits. A little careful flattery by their faithful courtiers might well persuade them that our applause and laughter represented the appreciation of the masses, and that they were still loved as much as they always had been, of course.

I have interviewed a substantial number of tyrants in my time, from Ayatollah Khomeini in Iran to General Galtieri in Argentina and P. W. Botha in South Africa. I have lunched with the head of the nastiest militia group in Lebanon, and drunk coffee at the *estancia* of a Colombian vigilante leader who boasted of the number of "communists" (that is, ordinary peasants) his men had killed. I have listened to one of the most notorious Palestinian hijackers eat his way noisily through a *meze* in Baghdad. I have shaken hands with murderers and torturers and embezzlers, in the hope of luring them into being filmed for television. It is not something to be proud of. Still, I have discovered that you do not have to pretend to agree with such people, any more than you have to pretend to share the views of politicians you interview. Politeness and a willingness to listen are all that is required.

You are usually safe enough with the heads of established governments, because they tend to obey the rules and leave you alone. Further down the social scale, at the level of bandits, gang leaders and militia bosses, you can get into serious difficulty; especially if they control everything around them and have no fear of the consequences. Most dangerous of all, though, is the crazed dictator who thinks he is omnipotent.

A friend and colleague of mine made the difficult journey to Uganda in 1973, at the height of Idi Amin's reign of terror. Amin was known for his towering rages, which could be sparked off by the slightest detail; and in his compound on the edge of Kampala he could kill or maim anyone he chose.

When the crew were ushered in, they found he was powering up and down his swimming pool, displacing vast quantities of water and breathing like a sea lion. He watched them as he swam, and they decided to take the risk of filming him. At last Amin reached his final lap, and hoisted his enormous bulk out of the water. At that moment the reporter saw that one of his huge testicles, the size of a honeydew melon, was hanging out of his swimming trunks. The cameraman seemed not to have noticed, and kept the shot wide enough for the giant gonad to be visible when the pictures were shown on television.

Amin walked down the side of the pool and lowered his bulk into a chair. This, clearly, was where he wanted to do the interview. The reporter was in some difficulties. If he suggested to Amin that he might want to hoist the stray object back on board, that could spark off one of his violent outbursts of anger. They might not even survive. If, on the other hand, the cameraman continued not to see, the pictures would be unbroadcastable and all the effort and risk it had taken for them to be there would be wasted.

In the end, the cameraman himself spotted Amin's ball, and zoomed in considerably to avoid it. The interview passed off well enough, Amin denying the accusations against him with a menacing joviality. But my friend said it required an immense effort of will not to look down at the vast testicle, as it lay in front of him on the chair like a particularly fine aubergine.

Kurt Waldheim was not a dictator; he was, in turn, a Nazi bureaucrat, a notably boring UN secretary-general, and a disgraced president of

Austria. But he had a nasty temper, and he is one of only two international leaders to have punched me.

It was during the Austrian presidential election of 1985, and Waldheim
was holding the last rally of his campaign, in the center of Vienna. The
cameraman I was working with, a tough, extremely dependable Scot
named Bill Nicol, had cleverly managed to edge his way onto the stage
beside Waldheim. Standing alongside him, I could see the upturned faces
glowing with pride: old faces, for the most part, with Iron Crosses pinned
to their ties and sometimes an empty sleeve or trouser leg to show what
they had sacrificed for Hitler. Now they had come out in large numbers
to support Waldheim, since for them no one whom the international
press had accused of being a Nazi could be all bad.

Waldheim was a rotten speaker, but with elements like this in the
audience even he could not fail to get a good reception. They cheered
him, and part of the crowd started up a song: It could have been the
Horst Wessellied, for all I know, but it was probably just the Austrian
national anthem. In those days most Austrians still believed the convenient fiction that the wartime Allies had begun to disseminate in 1945,
that Austria was Hitler's first victim. That was when they wanted to
wean Austria away from Nazi Germany.

After the war, the three Western allies were careful not to go in for
denazification too harshly in Austria, since they were in competition
with Russia, which occupied a sizeable chunk of the country. The fact
that most Austrians had enthusiastically welcomed the *Anschluss* in
1938 (though there were some notable and brave exceptions) and had
provided large numbers of recruits for the *Waffen-SS* had conveniently
been forgotten.

Until, that is, Waldheim's past began to leak out. He was not the kind
of Nazi who went around in jackboots, stomping on people's faces;
instead, he had created the conditions under which that kind of thing was
possible. He served in Yugoslavia, administering the German occupation.
The death warrants of resisters were signed, the torture of suspects was
arranged, but Waldheim didn't have to pull the trigger or plug in the
equipment himself; there were other people to do that kind of thing.

And now, after an undistinguished period at the UN (I remember the terror in his face and the way his hands shook when he met a group of gunmen during a half-hearted effort to broker peace in Angola), he was among his own people again. The crowd cheered, Waldheim held out his arms to them, Bill Nicol grunted that the camera was running, and I shouted my question over the roar of the crowd.

"Do you think you're going to win?"

"Yes, I do. You can see—zese people love me."

He was still beaming.

"Even though in today's British press there are accusations that you ordered the execution of several British prisoners of war?"

Actually, I don't think I got that far. He punched me in the stomach, just like Prime Minister Harold Wilson had, back in 1970. But although Waldheim was nastier and bonier than Wilson, I did not rate him as a puncher. Besides, I was wearing a large and rather expensive loden coat, which absorbed much of the blow.

His normally sallow face was distorted with rage, and had taken on an almost prunelike color.

"Vy are you asking me zese qvestions? You see, ze people love me."

He turned back to them, his face breaking into a ghastly rictus of a smile. And indeed all the old Mein Kampfers in the audience broke into a cheer, waving their empty sleeves and their crutches and hooting me for disturbing the great man at his devotions.

"You see," Waldheim repeated, the smile giving way to fury again, and leaning into Bill's camera lens so that his face became hideously distorted, "zey love me. I don't have to bozzer viz your qvestions. I shall VIN."

He turned to them again, and they cheered louder than ever.

Fortunately, an American camera crew had filmed Waldheim punching me, and gave us the pictures. The whole thing caused a certain sensation, even in Austria.

A couple of evenings later, the election result was declared in a vast and hideous Franz-Josef-gothic hall in the center of Vienna. Once again, Bill Nicol worked his way into a good position: so good that, as Waldheim and his family arrived, we were swept along with them. Suddenly, as the crowd carried us onto the platform immediately behind Waldheim, I felt an intense pain shoot up my right arm. The crush was too great for me to be able at first to see what had happened; then I realized who owned the expensive fur coat beside me, and I understood. Frau Waldheim, as tall and bony as her husband but still showing the remains of a certain hawk-like beauty, had dug her sharp scarlet fingernails into me.

"Ouch."

"I hope you are enjoying yourself," she hissed.

By the time I thought of an adequate comeback, Waldheim had been proclaimed president of Austria.

"Por favor, compañero, por favor."

A stout sixtyish comrade, one of the people who watched over the place, was pulling at me, her face screwed up like a dishcloth. I looked down: my offense was to have rested my hand on a glass case containing an old, yellowing piece of folded cloth. This, according to a typed notice, was a pair of Fidel Castro's trousers, as worn by the great man during his guerrilla campaign in the Sierra Maestra mountains in the 1950s. You could see the Sierra Maestra through the museum windows. Close by, a group of tourists was being told the story of Castro's attack on this building in 1953.

In those days it had been called the Moncada barracks. From it the Cuban military controlled Santiago de Cuba, the second largest city on the island. The barracks had been a place of unquestioned nastiness, where people were tortured and shot at random by the soldiers of President Batista. Bullets encrusted with human tissue had lodged in the walls.

Nowadays the glass cases around these walls were full of relics: the contents of the revolutionaries' pockets when they made their attack on the barracks, their hats and shoes, their guns, the Pepsi-Cola bottle they had filled with petrol. Everything about this place was holy, and Castro's wisdom and revolutionary courage were praised relentlessly on every hand.

And yet the photographs hinted that the callow young man who waved at the cameras as he was released from jail a couple of years after the Moncada attack was no wiser than the rest of us; just quick-witted, charismatic and rather lucky. And he had succeeded. HISTORY WILL VINDICATE ME, ran a quotation from Fidel across one wall of this shrine. It has, because his hagiographers were in a position to write it. History used to vindicate Stalin, Ceauşescu and the Shah of Iran.

Near the barracks I met a tough-looking university scientist who had gone into politics and was standing as a candidate for the 1993 election, which I was in Cuba to report on. He was a pro-Castroite, of course: There were no other candidates. What sort of a man was Fidel?

His eyes took on a faraway look. "Being next to someone of such genius is very difficult. The first thing he did was to take me by the hand and put me on the same level as he was. Of course I realize I'm not really on the same level, but it was an ethical gesture of modesty. I felt tremendous emotion, as if my heart wouldn't fit in my thorax."

Thorax? Ah, of course, he was a scientist. I looked at his inspired, faraway eyes and the determined mouth beneath them. This boy will go far, I thought. Assuming, of course, Castro lasts.

He has lasted since 1 January 1959. Yet it was his failure rather than his success to be the last Marxist ruler west of Beijing. There had been no smooth transfer of power to a chosen successor, no plan for continuing the system into the distant future. Everything rested on Castro.

Mental rigidity had become Cuba's primary characteristic. In another part of the barracks a school had been established. Wandering round, I saw a notice on a board in the corridor:

Requirements to be chosen as an exemplary worker: ideological firmness, modesty and simplicity expressed in an austere life without consumerist habits, the energetic and intransigent defense of state property, and the fight against petty-bourgeois individualism.

Since this was a nursery school, a cutout of Snow White was pinned above it.

Still, the old pictures of Marx and Lenin had mostly disappeared. After the collapse of the Soviet Empire their place had increasingly been taken by José Martí, the father of Cuban independence. Fidel read his writings when he was in prison, and underlined some of his leaden phrases in a book now on show at the Moncada barracks: "A lazy soul kindles no fire," and, more depressing yet prophetic, "Long service obliges you to continue serving."

We were in Santiago de Cuba because we hoped to get a word with Castro. But he was a difficult man to interview. In fact, as with other autocrats, you were never entirely sure you *wanted* to interview him, since he tended to go on talking for a very long time and expected that everything he said would be broadcast. That was what happened on Cuban television, and he assumed that everyone else would have the same interest. Not, of course, necessarily true. In 1998 he gave a three-hour interview to one of the big American networks, which used just nine seconds of it in their news bulletin: a usage ratio of approximately twelve hundred to one.

Castro was not a tyrant, but he was much too fond of the sound of his own voice. I once sat through a seven-hour harangue from him, in which he rambled on about a past so distant that you had to be in your sixties to remember it properly, and lectured his long-suffering people about the need for them to make further sacrifices; as though it wasn't enough of a sacrifice to have to endure seven hours of him on prime-time television with no opt-outs.

Its human rights deficiencies apart, I loved Castro's Cuba very much, and sympathized with its predicament immensely; but I found it hard to be totally enthusiastic about a man who set so little store by the physical comfort of his audience. However, the last time I heard him speak was on New Year's Day 1999, the fortieth anniversary of his revolution; and then he galloped so fast through his speech that he finished in under three hours, and took everyone by surprise. Many of the lower Party functionaries had only just begun to settle into positions where they could nap without being noticed.

There were two perennial questions in Cuba: What will happen when Castro goes, and How popular is he, in reality? Once, wandering around the old part of Havana with a camera crew, we were discussing his popularity among ourselves.

"There's only one way to find out," I said to the producer. "Let's just bang on any of these doors at random and film the answer."

The producer agreed.

"So which door?"

She pointed to one: a large, eighteenth-century affair which was largely held together by its ancient layers of paint, and sported a copper door knocker, green with age, in the shape of a woman's head. The cameraman (it was Nigel Bateson, a giant South African) said the camera was running, and I banged the knocker hard.

In a shorter time than I could have believed, a beautiful young woman pulled the door open.

"*Sí?*"

I explained in halting Spanish that we wanted to talk to her about Fidel.

"That's quite a coincidence," she said in excellent English. "My friends and I were just talking about him now. Come in and meet them."

All good stuff, of course, except that it seemed much too good to be true. Such an attractive woman, such good English, so swift and welcoming: I knew we would have problems convincing anyone that this had not been carefully set up, like those travel programs where everything works perfectly because it has been scripted and rehearsed time and again in advance.

It turned out that she was a ballet dancer, and her friends were also involved in the arts. They had been discussing how they could tell Fidel, whom they all admired, how hard life was and how much inefficiency and corruption you had to put up with in order to get by. Now they told us. It was superb.

"You see, we love and admire Fidel; he's like our father. None of us here knows anything else but him. And yet we want to be freer than we are. We want to be able to say what we like and read what we like and go where we like, and this is not possible in Cuba nowadays. So we have problems, and we don't know what to do."

A few days later we went to Santiago de Cuba and the Moncada barracks. Castro himself was going there to vote, and it was pretty clear that he would say something to the assembled foreign journalists. He liked microphones.

We chose our position with some care. Nigel planted his camera tripod in the best position, where it would catch the great man's eye as he passed. I stuck a large BBC sign on top of the lens.

It grew hot. People jostled and made jokes.

"Bloody snappers," Nigel grunted; photographers and cameramen wage a fierce world war with each other, getting in each other's shots and struggling for the best positions.

Our fixer, the television producer Rosalind Bain, who organized almost all my Latin American expeditions, thought about the question we should put to Castro if we got the chance.

"You know, King Juan Carlos offered Castro an estate in Spain recently. It wouldn't surprise me at all if the old boy was sick of all this and wanted to retire. You could ask him about that."

"All right."

A roar from the crowd outside warned us that Castro had finally arrived, hours behind schedule. His stature was considerable: a big, shaggy six-footer who still looked like a cigar-smoker even though he had long given up. His olive-green uniform was clearly new and clean, but in the heat it had started to take on the rumpled look that somehow belonged to him. His stomach hung over his belt, and there were patches of sweat under the arms.

He walked in a little vaguely, met everyone, stayed an oddly long time in the voting booth considering that there was no choice of candidate, then emerged to put his paper ballot in the box.

The Cuban journalists shouted out their questions, and he answered them with some care. Our sound recordist sweated in the ruck and pushed his boom microphone in closer.

"Get that fuckin' fishpole outta his face," shouted an American voice despairingly behind us.

"*Comandante!*" shouted a Cuban.

"Fidel," shouted someone else, more chummily.

I preferred something a little more formal.

"*Señor Presidente.*"

He turned, the heavy black eyebrows rising like the two halves of a hydraulic bridge, faint tobacco stains still visible on the beard that the CIA had once famously tried to eradicate. The dark gaze locked onto mine. In the West, I told the gaze, people were saying that the Cuban revolution was finished and that he was on the way out. Would he like to comment? Rosalind translated. He preferred her to me, as well he might: she was darkly handsome, with the flashing eyes Cubans love.

He stopped, and the crowd stopped with him. He snorted down his big nose, ran his fingers through his graying beard, and answered.

"I am a prisoner of the Revolution. I'm not a free man. If it were decided that I shouldn't continue, I would feel as though I'd been given a reward after all these years of struggle. Maybe someone else should take over in five years' time. I wouldn't feel sad."

There was a little intake of breath around me; this wasn't the answer the crowd had been expecting from Cuba's presiding genius.

He went on for some minutes, while the crowd sweated and heaved around him, cameramen hoisting their heavy cameras over their heads and pointing them down at him, photographers forcing their way between their arms and flashing their bulbs in his face.

I kept up the eye contact, creating a conversation between us so that he would forget the rest of the crowd who were sweating and shoving and trying to break in every time he paused for breath. I asked him if he was aware of the complaints of so many Cubans about their daily lives.

"People will have to go on fighting and working hard," he said, though it was no answer. "Everything changes."

A doorstep interview with Fidel Castro lasts almost as long as a set-piece interview with any leader in the West, and the only restriction on us was the sheer impossibility, even for a man as big and powerful as Nigel, to keep focused on Castro's face under such conditions. It didn't matter; we had what we wanted.

He took a last glum look at the eager, competitive journalists in front of him, and swept on.

"Fidel!"

"Comandante!"

The next night my colleagues and I had dinner in the kind of restaurant Cubans cannot afford to go to. A singer, luscious and dark, approached our table.

"To live in Havana," Graham Greene wrote in his novel about the island, "was to live in a factory that turned out human beauty on a conveyor-belt." She sang a corny old song for us, accompanied by a short, sweating guitarist:

> *Siempre que te pregunto*
> *Cuando, como y donde,*
> *Tu siempre me respondes:*
> *Quizás, quizás, quizás.*

"Whenever I ask you when, how and where, you always answer: Perhaps, perhaps, perhaps." She ended the song, her eyes holding mine longer than Castro's had. Then she went away and established eye contact with someone else.

Of course, when his term in office ran out, Fidel Castro did not head off to live in Spain; he just took another term. Everyone knew he would, especially since he had spent so much effort over the years getting rid of every conceivable political rival. Long service, as José Martí so depressively put it, obliges you to continue serving.

But what distinguished Castro from just about every other international leader was his utter self-confidence. He is prepared to speculate about almost anything in public. Another politician would have batted away a question about his long-term future. Not Fidel. In spite of the seven-hour speeches, the human rights violations, the rigidity of the system, the general atmosphere of decay, he still managed to cling on to the shreds of his old revolutionary glamour.

As far as I can remember, I have only experienced a certain sympathy for one of the various tyrants I have come across in my career. It happened in 1986, and I was in Paris as part of a swing through Continental Europe that would eventually take my colleagues and me to Liechtenstein to report on the wedding of the crown prince: a Ruritanian event that seemed likely to amuse everyone.

"So," I said, my feet on the desk, "tell me what's going on here."

The BBC Paris bureau on the rue du Faubourg St. Honoré, within a few hundred yards of the Champs Elysées and the Arc de Triomphe, is the pleasantest office the Corporation maintains anywhere. Some difficult correspondents have worked there alongside the pleasanter and easier ones, but the presiding genius of the place was a bundle of Gallic energy called Ginette, with whom I flirted and joked and commiserated for thirty years.

"John, *cheri,* I can't stand 'im," she said of various BBC people during that time; "'E's a fuckeur."

She was usually right.

Ginette worked absurd hours, making phone calls to politicians and academics, cutting out articles from the French press with a huge pair of blackened steel scissors, drinking *infusions* of different kinds, and making out filing cards in red and blue biro in a distinctively French hand. While being one of the most typically BBC people I knew, she was unfailingly patriotic, and exploded satisfyingly when I remind her that Paris has one inch more rainfall per year than London. But she knew everything that is going on.

"Well, we 'ave the little emperor 'ere," she replied to my question.

"Which emperor is that? Napoleon?"

"*Ne fais pas l'idiot,* John," she said severely. "The Emperor Bokassa. From the Central African Empire. It's now the Republic again."

"Didn't he eat someone? Schoolchildren? Or was it the leader of the opposition?"

It was the leader of the opposition. Ginette pulled some carefully scissored articles out of a file and showed me. There were also dozens of items about Bokassa's career from corporal in the colonial African army to captain, colonel, general, president and emperor, like an ambitious third-century Roman legionary; about his coronation, and the expensive regalia made for him in France; about his shooting down of protesting schoolchildren, and his overthrow by French troops; and about his trial, in which his French chef was the star witness. The chef explained how, whenever Bokassa felt low, he would order a slice off the leader of the opposition, whose stuffed carcass was kept in Bokassa's extra-large deep freeze. It was a story that would have delighted Evelyn Waugh.

Now, anyway, Bokassa had come to France and was spending his exile in a small château that he owned just outside Paris. It struck me as being a superb story; the chance to meet a crazed imperial cannibal doesn't come around all that often.

"*Mais enfin,* John, the *gouvernement* doesn't want anyone going to see him."

"How can they stop us?"

"Hah!"

This was France. The authorities had dug up the road to the château on the pretext that the telephone cables needed replacing, and no one was allowed to go in or out. They had also taken away the emperor's driving license, and warned him that if he spoke to even a single journalist he would be sent straight back to Africa immediately. In France there is a kind of presidential trade union whereby one president protects his predecessors, even if they are political enemies. In this case the Emperor Bokassa had been saying all sorts of scandalous things about the skeletal former president, Valéry Giscard d'Estaing, and President François Mitterrand wanted to ensure that nothing new reached the ears of the press.

"But maybe there is a way, *quand même.*"

There was. Somehow, Ginette managed to do what no one else had done, and fix an appointment with the world's best-known anthropophage.

We stopped at the nearby town hall to ask the way.

"Oh, you mean our little monkey," said the official I spoke to, himself a nasty, thin man with a wisp of a moustache; he was, predictably, a member of the far-right National Front. "Be careful—he may eat you."

There were five of us—television teams were a great deal bigger in those days—and we made a lot of jokes as we drove over the trenches and potholes that the French government had dug in the emperor's driveway in an attempt to keep him in and the press out. We were just in time: the road was still passable. By the next day it would have been completely blocked. The house itself was unremarkable but pleasant and compact: the kind of place a late nineteenth-century industrialist might have built for his mistress.

"Don't forget," said the picture editor, a particular friend of mine named Mike Davies, as we got out of our vehicle, "when he asks if you want a slice off the Sunday joint, just say no."

We gathered round the front door, carrying the camera gear. I pressed the bell. Someone imitated the sound of an ancient door creaking open, and we all laughed tensely.

At that moment the door really opened. A little man stood there, looking like an African Richard Attenborough, short and pudgy. He was wearing a red velvet jacket embroidered with gold thread, and a skullcap. Stray tufts of beard grew out of his jaw at angles that seemed to be purely accidental. He looked very sad. It was the Emperor Bokassa in person.

I introduced myself and my colleagues, and saw them grinning secretly to one another. The emperor seemed not to notice. He led the way into the darkened château.

Then I spotted it, and a feeling like an electrical current went down my spine. In his hallway, the emperor had a very large freezer; big enough to hold at least one medium-size opposition leader.

I wasn't quite certain how much English the emperor spoke, so I let the others go in ahead of me and pulled Mike Davies back by the sleeve.

"Get him into one of the rooms and keep him there while I look inside that."

The emperor led the way, and opened a door to the left. I caught sight of a throne, and paintings of Napoleon on the walls.

"Late King Faroukh," Mike muttered as he went in and engaged the emperor in some very loud but not altogether accurate French.

I stayed outside, pretending to fidget with the camera tripod. Then as Mike half-closed the door to the Throne Room I walked across the hall to the refrigerator. I was quite scared. Supposing there really was someone in there? What would I do?

It was a chest model, with the lid on the top. Glancing round at the Throne Room, I could hear the emperor's low, gloomy voice answering some question of Mike's about Napoleon. There was no one else around. I put my fingers under the lid, and lifted. My arms were weak with nervousness.

Inside, covered with freezer frost, were half a dozen lamb chops, a few frozen herrings, and some packets of peas and carrots. No heads, no ears, no fingers, or anything even more personal. I leaned down and reached deeper: just peas and carrots. Some ice cream. Several bags of ice. That was all. I lowered the lid, and in my relief and nervousness let it bang too loudly. The gloomy voice in the Throne Room paused for a second or two, then resumed.

Mike Davies and the others looked at me sharply as I walked in.

"I was just telling your colleagues here—"

I closed my eyes and shook my head a little. The others relaxed perceptibly.

"—about the way in which the French government has treated me."

I made soothing noises and shook my head again, this time at the way in which the French government had treated him. The emperor droned on, and I took the opportunity to look around.

The room was an elaborate memorial to a disordered personality. His court in exile had sat here once a week, listening to the imperial commands, until the French government had prevented them from turning up. It was probably quite a relief for them. We sat him down with his throne behind him and the portrait of Napoleon visible over his shoulder. The cameraman, Dougie Dalgleish, shifted him around. The sound recordist, Ron Hooper (who later became a cameraman and traveled with me around Russia), pushed a microphone up the imperial sweater and pinned it to the front of his shirt. The lighting-man, Tony Fallshaw, who would one day accompany me on all sorts of expeditions when he became a cameraman himself, shone lights in his face from different angles. Emperor Bokassa took it all with complete apathy. If we had asked him to stand on the throne and undress, he would probably have done it.

Napoleon looked out at us everywhere from paintings and engravings: life-size ones, and for the most part bad copies, the kind of thing you found for sale, often from the Bokassa's former subjects, in the corridors of the Metro. There was a lot of gold paint on the furniture. That made it imperial, at least to his mind.

The emperor was a fantasist, a sufferer from one of the more frequent delusions; only in his case he really had been an emperor, with the power of life and death over his subjects. I looked at him more closely. This anxious, sad little man had ordered hundreds of murders; his frown, now so predominant, had meant someone's painful death; his hands, moving nervously as though he were washing them in imaginary water, had struck those who had angered him; that mouth, now slack with despair, had closed on human meat. I was interviewing a madman.

And yet, as our interview wore on, I became more and more engrossed in his story, and found parts of it increasingly believable. I was the only one of our group who could understand what he was saying, and I missed plenty of things because he spoke so softly and his accent was so strong.

He had done many of the things he was accused of, he said, and he was profoundly sorry. He had indeed ordered his soldiers to shoot at the schoolchildren who were demonstrating against the introduction of expensive new uniforms.

"Which were made by a company owned by your own family?"

He nodded, contritely. To everyone else it had been a savage crime; to him it had been a mistake, easily enough made, which he now regretted. He would, he said, like to apologize for this. He could see it was wrong. He seemed to be looking to me to absolve him and make all the bad things go away; as though I were the Archbishop of Bangui and could crown him again, now that he had gotten that off his chest.

"Your critics say you're insane," I said.

For a moment I could see the embers of the old fires. Then they died down again.

"It was only the French. They wanted to make it easier to get rid of me. Giscard was behind it, calling me his cousin and taking all the diamonds and then doing this when his brother disagreed with me over the price. And then the paras knocked down the door of my office and pointed their guns at me."

It was tumbling out of him now, and I found it hard to keep pace with it all. It was just the monomania speaking, I told myself; and yet a certain crazy logic kept asserting itself in the mad, reddened eyes. The camera crew were getting restless, not understanding anything of the torrent that was pouring from him.

Some of it was an old story, some was entirely new. What it amounted to was this: Valéry Giscard d'Estaing had struck up a strange friendship with Bokassa—I saw letters from him in which he called Bokassa *mon cher cousin*—and used to visit him regularly in order to slaughter some of the Central African Empire's wildlife. Giscard encouraged his imperial mania, to the extent that French companies ran the entire mad coronation of 1977. It cost more than the entire gross national product of the Central African Empire for that year.

Giscard's brother, meanwhile, went into business with Bokassa for the mining and exportation of uncut diamonds from the Empire's mines. I saw the letters about that too, and they seemed entirely genuine. Then came the inevitable falling out over the price. Giscard's brother wanted more and cheaper diamonds; Bokassa claimed that the national interests of the CAE, which he had suddenly remembered, wouldn't allow it. You'll see what will happen, said Giscard's brother.

What happened first was the schoolchildren's demonstration, which was provoked by Bokassa's own lunacy and greed. The violence of its suppression caused an outcry around the world, and not long afterward, Giscard announced that France would step in to restore order in its former colony. And so the paras landed, captured Bokassa's palace, burst into his office, and tied him up. Then they turned their attention to the safe in the corner of the room.

"I used to keep a little pot of uncut stones in it, sixty-eight of them, just for myself. They were my own property.

"'You might at least tell me where you are going to take them,' I said to the paras.

"'Fuck off and shut your mouth,' the commander said—I can tell you his name, if you want to know it. 'We have orders to take them straight to the Elysée Palace.'

"They blew open the safe, and the para commander put the packets of diamonds into his pockets.

"And to think," he said, knuckling away the tear which had formed when he thought of his little pot of uncut diamonds, "that I regarded that man as my friend."

Afterward the French put Bokassa on trial. All his crimes came out in the evidence.

"So what about the cannibalism?"

"M. Simpson, I swear to you this was a complete lie. Never have I partaken of human flesh. The very idea is abhorrent to me. I am not a wild animal. I did things which were bad, I know; but not this, I assure you. You must believe me."

The strange thing was that I did. He fixed me with his crazy eyes, the brown of whose irises seemed to have leaked into the surrounding whites. I nodded. There was, after all, a certain plausibility about it all. If the French government wanted to stage something like this, accusations of mere despotism might not be sufficient to justify the act of taking control of the CAE in the eyes of public opinion. And what would appeal more to the French imagination, and better brand the emperor as a maniac, than detailed accusations that he had ordered his chief political enemy to be cooked?

I checked out the case later. These accusations came solely from Bokassa's French chef. He said in evidence that Bokassa would order him to cook slices of the frozen corpse, and specify which particular sauce he wanted. Then he would set to with gusto. There had been much laughter in court, and Bokassa had wept copiously. His defense lawyer, appointed by the French, had scarcely bothered with cross-examination.

A new Central African government, more liberal than Bokassa's own, eventually allowed him out of prison, and he slipped out of the country to his château in France. By this time Giscard had long been out of office, and the Socialist François Mitterrand had become president. Allegations about Giscard's diamond dealings had leaked out in *Le Canard Enchaîné* and other newspapers, but Mitterrand was clearly determined that Bokassa should not be able to tell any more of his story to the press.

We all posed for photographs with the emperor afterward, and went into the kitchen to meet his wives: jolly, plump ladies who seemed very fond of the little man. As we made our way back to the office I tried to explain the story to Mike Davies.

"You don't believe all that, do you?" he asked.

Weakly, I pretended I didn't. Journalists are always reluctant to appear credulous, and they take refuge in an assumed skepticism which eventually becomes a settled habit of mind. But there had been something believable about the emperor's story; and it was by no means out of the question that the French government should behave after this fashion. Why, I asked myself, should Mitterrand have gone to such extraordinary lengths to keep Bokassa quiet?

We were the only journalists, French or foreign, who managed to interview him. Later he decided, without warning, to return to what had once again become the Central African Republic to clear his name. He didn't succeed, of course. He was put away for life, and was said to howl at the full moon from his cell.

And then, since he was harmless, the government released him. He died in poverty in a hut on the outskirts of Bangui a few years later, still protesting his innocence. When the news of his death came through, I wrote an article for the *Spectator* about my visit to his château, the discovery of the deep freeze in the hallway, and my examination of its contents. We called it "The Silence of the Lamb Chops."

PART TWO

Part Two

7
Revolution

After nearly thirty years of hard traveling I still enjoy the business of getting on airplanes and arriving and checking into hotels as much as I ever
did; you have to, I suppose. There are of course certain destinations that
make the heart lift. But when a newspaper interviewer asks you for your
favorite place—it's one of those questions they turn to when things are
flagging—something special is required: as I say, Paris and Venice aren't
quite enough, somehow. So I tend to reply that Iran is my favorite country. It is certainly one of them, in terms of people, climate, landscape and
culture; though it would be a little truer to say that the whole of central
and south Asia, east of the Caucasus and south of Siberia, is the area to
which I feel the greatest attraction. The grandeur of the steppe, the clarity of the desert, the freedom of the hills, the dominance of Islam, the
seething cities of India and Pakistan: these are the conditions in which I
feel most stimulated, and most myself.

Until 1978 I had never been anywhere in this entire vast region. As for
Iran, I scarcely knew where to find it on the map; and it was something
of a revelation to me to discover that it was the same as Persia. Since the
beginning of that year there had been rioting in Iran, and it was getting

worse. Like most people, I found the details escaped me, but it seemed to be some kind of fundamentalist uprising against the shah. It also sounded extremely dangerous, and in those days I was still rather apt to feel worried about that kind of thing. Iran taught me that there are rules about revolutions and civil wars, as about everything else, and that if you apply the rules properly there is no reason why the most dangerous situation shouldn't be survivable.

In August 1978, though, I found myself on a plane to Tehran, feeling very uncomfortable. The police and army had been shooting down demonstrators in the streets. I read through a vast pile of press cuttings and specialized magazine articles as we flew, trying to understand what on earth was going on there. Everyone writing about the crisis seemed confident that the shah would survive the trouble, but there was no very clear idea what it was the protesters wanted. I saw a single reference to a particular religious leader, Ayatollah Khomeini, who lived in exile in Iraq; but beyond that, it simply appeared to be a matter of Islamic unrest—'fanatical' was a word I came across more than once—against a pro-Western, liberalizing ruler.

My excuse for going to Iran was slender. The man who was briefly the head of the Chinese Communist Party, Chairman Hua Guofeng, was making the first foray abroad of any Chinese leader in history, and I was following him around. His itinerary involved countries on the periphery of the Soviet Union which were in some way at odds with Moscow: Romania, under Ceauşescu; Yugoslavia, under Tito; and Iran under the Shah. All of them, too, were eventually to crumble under the weight of their problems. Anyway, Chairman Hua was about to arrive in Tehran, and I had come to report on it; though it seemed likely that I would spend more time reporting on the domestic upheavals of Iran itself.

The instant I appeared in the doorway of the aircraft and prepared to walk down the steps to the waiting coach, I knew I was going to like this place. The air was warm and had a delightful clarity, and the distant Elburz Mountains rose grandly from the plains, their topmost peaks glittering with snow even at the height of summer. There was a pungent smell in the air: the savor, I later came to realize, of central Asia. I felt at home.

I have often been back to Iran since then. For years at a time, when

I have offended the government, it has refused to let me in. But it has always relented at last, and as the fires of revolution have died down, going back has become easier. I have watched the convulsive changes there firsthand, but after twenty years it is at last a little closer to what it was that first day I arrived. It is more relaxed and freer nowadays than at any time during the past two difficult decades.

For those who know them, there is something deeply attractive about the people of Iran. The habitual, unselfish generosity that they show toward strangers is unusual even in the Islamic world. They also possess the rare ability to distinguish between individual people and the government of the country they come from. When the British government was being reviled daily in Iran, individual Britons were treated with kindness and respect. Maybe it comes from the Islamic tradition of treating strangers as guests; maybe it is the result of the long centuries during which individual Persians have had no voice whatever in the way they were governed, and therefore wouldn't consider blaming someone for what their government did. Yet at a time when British officials were being rude and dismissive to Iranians who had fled their country to escape persecution, and when gangs attacked and occasionally murdered innocent Iranian refugees in the streets of American cities, British and American journalists were treated well in Iran itself.

Once, during a time of great tension in Tehran, I was filming outside the place where Friday prayers were being held. The subject of the sermon was the iniquity of the British toward Iran, stretching back over the decades. The worshippers came boiling out into the street, chanting, *"Marg bar Englistan!" "Marg bar Thatcher!"* (Death to England! Death to Thatcher!) Standing out in the street filming them with a big BBC sign on our camera, we felt a little exposed. Or at least the cameraman did. I had seen this before, and was less worried.

"If you stand up on this wall you can get a shot of me walking through the crowd talking to them. Put a radio mike on me and you'll be able to hear what happens."

The cameraman was a gentle, rather paternal man not far short of retirement. "I really don't think you ought to do this, John."

The fact was, I had seen an American correspondent do precisely the same thing, and knew it worked. I insisted.

By now the crowd had stabilized, and had formed up in the road waving banners and beating their chests in time to their chanting. Even to someone who knew what was likely to happen, it was a little daunting.

But as I walked among them, explaining that I was from Britain, they would shake my hand and tell me I was welcome in their country. In the center of the crowd I spotted a large and rather excitable old man with a large sprouting beard and a turban. He was getting really worked up, beating his chest with both fists and booming out the responses:

"Marg bar Englistan! Marg bar Englistan!"

I could see the saliva whipping out around him, and his neighbors were moving away from him to give him more room. It seemed like the ultimate test of the theory. I edged up and stood in front of him.

"Good morning. I am from Englistan and I work for the BBC."

It was like the return of Empire. He bowed, took my hand and kissed it.

"You are very welcome in Iran, sir. I hope you like our country."

I assured him that I did. And indeed it felt very good to be among Iranians again. It also made excellent television.

"Well, I see why you're always going on about this place," said the cameraman when I rejoined him.

Many journalists who worked there during the revolution had reason to be grateful for the purely altruistic help of individual Iranians. A few weeks after this first visit of mine to Tehran, when the violence was even greater, a Canadian cameraman I knew was filming in a crowd when he did something that upset them: not speaking Farsi, he filmed the face of someone who was asking in Farsi not to be filmed. The crowd took this to mean that he was filming on behalf of the SAVAK— the secret police—and turned on him savagely. He broke away and ran off down the road, with the crowd streaming after him. Then, exactly as in one of those nightmares where you wake up sweating, he dodged into a side street and realized halfway down that it was a dead end.

He backed into a doorway, his camera held defensively in front of him, and waited for the crowd to catch up with him and kill him. And then the door behind him opened, and a woman pulled him in. She locked the door and piled some furniture in front of it. There was loud banging and shouting outside.

"Have you got something they want?"

"Film," he answered, his chest heaving.

"Give it to me."

He tore out some unexposed film that he didn't need and gave it to her. She went out onto the flat roof and shouted at the crowd, "Look, this is what you want. Take it."

Then she threw the film down to them. It unrolled like a New Year's Eve favor, and they grabbed at it and tore it angrily into little pieces. The woman meanwhile helped the cameraman over the roof and showed him the way to safety. She didn't want anything from him; she merely saw a stranger in trouble and, disregarding the danger to herself, felt it was her duty to look after him.

I quickly lost interest in the visit of Hua Guofeng, which had been my reason for coming to Tehran. What was happening here was of extraordinary importance, and I decided to stay and cover it. (In those days of relaxed budgets and low costs it was usual to spend a fortnight or three weeks on a foreign trip, just looking for interesting stories; nowadays the office becomes restless after a few days, and wants to know when you plan to pull out.) Nevertheless it wasn't easy. The pattern of events was that groups of people hostile to the shah's regime would gather in a mosque, and the mullahs would preach fiery sermons about the ungodly nature of the government. At the end everyone would come rushing out into the street and begin chanting slogans. The chances were, though, that someone would tip off the SAVAK, and they and the army would arrive in double-quick time and start shooting or arresting people. It happened every day, but the action would all be over within a few minutes, and unless you were actually on the spot you would miss it. We did miss it, day after day, and so did every other television team.

And then one Friday, as we were patrolling the streets of south Tehran looking for trouble, it happened. We chanced to be driving past a mosque just as everyone came pouring out. The army and the SAVAK were already waiting for them.

"Stop, stop," I shouted to our driver.

"Are you sure we're allowed to film this?" asked the cameraman I was with. He hadn't been captivated by the magic of Iran; he thought they were all a lot of dangerous lunatics. This cameraman may not come out of this episode particularly well, but he was a good and conscientious worker, and different things worry different people. Four years later in Beirut he stood his ground with great courage in the middle of an ammunition dump that was exploding all around us, and deserved an award for his spectacular footage.

Now, though, he was distinctly reluctant. He got out of the car too slowly and took too much time getting ready to film; and in doing so he attracted the attention of the SAVAK. One of the officers looked across and spotted us, and signed to the soldiers to arrest us. They picked us up bodily and threw us into the back of an army truck.

"This is all your fault," the cameraman said to me. The sound recordist said nothing. He wasn't looking very well.

We stayed in the truck for hours, right through the midday heat. There was no shade, and no water. The sound recordist was starting to look really bad, and seemed to be slipping in and out of consciousness. As for the cameraman, he had taken to groaning and rubbing his hands together. One of our guards felt sorry for us and went off to buy some watermelons. After four hours of thirst they tasted wonderful, but the effect was spoiled when one of the others told us to enjoy them because they would be our last meal on earth. I didn't feel I had to explain all this to the cameraman. Nor did I tell him, when they let us wash our hands with water brought from a nearby mosque, that the soldiers were suggesting we might like to take the opportunity to go and pray in the mosque before they shot us. I hoped they were joking, but I couldn't be altogether certain.

There was a telephone box only twenty yards away, and I could see it through a gap in the canvas at the back of the truck. I pointed encouragingly to it and made ingratiating noises. One of the soldiers stuck his rifle in my stomach. Soon, though, the cameraman's hand-wringing and the sound recordist's groaning made me decide that, come what may, I had to get out and ring the British embassy. This time I pushed the gun away from my stomach and climbed out. The soldiers didn't quite know what to do, but several of them pointed their rifles at my back as I walked toward the phone.

In my life, bathos never seems far away. Directly I got there I found that it took different coins from the ones I had in my pocket. I looked around: if I walked off to get change the soldiers would probably shoot me, yet there was no one else to ask. So I went back and asked the soldiers; and like true Iranians they not only pulled out the necessary coins, but insisted I should keep them as a present. Then they pointed their guns at me again.

I got through to the diplomat on duty. He sounded disgruntled, and explained that everyone was away playing tennis. I outlined our little problem and with great reluctance he agreed to do what he could. I came away feeling much better.

An hour or so later there was a crackling on someone's walkie-talkie, a shouted instruction, and the truck's engine started up. We were driven to a SAVAK office in south Tehran. (A few months later, during the revolution proper, I looked on and filmed as a crowd sacked this very building, killing the people inside and throwing the files out of the windows. My emotions were mixed.) Now we were made to wait in the office of a fierce-looking character in plain clothes, who spent most of his time listening to someone on the other end of the phone line.

"Bale," he would say, looking unpleasantly across at us. "Yes."

We certainly made a mixed bunch: the cameraman inclined to rub his hands and blame me audibly, the sound recordist lapsing into semiconsciousness, and me doing an impersonation of Alec Guinness in The Bridge on the River Kwai, announcing that we were being treated abysmally and that I would shortly be making my second formal application for us all to be released and for medical assistance to be given to my colleague. I also said that when I next saw the shah I would complain about this particular officer's behavior. None of it worked, of course.

Then came another phone call.

"*Bale,*" said the officer again; but this time it sounded different. He looked at me.

"Do you know Basingstoke?" he asked in excellent English. "My wife comes from there."

I immediately started praising Basingstoke and the famous beauty of its women, though as a matter of fact I had never been there. But I could see things were taking a turn for the better. And a few minutes later, after a tray of tea had been brought round and we had drunk it greedily, we were given a SAVAK car and taken back to our hotel.

"Phew," said the sound recordist as we drove away. He sat up.

"Are you all right?" I asked, rather anxiously.

"'Course I am. Just put it on to fool 'em."

"I still think you put our lives in danger unnecessarily," said the cameraman.

I didn't care. I looked out at the dusty streets of Tehran and felt great. I didn't even mind when the superior voice on the phone line from the British embassy cut across my thanks.

"As a matter of fact I didn't do anything," he said. "We never do in these cases."

The situation worsened. The demonstrators called it 'doing the forty-forty'—forty days after someone was shot dead by the army, the custom of Shi'a Islam dictated that there should be a gathering in his or her honor. And since all such gatherings were banned, the army would turn out and more people usually would be shot. The shah and some of his ministers thought this was the firmness they had to show; in fact it weakened their position every time it happened. When I went back to London at the end of August I put together a report that suggested that the shah's powers might be clipped, and that he would be forced to become a constitutional monarch. With hindsight I can see that this was always a silly judgment; yet it was the first time a British journalist had suggested that the shah's absolute power might be in danger, and the Foreign Office complained to the BBC that my report had been irresponsible and might weaken the shah's position. At that time the British ambassador, Anthony Parsons, had great influence with the shah, and the official British line was that the shah would survive this ordeal as he had survived others in the past. Tony Parsons was always kind and helpful to me, and I had a considerable affection for him. But to those of us who had seen what was happening on the streets, the shah's survival was beginning to seem less likely.

All in all, the shah was the author of his own downfall: much more, that is, than most of us are. In January 1978, when he had seemed at the height of his power, he had ordered one of his ministers to publish a scurrilous attack on the senior cleric who, back in 1963, had headed the last bout of trouble. The shah had survived that time, and the cleric had been forced into exile in neighboring Iraq. His name was Ayatollah Ruhollah Khomeini. The minister's article suggested that he was a homosexual, and a British agent. Khomeini's supporters, outraged by the second accusation even more than the first, came out onto the streets and were shot down. The forty-day cycle of demonstration/shooting/demonstration/shooting that eventually sent the shah into exile had begun.

Now, in the autumn of 1978, the shah was about to make the second big decision that brought him down. He put pressure on Saddam Hussein to force Ayatollah Khomeini out of his exile in the Shi'ite holy city of Najaf, in the south of Iraq. It was a foolish move: Najaf was almost impossible for Western journalists to get to, and Khomeini's practical influence was restricted to smuggling tape-recorded sermons across the border into Iran. Now, forced to leave Najaf, he took refuge in France. Everyone could go and see him there, and as a result his words were replayed to Iranians by radio, television and newspaper.

Soon after he had settled in the village of Neauphle-le-Château outside Paris, I went to interview him. He had taken over two houses on opposite sides of a small street. We filmed him crossing from one side to the other, and I had my first glimpse of the man whose revolution was to be an important part of my professional life for years to come. I had seen his features on posters and stencils and banners back in Iran, but now, looking at those beetling brows and that ferocious frown, I thought he looked like vengeance personified.

We set up our lights in the main sitting room of the house where he lived, and settled down to wait while he prepared himself for the interview. All the Western furniture had been taken out, and the floor was thick with Persian carpets. Around the walls were the large, comfortable cushions that Iranians like to lounge against. I practiced kneeling down. Then the door opened and he entered. You could feel the man's personality emanating from him: he was small, but he seemed to fill the room. He also looked extraordinarily clean: his robes were white and starched, and beautifully pressed. I wasn't quite sure what to do, so I said, "Welcome," and put my hand out to shake his, forgetting that some of the most particular Muslims feel they have to wash after touching a non-believer.

It was potentially awkward, but he dealt with it well. Looking down, he busied himself with the folds of his robe in such a way that it seemed he hadn't noticed my outstretched hand. It was done with such tact that I couldn't feel offended. Yet he showed no real interest in me at all: I was merely the megaphone through which he was about to address a message to the Iranian people.

TRANSCRIPT OF INTERVIEW RECORDED 3.11.78 IN PARIS

Speakers: Ayatollah Khomeini (non-staff), John Simpson (staff)

JS: Is it your intention to lead a revolution against the Shah, or do you simply wish to force him to change his policies?

AK: The Shah has ruled Iran as though it were his private estate, his property, to do with as he chooses. He has created a dictatorship, and has neglected his duties. The forces of Islam will bring this situation to an end. The monarchy will be eradicated.

JS: What kind of government do you wish to see in Iran, and what form would an Islamic Republic take?

AK: The Islamic Republic will be based on the will of the people, as expressed by universal suffrage. They will decide on the precise form it takes . . . But there are aspects of life under the present corrupt form of government in Iran which will have to be changed: we cannot allow our youth to be corrupted and our Islamic culture to be destroyed, and drugs such as alcoholic beverages will be prohibited.

Around us as we sat on the carpet were three of his aides, whose fates would shortly be determined by the experience of working with him. One, Abolhassan Bani-Sadr, became president and then escaped into exile; the second, Ibrahim Yazdi, was hounded out of government and spent his life as a dissident, in and out of jail; and the third, Sadeq Qot-bzadeh, became foreign minister and was then executed for treason.

Now they were all enthusiastic about the prospect that Khomeini's interview would be broadcast on the BBC, knowing it would be heard all over Iran. Of course I understood that this kind of thing often had a profound effect on the politics of the country in question, but a decision not to interview Khomeini would have been as much of a political move as the decision to interview him. If it was newsworthy, then we should report it and not bother our heads with the possible consequences.

There are Iranians in exile today who still blame me and the BBC World Service correspondent in Tehran at the time, Andrew Whitley, for creating the revolution by our reporting: as though the mood that brought the revolution about was not already fully in existence. And because strict factual accuracy isn't always one of the distinguishing characteristics of exiles, the story went around that Andrew would announce in his reports that the next big demonstration was due at such and such a time, and that as many people as possible should turn up. Foolish stuff, of course, but the shah himself became so exercised by these suspicions that he put pressure on the British embassy to control the BBC's broadcasts, and the Foreign Office in turn complained to the BBC. A careful examination of Andrew's broadcasting carried out after the revolution showed that the accusations had been entirely false.

And yet years afterward I was still getting anonymous letters accusing me of having received a half million dollars (the amount was always curiously specific) from Khomeini for broadcasting in a way that was favorable to the revolution. The fact that Khomeini's regime barred me from returning to Iran for seven years after the revolution didn't seem to affect any of this; but if you aren't objective and unbiased yourself, of course, you find it hard to believe that anyone else is.

Nevertheless the BBC had only its past to blame if people thought it had a political agenda in its broadcasting. The BBC Persian Service was set up by the British government in 1941 with the specific purpose of driving the shah's father, Reza Shah, from the Persian throne for his pro-Nazi sympathies. Only forty years later, Iranians of many kinds naturally assumed that the BBC still had a political purpose in what it broadcast. The moral is, don't allow your principles to be tampered with now, and you won't suffer for it in the future.

For the moment, though, I was only concerned with ending my interview with Khomeini as politely as possible. I got to my feet slowly, and realized that although he was forty years older than I was, his knees were a great deal suppler than mine. I didn't put my hand out this time, and he permitted himself something that I realized was a faint smile. Then there was a rustling of well-starched robes and he left to go on planning his revolution.

One November afternoon in 1978, the Tehran sky was dark with the smoke of fires as the demonstrators attacked public buildings and set up roadblocks on every street corner. The situation was now well out of the shah's control. I was really worried: partly because the rioters were going for anyone they thought might be British or American, and partly because I had left my camera crew in the center of town when things seemed much quieter, and had gone back to our hotel to ring the office in London. One of the main commandments of television news is that you don't leave your colleagues on their own in nasty situations. Our driver refused to take me back to them, on the grounds that it was too dangerous, and the taxis were all off the streets. There was only one thing to do: I had to walk.

I wasn't entirely inconspicuous in my checked sports jacket, and I sang to myself to keep my spirits up as I strode along, keeping to the side roads where I could. Whenever I came to a roadblock I glared at the demonstrators, as the Victorian general Sir Charles Napier (of "I have Sind" fame) is said to have glared at a tiger that attacked him. It worked for Napier, and it worked for me. They eyed me and they eyed my jacket, yet they fell back to allow me through as I came up to them. It was a long way to walk, but eventually I got close to the place where I had left the crew, only to realize that a half million people were thronging the previously empty streets. How could I conceivably find two men in this crowd?

But I did. In the far distance, bobbing over the uncountable heads, I spotted the absurd shape of the film magazine, shaped like Mickey Mouse ears, on top of our camera, turning as the cameraman found something new to film.

I couldn't believe my luck. Still, when I reached them they were so wrapped up in the drama of what they were doing that they weren't at all surprised to see me. They had obtained some remarkable pictures, but the crowd was worked up and very volatile, and we knew that something could happen at any moment. It did. A man started shouting out that his brother had been killed by the army, and the BBC hadn't reported it—which meant that the BBC was on the side of the shah.

Immediately people who had been perfectly pleasant to us a moment or two earlier, including one young man who had studied in Norwich and had just been telling me all about it, became caught up in the savagery of which crowds are capable at such times. They started to grab us, and I could see it would end in our being pulled to pieces. It had happened to other people that day.

Violent hands ripped at my jacket, and my own hands were trapped by my side. I could hear the others yelling and shouting, just as I was. It was getting desperate: a man was beating me in the face with a pole on which was pinned a portrait of Ayatollah Khomeini, as grim as when I had seen him at Neauphle, and blood was starting to run down my cheek.

I suppose it infuriated me that a little shrimp like this should beat me about the face simply because I couldn't defend myself. I roared with anger and dragged my arms free, and grabbed the pole out of his hands. All I could think of was hitting him back, and I got in a couple of satisfying whacks before I realized what I had to do.

"I am for Khomeini!" I shouted, waving the portrait of the old boy in the air. "*Javid* Khomeini!" Suddenly our molesters became our greatest friends, trying to lift us onto their shoulders (I quickly stopped that) and helping us to get through the crowd to peace and safety.

"Bit of luck, that," I said modestly, as we walked away. But the cameraman was the famous and much-missed Bernard Hesketh, who had his technical failings but possessed a fierce determination and an equally fierce sense of BBC propriety. He pulled me aside so the sound recordist wouldn't hear.

"I don't think you should have said that about Khomeini, John," he said.

"But that's what saved us."

"It's not right, all the same."

"But—"

He was already striding off down the road in search of more pictures. I didn't feel particularly proud of myself, but I was very glad to have got away with just a ripped jacket and a cut on the face. I had kept the picture of Khomeini, too. It was a keepsake to remind me how I had gotten away from a particularly nasty death.

One night a few weeks later, in January 1979, I found myself standing in the darkness, queuing up in the garden of one of Ayatollah Khomeini's houses in Neauphle-le-Château, waiting for a couple of tickets for his flight back to Tehran. The moment had come for his return, and he was willing to take a few journalists with him—but strictly on a first come, first served basis. I had been waiting almost seven hours so far, scarcely moving for fear one of the over-enthusiastic Iranian students who also wanted to go would step in and take my place. The temperature was well below freezing, and for years afterward my right shoulder ached as a result of that day's work.

I was there in defiance of explicit orders from my foreign desk. It was too dangerous to fly with Khomeini, they said, and anyway we had a crew and a correspondent in Tehran already. Why bother? There were so many reasons for bothering that I couldn't begin to list them, but the chief one was that having covered the growing revolution for so long, I couldn't bear not to be there for the culminating moment. And I didn't think it right to let something as important as Khomeini's flight home go unreported by the BBC.

There was, of course, a terrible mêlée in the darkness when the tickets arrived. Hundred-dollar bills were trampled into the mud or were caught by the freezing wind and blown away. Men wept. But no one fought harder than I. Years of rugby playing had at last paid off. I met up with the crew in a nearby café, and we headed back to Paris. There was only a ticket for Bill Handford, the cameraman, and me. His recordist, a huge character named Dave Johnson with a ferocious scar running down the entire side of his face, would follow on by the next commercial flight. He seemed relieved. For all his aggressive appearance, Dave was a gentle and rather discouraged man who preferred the company of his wife and cat to a life in the world's hot spots.

"Since this may well be our last night on earth," I said encouragingly, "let's have a really good meal."

We drove to the Train Bleu at the Gare de Lyons, where we were welcomed by the maître d'hôtel. He looked like the French ambassador at the Court of St. James; we looked like tramps, and I still had mud on my clothes from the scrimmage at Neauphle. Against his better judgment, though, he led us to a table. We read the menu. Dave, who disliked too much conspicuous expenditure, winced.

"'Ere, garçon," he called out.

The maître d' walked over as though someone was complaining about a cockroach in the soup.

"Three pounds for a portion of peas," Dave said. "You must be joking."

I soothed the maître d' in French, and we ate what might have been our last meal in silence. It was very good. Afterward, since we had several hours to wait before Khomeini's charter flight left, Bill suggested we go somewhere for a drink.

We went into a place called Le Rugbyman; Dave thought it looked like a pub, and I couldn't stop him. Inside, it seemed to be entirely inhabited by French second-row forwards. Ears had been chewed, noses broken. Enormous hands gripped glasses of beer. There was an appreciative rumble as Dave eased his bulk through the door.

"This isn't going to end happily," I said to Bill.

A skinny little man was playing the piano, and after a beer Dave went over to him.

"'Op it, Francisco," he said. The pianist hopped it. All around the bar, cauliflower ears pricked up: there was going to be a rumble. I hid my face. We were in enough trouble already, disobeying the BBC and facing a revolution.

But Dave eased himself onto the piano stool, and his huge fingers began playing beautiful thirties jazz. The small, red eyes around the bar softened. When Dave paused, someone called out for doubles for *les anglais*.

"Great pianist," I said chattily to a front-row forward. "Great rugby player too."

He gripped me by the hand so hard that tears came to my eyes.

Two hours later we said goodbye to Dave and boarded Khomeini's chartered Air France jet. An amusing gay steward explained to us that by special request there was no alcohol on board. A curtain blocked our view of the first-class section, where Khomeini and his advisers were sitting. We were back in steerage, and the students who wanted to shed their life's blood for the revolution were praying around us.

"This is a gloomy start," Bill said as the heads went down. He was a small, wiry, bearded yachtsman in his late forties, and I had always enjoyed working with him.

There was a colleague of ours on board, a radio reporter who was usually good company. Now, though, he was badly scared by the prospect of the flight and was gloomy and depressed. He went to sleep quickly. I found it harder to sleep, partly because Khomeini's supporters were so excited. For one thing they were going home, and for another, they thought there was a good chance the plane would be shot down by the shah's air force; which would mean they would go straight to Paradise as martyrs. This was precisely the possibility that made the correspondent so miserable.

It was light outside the plane by now, and people were starting to stir. The curtains dividing us from the first-class section parted without warning. One of Khomeini's aides came through and stood on an empty seat in the front row of the tourist-class section.

"I have a serious announcement to make," he said. There was a rustle of excitement. "We have just received a warning over the aircraft radio that the Iranian air force has orders to shoot us down directly we enter Iranian airspace."

More rustling: it was depressingly clear that many of our fellow passengers thought this would be the best outcome imaginable. As for me, I shrugged my shoulders and drank some coffee, and remembered 'Julius Caesar':

> Of all the wonders that I yet have heard,
> It seems to me most strange that men should fear,
> Seeing that death, a necessary end,
> Will come when it will come.

It wasn't that I didn't care whether I lived or died: I was thirty-four, and I had a wife and two daughters, and I wanted to live very badly indeed. But it wasn't going to be up to me. It would be up to a general with a lot of gold braid somewhere down below, and a pilot with his finger on the button of a missile.

If we weren't shot down, if we survived, I didn't want everybody to remember that I'd behaved embarrassingly badly. I looked across at Bill. He was sitting calmly in his seat, checking his equipment. He hadn't understood Qotbzadeh's French, but he knew exactly what was going on. Nearby sat the radio man, complaining and moaning to himself. I knew which one I wanted to be like; or perhaps, to be a little more honest, I knew which one I wanted other people to think I was like.

By now, anyway, there was something to do, which always seems to chase away the fear and introspection. Qotbzadeh beckoned us forward, and we went through the curtains and saw Khomeini sitting in the front row of first class, next to his son Ahmad. For a man who was returning from fifteen years of exile in order to start a revolution, he looked remarkably calm. I asked him that dreary, unimaginative broadcaster's question, how he felt. Deservedly, I was ignored. The grim head turned away from me and looked down. It was a few minutes later that a rather better-phrased question from a French journalist received the reply that went around the world.

"We are now over Iranian territory. What are your emotions after so many years of exile?"

"*Hichi,*" said Khomeini: Nothing.

It was no good trying to explain that as a Muslim cleric he had striven to banish every emotion within himself except the love of God; that he believed the love of one's country, or hope for the future, or even the desire for revenge, were all emotions that, divorced from the worship of God, had no value or meaning. For people everywhere, even in Iran, it seemed as though this personification of vengeance had no feelings whatsoever for the nation he had convulsed.

Our plane wasn't shot down, of course; it merely flew around and around for a very long time, waiting for permission to land, until we were all thoroughly airsick. Down below us the greatest crowd in human history was waiting for him, and as we made our final approach I could see the vast gathering around the airport buildings and along the route Khomeini would take into Tehran. On the tarmac I recorded a long piece to camera about what had happened and what the situation was now, and we all waited for Khomeini to appear at the top of the aircraft steps. It took a long time; but when he did, a roar came from the onlookers and was taken up by the enormous, expectant crowd outside the airport buildings.

By now, though, Bill and I had ceased to play any further part in things. Having come there against instructions, our job was to hand over to the correspondent and camera crew who were already in Tehran. It was deeply anti-climactic, but we were exhausted after working hard for nearly thirty hours. And although we could hear the noise as Khomeini met and addressed a crowd of thousands of mullahs in the main part of the airport, we left that to our colleagues and slumped down exhausted on the seats in the arrivals hall. A half hour or so later we were awakened when the doors opened and Khomeini appeared, being half carried by a group of very worried acolytes.

No one stopped us as we followed them into a side room. Nobody even seemed to notice we were filming as Khomeini lay down, apparently unconscious. Bill turned and looked at me, with a look on his face that seemed to say, "This could be one of the world's great exclusives." But of course it wasn't. After a while Khomeini opened his eyes and asked for water. He had merely fainted from the heat and from nervous exhaustion; and if he ever showed such weakness again, there was no one present to see it.

★ ★ ★ ★

The next twelve days were some of the most intense and exciting I have ever lived through. The shah had left Iran before Khomeini arrived, but his power structure was still more or less in place, and the prime minister he left behind him, the charming and brave Shahpour Bakhtiar, was still in office. (Years later Bakhtiar would be murdered in Paris by agents sent by the government in Tehran.) But now that Khomeini was setting up his rival government it was only a matter of time before the empty structures left over from the shah's rule collapsed and the new regime seized power.

The moment came twelve days later, on 12 February. I had been up much of the night, watching and filming at a roadblock outside our hotel. At 6:30 I was awakened by a loud grinding noise in the street outside. A column of twenty or more tanks was heading for a confrontation with the pro-Islamic militants: the Imperial Guard was on the move.

It was an utterly bewildering day. We drove round Tehran in the direction of gunfire, always managing to get there a little too late. Once, as we walked along a flyover we were buzzed by a pro-government helicopter, which seemed about to attack us; yet we didn't even get good pictures of that. But our luck had already started to change. We found a crowd attacking the SAVAK building where I had been held prisoner by the man whose wife came from Basingstoke, and filmed them.

By this time our driver had found out for us where the main action was going on and drove us there. There was no shortage of action anymore. Dave Johnson, the enormous piano-playing sound recordist, had joined us by this stage, and although he did not relish the action, he stayed connected up to Bill Handford's camera as we walked along a street toward the fighting, with bullets striking the walls a few feet above our heads. I was nervous enough: Dave, with his great bulk, must have felt that he offered an unfairly large target.

At the end of the street we at last understood what was going on: the crowds, and soldiers who had gone over to them, were attacking a barracks. The resistance had been strong at first, but was wearing down as we arrived. Soon a breach was made in the outer wall, and the soldiers inside began surrendering in their hundreds. For me, it was like watching the storming of the Winter Palace. I had reached the stage where filming the action was more important to me than my own safety, and I could see Bill had too. The fact that Dave stayed with us seemed to me admirable in itself. It was a dangerous time, and we were pinned down by gunfire in place after place. An American correspondent had been killed that morning, merely looking out of a window.

In North Tehran, in the foothills of the Elburz Mountains, we found a crowd gathering outside the Niavaran Palace, where the shah and his family had lived. These were really just local people, scarcely revolutionaries at all, and their motive seemed to be a kind of militant curiosity and a desire to loot, rather than hatred for the old imperial order. Their eyes flashed with excitement as they stormed into the grounds and saw the grand style in which the shah had lived. He seemed to have left everything behind him there. But the crowd was disappointed: the real revolutionary movement had sent some volunteers to make sure there was no theft or destruction, and the crowd obediently halted near the entrance to the palace, still avid to see the wealth of the monarch who had been overthrown. Looking through the windows, I felt a certain guilt, as though I were a looter myself. The shah had been no friend to the BBC, and as the originator of the plan to raise the price of oil in 1973 he was the cause of a good deal of economic pain in the Western world. I detested his record in human rights. But here at Niavaran he wasn't a monarch but a man who had been forced out of his country forever; and there was something poignant even in the showiness and poor taste that was evident as I peered through the windows of his palace.

By the entrance stood a sheepish group of several dozen men wearing nothing but their underpants. These were the Imperial Guards, "the Immortals," each of whom had taken a personal oath to defend the shah with the last drop of blood in his veins. Instead the shah had left them, and they had only defended him as far as their underwear. There was nothing grand about this revolution, any more than there was about the Russian Revolution. It was mostly absurdity and confusion.

We satellited our material from the television station at around midnight. While we were waiting for the satellite booking to start, there was a wild outbreak of shooting outside. Soon hundreds of rounds were hitting the building and coming in through the windows.

"The counter-revolutionaries are getting in! They'll kill us all!" someone shouted in rather good English from the passageway outside. From where I lay on the floor I looked around for somewhere to hide, and the only place I could see was a locker against one of the walls. I got into it for a moment or two, but felt distinctly foolish. The floor seemed a better place. In the end it turned out that there were no counter-revolutionaries anyway: it was just one group of excitable volunteers with guns shooting at one another. But a lot of people were killed or injured all the same.

As we were leaving, a man with a scarf tied around his head, revolution-chic–style, stuck his gun in my stomach and asked me who I was and what I was doing.

"Stop playacting, you silly wanker," I answered in English. I had been through a lot that day, and this seemed like the final straw. I pushed the gun barrel away.

"I speak English," he said grimly. "I went to university in Manchester."

Bad call, I thought. Then it seemed so ludicrous I grinned, and after a moment he grinned back at me. I could sense Bill Handford physically relax as he stood beside me.

"Perhaps you ought to be a bit more careful, John," he said gently as we walked away. I agreed. My instant's irritability could have gotten us both killed.

In the empty streets we and a group of other television people were given a lift back to our hotel in an ambulance reeking of blood. The sides and beds were covered with it.

A few days later, exhausted, we left Tehran. The bloodletting was beginning to frighten as well as sicken me; one of our team had to go to the airport every day to ship our film to London, and each time he had to deal with someone new because the others had been executed. When the British embassy organized the evacuation of Commonwealth citizens, it was agreed with the desk in London that we should film it and bring out the pictures. Someone new would have to take over.

The evacuation was carried out superbly well, headed by a young diplomat named David Reddaway, who escorted a column of cars and buses filled with very nervous people through the streets of Tehran to the British embassy summer compound in the north of the city. He stood up in the lead jeep like a tank commander, cutting a tremendous figure. I disliked him on sight for being so able and good-looking, but seven years later, when I met him again, he became one of my closest friends.

We were milling around with the evacuees, filming groups of people making the best of it and keeping calm and doing all the other things British people tend to do when they're frightened, when one of the other diplomats told me in passing that a call had come through for us from London. There was, apparently, a charter plane waiting at the airport to take us out. The pilot could only wait for another forty minutes, the diplomat said languidly.

Life suddenly speeded up, like fast-forwarding a video. Within a minute I had done a curious deal with the embassy: if we were given the ambassador's car and chauffeur to take us to the airport, they said, would we agree to take someone out with us? Who it was, I didn't want to know. I imagine it was a senior figure from the shah's regime who had worked in some way for the British, and whose life was now in danger. I agreed. We even managed to locate our luggage in one of the many trucks full of cases and packages.

The ambassador's chauffeur was a superb Pakistani, the car a rather grand Jaguar. We sped through the crowded streets with the Union Jack flying, at speeds that made me close my eyes. When there was no room in the road the chauffeur would mount the sidewalk and drive down that instead. It seemed to me like the last great imperial ride, while it lasted. Finally, as the airport came into sight, the chauffeur looked at me proudly. Thirty-five minutes had passed since we had spoken to the languid diplomat.

The pilot was waiting for us in the deserted terminal, and we packed all our gear into the plane. Then I stood and waited in the main road for the mysterious British agent to show himself. Time passed: no vehicle appeared on the long approach to the airport. No one was coming.

The pilot came up quietly beside me and looked meaningfully at his watch. I waited a few minutes longer, then nodded my head and turned. We had kept our side of the bargain. It was time to leave.

8
Death in the Square

For great empires, while they stand, do enervate and destroy the forces of the natives which they have subdued, resting upon their own prospective forces; and then when they fail also, all goes to ruin, and they become a prey. So was it in the decay of the Roman Empire: and likewise in the empire of Almaigne, after Charles the Great, every bird taking a feather.
—SIR FRANCIS BACON, *Of Vicissitudes of Things,* ca. 1625

With the comfortable hindsight of history, it seems so obvious. The Soviet Union and its empire in Eastern Europe was on its last legs in the 1980s; all it took for the whole rickety structure to begin collapsing was the decision of the reformist Communist government of Imre Poszgay in Hungary in the summer of 1989 to open the border with non-Communist Austria. Once a small hole had appeared in the Iron Curtain, the whole construct was immediately endangered. That, certainly, is the version that is nowadays being taught in the schools and universities of the world. Historians are even worse than journalists when it comes to self-assurance and pretending that the course of events is as plain as the nose on your face.

It wasn't like that at all, believe me. For a start, the Year of Revolution, 1989, was almost over before Marxism-Leninism appeared to be in any danger at all. The Communist authorities in China had faced down the determined, if muddle-headed, rebellion of the students in Tiananmen Square by murdering them wholesale. There were obviously problems, but until the very last moment—6:54 P.M. on the evening of 9 November, to be exact, when the East German government announced that the Berlin Wall was to be opened with immediate effect—there was no reason to think that anything important was going to happen. The West German chancellor, Helmut Kohl, who might have been expected to know that something was about to happen, was on a visit to Poland that day. I was with him, and at about 7:15 I heard some of his top officials whispering to each other about *Die Mauer.*

Something seems to have happened at the Berlin Wall, I told my camera crew in Warsaw; which must count as one of the twentieth century's more notable understatements. It took me more than twenty-four hours to make it to the Brandenburg Gate and report on perhaps the most exhilarating moment in modern history.

Although the Wall had been breached and the East German government was visibly collapsing, no one seriously thought that Czechoslovakia might be next.

"The regime in Prague is firmly in place," insisted one of the world's premier experts on Czech politics when I interviewed him on 14th November. The regime collapsed within ten days.

Next came Romania.

"Ceauşescu has such a tight grip on power, he could still be there in ten years' time," a leading authority on Romania told me on 10 December. On Christmas Day, Nicolae Ceauşescu and his unsavory wife, Elena—the Macbeths, as I came to think of them—had been put against a wall in the army barracks at Tergoviste and 120 AK-47 rounds were pumped into them.

"Mikhail Gorbachev and the system he heads seem to have come through the collapse of Communism in Europe in complete safety," said one television journalist with a good deal of assurance on 18 January 1990; it was me. On 19 August 1991 there was a comic-opera coup against him by the KGB, which had collapsed by the 22nd. In the days that followed, every element of the Marxist-Leninist state evaporated, from the command economy to the KGB itself (though of course plenty of the old elements were soon reconstituted in ways that were pretty similar). Gorbachev himself, an attractive figure whom I interviewed on various occasions—the first Soviet leader since Trotsky whom it was possible for Westerners to doorstep—was out of a job by the end of the year.

It was my great good fortune to have been on hand for every one of these cataclysms: the only journalist in the world who was, as far as I know, though I did arrive on the late side for the fall of the Berlin Wall. I was also lucky enough to have spent time in each of the countries involved, during the days when the Communist system seemed absolutely armor-clad and permanent. Without meaning to, Mikhail Gorbachev sparked off the entire process. He forgot the words of the private investigating committee that Tsar Alexander I set up to look into the causes of the Decembrist revolt in St. Petersburg in 1825: "The least relaxation of the autocracy would lead to the separation of many provinces, the weakening of the state, and countless disasters to the nation."

Gorbachev's promise—that it was possible to have a moderate, decent, democratic version of Marxism-Leninism—was the common denominator in each of the revolutions of 1989. It even played a critical part in the one revolution that failed: the student uprising in Beijing in May of that year. Gorbachev paid a visit to China. I went there to cover it, never expecting, anymore than he did, that his arrival would come close to bringing down the structure of Maoism. But thousands of students gathered in Tiananmen Square, outside the Great Hall of the People, where he was to appear, demanding the same kind of political and economic relaxation in China that he had introduced into the Soviet Union. Zhao Ziyang, the Reformist Party boss, gave them a measure of support. It was never clear whether he was hoping to use the student demonstrations to get rid of the old guard headed by Deng Xiaoping, but as it turned out they turned the tables on him. He has never been seen in public again.

The month I spent in Beijing, going almost daily to the Square and spending my time with the students, had a profound effect on me; and the massacre, which ended the demonstration on the night of 3–4 June remains one of the strongest and most painful memories of my life. Nowadays, of course, the Chinese government prefers not to talk about "the events," as they're known. Some leading figures in the government even try to give the impression that no such massacre took place; and as time goes on people in the outside world forget what happened, and even have their own doubts that there was any bloodshed. Maybe it was all the invention of the Western media, they say. Believe me, it wasn't.

It was early on the evening of Friday, 19 May, that we began to get reports of troop movements. We had set up our office in a couple of rooms in the Great Wall Sheraton, and it had become a center for information, with people continually coming in or telephoning. The 27th Army, to the north of Peking, was on alert status. Fifty trucks with soldiers in them had been seen on the western outskirts of the city.

The student leaders had decided to give up the hunger strike but not to leave Tiananmen Square. It was a belated response to Zhao's final appeal, and an attempt to ward off military action. It was now being reported that Zhao had offered his resignation. Deng Xiaoping wasn't after all a weak figure who could easily be toppled. He was still in charge. There was a sense of panic among the academics and intellectuals who had joined in the demonstrations on Wednesday and Thursday. I rang someone we had interviewed two days before and asked him for another interview.

"It wouldn't be timely," he said. He sounded deeply shaken.

Fang Lizhi, the respected scientist, was prepared to be interviewed. He had a record of taking risks. When the American embassy invited him to the Great Wall Sheraton for a banquet given by President Bush, he had turned up, only to be stopped by the police. Now he came to the Sheraton again. But he was so nervous, and his English became so confused, that he said nothing we could broadcast.

The leading figures in the Party held a joint meeting that evening with the military at the General Logistics department of the army in West Peking. Only four members of the Politburo Standing Committee were there. Zhao Ziyang had sent a message to say he was ill. It was both an affront to the others and an admission of defeat. The meeting took place in a large theater with the members of the leadership sitting on the stage. The audience was composed of military officers and Party members. They sat separately, divided into units and areas. Television cameramen from CCTV moved up and down the aisles filming the speeches on the stage and the reaction from the audience.

At midnight, an hour or so after the meeting had ended, an edited version of the proceedings was broadcast on television. Li Peng, wearing a black Mao jacket as though to symbolize the return to tougher and more disciplined ways, read out a statement.

> Until now we've been lenient. We've restrained ourselves for over a month. But a government which serves the people must take strong measures to deal with social unrest . . . The fate, the very future of the People's Republic of China, built by many revolutionary martyrs with their own blood, faces a serious threat.

Then it was the turn of the president, Yang Shangkun. Instead of standing and reading his speech, he sat at the table and spoke without notes. There was a teapot beside him, and he toyed with a cup.

> To establish stability around Peking and to restore normal order, we have been obliged to move troops of the People's Liberation Army to the vicinity of the city. If things are allowed to continue as they are, then our capital city will not remain a capital city.

There was loud applause at that, and the cameras panned across the width of the auditorium to show the full extent of it. Yang Shangkun tried to draw a distinction between the ordinary students, who had received such support from the people of Peking in the previous few days, and the troublemakers who had led them on: "I would like to make it clear that by sending in the troops we are not intending to deal with the students."

To those who listened over their radio sets in the Square, or heard it reverberating around from the loudspeakers near the Gate of Heavenly Peace, this was a clear declaration of war. Trucks full of supporters from schools, universities and factories headed for Tiananmen Square and drove wildly up and down the length of Chang'an Avenue, their great red and white banners floating in the wind. Groups of cyclists, hundreds at a time, bunched together and rode along at a stately pace, waving, chanting, singing, shouting. All over the city ordinary working-class people, who had mostly taken little part in the demonstrations, decided it was time to stand up and be counted.

As the troop lorries moved in toward the center of the city, people came out onto the streets and blocked them. They argued and shouted at the drivers and at the soldiers sitting stolidly in the back. Officers shouted into their radios and tried to persuade the crowds to let them pass. It was useless. Sometimes the soldiers themselves said they sympathized with the crowds and had no intention of taking action against them. Mostly they tried to ignore the shouts and insults. They were helpless, marooned in a sea of excited people.

These were not students, aroused by the oratory of their leaders, carried away by a quixotic demand for things they had only heard of in foreign radio broadcasts. These were the working people of Peking. Many of them were middle-aged. For the most part they maintained an eerie silence. As I walked through the crowd they fell back, politely, to let me pass. They all stared at me, looking at my clothes, my features, the notebook I was carrying. They were neither friendly nor hostile, merely uncomprehending; but when someone gave me a victory sign and I returned it, they exploded in cheering and applause.

I moved closer to the line of army lorries, which I could only dimly see ahead of me. In the distance there was chanting and shouting: "Go home! Go home! Go home!" The soldiers from one lorry had jumped out of their cramped seats and gathered around a short, heavily built woman who had brought them a bucket with soup in it. They ate noisily and greedily, while she watched and smiled. She wore short-sleeved blue overalls and her thick arms, folded over her chest, were bare. Her pleasant, jolly face was heavily lined. She smiled when we approached her, and when she showed her brown teeth and spoke to me I was enveloped by the smell of raw garlic:

> We are all Chinese. The soldiers are just human beings like us, and so I brought them some food. But I don't want them to go to the centre of the city. They are our children. They must love the students, not attack them.

It was hard to find anyone else who would talk to a Western camera crew. These were not articulate students who felt it was safe to express their views. Most of them remembered the days when speaking to foreigners was a punishable offense. They would smile when I asked them a question, moving away and shaking their heads. As for the soldiers, they appeared to have withdrawn into a glum silence of their own. It seemed cruel to try to make them speak. Their eyes followed me, but they said nothing and scarcely moved. They were not in any danger. They were humiliated but not threatened. There was no anger, no passion in this entire crowd. They had simply decided that the army would not get through.

Their motives seemed to be a modified version of those of the students. They disliked the security police, they disapproved of the stories of corruption in high places, they felt it was time for younger people to take over the government. Nevertheless they didn't echo the students' demands for democracy, and in the end they were prepared to use the fiercest violence against the army, when the students remained resolutely nonviolent. These were the People, in whose name the Communist Party had done everything for forty years. It seemed to me that this was their revenge on the politicians who had used their name. They had had enough of a system that supervised their lives and disrupted them at its own whim. Without having any clear idea what they did want, they knew they no longer wanted this. Probably they never had wanted it.

For the government, a new and more dangerous element had entered the situation. A senior official privately quoted Deng Xiaoping as saying earlier in the week, "As long as the workers and the peasants and the army are on our side, it doesn't matter about the students." Now, it seemed, the workers and students were uniting to neutralize the army. It was a magnificent victory for unarmed people. Even tanks had been stopped by the crowds. It showed equally a lack of determination on the part of the soldiers. One of the rumors going around was that the general commanding the 38th Army, based on the outskirts of Peking, had refused to issue his men live ammunition because his daughter was one of the students in Tiananmen Square. There were many such rumors. Most of them seemed to offer comfort and hope.

It was five o'clock on the morning of Saturday, 20 May. At the eastern end of Chang'an Avenue the sky was taking on a lighter tone. The orange light from the high streetlamps cast long, disturbing shadows. There were dozens of people on every street corner. They had been up all night, in case the miracle of the night before proved temporary and the tanks and trucks got through after all. A man labored past me, pedaling a trishaw with six people on the flat wooden boards behind him. They grinned at me and raised their fingers in the victory salute. It wasn't clear to me that the victory would last.

Once again I picked my way through the Square. The smell of disinfectant was strong, overlaying the other smells. In the dark I shuffled through the detritus on the ground: empty plastic bottles, cardboard from hand-drawn signs, leaves from the flowering cherry trees, bits of broken bamboo that had once carried banners, sticks from ice creams, cellophane bags from the frozen drinks the students endlessly sucked in the daytime heat.

There were sleeping bodies everywhere, wrapped in white banners with huge Chinese characters, or flags, or plastic coats the color of condoms, or tarpaulins. A girl lay with her arm across her boyfriend's chest and her head on his shoulder. Some people were sitting up now, their arms around their knees, looking dubiously at the lightening sky as if they were worried what the day would bring. I edged my way toward the village of tents and tepees in the center of the Square. A couple of marshals, their figures outlined against the sky, watched me coming and asked for my pass.

"BBC," I said to them. I'd left my pass in the hotel.

"Ah, BBC."

The word went round. People propped themselves up on elbows, sleepily, to look at this representative of an organization they all listened to.

Glass crunched underfoot: Xiaoping, little bottle. The sky was beginning to take on a glorious lighter blue, the clouds pink from the coming sun. I edged my way through the center of the Square, passing the Monument. Zhou Enlai's elegant calligraphy down its face glinted in the light from the sky. Ahead of me were the steps of the Great Hall of the People. There had been rumors that soldiers would come bursting out of the doors at sunrise. A hundred or so diehards sat on the lower steps to stop them. No soldiers appeared, and the sky was getting lighter by the minute.

People were thoroughly awake now, and a great cry went up as a truck with a hundred or so workers on the back careered down the street, sounding its horn. There were confused slogans, chants, bursts of laughter as it passed. Their faces were lit up by the dawn and by the exhilaration of it all.

The loudspeakers in the center of the Square, which were controlled by the students, crackled and made an announcement. It must have been good news. Everyone cheered, and the noise awoke the late sleepers. Near me as I sat on a low wall a couple stirred at the noise. The girl half cried with fatigue, and laid her head on her boyfriend's knees. He stroked her hair, looking across at the eastern sky. The red crest of the People's Republic over the Gate of Heavenly Peace, several hundred yards away, was still illuminated. The light from it shone faintly through the miasma that hung over the Square. The rising sun was taking over now. The blue flashing light of an ambulance passed me, and was obscured by a white banner. The disembodied light flashed eerily through the whiteness.

The street lights were switched off. I looked at my watch: 5:21. Even with the Square under occupation and the authority of the state challenged, the everyday routines were maintained. There was more crackling from the loudspeaker system: someone was putting on a tape. It hissed, and broke into the fourth movement of Beethoven's Ninth Symphony.

"*Freude!*" the bass shouted.

The word echoed round the Square, reverberating from the ugly Stalinist buildings, which were never designed to hear any such thing as Beethoven's notion of freedom. It was impossible for the heart not to lift at such a sound, at such a time. I watched the peaceful expression on the face of a man in his thirties who had spent the night on the pavement near me. He can have known nothing of Beethoven, but he pushed his conical straw hat back on his head and listened, the inevitable cigarette in his mouth.

The sound of morning coughing and hawking competed with the *Ode to Joy*. A man walked past me wearing a yellow headband with a skull and crossbones on it. A couple sauntered along close behind him, chewing something. Apologetically they reached up and wiped their hands on a banner over my head that proclaimed DEMOCRACY OR DEATH: something in the spirit of the man with the skull and crossbones.

Joggers were starting to appear on the edges of the Square now, men who had always come this way in the early morning and saw no reason why they should stop. A truck with reinforcements arrived, and young men and women dropped off the sides like people escaping from a burning ship. A cyclist circled round me and handed me a copy of *Beijing Science and Technology News,* which seemed to be all about the stopping of the army. The sun started to illumine the millions of shards of broken glass everywhere. It was morning. The army hadn't come.

There was martial law, but no force to back it. The suspension of everyday reality continued. The crowds stayed on the streets, the police wandered among them aimlessly, civil servants went into their offices and did no work, the shops stayed open. The patterns of everyday life continued, even though the government was unable to govern. At nine o'clock, a few hours after I watched the dawn in Tiananmen Square, the State Council issued three decrees:

Martial Law Order Number One. According to Article 89, Section 16 of the Constitution of the People's Republic of China, martial law is declared in the following eight districts of Peking municipality, with effect from 10 A.M. today, 20 May 1989.

The Peking Municipal Authority further issues the following three decrees.

1. Chinese citizens.

No Chinese citizen shall participate in any demonstration, protest or march in the martial law area, nor take part in any strike in the said area. It is an offense under martial law regulations to spread false rumors. Anyone who violates these provisions shall be liable to arrest by the duly constituted authorities, that is the People's Liberation Army or the police.

2. Foreign citizens.

(i) All foreign citizens must observe the martial law provisions, and all other relevant decrees.

(ii) No foreign citizen shall involve himself or herself with any activities by Chinese citizens which might violate the martial law provisions.

(iii) The People's Liberation Army and the police are authorized to arrest any foreign citizen who violates this decree.

3. Foreign journalists.

(i) All foreign journalists are strictly forbidden to incite unrest or issue reports which exaggerate the situation.

(ii) No foreign correspondent (including those from Hong Kong or Macao) may enter the premises of any government organization, factory, mine or university to undertake reporting or filming, without official written permission.

(iii) Any foreign journalist violating these provisions renders himself or herself liable to arrest by the People's Liberation Army or the police.

I went out very cautiously that morning with a cameraman colleague. We took a small video camera in a shoulder bag and looked for places where we could film without being seen. It was soon clear that there was no need for such precautions. No one cared about the martial law provisions, even though the government loudspeakers at the northern end of Tiananmen Square repeated them again and again. The students' loudspeakers in the center of the Square blared back Beethoven and messages of support from students in other cities across China. The war of the loudspeakers, which continued until the troops opened fire on the students on the night of 3–4 June, began in earnest that morning.

The danger hadn't receded. Overhead, helicopters buzzed the Square and dropped leaflets on the city which contained messages of support for Li Peng. People jumped into the air to grab them as they fell, then tore them into little pieces. Absurd fears were voiced over the students' loudspeakers:

> Dear friends and fellow-students, this is to warn you of two dangers which we have been informed about. We are told there are army snipers in high buildings around the center of the city. We have also been told that metal gratings in the streets may be electrified. Please be very careful.

That evening the students started building barricades. They dragged over the great concrete blocks with metal rails set into them which ran along the sides of Chang'an Avenue. Then they supplemented them with flimsier things: bicycles, blocks of wood, boxes, bricks and lumps of masonry from a building site beside the Beijing Hotel. There was a great deal of tension during the night, and few people slept well in the Square.

The next day, Sunday, a train full of soldiers pulled into the main railway station. The students had ten or fifteen minutes' warning and headed to the station, which was less than a mile away, in sizeable numbers. The soldiers stayed gloomily, silently, in their carriages as the students besieged them. Later, the train pulled ignominiously away. A proclamation from something called, vaguely, Martial Law Enforcement Headquarters put out a curious statement that afternoon that said that army maneuvers had now been stopped.

> The People's Liberation Army should continue to follow disciplined procedures. The army should love the people and take care of the students, and educate them to observe the law. We oppose any activities which are contrary to this endeavor.

No one thought the battle had been won, but everyone knew that the great mass of the urban population was supporting the students. Soon signs of a very Chinese form of resistance began to appear. The announcement of martial law was made on television by two news readers, Li Juanying and her male colleague Xue Fei. Xue read out the statement itself, never once looking at the camera and (most unusually for Chinese television) stumbling over the words. The following day a student banner appeared in the Square reading "Long Live Xue Fei!" Xue did not appear on television again. China Central Television had taken a liberal turn in the year or so before the demonstrations, and had been airing a considerable range of different views. It had also broached some difficult topics: inflation, the grain crisis, the failings of joint ventures. During the hunger strikes in the Square the news programs had shown pictures that had undoubtedly raised public sympathy for the students. They had also given a clear idea to the country at large of the size of the great anti-government demonstrations of 17 and 18 May.

There were other ways of fighting the government. There was sabotage in the preparation of the new banners that hung from buildings along Chang'an Avenue and elsewhere, enjoining citizens to avoid anarchy and obey the martial law decrees. Within a day or two, the squares of paper, each with a single character painted on it, began to curl and fall off. Guerrilla war was fought out in the pages of the newspapers. There was a constant flow of articles that presented the government's side, but even in the *People's Daily* there were other, contrary items. The sub-editors took to putting big, misleading headlines on foreign stories, as though they were commentaries on Chinese affairs. Thus:

MILITARY FORCE SHOULD NEVER BE USED AGAINST CIVILIANS

The Hungarian leader, Imre Poszgay, today commented on an official investigation carried out into the circumstances of the Soviet intervention in Hungary in 1956. It had been wrong, he said, for Moscow to send its troops in to suppress the Hungarian uprising.

Or:

OLD MEN SHOULD RETIRE FROM POLITICS

The Burmese parliament was told today that government ministers who reached the age of 75 should be encouraged to resign.

A newspaper in Shanghai carried a photograph of Winston Churchill giving a victory sign. These gestures were like partisan raids into enemy territory. They kept up morale and made the government look stupid. Each new example was greeted with delight by the students.

The Great Wall looped over the ridges and hilltops like the cordons the students used to rope off Tiananmen Square. For the five thousand years of China's recorded history the farmers here had had to fight hard to make anything out of the harsh land. The countryside was as dramatic as the watercolors Wen Chia painted to illustrate the work of the T'ang

Dynasty poet Tu Fu: peaks, standing rocks, winding rivers, fir trees, hermits, distant travelers. As we headed out beyond the Wall I remembered some of Tu Fu's lines:

> The empire is broken, but mountains and rivers remain
> In the city, spring grass and trees grow thick.
> Flowers shed tears for the times:
> Birds, resenting the alienation, shock the heart with their cries.

Eight hundred million people out of a population of a billion live in the countryside. If the cities were full of discontent and foreboding, the peasants had a great deal to be grateful to the government for. Before the revolution in 1949 the life of the peasants was wretched. Then the Communists leased out the land to them and things became better. But Mao Zedong, whose family were farmers, introduced one of his immense schemes of social engineering that did such damage to China. Anxious to prevent any gap between rich farmers and poor ones, he introduced a commune system. It was deeply unpopular. Poverty and lassitude overtook the countryside.

In 1979 Zhao Ziyang and Deng Xiaoping dissolved the communes and leased the land to the villagers on the basis of the numbers in each household. Farmers were allowed to sell most of their produce on the open market. As food prices rose in the towns and cities, the peasants began to prosper. For the ten years between then and the troubles in Tiananmen Square, the peasants had approved strongly of Deng Xiaoping's government. The news from Peking bewildered them and made them angry.

We stopped in the village of Bohaishuo, a half-day's drive away. It was a rambling place on a hillside, with dirt roads curving between the long, not unprosperous houses. It was like a village in Eastern Europe in the nineteenth century. Pigs rooted by the roadside. There was no electricity or water supply. In the middle of the village stood a mast with loudspeakers on it, which relayed the radio news every few hours. The whole village knew what was happening in Peking and the other cities of China.

Chickens and guinea-fowl scattered in front of us. Up the hillside, under the chestnut trees, goats were browsing. We were lucky in the house we chose first. The man who lived there was a sailor, and had traveled round the world to Europe. He had been to Antwerp, Southampton and Felixstowe. His face was pleasant and open over his dirty plaid shirt. Having seen so much of the world, he was less worried about talking to a foreign television crew at a time when Peking was under martial law.

Inside his house the straw burning under the cooking pot smelled almost like incense. He sat down on the family bed, which was a mattress laid over a clay-built stove to keep them warm in winter. Yes, he said, he did very well out of farming. His family earned 1,500 yuan a year, ten times what they had earned before Deng and Zhao reformed the agricultural system. He thought the students were stupid: they were putting everything in danger. Maybe China would sink back to the old ways if the present government was overthrown.

We filmed him pumping water from the well in the little courtyard. Then one of the neighbors arrived. The village Party secretary was worried that the sailor-farmer might be talking to the foreign television people. Not at all, said the sailor-farmer, they had just wanted to film him using the well. He looked at us expressionlessly.

I went with our translator to see the Party secretary. He was an engaging old man in his late sixties with a witty, evil face. His mouth was filled with ill-shapen, misplaced teeth, mostly capped with gold; he carried his savings around with him. He was badly wall-eyed, but he turned his strabismus to his own advantage. The translator and I sat on chairs side by side, and as he, too, perched on his bed above a clay stove he kept his left eye on me and his right on the translator. Over his head was a Chinese calendar with a picture of Marie Antoinette on it: a curious thing to find in the house of a Communist Party official. One of his many sons sat silently beside him. Every now and then he refilled our cups from a giant enamel teapot.

In village terms, Liu Qingshang was seriously rich. Taking one of his eyes off us and shifting it to his son, he told me he earned 10,000 yuan a year: a thousand from pears, a thousand from chestnuts, six thousand from chickens, two thousand from other things. The translator, who had been working out the amount of land Liu farmed with his sons, suggested that he probably earned 100,000 yuan a year. Liu laughed, pleased at the compliment.

"If I earned that much I'd go and live in Hong Kong."

He had helped the resistance against the Japanese in the War, running messages and hiding weapons. I told him that my uncle had also fought the Japanese in the War.

"Salute!" he shouted, and slapped the palm of my hand with his.

I hoped this might encourage him to record an interview with me, but he was too canny for that.

"I follow Party discipline," he said.

Since 1949 he had been purged no fewer than four times, and each time he had made a comeback. He was a village Deng Xiaoping.

"I'd be in Peking running the country if it weren't for one thing. Guess what it is?"

I looked at his dishonest, amusing face and tried to work it out.

"I can't read or write!"

He roared with laughter, perhaps at my discomfiture. His physical appearance apart, he would have made a good living out of the rich pickings that "everyone doing business" offered.

> Everyone here supports Comrade Deng Xiaoping. He's done everything for us. As for those students, they just piss in the bed and spoil it for everyone.

He pointed graphically at the communal bed he was sitting on. The words seemed familiar. Afterward I remembered: Charles de Gaulle had used the expression *chie-en-lit* about the students in Paris in 1968. But Liu Qingshang wouldn't repeat even these loyal sentiments for our television camera. He was too canny for that. Four purgings were enough. Who knew what might happen next?

There was a great deal of handshaking as we left. With a kind of good-natured cunning he asked the translator for his name and work unit number. A report would have to be prepared about all this. The translator refused. He was a strange man, a poet and writer who had attached himself to us in a way which no one could now remember. His English was very good, but our other Chinese helpers were certain he was a spy and would sometimes refuse to talk if he was in the room. I found his company very pleasant, but even I became nervous when he wrote down everything we said in a large school exercise book. When I asked him why he did, he said he was planning to turn his experiences with us into a short story. Here in the village, however, he became anxious when the Party secretary wanted to know his identity. I intervened.

"Who knows," I asked the Party secretary, "what might happen next?"

He laughed a great deal at that. He was still laughing as we drove off. I could see his straw hat waving for a long way down the road.

Tiananmen Square had changed. There were fewer people there now, and many of them came from provincial universities. The Peking students had mostly gone back to their studies, though they were ready to turn out again at the hint of trouble. The Square was less pleasant. The makeshift latrines stank with the sweetness of feces and the acid of urine. The marshals were more officious in demanding passes. The leaders argued among themselves and were rarely seen.

It was a relief to walk down the western arm of Chang'an Avenue, past the Gate of Heavenly Peace, to the main entrance of Zhongnanhai, the leadership compound. A thousand or so students were blockading the gateway, standing or sitting opposite it while twenty or more soldiers sat facing them under the portals of the gate. It was a gesture, nothing more; the Party and government leaders, who lived inside the compound, rarely used the formal front gate, and the side gates, which they did use, were free of demonstrators. Still, it was a serious indignity. Someone had hung placards round the necks of the two ceremonial lions on either side of the gateway. The slogans demanded the resignation of the government and the introduction of democracy.

There were speeches, and the occasional entertainment: dancing, drumming, flute-playing. The soldiers sat with their legs crossed, looking straight ahead of them. No one taunted them, but once when a soup kitchen handed out food to the students I saw a young man go up to the line of soldiers and offer them a bowl of rice and chopsticks. They continued to stare straight in front, and one of the student marshals pulled the young man away. Everything the students did in April and May was reminiscent of 1968 and the Woodstock period, but nothing was more evocative than this.

As we were filming the crowd from the vantage point of the soldiers, I saw an old man craning through the heads to watch these goings-on. You could tell from his wrinkled brown face he had never dreamed that ordinary people could be allowed to heap such indignities on the Party and the government. He was amazed and shocked and yet, I thought, felt a sneaking excitement at it all. Perhaps even the most timid and obedient servant of the state derived a private, guilty pleasure from the iconoclasm of others.

All this time the government had slowly been growing in strength. Military units were ordered to hold study sessions on the speech Li Peng had made the night before martial law was imposed. Messages of support came slowly and sometimes reluctantly for Li Peng. After four days only twelve out of thirty-nine provinces and major cities had given him their backing. Most of the local Party bosses were waiting to see which way the wind would blow. There was an attempt by Zhao Ziyang's allies to summon an emergency meeting of the National People's Congress, which would have brought things to a head and might have voted against Li Peng. The chairman of the Congress, Wan Li, had been on a visit to Canada and the United States and was now, according to Zhao's supporters, flying back to Peking to call a meeting. Instead, his plane flew to Shanghai, and he was said to be ill. A week after the introduction of martial law he issued a statement, which said that while the students were patriotic, the demonstrations were being manipulated by a handful of people.

Later, a high-ranking source that usually had been reliable in the past told us that Deng Xiaoping, who had not been seen in public since Gorbachev's visit, had been traveling around the provinces demanding assurances of support from the senior commanders of the People's Liberation Army. On 18 May, we were told, he flew to the city of Wuhan, where he summoned the generals commanding all seven of China's military regions to a conference. Six of them agreed to give him total support. The seventh was more equivocal. He was the general commanding the Peking region.

Slowly, the government machinery was starting to regain its self-confidence. There were more anonymous people with cameras in the Square, filming the leaders, especially when there were foreign journalists about. Strange incidents that placed the students in a bad light began to occur. On Tuesday, 23 May, a teacher, a journalist and a worker from Hunan, Mao Zedong's province, walked up to the gateway and threw ink at the huge portrait hanging over it. Mao's bland, moonlike face was not badly defaced—a blot hit his left eyebrow, and others spattered across his neck and jacket—but this was iconoclasm of a serious kind. A group of students standing nearby seized the three men and handed them over to the police. They were taken to a bus, where a CCTV reporter interviewed them. None of them would say why they had done it. The students were certain they were agents provocateurs, whose task was to show that crimes against decency were being committed because of the occupation of the Square.

Later even more disturbing things happened. A lone soldier drove a truck into the Square, parked it, and ran off. The students examined it and found it was full of rifles, ammunition and hand grenades. Again, they handed it over to the police at once, and helped to unload it. A security policeman with a video camera filmed the incident. Later, when the government had regained control, CCTV broadcast a carefully edited video, which purported to show that the students were armed and violent. This incident featured strongly in it. So did the defacing of Mao's portrait. There were also numerous shots that, the commentary said, showed foreign agitators suborning the students. I thought I recognized myself among them.

An hour after Mao's portrait was attacked, the sky, which had earlier been clear, began to darken. Soon black storm clouds were heading from the west. We had come out to see the ink-spattered painting, but we found ourselves instead filming a wild storm. The rain fell harder and faster than I had ever seen. In a few minutes my thin tropical suit was soaked through, and a pen in my inside pocket started to leak ink all over my jacket like black blood. Truckloads of demonstrators careered across the road, skidding on the wet surface. The wind whipped the red and white banners and sent them streaming across the Square. It lifted tents bodily and blew them away, leaving the people who had been sheltering in them exposed and frightened. It whipped up the rubbish and swept it out of the Square altogether. It lashed the Monument and blew down the tepees around it. The air was full of sticks and tarpaulins and sheets of plastic. They wrapped themselves round trees and streetlamps, or flew off into the distance, like the spirits of the dead. The loudspeakers shook on their posts, pouring music and instructions into the rain and the empty Square. At last the stench of disinfectant and urine was washed away.

Most people fled when the wind came up and the sky darkened. They took shelter in the underpass which went from the Square to the Gate of Heavenly Peace, thousands of wet, dispirited people crammed together, their light clothes steaming. Some diehards rode out the storm. We filmed a man whose picture went round the world: naked to the waist, held in position by a friend, he perched on the marble rails of the Monument and defied the elements, his arms raised in twin victory signs. He was doing it for our benefit, but it seemed to symbolize the spirit of the entire protest.

Soon there were only a few dozen students left in the Square. A platoon of soldiers in sou'westers could have solved the government's problem. We were on the northern side of that vast expanse, obliged to stay there because the cameraman, Eric Thirer, was a perfectionist and the pictures were stunning. The wind lashed the rain at us, and whipped it toward us across the empty, flat expanse of paving stones. In the distance three figures came battling toward us, sometimes leaning into the wind, sometimes blown along by it as it veered. They tacked in our direction like small boats in a stormy bay. As they reached us one of the students started taking off his flimsy raincoat. It was a difficult operation, but when he had it free he thrust it toward me. It was a gesture of thanks to us for being there. I couldn't accept it: I was wet through anyway, and he had nothing on but a T-shirt and shorts. In the end he accepted it back, but knelt down in the rain and kissed my hand. In that storm I felt like King Lear with Tom O'Bedlam.

I first heard about the statue in the house of one of the artists who had been working on it. It had to be created in great secrecy. The authorities would regard it as the ultimate provocation and would do everything they could to prevent its being erected. The idea had come not from the student leaders themselves but from a small group of students at the Central Institute of Fine Arts. They constructed it from a small maquette model in a courtyard of the Institute, building it up with a mixture of fiberglass and plaster of Paris. It was clearly inspired by the Statue of Liberty with its lamp, but in other ways the flowing hair and the girlish, European features owed something to the French figure of Marianne. Chai Ling, the student leader who had been most enthusiastic about the plan, called it a symbol for the movement. We smuggled her into our hotel shortly after the statue was erected and interviewed her. She sat smiling her gentle smile, her feet scarcely touching the ground. In the white top and green shorts she wore she looked like a schoolgirl. She was passionate about the statue. Was it a Statue of Liberty? Or the Goddess of Democracy?

> She is the Goddess of Democracy, of course. She is the symbol of our hopes and aspirations, she represents the fruit of our struggle. The government is making all kinds of slander and accusation about her, but we resist its propaganda.

On the night of 29 May the statue was brought into Tiananmen Square in three parts, on the backs of flatbed bicycle rickshaws. Flimsy-looking scaffolding was in place by the next morning. That evening there was a festival of drumming and dancing around the shrouded statue, and then she was uncovered. It was a master stroke. People came flooding back to the Square in such numbers that Chai Ling and the other leaders called off their fruitless argument about whether and how they should abandon Tiananmen Square. Standing opposite Chairman Mao's portrait (a spare copy of which was raised into place within hours of the desecration) the statue held up her torch of freedom almost in his face. It was extremely effective, and deeply offensive to the government.

On the night of Friday, 2 June, the army moved in. This time they didn't come by truck and tank, they ran in groups of a hundred at a time. Choosing their routes carefully, they had worked through the side streets. By the time the students and those who supported them realized what was happening, they were almost in the Square. I ran too when I heard the news, following the sound of drumming. The streets were empty and dark, but I knew them well by now. I was alone, and hoped I would be able to find a camera crew.

I turned the corner into Chang'an Avenue. Heaps of military equipment lay in the middle of the streets. Lines of young men were being forced down the farther side of the road. They'd moved the students out of the Square, I thought.

"What's happening? Does anyone speak English?"

No one spoke English. I pushed my uncomprehending way through the crowds. There were so many things I couldn't work out. Why were the crowds so big? Where were the guns?

Then I realized. The soldiers were the prisoners. The equipment was their equipment. They had been stopped again. You could see they were exhausted from running. They had no spirit in them. Down beside the Beijing Hotel several hundred of them were sitting down, some in the road and some in a building site. They were hemmed in by a thick crowd of exultant people. From time to time someone would grab a portable loudspeaker and boom some message at the luckless soldiers. As before, they sat there and took it. Their officers looked at the ground. They had no orders, no idea what to do next.

I met up with a BBC camera crew. We filmed the lines of soldiers on the other side of the road, though they were often hostile to us. Then we went back to the large group beside the Beijing Hotel, their white shirts and green jackets startlingly bright in the camera lights. The officers were negotiating with the student leaders. As we filmed, one of the officers shouted an order and about two thirds of the group stood up, stretching their aching legs, and formed up in the road. The others stayed where they were. They and their officers, it seemed, had sided with the crowd. The others were going back to their barracks.

They marched down the dark side street. We followed, filming them as they went. They took no notice of us, and we moved in and out of the ranks. They were walking slowly, with little discipline. Bob Poole, the cameraman, found himself behind an NCO carrying a white plastic can. Perhaps it had contained drinking water. The camera light suddenly angered him. He lashed out at it with his plastic can. His act of resistance rallied the other soldiers. They gathered around us, shouting and pulling at us. The light came off the camera and was smashed. They began wrenching at the cameraman, getting him away from me and the sound recordist. I was shouting now, at the soldiers and at the cameraman.

"Hold the camera down, Bob."

He managed to lower it from his shoulder, and that calmed them for a little. But the man with the can came back and shouted at us, and the violence started again in the dark, narrow street. Bob was pulled away from us again, into the pool of green uniforms.

The next moment someone was shouting back at them in Chinese, and three students moved in between the soldiers and us. The soldiers released Bob. We got away quickly, back down the street toward the bright streetlights of Chang'an Avenue. I tried to thank one of the students. He shrugged.

"It's our duty," he said.

The soldiers headed off into the darkness, disappointed at the failure of their momentary attempt at revenge.

The next night, Sunday, 3 June, everyone was expecting them to come back. It was humid and airless, and the streets round our hotel were empty. We set out for the Square, a big conspicuous European television team: reporter, producer, cameraman, sound recordist, translator, lightingman, all complete with gear. A cyclist rode past, shouting and pointing. What it meant we couldn't tell. Then we came upon a line of soldiers. Some had bleeding faces, one cradled a broken arm. They were walking slowly, limping. There had been a battle somewhere, but we couldn't tell where.

When we reached Chang'an Avenue it was as full of people as it had been at the height of the big demonstrations. It was a human river again. We followed the flow of it to the Gate of Heavenly Peace, under the restored portrait of Mao. There were hundreds of small groups, each concentrated around someone who was haranguing or lecturing them, using the heavy public gestures of the Chinese. Other groups had formed around radios tuned to foreign stations. People were moving from group to group, pushing in, crushing round a speaker, arguing, moving on, passing new information.

For the most part these weren't students. They were from the factories, and the red cloths tied round their foreheads gave them a look of ferocity. Trucks were arriving from the outskirts of the city, full of young workers. They waved the banners of their workplace, singing, chanting, looking forward to trouble.

People were shouting: there was a battle going on between tanks and the crowd somewhere to the west of the city center. Details differed. I had trouble finding out what was being said. I watched the animated faces, everyone pushing closer to each new source of information, pulling at each other's sleeves or shoulders. Tanks and armored personnel carriers, they were saying, were heading for the Square. They were coming from two directions, east and west. The crowds couldn't stop them.

"It's a different army. It's not the thirty-eighth!"

The man was screaming it, clutching at our translator, pulling his arm, wanting to make him understand the significance. It had been the 38th Army that had tried to recapture the city the previous night, and on the night before martial law was declared. The soldiers had been unwilling to do their duty. These were armies from the outside, the rumors said, savage armies that didn't care who they killed. It wasn't true. The soldiers that moved in to Tiananmen Square were indeed from the 38th Army. They were just as savage as any outsiders.

We pushed on toward the Square. Several thousand people were standing there motionless, listening to the loudspeakers high above our heads: the government loudspeakers.

Go home and save your lives. You will fail. You are not behaving in the correct Chinese manner. This is not the West. It is China. You should

behave like good Chinese. Go home and save your lives. Go home and
save your lives.

The voice was expressionless, epicene, metallic, like that of a hypnotist. I looked at these silent, serious faces illuminated by the orange light
of the streetlamps, studying the loudspeakers. Even the small children,
brought here with the rest of the family as part of an outing, stared
intently. The words were repeated again and again. It was a voice the people of China had been listening to for forty years, and continued listening
to even now—but no one did what the hypnotist said. No one moved.

And then suddenly the spell broke. People were shouting that the army
was coming. There was the sound of violent scraping, and across the
avenue people were pulling at the railings set in concrete and dragging
them across to form a barricade. Everyone moved quickly. The crowd was
acting as one, suddenly animated. Its actions were fast and decisive, and
sometimes brutal. They blocked off Chang'an Avenue. We began filming,
flooding the sweating enthusiasts with our camera light. Young men
danced round us, flaunting their weaponry: coshes, knives, spears, bricks.
A boy rushed up to our camera and opened his shabby green windcheater
like a black marketeer to reveal a row of Coca-Cola bottles strapped to his
waist, each filled with petrol and plugged with rags. He laughed, and
mimed the action of pulling out a bottle and throwing it. I asked him his
age: Sixteen. Why was he against the government? No answer.

Our translator heard that the army would move in at one o'clock. It
was half past midnight now. In the distance, above the noise of the crowd,
I thought I could hear gunfire. I wanted to find a vantage point from
which we could film without being spotted by the army. But the tension
that bonded the members of the crowd together had a different effect on
us as a team. It was hot and noisy. We argued about whether we should
have interviewed an English-speaking doctor we had met a short time
before. We started shouting. It was all very trivial. The producer wanted
to gather more background material for the documentary we had been
working on. I argued that we needed to prepare ourselves for the coming
confrontation, worried that it would take us by surprise unless we had a
plan of action. The cameraman, impatient with us both, wanted to get on

with filming the scene in front of him. Both of them were right. Made angry and petulant by the airlessness, the heat and the sense of coming violence, I headed off on my own to find the doctor whom we should indeed have interviewed earlier.

I pushed through the crowds, immediately feeling better for being alone. There were very few foreign journalists left in the Square by now, and I felt conspicuous on my own. Yet I also felt good. People grabbed my hand, thanking me for being with them. I gave them a victory sign and everyone around me applauded. It was hard to define the mood. There was still a spirit of celebration because so many people were out on the streets in defiance of the government; but it was giving way to a terrible foreboding. There was also something else, something I hadn't seen before in China: a reckless ferocity of purpose.

I crossed into the main part of Tiananmen Square and headed for the village of tents. I had spent so much time in the Square that I felt I knew each tent, each smell. A young couple clung to each other, her head on his shoulder. I passed close to them, but they didn't look at me. I thought of passengers on a sinking ship, waiting for the killing shock of the cold sea. A student asked me to sign his T-shirt. It was a gesture from an earlier, happy time, and I suspected I would be doing it for the last time. I signed the loose material at the back, below the collar, and he turned to face me. He had thick glasses and a bad complexion.

"It will be dangerous tonight," he said. "We are all very afraid here."

He grabbed my hand and shook it with a great intensity. His grip was bony and clammy. I asked what he thought would happen.

"We will all die."

He straightened up and shook my hand again. Then he slipped away through the tents.

The camp was dark. A few students were left there, but most of them had gathered around the Monument in the center. I could hear the speeches and the occasional burst of singing: the *Internationale*, as always. They were about to pay the price for rebelling against the Communist system, and they were singing the Communist anthem while they waited. Here, though, it was quiet. I looked up at the face of the Goddess of Democracy, thirty feet above me. The symbol of all our aspirations, the fruit of our struggle. I loved that statue. It seemed disturbingly fragile, very easy to tear down and smash.

The speeches and the songs continued in the distance. Then they stopped. There was a violent grinding and squealing: the familiar sound of an armored personnel carrier. I heard screaming. Behind me in the avenue everyone was running. The APC was driving fast down the side of the Square. It seemed uncertain of its direction, one minute driving straight for Chang'an Avenue, the next stopping, turning, stopping again, as if it were a big animal looking for a way of escape. There was a scream and a sudden angry roar. The vehicle had crushed someone under its tracks. It turned in my direction, and started moving. I felt another kind of panic now, but it wasn't fear for myself. The action was starting and I was separated from my colleagues. In times of danger, the professional code runs, you stay with your colleagues and help them. I didn't want to earn a reputation as someone who disappeared when the trouble started.

The vehicle went on careering back and forth. It must have knocked down six or seven people. Later I saw one of the bodies, the legs wrenched off at the knee by the metal tracks. By now the APC was being hit repeatedly by Molotov cocktails and was on fire. Somehow it managed to escape, barging its way through the crowds with a crowd of angry attackers behind it. It fled along Chang'an Avenue to the west.

Then a second armored personnel carrier came along the Avenue, alone and unsupported like the first. The crowds knew that with their numbers and their petrol bombs they had the power to knock it out. They screamed with anger and hatred as it veered in different directions, trying to find its way through the crowd, not caring who it knocked down. The Molotov cocktails arched over my head, spinning over and over, exploding on the thin shell of armor that protected the soldiers inside. Still the vehicle carried on, zigzagging, crossing the Avenue, trying to find a way through the barricades. A pause, and then it charged head on, straight at a block of concrete—and stuck there, its engine roaring wildly.

A terrible shout of triumph went up from the crowd then, primitive and dark. The prey had been caught. The smell of petrol and burning metal and sweat was in the air, intoxicating and violent. Everyone round me was pushing and fighting to get to the vehicle. I resisted, and then saw the light of a television camera close beside the trapped APC. I guessed that my colleague, Ingo Prosser, was the only cameraman brave enough to be that close. Now I was the one who was fighting, struggling to get through the crowd, pulling people out of my path, swearing, a big brutal Englishman larger and stronger than any of them. I tore one man's shirt and punched another in the back, desperate to get to my colleagues.

All round me people seemed to be yelling at the sky, their faces lit up. The vehicle had caught fire. A man, his torso bare, scrambled up the side of the APC and stood on top of it, his arms raised in victory, the noise of the mob welling up around him. They knew they had the vehicle's crew trapped inside. Someone started beating at the armored glass with an iron bar.

I reached Ingo, the cameraman, and pulled at his arm to get his attention. He scarcely noticed me amid the buffeting and the noise and the violence and just carried on filming. He and his sound recordist and the Chinese lighting-man and I were a few feet from the burning vehicle: close enough to be killed if it exploded or the soldiers came out shooting, but I couldn't persuade them to step back. So we stayed there, with the heat beating against our faces as people continued to pour petrol on the bonnet and roof and smashed at the doors and the armored glass. They wanted to get at the soft, vulnerable flesh inside. What must it be like in there? I could imagine the soldiers half crazed with the noise and the heat and the fear of being burned alive.

The door at the rear of the vehicle opened a little. The screaming round me rose even higher then. A soldier pushed the muzzle of a rifle out, but it was snatched from his hands and suddenly everyone was grabbing his arms, pulling and wrenching until he finally came free. Then he was gone. I saw the arms of the mob flailing above their heads as they fought each other to get their blows in. He was unconscious or dead within seconds, and his body dragged away in triumph.

A second soldier showed his head through the door and was immediately pulled out by his hair and ears and the skin on his face. I could see him clearly for a few instants: his eyes were rolling and his mouth was open, and he was covered with blood where the skin had been ripped off. Only his eyes remained, white and clear, but then someone was trying to get them as well, and someone else began beating his skull till the skull came apart and there was blood all over the ground, and his brains, and still they kept on, beating and beating and beating at what remained.

Then the horrible sight passed away, and the ground was wet where he had been.

There was a third soldier inside. I could just see his face in the light of the flames, and some of the crowd could too. They pulled him out, screaming, wild at having missed out on the killing of the other soldiers. It was blood they wanted, I knew, it was to feel the blood running over their hands. Their mouths were open and panting like dogs, and their eyes were expressionless. The Chinese lightingman told me afterward they were shouting that the soldier they were about to kill wasn't human, that he was just a thing, an object, an animal that had to be destroyed. And all the time the noise and the heat and the stench of oil burning on hot metal beat at us, overwhelming our senses, deadening our feelings.

Just as the third soldier was pulled out of the vehicle, almost fainting, an articulated bus forced its way fast through the crowd and stopped with great skill so its rear door opened just beside the group around the soldier. It was the students. They had heard what was happening, and a group had rushed over in the bus to save whomever they could. It was as noble an act, I think, as any I had come across. The students—there were four or five of them—tried to drag the soldier on board by force, but the crowd held on to him, pulling him back. By some mischance the bus door started to close. It seemed the soldier's life must be lost.

I had seen people die in front of me before, but I had never seen three people die one after the other in this way. Once again the members of the crowd closed around the soldier, their arms raised over their heads to beat him to death. The bus and the safety it promised were so close. I couldn't look on any longer, a passive observer, watching another man's skin torn away or his skull broken open, and do nothing. I saw the soldier's face briefly. It expressed only horror and pain as he sank down under the blows of the people around him. I started to move forward. The ferocity of the crowd had entered me, but I felt it was the crowd that was the animal, that wasn't human.

The soldier was hanging limply in the arms of the crowd and a man was trying to break his skull with a half-brick, bringing it down with great force. I screamed obscenities at him, stupid obscenities since no one could understand them, and threw myself at him, catching him with his arm up as he prepared himself for a final blow. He looked at me blankly, and I felt his thin arm go limp in my grasp. I stopped shouting. He let me take the brick away and I threw it under the bus. It felt wet. A little room had been created around the soldier, and the students who had tried to rescue him before were able to get to him and pull and push him onto the bus by a different door. The rest of the mob hadn't given up, and some of them swarmed onto the bus to try to kill him there, but the students formed a protective block around him and they gave up. He was safe.

The vehicle burned for a long time, its driver and the man in the front seat beside him burning with it. The flames lit up the Square and reflected on the face of the Monument, where the students had taken their stand. The crowd in Chang'an Avenue had been sated. The loudspeakers had stopped telling people to save their lives. There was silence.

The students sang the *Internationale*. It sounded weak and faint in the vastness of the Square. Many were crying. Maybe some students had taken part in the violence, but those in the Square itself had been faithful to the principle of nonviolence. I began to realize why the two armored personnel carriers had been sent in on their own. They were intended to be sacrificial victims. The army commanders had known that one or both of them would be caught. It was a way of stirring up the emotions of the ordinary soldiers, so that when the moment came they would have no pity for the demonstrators.

My colleagues and I wanted to make sure our pictures survived if we were arrested or shot, and I told the others we should go back to the Beijing Hotel and come out again later. I feel guilty about that now. We should have stayed in the Square, even though all the other camera crews had left and staying might have cost us our lives. Someone should have

been there with the demonstrators when the army moved in, filming
what happened, showing the courage of the students as they were surrounded by tanks and the army fired into them as they advanced. One
or two Western newspaper journalists stayed with them, anonymous in
the crowd. With our conspicuous equipment, we could not have been
hidden, but we should have stayed too.

We didn't. We took up our position on the fourteenth floor of the
Beijing Hotel. From there we got the famous pictures that were seen all
around the world. Everything in them seemed gray and distant, though.
We saw most of what happened, but we were separated from the noise and
the fear and the stench of it. We saw the troops pouring out of the Gate
of Heavenly Peace, bayonets fixed, shooting first into the air and then
straight ahead of them. They looked like automata, with their rounded
dark helmets. We filmed them charging across and clearing the northern
end of the Square, where I had seen the young couple sitting and waiting
for the shipwreck. We filmed the tanks as they drove over the tents where
some of the students had taken refuge. Maybe the young couple, or the
boy who asked me to sign his T-shirt, were among them. Those who were
closer than we were said they heard the screams of the people inside the
tents. We filmed as the lights in the Square were switched off at 4 A.M.
They were switched on again forty minutes later, when the troops and the
tanks moved toward the Monument itself, shooting first in the air and
then directly at the students, so that the steps of the Monument and the
heroic reliefs that decorated it were smashed by bullets.

Once or twice we were shot at ourselves, and a Taiwanese photographer in a room two doors from ours died from a bullet wound as he
stood on the balcony. During the night the security police came to
arrest us in our room. The young Chinese student who had been our
lightingman, Wang, had opened the door to them and then tried to shut
it when he saw who was there. A uniformed hotel porter grabbed him
by the sleeve, and two men in suits stood behind him. Wang shouted out
and I ran over. I pulled him away from the porter, and confident in my
ability to keep the door shut against the three of them if necessary I
peered through the gap between the door and its frame. Wang kept trying to translate, but I pushed him away.

Foolish things come to one's lips at such times; I shouted out that the British ambassador would be very angry if they persisted in trying to enter the room, and that unless they left at once I would ring him myself. The threat was more than usually empty: I had not visited the British ambassador in Peking and knew nothing of him, but my experience of a number of his colleagues was that they wanted nothing to do with such difficulties.

Curiously, it worked; perhaps it was my tone of voice. The pressure on the other side of the door relaxed, and there was grumbling as the three of them moved away. They did not come back. After that, Wang stuck close to me, convinced that I exerted some occult power over secret policemen that would protect him. I liked him: he was bold and amusing, and stayed with us long after all our other Chinese helpers had evaporated.

Meanwhile the crowds below us had regrouped on the Avenue, shouting their defiance at the troops who were massing at the far end. Every now and then the crack of a rifle would bring down another demonstrator, and the ambulances or the flatbed bicycle rickshaws would hurry them away to hospital. I had given up trying to clear the balcony of everyone except the cameraman and me. The Chinese who had taken refuge with us couldn't be prevented from seeing what was happening.

One of them was a student leader who had come to our room because we were foreigners. I shouted at her to get away, that it was too dangerous, that only those with a job to do should stay out there. She refused, turning her head away from me so I wouldn't see that she was crying, her hands clenched tight enough to hurt. She was determined to watch the rape of her country and the utter destruction of the movement she and her friends had built up in the course of twenty-two days in the Square.

I recalled the lines of another T'ang Dynasty poet, Tu Fu's friend and master Li Po: *If you try to cut water with a sword it will just run faster.* But the river of change had been dammed, and below me on the Avenue where it had run, people were dying all the time. Beside me, the cameraman stirred and started filming. Down in the Square, in the early light, the soldiers were busy unrolling something and lifting it up. Soon a great curtain of black cloth covered the end of Tiananmen Square. What was happening there was hidden from us.

Chai Ling, the best-known of the student leaders, stayed in the Square until the end. Later she recorded her impressions of what happened, and the tape was smuggled out to Hong Kong. These are extracts from it.

I was the general commander in the Square. There were also some other student leaders like Li Lu and Feng Congde [her husband]. At 9 P.M. all the students in the Square raised their right hands and made a vow: "I swear to promote the democracy and prosperity of my country and to prevent it from being overthrown by a handful of people. I am willing to give my young life to protect Tiananmen Square. I am willing to give up my life and my blood to protect the people's Square until the last one of us dies."

We knew this was a war between love and hate. This was not a war of weapons against weapons. We knew that if we used truncheons, bottles and sticks to fight the speeding tanks and the sub-machine guns, our demonstration was bound to fail. We decided to sit there quietly and be prepared to be sacrificed for the peaceful pro-democracy demonstration. We embraced each other. Our eyes were full of tears. We were waiting for the moment to come.

All the people on the outside edges of our gathering died. At least two hundred students in tents were rolled over by tanks and crushed to death. In the Square, nearly four thousand people died. After the massacre the executioners even burned all the corpses to eliminate the traces of their violence. The symbol of our movement, the Goddess of Democracy, was smashed to pieces by the tanks.

For each and every Chinese who has a conscience, please put your hand on your heart, please think of these young children, hand in hand and shoulder to shoulder, sitting quietly beneath the Monument, watching the blows of the murderers with their own eyes.

A student from Qinghua University takes up the story:

By 4 A.M. all the lights in the Square were turned off. The pop singer, Hou Dejian, decided to negotiate with the army for a peaceful withdrawal of the students. By 4:40 we were starting to withdraw. All the Square's lights were switched on again, and we saw endless lines of troops marching toward us fiercely. They held sub-machine guns and weapons I had never seen before. The police began hitting students fiercely with electric cattle prods and sticks with iron nails. Before long, scores of students were bleeding heavily. We were forced to retreat up the steps to the level of the Monument. We still held hands tightly and sang the Internationale.

I then realized we were completely surrounded by soldiers. Only one small opening remained, in the direction of the Military Museum. The armed police kept hitting us with full strength, and we finally fell down into the Square. Then the sub-machine guns started.

We were forced to retreat back up the Monument steps. The troops started to shoot at us again. Groups of workers and citizens, not students, became really anxious and they took up wooden sticks and rushed toward the soldiers. The Autonomous Federation of Beijing University Students announced the students would leave. It was not yet 5 A.M.

By then the only opening in the lines of troops was filled by tanks. A group ran forward and tried to open an exit among the tanks for the retreating students. Most were shot and killed. We finally opened a small exit amidst the tanks. I and three thousand students escaped through that opening. We ran and ran without stopping amidst the shooting.

Chai Ling's estimate of the number killed was too high. When universities resumed in the autumn of 1989 the student roll calls showed that relatively few were missing: perhaps several hundred in all. Most of them would have died in the Square. The most reliable estimate of deaths in Peking put the figure at between 1,500 and 3,000. Most of those were ordinary citizens, people who had come to hate the Communist system and the government, and who were not bound by the nonviolent ideals of the students.

As the sun came up that Sunday I looked down at the avenue, which had become so familiar to me as it took on its latest, unfamiliar transformation: a field of fire for the army. Bicycles rode up and down, bells jangling angrily, swerving in and out among the lumps of concrete, the burned-out cars and the wrecked buses. To my right the avenue was empty. Anyone who ventured there was shot immediately. I lay down on the balcony and slept for a few minutes, but was wakened by a wild volley of shots. Twenty soldiers were walking down the road in a group toward the crowd, firing up at the buildings. Wang peered over the balcony and a bullet cracked close to him. He glanced at me, shocked for a moment, then laughed. The firing became heavier. I looked over now and saw why: two helicopters were approaching from the east, and the soldiers wanted everyone to keep their heads down.

I watched through binoculars as the helicopters landed, one after the other. It wasn't very sensible, but I had to see what was happening. We were several hundred yards away, too far to be able to identify the men who got out, but there were long lines of soldiers on parade to greet them. Maybe it was Li Peng or Yang Shangkun. Maybe it was Deng Xiaoping himself. They walked over to a heap of white plaster where the statue of the Goddess of Democracy had stood. Soon smoke began rising from the northern part of the Square. It came from burning tents—maybe from burning bodies too. The smoke drifted eastward with the wind and joined the smoke from an ambulance in the middle of the road which had crashed and caught fire.

There was another burst of fire, and directly below me a woman fell to the ground. Three men came running over, bent double, and put her on the back of a flatbed trishaw. The driver pedaled off fast, hoping to get out of range as quickly as he could. Another body, covered with blood, was driven past. One leg seemed to be missing. At the crossroads to my left a small crowd gathered round a car and pulled out a policeman. His hat and uniform were pulled off him roughly and heaped on top of the car. In the end they let him go, still in his underclothes.

We had heard that security policemen were manning the door of the hotel and searching everyone who came in or left. Somehow the cassettes we had shot all through the night had to be taken to our main office, where they would be edited, and copies sent to Tokyo and Hong Kong by plane for satelliting to London. There was no point in hanging about any longer. I put the cassettes in my socks: I couldn't think of anywhere more sensible. As I walked down the vast corridors of the Beijing the cassettes clanked and I could only walk slowly. Ahead of me as

I came out of the lift was a group of security policemen in plain clothes by the door. They were searching someone who was trying to leave.

I walked toward them. To have stopped would have looked suspicious. I could smell the stale sweat of a long and difficult night on myself. The floors were highly polished and the hall echoed to the sound of the cassettes clanking. It was both ludicrous and nerve-racking, and there was a distinct temptation to laugh. I made my way around the kiosk in the middle of the hallway where they sold carved jade and ivory. Everything was arranged as tidily as if there had been no massacre. There was just the empty area between the kiosk and the main door now, and the security policemen were starting to turn their heads to look at me. At that instant there was a loud and prolonged burst of firing outside. The security policemen crowded round the glass doors to see what had happened. I pushed my way through, excusing myself politely. They didn't look at me. I got a little way down the ramp then pulled the cassettes out of my socks and ran for it. The pictures of the massacre would be seen after all.

9
Tumbling Down

Why did you not take this down 20 years ago?
—Graffiti on Eastern side of Berlin Wall, January 1990

It was a pleasant-enough flat, though the rooms were small. From the window you could see the Reichstag, the Brandenburg Gate and the empty site between the inner and outer Wall where Hitler's Führer-bunker had once been. It was the kind of property that would command big money when Berlin was eventually united. The present occupant was finding it difficult to pay the absurdly low rent, which the East German authorities were still charging.

"I have a wardrobe full of expensive suits," he said. "Before long I may have to eat them."

His attractive Russian wife smiled at him and stroked his thin gray hair affectionately. He began to smile too, but he was a worried man. All around us were the accoutrements of a prosperous existence: bottles of Scotch, books from the West, an expensive hi-fi set, some good records and tapes. And now he had nothing except these things, and no means of earning a living. He had not been trained for that. I felt as though I were in the apartment of a Romanov prince after the 1917 Revolution. But this was no minor royalty. Günter Schabowski had been the general secretary of the Communist SED in East Berlin and a member of the Politburo—one of the most powerful men in East Germany.

Erich Honecker had been overthrown and was in disgrace, the SED had been thoroughly reorganized and had changed its name to the PDS—the Party for Democratic Socialism. All the old figures like Schabowski and Egon Krenz had been thrown out of the Party by early December. Krenz had become a wealthy man. He had sold his story to the right-wing tabloid *Bild* in West Germany for a fee that he insisted was not as high as 1.5 million Deutschemarks. Günter Schabowski refused to do that kind of thing. But he was hoping to earn some money from writing his own account of the collapse of Marxism-Leninism in the GDR.

I had come to see him to ask about one single episode in the chain of events that brought about the SED's downfall. Time and again people in East Berlin had spoken about the miraculous way in which the opening of the Berlin Wall had been announced to the world on the night of 9 November 1989. In East Germany this had now taken on something of the supernatural aura of the Angel of Mons or the leaning Virgin of Albert. Everyone who watched the moment on television had different versions of it. Some said an East German radio correspondent had come up and handed him a piece of paper, which he had then read out. Others said the paper was brought in by a messenger whom no one recognized.

"If you find out how that announcement came about," a minor government official said to me, "you must tell everyone. It's the great mystery of our time."

"There was something very strange about it, I know that," said a Marxist historian. "No one has been able to explain it satisfactorily. I'm positive that the Politburo didn't intend it to come out like this."

Some senior figures in the opposition, whose lives and careers had been radically changed as a result of the announcement, seemed to regard it almost as an occult intervention in Germany's affairs.

"It was a miracle," said one senior CDU official in East Berlin. "We still don't know who wrote that small piece of paper which ordered the Wall to come down. It was read out in a most extraordinary way at the end of a press conference. It created such amazement. Even the man who read it out was amazed."

The man who read it out was Günter Schabowski. I had come to his flat to find out if it really was the Finger of God that had placed the piece of paper in front of him. It took him a long time to decide whether to tell me. He had, he said, refused to talk to everyone else. There was silence.

His wife made tea in the kitchen. His pet parrot squawked. The lift clattered into life outside his front door. Finally an innate courtesy overcame him, even though he felt he might be lowering the value of his own exclusive account of the Miracle of the Wall. He decided to talk.

At the time, Schabowski was the Central Committee's secretary for the media as well as being a member of the Politburo. He had a reputation as a straight and honest man. He wasn't scared to go into the streets after the fall of Honecker and argue out the unpopular policies of the SED with ordinary people. Shortly before 7 P.M. on the evening of 9 November he gave a press conference to announce the latest decisions of the Council of Ministers. Much of it dealt with the new philosophy of the Party. It was now accepted, he said, that the GDR was a pluralist society. There were details about the forthcoming Party conference.

Schabowski came to the end of these announcements. There was an awkward pause. The three hundred journalists who were sitting there became restless. He whispered something to the man next to him, and shuffled his papers. The man next to him leaned over. A piece of paper appeared in Schabowski's hand. He read from it slowly and hesitantly.

> This will be interesting for you: today the decision was taken to make it possible for all citizens to leave the country through the official border crossing points. All citizens of the GDR can now be issued with visas for the purposes of travel or visiting relatives in the West. This order is to take effect at once.

Everyone started talking. A correspondent from GDR radio stood up and asked for more details. Schabowski had used the expression *unverzüglich* ("at once, immediately"); when precisely did that mean? Schabowski gave no clear answer. He was still holding onto the piece of paper. A crowd of journalists gathered around him, trying to find out further details. How soon was *unverzüglich*? Schabowski was confused and tired.

"It just means straightaway," he said.

The art of politics is to create the illusion of competence. An illusionist who admits to letting the doves escape from his inside pockets is an illusionist who has given up all hope of a return booking. Sitting in his flat overlooking the Brandenburg Gate, Günter Schabowski was at first unwilling to admit to any confusion in announcing the breaching of the Wall.

"I finished giving my information about the Central Committee business, and then I turned to the next item on the agenda."

I pressed him. Finally he admitted it. The mysterious piece of paper, the note, which had been passed to him by some superhuman agency, written with the pen of an angel, was the typed-up note of the decision the Politburo had reached that afternoon. It had been on top of his sheaf of papers when he came into the press conference. Somehow it became mixed up with the rest. So instead of reading it first he had to go through Any Other Business, in the hope of coming across it later. He discovered it at the bottom of the pile. End of miracle.

The decision had been made by the full Politburo a few hours before on the afternoon of 9 November. It was an acknowledgement of the anger building up in East German society over the inequity of the rules governing permission to visit the West.

"The fact that some were allowed to go and some weren't was silly and Kafkaesque. It demanded a solution, but it had to be done quickly. We didn't have time to think about it carefully. We had to make our draft program public fast, and that had to be in it. There was already the draft of a special law on the subject in existence, and so we in the Politburo decided to instruct the government to take some of the points from this draft. It had to be written in a way people could understand. We didn't want it to be in a kind of india-rubber language which could be stretched in one way or the other. We wanted to make it quite clear: if you want to go to the West, you can go. Full stop. There would have to be some transitional measures, because most people didn't have passports. But our aim was to have a system like you do in the West, whereby if you have a passport, you can leave the country."

I was unwilling to interrupt the flow, in case he decided that he'd told me more than enough already. But it was important to know whether the members of the Politburo understood the significance of what they were doing. Had anyone, for instance, suggested at the meeting that this was really the end of the Wall, and might well be the end of Communist government in the GDR—the end, indeed, of the GDR itself?

"No one realized. No one said anything like that. No one really thought about the result. We knew we had to take this step. As for its leading to the end of the GDR, none of us expected that at all. And I have to say that none of the opposition groups in the country expected it either. We hoped, quite simply, that this measure would create a better GDR, more open to human rights and so on. We thought the Wall was stable, I must say."

In its way, then, it was a kind of miracle. Without the suddenness of the announcement, the impact of the opening of the Wall would have been less. Without the great outflow of surprise and delight at the Berlin Wall, the tidal wave that swept across Czechoslovakia might not have happened as it did. And without the suddenness of the revolution in Czechoslovakia, people in Romania might not have been emboldened to come out and challenge Ceaușescu.

The nuclear reaction required a powerful detonating explosion. That had been provided by Günter Schabowski. Now he sat in his small but disturbingly expensive flat overlooking the Wall, which he had helped to demolish, wondering how he was going to make a living. His papers had been mixed up by the finger of history.

The first news that people could pass freely to the West was broadcast on an East German television news bulletin at 7:30 that evening. The pictures of the celebrated press conference by Schabowski were broadcast, but there was little explanation. Immediately the switchboard of the television station was swamped with callers trying to find out more. The director of news ordered that Schabowski's announcement should be repeated at regular intervals through the evening. By now too, it was being reported on West German television. People in East Berlin were switching backward and forward, watching the coverage.

The message was relayed to the West German Chancellor, Helmut Kohl, who was on his official visit to Poland. A few minutes later he was stopped by a West German television reporter as he arrived for a formal dinner. Kohl was not a man to match great occasions with inspired sentiments. His concern was with the outflow of East Germans to the West:

> The solution cannot be for many people to come to West Germany.
> Living conditions should be improved in East Germany, so they stay
> there. It's in our interests that they should stay.

In Berlin itself, people were starting to head out into the streets to see
what was going on for themselves. Schabowski's slightly vague expression, that people would be able to obtain exit visas *unverzüglich,* immediately or at once, seemed unlikely to mean that anyone could cross that
night. In a society inured to waiting for everything from officialdom, it
was hard to think that police stations would issue the necessary piece of
paper so quickly. At the Invalidenstrasse crossing, a little to the north of
the Brandenburg Gate, the first East Germans to arrive there at around
nine o'clock were told by the officer in charge that they would need a
stamp in their identity cards. This, he said, could be obtained only from
their local police station. They went away, disappointed.

About a mile farther north, at the Bornholmerstrasse crossing point,
the situation was altogether different. Shortly before nine thirty a couple in their late thirties decided to test out the system. They walked
through to the glass-fronted booth where the border guard sat. He gave
them a smile and said they could go through without a visa. He promised them that there would be no problem as long as they came back
through the same checkpoint that night. Several journalists saw them
coming through to the western side, but they were so matter-of-fact
about it all that it seemed as though they were Westerners returning. No
one stopped them to ask them questions.

Erich Knorr, an engineer in his mid-forties, had been out late that
evening in East Berlin, seeing friends. His wife had left him a few
months before, and his daughter was at university. His flat was cold and
uninviting as he let himself in. Automatically, he went over to turn on
the television. The sound of voices made things seem a little less lonely.
He was still not used to living by himself. It was around ten thirty, and
the station he had switched on, SFB in West Berlin, was showing a discussion program of some kind. Knorr was making a cup of coffee when
he caught the words, "And now we're going over to our reporter at the
Invalidenstrasse crossing point."

Idly, thinking there might have been some shooting incident, he wandered back into the sitting room. The reporter was talking excitedly in front of a crowd of a few dozen people. As he spoke a young man came running up out of the darkness and shouted at the camera, "They've opened the checkpoint in the Bornholmerstrasse!" Erich Knorr knew now that the unthinkable had happened. He lived close to the Bornholmerstrasse, in the Schönhauserallee. He rang a girl he knew to see if she wanted to come with him to the West, but she said she was too tired, and didn't believe it anyway.

He left his coffee untasted on the table and set off. Out in the street he broke into a run. As he turned into the road that led to the crossing point he ran into crowds of people heading in the same direction. There were people of all ages, many with young children who had been wakened up so the whole family could experience this extraordinary moment. Knorr was unencumbered by wife or family. For the first time in weeks, being on his own was an advantage. He pushed through to the front.

He could see the checkpoint now. They were letting people through very slowly, checking their identity. A big crowd had built up. From time to time there was chanting:

"Take the Wall down! Take the Wall down!"

There was no anger, but there was real impatience at the slowness of it all.

Then the border guards came pouring out of the building, about a dozen of them, and Erich thought there was going to be trouble. He'd worked his way almost through to the front by now, and he was afraid that if they charged he might be injured. But the guards ignored the crowd. They fanned out in front of the post and started shifting the heavy blocks of concrete that lay across the street to prevent cars from passing through more than one at a time. The gates opened. An officer made a gesture with his hand, like a doorman at a hotel. There were no more formalities: the way to the West lay open. Everyone cheered and shouted and sang, and they surged forward, ten abreast.

At that moment, where the road passes over two Stadtbahn lines, one serving the East and the other the West, a couple of trains happened to come along at the same time. As they passed the Bornholmer crossing they both stopped and hooted their horns, while the passengers waved and blew kisses. Erich Knorr was shouting and weeping with the rest of them now, and when he reached the other side of the Wall, people came running out of the houses and flats on the West and offered them things: cups of coffee, glasses of champagne, flowers and West German Marks. Erich saw someone throwing a handful of useless Ostmarks, the non-convertible currency of the East, into the air. The little notes were picked up by the mild November wind and fluttered over the heads of the crowd. Everyone cheered to see them go.

> I can't tell you what it meant to us. All these years we'd been bottled up in our little part of Germany, second-class citizens that nobody wanted, in a country most of us didn't really want to be in. I'd been a prisoner, and suddenly I wasn't a prisoner any longer. I could have shouted and sung and waved my arms. I couldn't stop smiling. A girl came up and gave me a kiss, and I thought I was really in heaven.

A crowd control van belonging to the West Berlin police drove up. Someone made an announcement:

> Everyone should stay calm. No need to get excited. Buses are coming to take you to the Ku'damm.

The crowd cheered. Erich didn't want to wait for the bus. He took the U-bahn to the Kurfürstendamm. The city authorities had just decided that it should be free, since most of the people using it would be unable to pay.

> I got out at the Ku'damm station and walked out into the street. The lights just seemed so bright, and there was so much money about. I felt like some country cousin, shabby and poor and innocent, somehow. It was a little too much for me, the emotion and everything. I'd been planning to wander round the shops and see what there was to buy. But suddenly I didn't feel like that any more. I just walked down to the Gedächtniskirche [the bombed church which has been left unrestored as a memorial] and stood there looking at it in the darkness. The last time I'd seen it was 12 August 1961, the day before they built that accursed

Wall. I was nineteen years old then, and now I was forty-eight. I'd never been allowed to see the West in all that time. I was too sad to do any more rejoicing. I just went back to my flat and went to bed. But it was a wonderful memory, all the same.

A British student, Sean Salsarola, was in West Berlin when he heard the news on an East German radio station. He ran to Checkpoint Charlie and made his way into the East at around nine o'clock. Almost everyone at that point was heading in the opposite direction, but Sean had a plan. He headed for the Grand Hotel, farther down the Friedrichstrasse, an expensive place on Western lines where most of the foreign television crews stayed. In the lobby he spotted a cameraman and sound recordist. It was Ingo Prosser and Mark McCauley, who had filmed the massacre in Tiananmen Square with me. They were working that night with one of my colleagues, Brian Hanrahan, and Sean's knowledge of East Berlin was invaluable to them as they filmed their remarkable pictures of the night's events.

Elsewhere, the night was loud with singing, cheering and chanting. At Checkpoint Charlie people were singing, suitably enough, the song "Wilkommen" from the musical *Cabaret*. An elderly woman came through in slippers and nightclothes with a coat over the top, explaining that her daughter had telephoned her from the West and said, "Mama, Mama, you can come to West Berlin to see us." So there she was. A young waiter had just come through a checkpoint from the East when a middle-aged West Berliner came up to him and put a 50-Mark note in his hand.

"Go and buy yourself a beer. There'll never be another day like this."

A West Berlin teacher took advantage of the open border to drive into the East to see some friends. Then they all headed back.

"The border guards stopped me as I came through. 'Have you got anything to declare?' 'No,' I said, 'only four Easterners.' "

At the Sonnenallee crossing, which was also crowded with people, a group of young people from the West clambered onto the roof of an East German watch tower. A few hours before they might have been shot dead for attempting it. Now the officer in charge just stood and smiled indulgently at them.

"Be careful you don't fall down," he said.

A little farther along the border a group of people struggled to raise the barrier across the road.

"This is crazy," said an officer, "we haven't opened that for years. It's completely rusted up."

Policemen from East and West gathered in the middle of the street, talking to each other for the first time.

People crammed the Ku'damm all night long. The air was filled with the sound of car horns, and the long lines of Trabants and Wartburgs filled it with something else as well: the blue clouds of their unrestricted exhaust gas. The Ku'damm stank, but nobody cared.

Joe's Biersalon in the Ku'damm was the place where a lot of Easterners congregated. Joe had fled from the East himself in 1961.

"Tonight," he announced, "anyone can pay in Ostmarks."

He lost heavily on the exchange, of course. But he probably lost more over the distinctive beer glasses from his bar. Dozens disappeared as souvenirs.

"*Mensch, bin ick denn hier uff'm anderen Planeten?*" someone asked, in a heavy Berlin accent: "Hey, man, am I on another planet?"

But it was the Wall itself that was the great magnet. As the crowds gathered, the boldest spirits started to test the extent of the East German government's commitment to the new era. Where the Wall starts to bulge out in a semicircle to take in the area round the Brandenburg Gate, two young men in their early twenties vaulted over the low railings and stood beside it. In the arc lights on the western side the wild graffiti— pleas, accusations, and endless names of people and places—stood out like colored clouds around their heads. One made a stirrup of his hands and launched the other upward. Fingers scrabbled until he found a purchase. He got to his knees, then stood, then raised his arms over his head, fists clenched. The crowd roared. A new Germany and a new Europe, for good or ill, was being born.

It took me hours to get to Berlin after the announcement that the Wall was to be opened. I had been in Poland, covering Chancellor Kohl's visit, and I had to fight my way on crowded planes across Central Europe.

When I arrived, the party was still going on. Trabants were everywhere, crammed with laughing, singing, shouting people. Groups wandered along the streets, a half dozen abreast, arm in arm. The road that leads to the Brandenburg Gate on the western side, the Street of 17 June, was crammed with cars and people, eight or nine lanes across. The lights of several dozen television organizations were directed onto the Wall. More faintly they illuminated the Gate, which rose above it surmounted by the Quadriga, an unreal green in the floodlights, Victory's back toward us as she faced down the Unter den Linden in what had the previous day been hostile territory.

It was then that I saw a sight that I, as a latecomer to the festivities, had never thought to see. Hundreds of people were standing, sitting, squatting, dancing on top of the Wall. Some held sparklers, and waved them in neat childish circles or described outlines with them in the cold night air. There was singing: *Geh'n wir mal rüber, die Mauer ist weg* ("We're going over, the Wall's gone") and *Krenz, wir schlagen Dir die Tür an* ("Krenz, we're knocking on your door").

I had a lot to do, to prepare myself for a live broadcast, but I could not help looking round all the time at the unthinkable sight: something that had been the symbol of division and cruelty for nearly three decades had become a symbol of sheer delight. I remembered all the times I'd been here in the past: times of tension between the Germanies, times when political leaders came to make their ritual condemnations of a division of Europe and of Germany with which they were thoroughly content. I looked up at the watchtowers from which everyone who came close to the Wall was once photographed as an obscure form of intimidation. Now the guards were leaning out and a number of them joining in the singing. The following morning they would be clambering around on top of the Wall as well, grinning at the western side, which was no longer forbidden fruit for them.

I duly stood in front of the Brandenburg Gate in the television lights and answered questions about an exciting present and an unknowable future. Halfway through a reply, as I was speaking to one of the largest television audiences for any news program in British history, the satellite link with London was accidentally cut. It was an absurd and humiliating moment. I slunk away from the camera position feeling deeply depressed. And then I looked across at the Wall and saw how trivial it was to worry, on a night of such unparalleled pleasure for so many people. My colleagues, all of them good friends of mine, walked with me along the line of the Wall in the direction of the Potsdamerplatz. It was a dirt path through woods and bushes, which had been the center of government in Berlin. Hitler's Chancellery and his bunker had once lain on the other side of the Wall. But the destruction of April and May 1945 and the tourniquet of the Wall itself had turned the heart of the city back to its origins, like the Forum in Rome, overgrown and haunted by wild animals.

Now though, the crowds moved along the pathway so thickly that it was hard for us to keep together. And all the way along there was the sound of hammering. People were beating at the Wall with pickaxes and chisels by the light of candles, anxious to demonstrate their mastery over something that had mastered them for so long. Great shadows were thrown across the face of the Wall as the picks were raised. The shuddering of steel against concrete jarred onlookers as well as the would-be demolishers. But their persistence was paying off. They crashed away at the joints between the slabs of concrete and made holes like wounds, so that in some places you could peer through into the wide no-man's land beyond. There, one of the busiest intersections in pre-war Germany, the Potsdamerplatz itself, had been transformed into an open strip of land nearly a quarter of a mile wide between the eastern and western sections of the Wall, planted with great arc-lights to detect escapees.

As the hammering went on, there was an eerie echo that seemed more than just an echo; and when the man with the pickax on the western side paused to ease his aching muscles, the sound continued from the other side. A roar of delight broke out as everyone realized the Wall was under attack at the same place from the eastern side as well. At last another wound was opened by alternate strokes from East and West; and by the light of candles and torches a hand came through the small gap, and the man with the pickax on our side shook it. At such a time, genuine miracles seemed to be taking place.

We wandered back to the Street of 17 June. The vans selling wurst were doing a good business. So were the stalls where they were pouring out steaming cups of Glühwein. As the steam rose it took on the bluish color of the television lights focused on the Brandenburg Gate. From a girl with an excited face and high voice I bought an early copy of the following morning's *Bild* newspaper, crude, raw, nationalistic. There was the picture in color of the crowds standing on the Wall at the Gate, a hazy version of the real thing, which was bright and sharp in front of me in the chilly night air. DEUTSCHLAND UMARMT SICH, it said: "Germany embraces itself." And in larger letters underneath, "EINIGKEIT UND RECHT UND FREIHEIT," words from the national anthem: "unity and right and freedom." All around the front page was a border of black, red and gold, the national colors of a Germany that was suddenly becoming much bigger and more powerful.

The following days were unforgettable. I went to Glienicke Bridge, where the far southeastern spur of West Berlin reaches out toward Potsdam. I had last been there in February 1986 when the Soviet dissident Anatoly Shcharansky was released in exchange for East German spies held by West Germany. Then it had been white and frozen, and the iron bridge with its red flags fluttering at the other end had seemed like the gateway to another world. Shcharansky's tiny figure appeared from a Russian car, which had stopped at the center of the bridge. He was escorted over to an American vehicle and driven away. The East German spies, a busload of them, were changed over to another bus. Soon it began to get dark. Over the snow-covered bridge a light came on and illuminated the red flag. It was like every Cold War spy novel ever written.

Now Glienicke Bridge was just another way across a river. Bus services from East and West put it back on their schedules after 28 years, and this time they were delivering shoppers, not spies. Children bounded around their parents in the unseasonably warm air. The sunshine lit up the faces of people who had once stared across the bridge and could now walk across it at will. The East German border guards smiled and banged their gloved hands together and scarcely bothered to look at the identity documents that each person obediently tendered.

We filmed down by the waterside. An East German patrol boat spotted our television camera. A few days before, its job had been to search the cold waters for any sign of people swimming across, and shoot them if necessary. Now it staged a little display for us, speeding past and turning suddenly so the spray rose up in an arc and made rainbows in the afternoon sunshine. As the patrol boat passed them a flock of wild ducks exploded protestingly into the air, wheeled overhead, and eased themselves down onto a quieter stretch of water. We went back to the bridge and watched the lines of people heading eastward across it. They were carrying the shopping they had bought with their own hard-currency savings and with the 100 Marks that Bonn had given them as a celebratory gift. A dog-end of quotation from a Shakespeare comedy floated across my mind: "You happy winners all."

No country, perhaps, has come out of a major war and behaved as well and as modestly as West Germany since 1945. It has rejected its twentieth-century history almost in its entirety. For much of the forty-five years after Hitler the most frequent complaint of its neighbors and allies was that it failed to translate its economic power into military or political power: not a complaint leveled at Germany previously. Bonn became the quiet capital of a state that was preeminently modest. Diplomats and foreign correspondents who were assigned there would groan inwardly at the worthy boredom that lay ahead of them.

Now, within a few November days and nights, that had all changed. Helmut Kohl, the bumbling chancellor whose clumsiness had gotten him into all sorts of problems in the past, suddenly became the modern Bismarck. He was unifying Germany. People who had paid little attention to the Federal Republic in the past paid attention to it now. Tadeusz Mazowiecki, the Polish prime minister who had been a Solidarity journalist, remarked that repressed hopes were springing into life. It was true; but so were many repressed fears.

Chancellor Kohl had first arrived at Warsaw Airport on the afternoon of 9 November—the day the Wall was breached. He was followed down the aircraft steps by dozens of German businessmen, each with a briefcase bulging with plans and agreements. Over the next few days they fanned out across Poland, signing agreements and partnership deals. My colleagues and I followed them around. We were interested in the scope of Germany's new involvement in its old economic hinterland in Central Europe.

In an elderly office block of the Stalinist period in Warsaw the workmen were in. They were nailing down carpets, replacing bits of damaged woodwork, putting in new electric wiring. The Foreign Investment Agency of the Polish government was being set up at speed. The head of it, Zdzislaw Skakuj, sat in the only office they had completed. A little brass model of a ship was on his desk, and he played with it from time to time. He was a marine engineer by training, not a businessman, but he had a plain, straightforward manner, and had been chosen because of his ability to negotiate a contract. His job now was to negotiate contracts with countries that wanted to put money into Poland. Chief among them, by a long way, was the Federal Republic of Germany. Of 600 schemes, West Germany was responsible for 248, the United States for 36, Britain for 30 and France for 22.

> I am pleased as a government servant to see this, but as a Pole I am not so pleased. As a government servant I am worried that a reunited Germany will absorb more German money and attention than the rest of Eastern Europe; as a Pole I hope it does. But then, as a Pole I hope that a reunited Germany doesn't become so rich and powerful that it dominates us again. We have had a long history together, and now we need money urgently. It is my job to get that money from anywhere, but to be honest with you I would be happier if it came from other countries as well as Germany. In 1939 we needed help from Britain and France against the Germans. Now we are not against them, but I think we need your support just as much. You know, it's funny: when they invaded Poland in 1939 I was eight years old. A German soldier fired his gun at me. Now they're here again. And this time we want them, and it's my job to make sure that even more of them come.

The possibility that a united Germany would have a united Berlin as its capital raised the question of the seaport that would serve it. In the past, the seaport of Berlin was Stettin. Now, as Szczecin, it belongs to Poland. Soon after the collapse of Communist rule in Poland, the West German embassy sounded out the new foreign minister on the possibility that

Szczecin might be turned into a free port. A Polish government official had precisely the same divided views on this as Zdzislaw Skakuj had about German investment.

> If Szczecin were to be a free port serving Berlin, that would mean tremendous growth for the entire area. At the moment it's quite depressed. But think: the growth in trade would have a big effect on the agriculture of the region, because it would have to feed the city and it would be easier to export food from there. The farmers badly need new machinery, and the banks, foreign and Polish, would lend them the money. It would be a good investment. We could see a period of tremendous transformation, and this would spread out from Szczecin all along the Baltic coast, and right down to the German border. And then perhaps our children will say to us, "Whatever happened to Poland?" Because it'll be swallowed up completely. It'll cease to exist. We'll be wealthy, but we'll be working for somebody else.

The shifting of international boundaries, the movement of hardworking Germans farther and farther eastward, the savage wars of conquest mean that across a swathe of two or three hundred miles from the Baltic coast to the Black Sea there have been colonies of Germans since the twelfth century; sometimes earlier. All the large towns and some of the villages have two names, one German and one Slavic. The immigrants suffered and made others suffer. Germans in Czechoslovakia and Germans in Danzig and Stettin were a contributory cause of the Second World War. After 1945 they were forced out as cruelly as their own government had forced others out in the past.

With the memory of the breaching of the Berlin Wall still strong, Helmut Kohl came back to Poland to complete his official visit. When his host, Mr. Mazowiecki, invited him to give formal, public recognition to the Oder-Neisse line dividing East Germany and Poland, he declined. His foreign minister, Hans-Dietrich Genscher, spoke of the border as fixed; but Genscher was a Free Democrat, and his party had nothing to gain from the far right. Kohl had a considerable amount to gain by heeding the nationalist voices. He went to Silesia in the southwest of Poland to meet the submerged colony of Germans that once dominated the area.

It was strange to see them. In the pleasant towns and prosperous villages which seemed to an outsider to be entirely Polish, they surfaced as though the previous forty-five years had never been. They were survivors from a terrible upheaval, coming out into the open for the first time. People with names whose Polish spelling could not hide a German pronunciation came out to cheer and wave the German colors. Karel Szulc, who called himself Karl Schultz on everything except official documents, said his family had lived in the area for four hundred years. He happened to be a Communist, and identified with Poland rather than with either part of Germany.

> The Germans regarded us as Poles, the Poles regarded us as Germans. This area was hit badly when the Russians invaded, because they identified us as Germans. I spoke German before I spoke Polish. Now I'm bilingual. My father was taken by the Russians and put to work in a coalmine in Siberia. Then at the end of the War, when hundreds of thousands of Germans were forced to leave, we stayed. Quite a few others managed to as well. At that time, by comparison with Germany, Poland was a land of plenty.
>
> But then they forced collectivization on us, and they began to repress us. They destroyed all the old German monuments, all German libraries, even German books. For two or three years after the War, when we wrote the word "German" we had to write it with a small "g". I was given the task of collecting all the German books from my school and taking them to be pulped. Each day I used to look at them carefully as I carried them along, and decided which to keep. I hid them behind the big cupboard in our kitchen.
>
> I ran for election to the Polish Sejm a few years ago. When I went to canvass in a shoe factory a woman said, "How dare you run for the Sejm? You're a German." But I still got 18 percent of the vote. Things are much better nowadays. That's why I'm a loyal Pole. But even so, there are local authorities which don't allow German libraries or schools. And for years anyone with a German name who applied for a passport to go abroad would automatically lose his job. But I see some things from the Polish point of view. All this reunification is very worrying.

When Helmut Kohl appeared at one rally in Silesia, a German brass band welcomed him and there was German beer. Everything and everyone was decked out in black, red and gold. HELMUT, DU BIST AUCH UNSER KANZLER, one banner read: "Helmut, you are our Chancellor too." They were no longer ashamed to admit their Germanness. Kohl, in a speech, appealed for a new start, where Poles and Germans could learn from their history. Some Poles were deeply offended by the hint that Germans should forgive Poles just as Poles should forgive Germans.

In a grim auditorium in an outer suburb of Warsaw, a man climbed onto the stage and called for quiet. The two hundred or so people milling round stopped to listen.

"It's no use trying to make your claims without filling in the proper forms," he said. "You collect them down at the other end of the hall. Then you can come up this end again and ask us for help."

The acoustics were bad, and many of the people gathered there were hard of hearing. All of them had a claim on the government of Germany for their treatment during the Second World War. There were survivors from Auschwitz and Ravensbrück, former workers from slave labor camps, prisoners of war, men and women whose houses and families had been destroyed. I spoke to one woman who was arrested with her husband after only a few weeks of marriage. They were sent to separate camps, and he died almost immediately.

"He was such a sweet boy," said this old, stout woman in a woollen hat and scuffed brown boots. She still wore a wedding ring, and forty-eight years afterward the tears brimmed over just as readily in her vague blue eyes.

Yet the survivors were cheerful enough, pushing forward eagerly in the hope that after so long they might at last be about to receive compensation. They had been deprived of their rightful payment by Soviet sharp practice. The Allied Powers agreed at the end of the War that West Germany should recompense those in Western countries for the crimes of the Nazis, while East Germany would pay those in the Eastern bloc. The money was collected by the Soviet authorities and never redistributed. Now the West Germans were taking on this burden as well.

"What do you think about the Germans?" I asked them.

"I used to be very bitter about them," one attractive, middle-class woman said.

She had been at Ravensbrück, and had never been able to bear a child as a result of the injuries she received there.

"But I am a Christian, and I realized at last that I had to forgive. I am glad that they are here. We need all the economic help we can get."

An older woman, poorer and with a face marked by the years of unhappiness and struggle, moved across when she heard that. She said, "I saw them on television, singing that national anthem of theirs beside the Berlin Wall, and I knew we were in for trouble. Poor Poland: we can't get our land back from the Russians, and now the Germans will start demanding Silesia back from us. I remember 1939. You wait: it's all going to start again."

A PanAm jet took off from Tegel Airport in West Berlin and flew noisily over the city, linking it to the real world. It passed over the Unter den Linden to the West, banking steeply. I walked through Marx-Engels Platz, talking to a former Communist in his mid-thirties, and watched it go. To people on this side of the Wall, it must once have been a galling sight: a reminder of their imprisonment. Now, in March 1990, they were free to pass through to the real world themselves, though the non-convertibility of their currency was another, subtler form of imprisonment. I had been away for most of the five months since the Wall was breached. In that time there had been a change of mood.

My companion was loudly dressed: red shirt, orange scarf knotted round his neck, black trousers. All his energy, his enthusiasm, and the intensity of his inner life seemed to have gone into his appearance.

> We lost our chance of self-government here when the SED collapsed. Krenz should have said "I've kicked out Honecker and taken his place," but he didn't. He should have said, "I'm only a transitional figure. I'm going to abolish the Politburo, I'm going to reconstruct the Party, I'm going to hold free parliamentary elections." And he should have said, "Yes, we admit it, the local elections were manipulated. I'm going to clear up the whole mess." But he didn't do any of that. He just tried to play politics like all the others. He gambled it away.

The former Party member and I headed across Marx-Engels Platz in the direction of the old Party headquarters. It was Sunday, and people were out in their thousands, thronging the streets, lying on the grass, laughing and joking, altogether unlike the old GDR way of behaving. The date was 18 March: the day of East Germany's first free elections. But the former Party member wasn't entering into the atmosphere of it all. His strong accent echoed out over the pleasantness of the scene.

> You hear people saying all the time now that reunification couldn't be worse than what we had in the past. Well, that's probably true. I hate the stupid bastards for what they did to this country, the way they fucked it over. But all that euphoria from last November has gone.

He gestured at the scene in front of us, taking in the picnicking families, the dancing children, the entwined couples.

> What you see here, this is all because it's a nice day and people are doing something they haven't done for, what is it, fifty-seven years here: they've voted for the party they want to vote for. Great, that's great. But we all know that we're being taken over here, and that's not a nice feeling. We used to have lousy jobs with no real money attached to them, but at least we held on to them for the whole of our working lives. Now the West Germans are going to come in and say, "What is this shit-heap, man? We're closing it down, and fast." And then nobody's going to be looking out for us. And they're going to come round to the chicken coops where we live, that we're paying peanuts for, and they're going to say, "You wanna go on living here? That'll be two thousand Marks a month." And if you don't pay, you're out on your ass. This is going to be a poor country. Only it won't be a country any more. It'll just be the part of Germany that doesn't do so good.

He had a point. Details were emerging all the time of the terrible backwardness of the place. A man lounging by a factory production line said on television that his pay was still what it had been thirty years before, and his methods of working were the same as they'd been thirty years before as well. An environmentalist stood in an open field and pointed to an evil green liquid bubbling up in the middle of a brackish pool of water. It was the chemical outflow from a fertilizer plant, which had sprung a leak and was poisoning the entire area. In the Harz Mountains the trees had been so damaged by acid rain and other forms of pollution that the bird population had fallen drastically. The fieldmice who were the natural prey of hawks, owls and eagles were living and breeding almost without hindrance. Now they were beginning to constitute a plague of biblical proportions. A gynecologist explained why she hadn't been able to set up in private practice in a provincial town outside Berlin. First, she hadn't been able to find two rooms together, so she could have a waiting room and an examination room. Second, the water supply in the town contained so much nitrate that it wasn't safe to treat patients there anyway.

The area around the town of Bitterfeld is perhaps the dirtiest in Europe. Your clothes are grimy after an hour or so; your hands and face have a film of oily dirt on them. There are pesticide factories, aluminium-smelting plants, ten lignite-burning power plants, a dye-making factory. Five employees of one of the pesticide factories have died of cancer within four years. Carbon disulphide escaping from the machinery in a plant that spins cellulose fibers has been measured at concentrations ninety times the danger limit. It can cause brain damage. Farmers outside Bitterfeld find it hard to get their animals to breed. Children in the town are more than twice as likely to contract respiratory diseases as children elsewhere. Their bone growth is retarded. A West German study found that life expectancy in Bitterfeld was five years shorter than average for men and eight years shorter for women.

West German television devoted hours of discussion to the question of the GDR's industrial and economic position. On one program a Frankfurt banker was pessimistic about the short-term effects of reunification.

> They're at least thirty years behind us. I find it funny to listen to the British and the French and the Poles worrying that our new Germany is going to be a super-power. I think it'll take us at least ten years to get the GDR up to our standard, and it's going to cost a great deal of money. Maybe at the end of that time we'll be rich again, but in the meantime

it's going to be like taking out a mortgage on a really expensive second home. Only this home has sixteen million people in it, all demanding our money.

But on this Sunday, halfway through March 1990, it wasn't at all clear what the shape of the GDR's future would be, or what precisely people were voting for. Chancellor Kohl, having given the impression that the two Germanies would be reunited in a matter of months, now seemed prepared to put it off until 1992 or even later. The Soviet Union, Britain, France and the United States were all relieved. The pleasure for most East Germans seemed to lie not so much in thinking about the future as in taking part in the act of voting. The last genuinely free election in this part of Germany was in 1933, when the Nazis were voted into power. You had to be older than the former mayor of Berlin and former Federal Chancellor Willy Brandt to have voted in that election; and he was now seventy-six.

I had expected the former Communist Party headquarters to be a gloomy place on a day like this. Not so. It had purged itself of the old Party bosses and changed its name. It had two popular leaders, Gregor Gysi and the ex-prime minister Hans Modrow, both of them widely respected by non-Communists. The old Communist Party building was ugly and lowering: Nazi architecture, Stalinist overtones. But today it was transformed. All across the frontage the former comrades had hung canvases spray-painted with the kind of art you found on the Berlin Wall: heavy pictograms of defiance and confusion and color. Where Marx and Engels, Ulbricht and Honecker had once hung, there were big portraits of Gysi and Modrow, also in spray-paint style. German rap music blared from the man-size loudspeakers on either side of the main doors:

> This is the Party that can solve your problems,
> Solve the problems of ev-ry-one.

Thousands of people lay on the grass and listened. A girl was walking around wrapped in an East German flag. Another flag was being used as a tablecloth by a group of teenagers who were eating sandwiches. There was a stream hundreds strong going into the building.

The workers and peasants to whom the German Democratic Republic was dedicated would never have come here in the past. Now they were flooding in to see what it was like. Everything was open. Most people, carrying little paper flags with the East German insignia of hammer and compasses on them, were content to hang around the ground floor. That was where the bands were, and the restaurant with a jokey quotation from Marx over the place where you could buy cheap sausages and potato salad: Der Mensch sollte nicht mit Kohl vorliebnehmen, wenn er edleres Gemüse erhalten kann. ("A person shouldn't make do with cabbage if he can get nobler vegetables.") The joke lay in the German word for cabbage: Kohl. There were other jokes too: "We don't want to be Kohlonized," and simply "Germoney." This was the last-ditch stand of East German nationalism, and it was remarkably lively and enthusiastic.

I went upstairs. The corridors were empty. The rooms were small, and they still had names from the old SED days on the door: secretary for agitation and propaganda, secretaries for the economy, secretary for inter-German relations. They were all empty. Many of them had newly issued pictures of a smiling Lenin on the wall, with a sticker that said "Look up—the future's good!" Some even had that rarer phenomenon, a smiling Karl Marx. One door had a brass plate on it from the old, unreconstructed days of Honecker: Problems of Peace and Socialism. The room, when I opened the door, proved to be entirely empty, its walls bare from ceiling to floor. It smelled of dust and stored newspapers. There were no answers to the old problem.

The Wall divided Berlin into unequal portions. Most of the grand buildings in the old city center fell into the East. The West was essentially suburban. The Unter den Linden is a severe North European imitation of Rome, lined with temples in dark gray granite. In the winter, in the rain, after dark, it is gloomy and foreboding. This Sunday, in the sunshine, it was delightful. Four West Berliners coursed along the road on roller skates. Two exquisites, also from the West, posed by a bench near the Grand Hotel. One wore an apricot-colored jacket in crushed velvet. The other wore a black leather jerkin and thigh-high black boots. A dog like an Irish wolfhound lay beside them in the sunshine. Compared with such extroverts the East Berliners were dowdier and more sensible, but they may have enjoyed themselves at least as much. A little admiring group had gathered round a couple of West German motorcycles, parked on the sidewalk. The owners affected not to notice them, and talked loudly to each other about speeds and maneuverability. A group of far right-wingers from West Berlin pushed their way through the easy-going crowds. Their heads were shaven and they wore heavy boots. Their T-shirts said in English, "Have A Nice Day—Or Else" and "Sid Vicious Was Innocent But Sick."

Outside one of the more somber buildings along the Unter den Linden, the memorial to the victims of Fascism and Militarism, a crowd had gathered round the two unfortunate soldiers on guard duty there. They wore the flattish helmets of the GDR army, and despite the warmth of the spring day they were in greatcoats and boots. They held their rifles balanced on the palms of their hands, taking all the weight of them on their outstretched arms. It was a part of the Prussian drill, like goose-stepping, designed to show that soldiers can endure any physical trial because they are essentially fighting machines. The Prussians exported the drill to imperial Russia in the eighteenth century, and the Soviet Union imposed it on its allies after 1945. Outside the Memorial to Fascism, Prussian drill had come back home.

A boy on crutches eased his broken ankle forward until he stood beside one of the soldiers; then he handed one of his crutches to a friend, who went and stood on the other side of the soldier. Together, they shouldered arms with them while their friends laughed and took photographs. A few months previous they would all have been arrested. Now the policeman on duty simply smiled indulgently, while the soldier himself frowned for the photographer and tried to look military. Inside the building, a small granite temple, a flame burned in a faceted cube of yellowish glass, like a new type of cooking stove at an Ideal Home exhibition. A little old man stood beside it in a belted raincoat, boots and a red crash helmet. Somehow he looked military as well. He was a little cracked.

"I am a Communist, and I remain a Communist," he told a small crowd of teenagers.

They giggled with embarrassment and began to melt away. He saluted the flame and turned to face me. He hadn't shaved for some time, and hair grew irregularly around his face.

"He's just a loony," someone said.

A fussy statue of Frederick the Great dominates the avenue. Elsewhere, East Berlin is an ugly collection of post-War glass and concrete: the kind of place where the engineers took care of the architecture to save money. But the Unter den Linden has been reconstructed much as it was. It is boastful and unlovable, like Wilhelmine Germany. Even the great Protestant cathedral, which the Communist authorities never finished restoring, carries a verse about victory on its frontage: UNSER GLAUBE IST DER SIEG DER DIE WELT ÜBERWUNDEN HAT ("Our faith is the victory which has overcome the world.")

The Marxist-Leninists did much the same with quotations from their scriptures. I thought of Bonn, comfortable, small, bourgeois, unpretentious, and contrasted it with all this. If a country's capital is an expression of its personality, then a united Germany would be inheriting an unpleasant personality indeed when it moved back into its old quarters. There was something about the Unter den Linden that encouraged noise and aggression.

Now there were posters on every wall, beckoning voters to one part or another of the political spectrum. There were obscure personal shafts:

"Anyone who played the *BLOCKflöte* (recorder) in Honecker's orchestra cannot play first fiddle in a democracy."

"The CDU has been partners with the SED since 1949. The honorable alternative is to vote SPD."

"Don't Worry, Vote Gysi!"

"The future has a new name . . ." (but unfortunately someone had covered it up).

"We're fighting for every millimeter: The Greens."

"Modrow—the best reason for voting PDS." (But they had to print the full version of the SED's new name alongside it.)

"To all tenants: now at last you can choose—between higher rents and getting notice to quit! Vote for your tenants' rights coalition, CDU-FDP-CSU" (the government coalition in the Federal Republic).

"The left you have. You don't want the right. Vote for strong center—the Union of Free Democrats."

"Hello! Do you remember 1914? Was there anyone who wasn't inspired by the Kaiser and his war for the Fatherland?

"And 1918?

"Do you remember 1933, and the huge jubilation for the new Chancellor with no opposition?

"And 1945?

"And today there's a headlong rush for 'unity' at any price.

"So vote with awareness and conscience, so that tomorrow you won't have to crawl away and hide."

But the voters did vote for unity after all. That night, at an ugly glass-and-concrete social center, the CDU celebrated its relative victory. There was Country and Western music in German, and a curious mixture of the smart and the rough in the crowd. A blonde woman in an expensive leather suit edged her way past a group of youths in T-shirts, and watched as one laughed and swept his hand across the table, knocking several glasses to the ground. The others cheered.

The chairman of the CDU in East Germany, Lothar de Maiziere, announced to the crowd that they were winning 49 percent of the vote, compared with 22 percent for the Social Democrats and 16 percent for the former Communists of the PDS. It hadn't mattered that the CDU had been a meek and silent part of the Communist coalition in East Germany for decades, nor that one of its leaders was discovered shortly before the election to have been a security police informant. A vote for the CDU was a vote for union with West Germany as soon as possible.

It was, in its way, an aspiration: if you vote to join a rich country, perhaps you will become rich too. Chancellor Kohl gave them the impression, which was later denied, that the East German Ostmark would be converted to West German Marks at a rate of 1:1. A vote for the CDU was a vote for maintaining savings, pensions and incomes at a decent level. Later, Kohl was obliged to promise that there would be a 1:1 exchange for the majority of private savings. There was something else about the election. Time and again during the campaign I had had the impression that voters and candidates were just doing what they thought people did in democracies. They were acting out a role rather than doing something that was natural to them. It wasn't surprising: nothing came naturally in the GDR except obeying orders. And now there were no orders to obey, only economic imperatives.

The next morning I went back to the Wall. Once it had been the central metaphor for the GDR, just as a booming economy had been the central metaphor for the Federal Republic. There was the constant murmuring of hammers, as people on the western side chipped away at the spray-painted surface and loosened pieces to sell or keep as mementoes. There is no hammering on the eastern side, partly because there was less spray-paint. But there was some. The unthinkable had happened: if people were free to write on the eastern side of the Berlin Wall, the East really was free at last. On the other side the slogans had been painted thick and deep for decades. Here they were new:

THE WALL HAS FALLEN, THE OTHERS WILL FOLLOW
1990: GORBY'S YEAR
EAST OR WEST, DOWN WITH THE NAZI-PEST
FUCK TO DENG
28 YEARS ARE ENOUGH

Someone had painted a life-size doorway on the Wall, with the door slightly ajar. Elsewhere there was the familiar joke:

LAST ONE OUT TURN OFF THE LIGHTS

In Berlin there was more to the joke than there usually is. The East German army was simply melting away. According to one estimate, 40 percent of its effective force had crossed into the Federal Republic by March 1990. The evidence lay beside Checkpoint Charlie. The stalls still sold neat little packets with pieces of the Wall in them (five Marks for a small one, ten for a larger), and hired out hammers and chisels so you could break off your own pieces. But now they had a new stock in trade:

army hats. In places they were piled up, eight lines wide and six or seven deep: light blue fur hats of the Soviet army, darker ones from the East German army, hats of border guards, officers' hats, peaked caps, even the occasional Stasi hat. East German greatcoats hung from the branches of the trees overhead, as if the revolution had been hanging Communists. There were shoulder flashes and cap badges, belts and gaiters and water bottles, and a tank commander's leather helmet. That was being sold by an Egyptian, whose piles of hats were the largest and most expensive. He said,

> I saw a man come through from the East in civilian clothes, carrying a big bag. He pulled everything out. It was all his uniform, even the boots. And a lot of documents about the tank, with his orders and everything. I laid it all out to sell, and five minutes later two men in civilian clothes, they looked like officers, one with a British accent and the other an American, bought all the papers. I've sold most of the uniform now. It's rare. The tank commander just carried on walking after I gave him the money. He won't be back.

A little later I was talking to another stall-holder, a West German expert in GDR militaria. His trestle table was covered with East German medals and badges. He told me,

> You see them all come past here: not just Easterners, but Poles and Russians. Most of them are going to the West illegally, and they stop off to get a little money for the journey. We don't pay them much. Directly the Wall comes down and Germany is reunited, no one will want these things except a few collectors like me. The tourist trade will be gone.

He picked up a cheapjack medal in imitation bronze and dangled it for me to look at. Für Treue Dienst, it said: "For Faithful Service."

"Cheap shit. But it's worth a little to a collector."

A man came uncertainly toward us, from the direction of East Berlin. His hand was in his pocket. He was in his mid-forties, with a tired, worried face.

"I've heard you buy things," he said. "Are these medals of any interest?" He said it as though he expected to be rebuffed.

"Yeah, I'm interested. These aren't bad."

The East German smiled. He was a dignified man in his way, tall and straight. One of the medals had a double X on its ribbon of black, red and gold. I asked him what it was for.

"Twenty years' service in the army of a country that doesn't exist any longer, that's what it's for. Twenty years of my life wasted."

The dealer gave him twenty Marks. He looked at the notes and smiled at me.

"I'm going to use this to buy some real coffee, ground from coffee beans, to take back to my wife in the East. It's her birthday. So you see, maybe twenty years of my life have a value after all."

He made his way toward the shops farther down Friedrichstrasse. I bought the medal. FÜR DEN SCHUTZ DER ARBEITER UND BAUERN, it says on the reverse: "For the protection of the Workers and Peasants." It's as unconvincing, as gimcrack, as the State that issued it. I have it in my hand as I write, but what I remember when I look at it is the bitterness as its owner said, "Twenty years of my life wasted."

PART THREE

10
Strange Places, Questionable People Taking a Chance

Look if you like, but you will have to leap.
—W. H. AUDEN, Leap Before You Look, 1940

It was guilt that first took me to Baghdad.

In the early 1980s I met a smart-looking young Iranian at a reception of some kind. He was generous about my reporting of Iran, and it became clear he was looking for a job at the BBC. After that he would ring me up and tell me snippets of information about Iran. When I checked them out, they were usually correct. After that I paid him occasional amounts of money for work he did, but although I liked him I never quite trusted him enough to get him a job with the BBC. If I had, he might still be alive today.

Instead he went to the *Observer*. They obviously didn't trust him too much either, because although they printed his material from time to time they never gave him a staff post. Poor Farzad Bazoft: he always felt he had to try harder and go a little bit farther in order to impress the people he worked for.

In particular he went to Iraq. As an Iranian, whose country fought a savage war with Iraq from 1980 to 1988, it was a dangerous thing to do; especially since he had nothing more substantial than a British travel document. Between 1987 and 1989 he traveled to Iraq five times. The last time was in September 1989, and on the day he left London the news leaked out that a huge explosion had taken place the previous month at the Iraqi government's weapons manufacturing plant at Al Qa'qa near the town of Al Hilla, sixty miles south of Baghdad.

It was typical of Farzad Bazoft that nothing would prevent him from finding out what had happened. If ever there was a true martyr for the faith of investigative reporting, it was Farzad. He used his considerable charm on an attractive British nurse living in Baghdad, Daphne Parish, and persuaded her to drive him down to Al Qa'qa.

There was no question of secrecy. He asked an Iraqi minister and the information ministry for help in going there, and told the *Observer* over a heavily tapped phone line precisely what he was going to do. It was a gamble, of course; but Farzad was a habitual gambler.

They picked him up as he was leaving Baghdad Airport at the end of his visit. In his luggage were some samples he had gathered from the roadside at Al Qa'qa; presumably he wanted to have them analyzed back in London to reveal what type of weapon had exploded there the previous month. He was tortured, and eventually confessed to everything they wanted: in particular, to spying for the British and Israelis. Mrs. Parish refused to confess, because she had done nothing wrong. When the Iraqi authorities put them together Farzad tried to persuade her to do as he had. It would, he said, mean that she would be released.

It didn't, of course; it just meant that the Iraqis had the grounds they wanted in order to execute Farzad. At their trial, Farzad was sentenced to death and Mrs. Parish to fifteen years. No one translated the sentence for them or told them in court what was going to happen. A British diplomat had to break the news to Farzad that he was to be hanged as soon as their meeting ended. He took the news as well as he could. A moment or two before, he had been talking about his hopes that international pressure would work in his favor. Now he sent his love to his family and his former girlfriend, and his apologies to Mrs. Parish.

"I hope the world will decide, after I'm gone, what kind of person I have really been," he said. Minutes later he was taken out and executed. Mrs. Parish was released after ten difficult months in prison.

Hanging Farzad Bazoft was Saddam Hussein's first open defiance of the Western world. Mrs. Thatcher had asked for his release, and called his execution "an act of barbarism." If the British tabloid press hadn't been so hysterical about it—they love insulting people from a safe distance—it is possible Farzad would have been pardoned.

All this made me determined to go to Baghdad for myself. In May 1990, six weeks after Farzad's death, I arrived there with a small BBC team and several other British journalists. There were daily demonstrations outside the British embassy complaining about the efforts the British government was now belatedly making to stop weapons technology from reaching Iraq. We were virtual prisoners in our hotel, and no one in the streets wanted to meet our eyes as we walked around with our minders. Sensible people knew that Western journalists were dangerous.

Given Farzad Bazoft's experiences, I made an unforgivable mistake. The Ministry of Information decided to impound all our video cassettes (I had said something in a broadcast about the total surveillance under which we were working, and that upset our minders) and the producer, Eamonn Matthews, wanted to stay on for a day to get them back. When I realized how determined he was, I should never have left. Anyway, the rest of us went home, but Eamonn was picked up at the airport the following day exactly as Farzad had been. He was threatened and roughly treated, and kept a virtual prisoner overnight. When he walked into the *Newsnight* office in London his face showed clear signs of the stress he had been under. As for me, I assumed I wouldn't be allowed back into Iraq. I wasn't too upset about that.

On 2 August 1990 I was on holiday in southern France. Within three hours of hearing on the radio that Saddam Hussein had invaded Kuwait, I was on a plane back to London. That was the last day off I was to have for the next six months.

As the days passed, negotiation failed to dislodge the Iraqi forces and an international coalition was assembled. I tried to think where I would most want to be. There was London, of course, where I could appear in the studio each night and pull everything together—but that was much too safe and boring. There was Saudi Arabia, where the coalition forces would assemble—fine, but it was likely to be far too highly controlled. Anyway, I don't really like the idea of being on our side, with our troops.

I enjoy the company of the British army, and I have come to realize that it is without question the best-trained in the world, but I don't like to do my reporting in the company of friends. I prefer the principle of antagonism.

There were considerable problems, of course. For one thing, I had left Iraq four months earlier assuming that the authorities there would never let me back. For another, the Iraqis were already taking British and American and European expatriates hostage, and Farzad had been executed there merely for doing his job. The risk seemed to be extremely high, both personally and professionally. Put a foot wrong, and I might be strung up. Fail to get in, and I might spend the rest of the crisis at Television Center. Yet having identified Baghdad as the place to be, I couldn't now back away from it. I decided to put everything I had on this single throw of the dice. A long career of risk-taking has taught me that gambles tend to come off; it's the failure to take the plunge that you usually regret later.

The BBC didn't like it. There was a lot of hemming and hawing. Perhaps it was because of concern for me; or perhaps they were working out how much they would have to pay out if I became (a) a hostage and (b) dead. All right, I suggested, but let's just see if I can get permission to go there in the first place; no point in worrying about whether I should before we know if I can. It's an argument I've often used: the powers that be feel they haven't had to make an irrevocable decision, and yet a momentum is building up, which will make it more difficult for them to say no later. For me there was an added attraction: since Britain had cut its diplomatic relations with Iraq after the execution of Farzad Bazoft, applying for visas would have to be done in pleasant places like Paris, Geneva and Amman.

I went to Paris first. The Iraqi ambassador was sitting in his office watching an afternoon soap opera on television when I was shown in. He had been brutally handled in a BBC television interview the day before, and I wanted to smooth his ruffled feathers. Merely because his government and ours were at loggerheads over something didn't mean that the BBC should treat him as an enemy.

Years before, just before I was sent to South Africa, the BBC's head of news and current affairs, a wily old Ulsterman called Waldo Maguire, handed me a single piece of flimsy copy paper, an ancient minute which the BBC's board of governors had sent to the director-general at the beginning of the Second World War. The BBC's broadcasters should, it said in its smudged old type, address even German listeners as if they were having a conversation with them in a neutral café. "Above all," it concluded, "there can be no room for ranting."

Absolutely. So we were chatting in a civilized way about this and that, when the phone rang. It was someone with information that a well-known member of the Saudi royal family had lost six million francs at the gambling table in Nice the previous night. The ambassador gave instructions that this juicy little item of black propaganda should be passed around to the Arab journalists in Paris, and beamed at me.

It seemed an auspicious moment.

"Would you help me get a visa to Baghdad?"

"Why not?" The ambassador smiled.

I was delighted, not knowing that "Why not?" is the polite Arab response to an impossible request.

After that, with my friend Mike Davies as producer and picture editor, I processed through the Middle East reporting on the growing crisis and trying to find a way to get to Baghdad. We started in Cairo, moved on to Jerusalem, and ended up in Amman. I went to the royal palace to ask King Hussein for help, and one of his superbly suited assistants replied, "Why not?"

I queued up outside the Iraqi embassy in Amman for hours in the hot sun. The only way to get in was to trick the guard into opening the door a crack, then pushing through. It still didn't do me any good: once I was inside the press attaché said, "Why not?"

Just as I was about to leave for London, I heard that Tariq Aziz, the Iraqi foreign minister, was coming to Amman to give a press conference. I asked a couple of questions during the course of it, in order to imprint myself on his consciousness, then doorstepped him as he left.

"Would it be possible for the BBC to visit Baghdad?"

"Why not?" he said, as he climbed into his expensive limousine. This time, though, I had the faint sense that he meant it.

The following day the Iraqi embassy in London called. Our visas had come through.

I felt like a condemned man heading off in a tumbril. It was still only a couple of weeks after Iraq's invasion of Kuwait, and we were the first European television team to be allowed into Baghdad. With me was Ray Gibbon, who had covered the Sabra and Chatila massacre with me and was now a cameraman in his own right, and a freelance cameraman who later left Baghdad when we needed him most. As the three of us left the InterContinental Hotel in Amman people shook our hands with a particular intensity. At the airport there was a camera crew from one of the television news agencies to film us leaving.

"Would you mind if I did a quick interview with you? You know, just in case."

I did know: I'd interviewed people just in case something happened to them, too.

Another group of television people was waiting at the Iraqi Airways check-in for the Baghdad flight. They came from Cable Network News, CNN: still not very big or very important. This trip of theirs to Baghdad would establish them with the Iraqis, and as a result of their presence in Baghdad during the run-up to the war and the war itself they would pole-vault themselves way ahead of the other American television companies in terms of international awareness. I had always liked CNN because of its lack of pretension and its concentration on news, and I had quite often appeared on it as an interviewee. Since the BBC had not yet started its own television world service yet, there was no competition between us.

As we lined up at the check-in desk I talked to the CNN producer. His name was Robert Wiener: a witty, quick-thinking man, more intellectually rounded than the usual run of American television news producers, and not concerned (as so many people in this competitive business are) to put you down in order to establish their own position. I took to him at once—particularly when he told me he'd come across a rather favorable review of a book I'd written. This would turn out to be an important trip for Wiener. As a result of it he would become the chief architect of CNN's success in Iraq over the next six or eight months, and therefore, by extension, of its new importance in the world.

"So why are you going to Baghdad?" I asked. What I meant was, the chances must be quite strong that something unpleasant will happen to us all; why should you voluntarily put your head in the noose?

"Because it's the place to be," he said.

I knew then that he'd been through all the same thought processes as I had, and had come up with the same answer. Once we had established ourselves in Baghdad we were to slip into an atmosphere of much greater competitiveness, which was a pity. But before the air war began five months later he played a significant part in my decision to stay there when other people were leaving.

"I was in Saigon when Americans pulled out in '75," he went on. "And I decided to leave before the Viet Cong came in. I've spent the last fifteen years trying to make up for that. I don't want to have to make up for anything again."

Landing in Baghdad was disturbing and eerie. The airport was almost entirely deserted: this was the only flight of the day, thanks to the UN sanctions. I was the first person off the plane, and found myself in the arrivals hall before the large group of security men expected. As I walked in they scattered like snooker balls to the outer edges of the hall to watch and listen. Outside, as we piled up our gear and suitcases, the savage heat wrapped around us like a barber's heated face-towel. It was too hot even for the flies. We took the only taxi we could find, cramming uncomfortably into it, and had to keep the window tightly shut. When, unable to breathe, I opened it, the hot wind burned my face and I had to close it again.

The streets were silent and empty. It wasn't just the heat: people were terrified of what might happen, and mostly stayed indoors with their families. At the hotel, though, they were genuinely welcoming.

"Alas," said a man who had taken a British Council course in English literature, "we see regrettably few of your countrymen now."

"Will things be very bad?" asked one of the dark, lusciously beautiful women whom Mesopotamia produces, with a touching anxiety. "Please remember," she added, as though I had the power to halt the coming air strikes, "that it's not our fault."

She glanced meaningfully at the icon of President Saddam Hussein on the wall. That was as close to political comment as you could get to in Iraq without knowing someone well enough to trust them.

The same charming officials greeted me with ironic smiles. No one mentioned the confiscation of all our tapes at the end of my previous visit. They were witty and feline in turn, as though they had served their apprenticeship at the Sublime Porte rather than in one of the fiercest dictatorships around. It's easy to convince yourself that because you have good personal relations with senior people in a government like this you will be protected in some way if things go wrong. As Farzad Bazoft discovered, that isn't the case. In Iraq you are on your own. Your highly placed friends will shrug their shoulders and smile with ironic apology at the latest unfortunate bow-stringing. They have their own careers, their own lives, to protect.

On that first afternoon, Saddam Hussein visited some of the British hostages from Kuwait, accompanied by Iraqi television cameras, and stroked the hair of a young English boy as he talked to the parents. There was absolutely nothing wrong with that in an Arab context, but in the Anglo-Saxon world in particular it set everyone's teeth on edge. I was still meeting officials when these pictures were broadcast, and in between handshakes I tried to make out what was happening on the screen in the corner of the ministerial office. Were the hostages going to be released? What was Saddam saying? The officials were vague and unwilling to commit themselves. It was immensely frustrating, especially given that I was going to have to build my evening's report around the incident. Also, we needed more pictures. Could Ray film from the official's window?

"Why not?"

We got a series of rather fine panoramic shots of the city skyline in the setting sun.

Going to the television station was extremely worrying. In the hot darkness soldiers patrolled the empty roadway. Our driver, the wiry and unshaven old Mr. Hamid, wasn't allowed to stop anywhere near the entrance. An armored personnel carrier sheltered in an entry, its gun pointed directly at Ray and me as we labored along on foot, gripping our edited video cassette and hoping to be in time for the fifteen-minute satellite booking, which was due to start in only five minutes.

The soldiers inside didn't share our sense of urgency. We had no written permission to enter, and there was no answer from the office of the ferocious woman who was in charge of television news. Time passed. I paced up and down, sweating and brushing away the flies, which had now come out with a sleepy intensity. Saddam Hussein looked down at me from a variety of pictures: desert sheikh, soldier, statesman. The clock ticked into our satellite time.

Finally, my patience snapped. I wrenched open the door that led to the main television complex, scarcely caring whether they shot me: all that mattered was to make the satellite. Ray came with me. There was some angry shouting, but no one quite had instructions to kill us. I looked back: the officer was resignedly waving one of his soldiers, a small moustached Saddam clone, to follow me. In the darkness of the courtyard there was the smell of sewage, and my ankle turned on the broken pavement. Feral kittens playing in an abandoned oil drum squeaked and scattered.

The woman who had the power to broadcast our material or withhold it was handsome and dark, with hair pulled back hard on her head like Eva Perón's. She was exhausted: each day she worked sixteen or seventeen hours in the intense heat. But exhaustion had made her poisonous. When I asked her questions about the satellite she repeated my words to me mockingly; the handsomeness left her face and was replaced by a Rosa Klebb expression of contempt and anger.

Ray put the cassette into the player and ran through it to show her what we intended to transmit.

"Take that out," she snapped, as an innocuous shot of the city skyline appeared. No good trying to tell her that a senior official at the Information Ministry had let us film it from his window: She worked for the Interior and Security ministries, which in a society like this far outranked mere Information. She took further offense at a shot of one of the giant portraits of Saddam in the city streets, at a woman carrying a bundle on her head, and at the awful monument to the war with Iran — crossed scimitars a hundred feet high, held in giant hands modeled from those of Saddam himself. I could have understood if her objection had been aesthetic. It could scarcely have been on security grounds, since pictures of the arch appeared every night on Iraqi television news. Why, then?

"No discussion," said Rosa Klebb, and her mouth shut like a mouse-trap.

What Saddam had said during his meeting with the British family was that women and children taken hostage in Kuwait would be able to leave. They were brought up by coach to Baghdad and flown out from there. Over the next week or so this was to be the staple of our reporting.

Many of the women reacted superbly. They smiled and kept calm while the cameramen sweated and shoved around them. They talked in terms of quiet affection about the husbands and sons they had been forced to leave behind, and whose fate was completely unknown. Many had no homes to go to in Britain, and no certainty about their future income. Yet they spoke about getting back to nice cups of tea and the greenness of England as though nothing had changed since the Blitz. They fought back the tears for the sake of their children, and busied themselves with their luggage so that the cameras couldn't pry into their emotions.

Others complained. Their meals were cold, they couldn't use the swimming pool in the luxurious hotel that the Iraqis had set aside for them in Baghdad, the journey from Kuwait had taken too long.

"My little boy is used to proper food—burgers, fish fingers, chips, things like that. All this rice and vegetables upsets his tummy."

Many complained that the Foreign Office or the British embassy had failed to help them enough, and seemed to feel it was all the government's fault, as though Saddam Hussein were an act of God like drought or flooding, and Mrs. Thatcher should do something about it.

"I don't see why we should suffer because of her and President Bush," said one affronted woman.

Another agreed. "If she's going to call Saddam a dictator, why didn't she wait till we were safely out of Kuwait?"

A British girl of around eighteen announced proudly that she'd been forced to take the Iraqi soldiers to her father's hiding place in Kuwait. They wouldn't have let her leave otherwise, she explained. The Iraqis had announced that the penalty for hiding from them could be death, though in this case nothing happened to him. Perhaps they thought he was sufficiently punished by having such a daughter.

The British tabloids loved it all. They weren't allowed into Iraq, so they interviewed the women as they came through Amman. JOURNEY THROUGH HELL was the way one headline described the trip by air-conditioned coach from Baghdad. "Burning desert," "torturing thirst," "fiends," "evil," "sobbing," "loved ones' anguish": the hacks' *Roget's* was in constant use. There was a hint of strategically ripped clothing, of beautiful white women menaced by lustful natives.

THATCHER WARNS EVIL SADDAM said the first poster I saw when I went back to London for a break. Some of us, I thought, have been writing and broadcasting about the unpleasantness of Saddam Hussein's regime for years, while the British government regarded Iraq as a good customer for weaponry of all kinds.

When the newspapers put a compulsory "evil" in front of someone's name, you know there's a particular need for coolness and rationality. And to prove the superiority of our civilization over Saddam's, someone threw a brick through the window of the Iraqi Cultural Center in the Tottenham Court Road.

I went back to Baghdad after a week or so, and stayed on for two months, from September to November 1990. This trip, the third of six to Iraq, was the foundation stone of my entire reporting assignment in Baghdad. I got to know more and more people, both officials and private citizens, and started to find out what made the place tick. I grew to love it, and to sympathize with it too: Iraq seemed to me like a hijacked plane being flown to an unknown destination. A man whom scarcely anyone wanted as their president was holding a gun to the pilot's head, and the passengers and the rest of the crew were terrified to say a word or stop him. The fact that British industry, with the enthusiastic encouragement of the British government, had supplied the hijacker with his gun and the bullets for it made it all the worse.

Soon I settled into a routine. We had been moved from the Sheraton to the Al-Rashid Hotel: one I had always steered clear of. The advertisement for it at the airport: "The Al-Rashid: More Than Just a Hotel."

How much more, I wondered? It had been built for an Arab summit conference during the Iran-Iraq War, and was equipped with slabs of concrete set at an angle above each window, to deflect any shrapnel from exploding missiles. The entrance hall of the Al-Rashid was enormous, and with its white marble and its stained-glass windows it looked like a recently built crematorium. Until the press contingent swelled to such size that every available secret policeman had to be drafted in to watch us, there would always be a half dozen of them, sitting in the lobby in their suits and Saddam moustaches, reading their newspapers and watching the comings and goings.

There were usually some peace tourists there too: well-intentioned people who hoped to prevent the war by coming to Baghdad to demonstrate with the Iraqis or try a bit of freelance negotiation. Others were attracted to trouble and media attention like bluebottles to a dustbin. Many had come to plead for the release of their fellow citizens whom Saddam Hussein was holding hostage. The most prominent of them were given an audience with the great man himself. You could see them occasionally on television, bowing over his hand. That wasn't necessarily intentional. Saddam, a man of around five feet seven, deliberately held his hand out quite low when they came forward to shake it, and gave them a little pull, which meant they lowered their heads automatically. His court photographers waited for that instant, and the next day's newspapers would show them inclining their heads to greatness.

A banker friend of mine in London had advised me not to stay at Al-Rashid. His company had loaned a large amount of money to the company that built it, and among the costs was an item for Swedish built surveillance cameras, which were fitted into the television in each room so that the security people could watch you as you watched television—or did anything else, of course. It was fashionable for those who could afford it to hold their wedding receptions and honeymoons in the Al-Rashid, and shortly before I arrived there was a minor scandal when it was discovered that the security men in the hotel were selling videos of the honeymooning couples in the Bazaar. A recent bridegroom, it seemed, had recognized himself and his wife. As far as I was concerned, there was never much for the spooks to watch—unless they liked the sight of a large man in his underwear looking through his library (as ever I brought ten or twelve books with me, large Victorian three-decker novels and collected poems mostly, in case I was taken hostage or put in prison) or playing music. I would listen to Shostakovich, Mozart, Stéphane Grappelli, Fred Astaire, Elgar. Then I would sit and look out at the view, and wonder what it would look like when the aerial bombardment started.

For me, the greatest pleasure was to take a car down to the Tigris River and stroll around the ancient part of the city. The Baghdad of Haroun al-Rashid, the circular city that was the most advanced in the world in the eighth and ninth centuries after Christ, was utterly destroyed by the Mongols in the thirteenth century; so there is no sign of it whatsoever in modern Baghdad. But along the river bank are the university and the Bazaar and other ancient buildings—often disregarded and falling apart, but recognizably of the time.

I would wander through the Bazaar, with the coppersmiths' hammers ringing in my ears and the old women calling out humorous endearments and the sellers of fruit and cloth and jewelry coming out to offer me tea and begging me just to look, no obligation, because the quality and beauty alone would steal my heart. The shopkeepers soon became familiar to me, and I learned how to bargain with them, setting aside an hour or more to look at their wares and starting the bidding, not only at prices that were absurdly low, but for objects I had no interest in. After half an hour's banter and three or four cups of strong mint tea, I would suggest that if the merchant wanted to make a sale he should throw in whatever it was I was really interested in: a carpet from Bokhara, perhaps, or a piece of curiously carved lapis lazuli, or a British medal struck for some Mesopotamian campaign, or a collection of cups and saucers with the face of King Faisal on them. Then the shopkeeper would relax a little, and the real battle would begin.

I never scorned the quality of the goods on offer, as you are advised to do, though I would always show I had spotted the faint chip or the mended crack. Instead I would praise whatever it was I wanted to buy, and then offer a price that I thought was low but realistic. Sometimes I would have to say goodbye and leave—once I was even getting into the car before the merchant ran up and agreed to the deal—but I always got what I wanted.

One merchant had a beautiful early 1920s gramophone with a brass horn and a wind-up handle on his top shelf. I first discovered it while I was up a ladder, mountaineering for books; and it took me three visits before I could get him to agree to a price I thought was reasonable. One Thursday evening, together with some friends, I went to pick it up.

Almost all the rest of the Bazaar had closed down. Like an illustration in an old manuscript, the yellow light from a hurricane lamp in the shop window shone through the dark archways. Our footsteps echoed through the passages. The smells of the day's commerce, of the fruit and vegetables, the coffee, the hideous joints of meat, lingered in the darkness. The old man was still sitting in his shop, and he grinned victoriously at me: by coming I had shown I had accepted his price. With unlikely agility he swarmed up the ladder in his bare feet and snatched the whole perilous contraption for me. On the way down he paused.

"Want record?"

I nodded. He gripped a selection from a leaning pile and carried it down. I knew then that I had paid too much for the gramophone; bazaaris in Baghdad don't hand out presents unless they feel a very powerful moral obligation. I didn't care, because the thing was so lovely, with its little image of the dog, head turned, listening, and the words HIS MASTER'S VOICE painted on it, and its beautiful brass horn. My colleague Mike Davies took it from me, and on a bench in the darkness started to reassemble the whole thing, almost by touch. Like a surgeon, he held out his hand for a record. It was too dark to read the labels, so I handed him the topmost one from the small pile I was holding. Mike placed it on with care, and wound the handle.

Then came the miracle. In the medieval darkness there was a hoarse, scratching sound, and the horn began to speak.

> *Runnin' wild, lost control*
> *Runnin' wild, mighty bold.*
> *Feelin' gay, reckless too,*
> *Carefree mind, all the time,*

Never blue.
Always goin', don't know where.
Always showin' I don't care.
Don't love nobody, it's not worthwhile.
All alone, and running wild.

The echoes of Duke Ellington and his Famous Orchestra had faded into the recesses of the ancient stonework before we started clapping.

Why did the Iraqis want us there? Why should a government that had been so paranoid about foreign journalists a few months earlier now invite them to Baghdad in such large numbers that the pool of English-speaking spooks was drained by the effort of following us around? (One side effect was that there weren't enough of them to listen in on our phone calls; realizing this, I started dictating the weekly column I was now writing for the *Spectator* by telephone. Better still, none of the snoopers the Iraqis used in London were *Spectator* readers, so the authorities in Baghdad didn't find out what I was writing. That in turn emboldened me, of course, and I found myself writing things about Saddam Hussein that would have driven the Iraqis crazy if they had known.) Now, though, there were well over a hundred journalists from the main countries, and the main news organizations, of the world; and there would be more to come.

The man who had invited them in was the chief civil servant in the Information Ministry, Najji al-Hadithi: a handsome, elegant man who had spent seven years in London as press attaché, and spoke English superbly. Somehow he had managed to persuade his minister to approach Saddam Hussein himself with a plan: that Iraq should now regard Western journalists as useful to its own purposes.

It worked—and having agreed to allow me in, together with the leading American networks, Iraq gradually opened the doors until every major British broadsheet newspaper, and every major American, French, German, Spanish, Italian, Canadian and Japanese news organization, plus plenty of others, had its own representative in Baghdad. But I was the correspondent who was allowed to stay the longest.

It was because I got on so well with Najji al-Hadithi. He liked Britain
and the British, and he had a British sense of humor. One evening, a
couple of weeks before the air war started, I took the BBC news editor
to see him. We had spent the day at the ruins of Babylon.

"I've been showing Mike here what the rest of the country is going
to look like soon," I said.

There was a silence. Oh Christ, I thought, why do I let my habit of
making jokes run away with me? I was staring down at the carpet at the
time, and I let my eyes stay there for a bit. Then I looked at al-Hadithi.
He was rocking with silent laughter.

One evening in October he invited me to a dinner party. It was a
beautiful night, with the first hint of coolness in the air after the ferocity of summer. A crescent moon hung in the black sky with a single star
below it, like the Arabic letter B. The table was set outside, and the terrible New Town architecture of Saddam-era Baghdad was invisible. We
could have been dining in the circular city of Haroun al-Rashid.

"And how is dear old England?" asked the man on my right, a weaselly
fellow who seemed to be making fun of me.

Dear old England, I said, was fine.

"And where are you from?"

Suffolk, I told him.

"Ah," he said, getting his fricatives mixed up with his sibilants, thinking I meant Sussex, "Suffolks—Brighton, the Old Ship Inn, Eastbourne."

Something like that, I said.

"And how is Orpington? And Newcastle? And Edinburgh?"

When last heard of, I assured him, they were bearing up.

"When all this is over," he said with a softening in his voice, which
gave me a sudden sympathy for him, "I would love to see Edgware Road
again. And High Saint Kensington."

I didn't allow my face to change, but he knew he had made a mistake. It was as though I'd spoiled his dreams. He turned away from me
at precisely the moment I felt most drawn to him.

By now, though, the conversation on my left had become interesting.
Najji al-Hadithi was sitting immediately next to me, with the American
journalist Carl Bernstein, of Watergate fame, on his far side.

"Kuwait is now, and always will be, a part of the motherland," al-Hadithi said to him, dangling from an elegant hand a set of worry beads made from some attractive semiprecious stone.

"What you're telling me is that you aren't planning to withdraw," said Carl Bernstein, pointing a stubby finger at al-Hadithi.

The beads clicked with a faint irritation.

"Why," I broke in, "do you allow so many foreign journalists to come to Baghdad, when you used to keep the doors so firmly shut?"

"Because we want you to see that we are human beings like yourselves. So that your readers and viewers will see it. So that if, God forbid, President Bush decides to bomb us, you will know who you are bombing. You are a form of protection for us."

"What you're saying—" Bernstein began. But his probing finger froze in midair. Najji al-Hadithi was already talking to someone across the table.

It was an intelligent strategy, and in the end I think it worked. I hope it did. And if, by being a small part of Najji al-Hadithi's strategy, we helped to persuade the United States that Iraq wasn't another Vietnam or Laos or Cambodia that could be carpet-bombed because there were no Western eyewitnesses to tell the world what was happening, then I'm proud to have been there.

The Gulf War was the first (or perhaps, if you count the Falklands War, the second) since the Second World War in which it was essential not to have large-scale casualties. If Winston Churchill had promised in 1942 that German civilian casualties would be avoided where possible, he would have been howled down by a public opinion that longed for Germany to suffer just as it had made other countries suffer.

The Gulf War ended precisely when President Bush began to get nervous about the pictures of death and destruction that were coming in from the desert. Public opinion in Britain and America wanted a war fought, but it didn't want a huge body count. And quite rightly, I believe. There are no nice, comfortable wars; but if we are still stupid enough to fight them, we might as well do it with a minimum of bloodshed. The problem was the million deaths *after* the war, caused by UN sanctions and Saddam Hussein's reaction to them.

I liked Najji al-Hadithi a lot, though I must have been a real trial to him. One morning in November I received an invitation to come over to his office. In front of him on the desk lay a pile of *Spectators,* each open at my article. There must have been ten of them at least.

"Oh, John."

I tried to explain. I was a writer; that was what I did. I couldn't not write, and it was my duty to get my material out in the best way possible.

A portrait of Saddam Hussein hung over his desk, and he glanced toward it.

"But the things you said."

"You know it's all true, Najji." Might as well go out frankly as try to grovel, I thought.

"It's not true at all," he said instinctively. Then, "You mention this elegant government official who speaks almost perfect English. Might I ask—"

"Najji, you know perfectly well it's you."

"H'm." There was a pause. "Please, if you must write about our country, don't speak disrespectfully—" Another glance at the presidential portrait.

"Of course not, Najji."

I could let up now, I thought: I'd be staying.

A few days later the Iraqi government was threatening to hang any of the foreigners in Baghdad who had taken refuge at the various Western embassies. The thought that the determinedly jolly, brown, plump men and women whom I had filmed camping out at the British embassy and splashing around like seals in the swimming pool might suffer a fate like this was quite intolerable. Yet was it so very different from the Western commentators, particularly in the United States, who were starting to talk of turning Baghdad into an empty car lot, or back into the Stone Age, by aerial bombardment?

I thought of this as I sat in a Baghdad teahouse looking through the open window at the greasy waters of the Tigris below. The room was cooled by slow overhead fans. There was the sound of loud laughter, and of ivory dominoes being slammed victoriously down on wooden tables. A waiter with a gotch eye and a badly scarred face came over with a dirty tray of lemon-flavored tea. Rough faces, dark and unshaven, grinned wolfishly at us from around the room. As far as I can remember, no ordinary citizen of Iraq ever once insulted or threatened me during my entire six months in the country. A cripple shuffled across to us, called each of us "Lord" and took our shoes away to be polished.

Our driver had brought us here: an upright brown little cock-sparrow of a man who was of course working for the *Mukhabarat,* Iraq's fearsome intelligence organization, but nevertheless gave us good service. His name was Hattem.

"Mr. Hattem number one driver?" he would ask.

"Absolutely, Mr. Hattem," I would reply. It was a ritual.

He was always on duty half an hour before the appointed time, and recently, with some embarrassment, he asked for the afternoon off. It turned out that his wife had given birth to their fifth child the day before, and this was his first chance to see him.

Now Mr. Hattem was showing us the complexities of the Turkish versions of backgammon: *Adi, Mahbous, Gulbaha, Chesh-besh,* and another whose name I never caught. Mr. Hattem threw the dice with a tremendous flourish, and went on to make a series of moves that none of us could understand, let alone copy. Out of the game, I sat back and surveyed the scene. Fat-bellied men in grubby white dishdashas knocked back tea or banged their fists on the table or laughed. Pictures of the Prophet Mohammed and of Haroun al-Rashid looked down at us from the walls. The cripple worked away on our shoes under a tree in the courtyard outside, joking with a small group of friends. This was *douceur de vie* as the poorer people of Iraq knew it. It had nothing to do with the savageries of Saddam Hussein and his government, but they would suffer equally if Iraq were indeed turned into a parking lot. Of course, these were the kinds of thoughts his officials hoped we would have. Yet what they really amounted to was an appreciation of how pleasant Iraq could be, if only Saddam Hussein were no longer in power.

In all this time I hadn't actually met the man himself. I had seen him in the flesh, had even been in a group that was allowed close to him; but I hadn't actually shaken his hand or looked him in the eyes. It was, I told myself, only a matter of time. The application was in, and the officials spoke of "when" rather than "if." Then in November 1990, just as we were about to arrange the details, I suddenly couldn't get in touch with the officials anymore. Somehow they were never in when I called; and when I spoke to Najji al-Hadithi about it, he went into "Why not?" mode.

I knew why it was. Saddam Hussein couldn't allow anyone to edit his words, and I had warned the officials that we would not be able to run an hour and a half of Saddam uncut. We didn't allow that to any British politician, so we certainly couldn't allow it to the president of Iraq. It was a standoff; and the Iraqis solved it by offering the interview to Independent Television News instead. ITN said yes at once.

I was furious, and decided to go back to London. There was a certain calculation in it as well: I was tired after ten weeks' work in Baghdad without a break. Then again, Margaret Thatcher had just resigned as prime minister, and I wanted to cover the campaign for the succession. Probably I'd have left Baghdad anyway; but I didn't tell the Iraqis that, and several of the officials were gratifyingly apologetic.

I had one last dinner with my colleagues in our favorite restaurant, and afterward asked if anyone wanted to walk back to the hotel instead of driving. A Dutch correspondent who was with us volunteered to come with me. There seemed no reason to be worried.

We stopped on the Jomhuriya Bridge across the River Tigris and looked across at Saddam Hussein's palace—one of the many—lying in darkness on the other bank. Would there really be a war?

There was the sound of a police siren. Two cars came swerving up and mounted the sidewalk, and four men waving guns got out and ran over to us. One of them, a man of about fifty, wore a uniform with a big unwinking eye embroidered on the shoulder-patches. When I refused to take my hands out of my pockets he screamed that he would throw me into the river. I took no notice, of course: I guessed he wouldn't go through with it. Instead he called for reinforcements.

So there we stood, on the Jomhuriyah Bridge in the darkness: the poor Dutch correspondent who was more nervous than ever, me with my hands in my pockets pretending not to be worried, four police cars with flashing lights, eight policemen, and at least eight guns. The most senior of the reinforcements swaggered across to me. Baghdad isn't a town where people talk back to policemen. I cut him short as soon as he started shouting at me in English, which was quite good.

"I work for British television," I told him, choosing my words with as much care as a lawyer or a writer of advertising copy, "and British television is interviewing president Saddam Hussein tomorrow morning. If I see the president tomorrow morning I shall complain to him personally about your behavior. Please give me the names of all the policemen here."

I can't think when I've said anything that had a more gratifying effect. His face went a strange prunish color and he ran over to his car. Grabbing the two-way radio, he started yelling down it in Arabic. I could only distinguish the words "British," "television," and "Saddam," but there was no doubt a bull's-eye had been scored. Even the Dutch correspondent perked up a little. When the flow had stopped I asked the policeman what was happening. He merely held his hand up and stared out across the river as though his life was passing before him. He was a man in a career crisis.

Twenty minutes later, down the dark, empty street, came the sound of an old car. It was a beat-up Volkswagen Passat of indeterminate color, lots of dents in the bodywork, and a wire coathanger for a radio aerial. It stopped at the end of the row of flashing police cars, which were ranged along the pavement like fairground stalls, and a slight figure climbed slowly out. He was in his early twenties, yet the senior policeman I'd been talking to actually bowed to him. As for the others, they fell back in case he might catch sight of them.

"Hi," he said.

His tie was loose, his expensive suit was rumpled, and he looked exhausted. Obviously he was very high up in one of Saddam Hussein's many secret police forces; even so, there was something about him I felt was rather amusing and skeptical.

"Is it true you told these men you would report them to Saddam tomorrow morning?" His English was superb.

"Something like that," I said.

"If I drive you back to your hotel and no action is taken against you, will you agree not to say anything about it to Saddam?"

"It's a deal."

I thought the Dutch correspondent was going to faint with relief. As for the policemen, they fawned on us as they queued up to shake hands.

We crammed into the Passat for the quick journey to the hotel. I tried to draw him into conversation about what he did, and the situation, but he grinned and shook his head.

"It's been nice knowing you," he said.

For me, it was an eye-opener. Even failing to interview Saddam Hussein conferred a certain power.

A few hours later I was at the airport. Here, too, the security men were rather nervous. A few weeks before, their colleagues had run a scam in which one of them opened your wallet to look at your money while the other started pulling things roughly out of your hand luggage. As you started yelling at the man with the hand luggage, the man with the wallet palmed some money out of it. One of our people lost $300, and another a good deal more than that. I complained to the Ministry, and although they wrote me a letter saying there was no foundation whatsoever in my accusation, one of the minders told me a couple of security men had been hanged. I felt bad about it until I reflected that they could well have been the men who arrested and beat up poor Farzad Bazoft at the airport.

Anyway, there was no repeat of the old scam now: the security men were polite and very correct. But they still wanted to know what we were taking on board. I had packed the body of my "His Master's Voice" gramophone in my biggest suitcase, but I was carrying the brass horn with me as hand luggage.

"What's that?" asked the security man. I handed it to him.

"It's an Object," I replied.

He took it out of its wrapping and examined it. Then he showed it to his superior.

"*Murmur-murmur-murmur*-object," I heard him say.

"Object?"

The security man nodded.

"OK, no problem," said the boss.

I took my Object on board the plane, and stayed away from Baghdad for almost a month.

When I came back in mid-December, things had changed. Mr. Hattem was much more subservient to our minders, and wouldn't take us anywhere without consulting them. Once we missed an entire story because of this, and in anger I turned to our second driver, the elderly, lopsided, mildly unreliable and distinctly alcoholic (not to say unsuitably named) Mr. Ramadan.

There were other, more important changes. Saddam Hussein had ordered the release of all the foreign hostages ("You really must call them 'guests,' Mr. Simpson," the censor feebly insisted) who had been taken to likely targets in Baghdad and elsewhere and held prisoner there. This was a decision of considerable importance to the Coalition forces headed by the United States; public opinion at home would have been much more reluctant to support the air war if it had seemed likely that ordinary Americans, Britons, Frenchmen and others would be killed by the bombs and missiles.

The man who persuaded Saddam Hussein to give up one of the best cards in an otherwise rather empty hand was Yasser Arafat, the Palestinian leader. Poor old Yasser: he has never been loved in the West. But he was a man with a remarkable degree of personal courage, and although he always liked to wear military uniform and at one time seemed distinctly fond of side-arms and AK-47s, he was always instinctively a man of compromise. His argument had been that if Saddam Hussein let the hostages go, this would weaken the moral argument of the United States. It was a tactical mistake, and Saddam Hussein came to hate Yasser Arafat for having suggested it. But for the time being they were still friendly.

Palestinians generally had swung in Saddam's favor when, early on in the crisis, he offered to withdraw from Kuwait if Israel would withdraw from the West Bank. Yasser Arafat, whatever his private feelings, had come out publicly in support of Iraq in the crisis, and had settled in Baghdad for the duration.

One morning, shortly before Christmas, I went round to his house to record an interview with him.

TRANSCRIPT OF INTERVIEW WITH YASSER ARAFAT, 17.12.90

JS: Will there be a war?

YA: No. I can tell you that there will not be a war. I promise it: you will see. Something will happen: there will be an agreement. You must not think President Bush is so foolish. You must not think the Arab brothers are so foolish. War is a terrible thing. Nobody wants it. President Bush will compromise.

JS: Will there be acts of terrorism carried out by Palestinian groups?

YA: I do not think you will find this is so.

JS: You will stop them?

YA: I will ensure they do not happen.

It certainly looked at that stage as though Arafat would be right about the deal. President Bush was starting to talk of "going the extra mile for peace," and the Iraqi press was announcing a major diplomatic victory for Saddam Hussein. As for terrorism, I was to see for myself how ferocious Arafat could be in curbing it, if he chose.

After our interview we went in to lunch, Arafat holding my hand lightly in his own. It wasn't an intimacy I would have sought: his hand was bandaged and coated with ointment, and it stuck to mine audibly. His doctor, some months earlier, had warned him that his strange habit of sleeping during the day, getting up at six or seven in the evening and working throughout the night meant that he wasn't getting enough sun. If he couldn't change his ways, the doctor had said, he must use a sun-ray lamp—but never for more than a few minutes at a time. Arafat, always tempted to overdo things, stayed under his sun-ray lamp for forty-five minutes and burned himself badly. Hence the bandages.

A dozen or so people were politely standing, waiting for us in the dining room, and sat down only when we did. Arafat's conversation was interesting and amusing, but I was fascinated by the large, dark, humble character at the foot of the table: it was Abu Abbas, the Palestinian terrorist leader who had carried out the attack on the Italian cruise ship

Achille Lauro in 1986, and whose forces had landed on the Israeli coast in May 1990 and had been wiped out. That particular effort had infuriated Arafat, who had told him he would cut his hands off if he tried anything like it again.

"You know our Arabic expression, 'cutting someone's hands off,' meaning to render them incapable of action?"

"Yes," I said.

"I told him it would not be a figure of speech in this case." Arafat laughed hugely.

I could hear Abu Abbas with his head deep in the foodstuffs from a distance: he wasn't a discreet eater. But he was certainly a tamed man. His eyes scarcely met those of anyone else, and he never even looked in Arafat's direction.

In the third week in December I started getting discreet visits from a very senior figure indeed: someone who saw Saddam Hussein on a regular basis, and for reasons that were difficult to work out told me in detail what Saddam had said and what his mood was. This man, whom I nicknamed "Bertie," persuaded me that I should go public on Saddam Hussein's determination not to withdraw from Kuwait before the deadline imposed by the United Nations. Like the United States and British governments, I was inclined to think that Iraq would pull back at the last moment and leave the Coalition forces embarrassingly exposed. Bertie was absolutely certain this wouldn't happen, and he was right. Thanks to him, so was I. This, for instance, is what I told one interviewer over the line from London.

TRANSCRIPT OF RADIO 4 INTERVIEW, 2.1.91

Q: So what's your estimate now? Do you think Saddam will pull back from Kuwait?

JS: I think we can be certain that he won't. People who have seen him in the past day or so have told me that he is determined to stand and fight. He told one visitor that if he pulled his forces back now, there would be an uprising against him in the army and he might not be able to cope with it. If he feels it's essential to his own survival in power to face a war, he'll certainly do it.

I could hear the skepticism in the interviewers' voices, but Bertie had convinced me not only that what he told me was accurate, but that it was important to make it public. Of course the possibility existed that Saddam Hussein knew Bertie was talking to me—the Al-Rashid hotel wasn't exactly the most secure place to have a conversation—and was feeding him this line in order to strengthen the Coalition powers' belief that he meant what he said. Somehow, though, I didn't believe that. Not wanting to identify him, I pretended when I first wrote about this period that I had gathered my information from a range of people who met Saddam Hussein. The reality was a lot easier than that; and my colleagues became used to seeing the distinguished-looking Bertie coming to look for me and going off with me into the next room for a talk.

In report after report I pressed the same line until it became an act of faith for me; and when, on the day when James Baker, the US secretary of state, met the Iraqi foreign minister Tariq Aziz in Geneva and ITN reported that Tariq Aziz was bringing with him an offer of conditional withdrawal, I wondered if I had got it terribly wrong. But he had brought no such thing; and the meeting broke up without the possibility of a diplomatic settlement. That evening I saw Bertie again.

EXTRACT FROM NOTES OF MEETING WITH BERTIE, 7.30 P.M., 13.1.91

Acc[ording] to B. S[addam] was in his hardest and most aggressive mood today. S[ai]d Iraq wd only have to face 2 waves of airstrikes, and B[agh]dad wd be so destroyed and loss of life so huge that international opinion wd be revolted and wd force the US, Br & others to stop. Result: diplomatic victory for S.

Wdn't S be killed? No, because his bunker is impenetrable. He will survive, even if tens of thousands die.

Where is bunker? B too nervous to say. He is driven in with curtains on car windows closed.

Cd he open the curtains a touch and see? B: They wd want to know why I shd do a thing like that.

But does he think it's near here? B, looking round room: Subject not a good one to discuss.

In fact we had a pretty good idea on 11 January where the bunker was. Saddam Hussein was due to appear at an international Islamic conference at the government center immediately opposite the Al-Rashid Hotel. Our minders by now were so unnerved by the prospect of the approaching war that their control over us was becoming increasingly lax. As a result we and the television organizations we worked with were able to station camera crews at every entrance to the conference center, in the hope of getting something more than the official pictures of Saddam Hussein. We might even get a word from him, we thought.

I sat in the hotel, watching Iraqi television's live coverage of the meeting. On cue the great man appeared on stage, holding out his arm in the affected way that is his trademark, while the audience went wild. I looked forward to the pictures the camera crews must be getting. But when they came back, each of them said that Saddam hadn't come past him. That convinced me. We had long heard rumors that his command complex was based under our hotel: this indicated that there were underground roads and passages from the complex to enable him to reach the various important government buildings in the area.

(More evidence came soon after the air war had begun. For some reason I looked out of my hotel window in the early hours of the morning, and saw a team of men in black clothes, black gloves and black balaclavas drive in on a flatbed lorry and take up position in an empty yard below the hotel. On the back of the truck was a remarkably sophisticated air defense system, a battery of missiles that twitched and turned all the time as their radar systems picked up the faintest of signals from the sky.

That night there were no attacks on the center of the city, and the men in black left shortly before dawn. But I couldn't think of any reason why they would want to defend a building site or the back of our hotel, unless Saddam Hussein was underneath. He was. A large village existed underground, with its own sophisticated communications and power systems, manned—according to Bertie—by a number of former Soviet officers.)

So there we were, living and working a hundred feet or so above Saddam Hussein's head. We were his protection. And if he knew it, the Coalition forces did as well: the European company that had built much of the bunker had handed over all the blueprints to them. The outlook wasn't good. The American embassy in Baghdad, before it closed down, had warned everyone who stayed that they could expect to be killed by the bombing. President Bush himself had phoned the editors of the big American organizations represented in Baghdad and begged them to pull the journalists out. And since journalism in the United States is less noted for enterprise and courage now than it once was, the big organizations (with the exception of CNN) obliged.

If we were all so certain we were going to be killed, why did we stay? In my case it was a complex mixture of motives.

First, perhaps, was the sense of duty. I wanted the BBC to have proper coverage of whatever was going to happen. No one had forced me to go to Baghdad in the first place, and now that it had become dangerous it didn't seem right for me to pull out and leave the job to someone else. I remembered very strongly the experience of the CNN producer who had left Saigon before the Viet Cong takeover, and had spent the years since trying to make up for it. I didn't want to have anything to make up for.

Second, I was too interested to want to leave. What would it be like, to be under the greatest aerial bombardment in human history? I didn't want to read about it afterward in the newspapers.

Third, I had undertaken to write a book about the crisis, and I didn't feel I could simply walk out before the final part began.

As for the desire for glory, that didn't play much of a part at all: The chances of ending up dead and forgotten were too great. It is true, though, that I found the excitement enjoyable—but I would have to survive if I were to be able to enjoy it fully.

Months later, a particularly skillful interviewer pressed me to say why I had remained in Baghdad. I went through these answers, but they weren't enough. She forced me to go a little further.

Transcript of *Desert Island Discs* interview, 10.5.91

Speakers: Sue Lawley, John Simpson

SL: But these things—I mean, it's not really enough to risk your life to write a book, is it?

[Pause]

JS: I suppose it's just that I'm a bit of a chancer, that's all.

And although I wish I had put it in more attractive terms, that's exactly what it was. I couldn't say why, but I thought I would probably survive; if I did, the benefits of seeing the war firsthand would be considerable in every way.

And if I didn't? Perhaps my upbringing has given me a rather Victorian view of life and death. I find it hard to accept the contemporary view that life of any kind, no matter how restricted and feeble, is better than no life at all. The thing doesn't seem to me to be worth clinging onto at all costs, regardless of its quality. Like an ancient Roman, I would prefer to get out while I'm ahead; and if that involves taking my chances in an air war of extraordinary proportions, so be it. I wouldn't like to be forgotten too soon, or ignored too completely, but once the party is over, it seems to me that one should know when to leave.

Strange though it seems, the usual Wednesday race-meeting took place on the afternoon of 16 January at the Baghdad Horsemanship Ground. I wanted to film it, but the Ministry of Information wouldn't give us permission. Perhaps they thought it detracted from the high seriousness of the moment.

The weather was beautiful. The blue sky was streaked with pink cirrus, and the dust thrown up by the horses' hooves was turned to gold by the late afternoon sun. The punters wore flat caps and tweed sports jackets over grubby white dishdashas, so that they looked as though they had been transported from Punchestown or Naas or some other Irish racetrack. They were as enthusiastic about the horses as ever, and crowded forward to bet at the Tote windows on Sheherezade or Lulu in the 4:10. I queued up to watch, but was reluctant to put any money down. To lose a bet would seem like a very bad omen indeed at a time like this.

"Is Ass-cot as nice as here?" someone asked me.

"Absolutely," I answered soothingly. Maybe in Iraqi terms it was: a place where you could get away from the horrible pressures of Saddam's Iraq. They drank local beer from the can, and wiped their mouths expressionlessly as they watched the favorite lead the field to the winning-post. At the Baghdad Horsemanship Ground, as in Iraqi elections, the favorite invariably wins. The betting depends on guessing which horses will come in second and third.

"There will be no war," said a big, sweating bookie with a brick of notes in his hand. "Nobody wants it."

It was a good job, I thought later, that he hadn't put any money on it.

That night I produced what I intended to be the best report I had ever done. It started off with some superbly elegiac pictures of the River Tigris enshrouded in mist; it contained moving, gentle shots of a group of Iraqi schoolgirls at their morning assembly, then moved on to the empty city with a cat running through the shot to tell my girlfriend, who liked cats, that I had been thinking of her, and went on to show the preparations ordinary Iraqis were making against air attack: taping their windows, and so on. Finally, over a sensational shot of the nighttime skyline of Baghdad, there came the sound of the first air-raid sirens of the war.

"That deserves an award," the picture editor said, as he spooled back to the start and pressed the "Eject" button. He was going off to satellite it to London.

I didn't really expect to live long enough to get an award. I thought it was more likely that I would be dead by the next evening, and I wanted my last report to be the best I had ever done. Back in London a few months later, having survived, I thought I would see what it looked like. When I watched it, I realized that the editor of the *Nine O'Clock News* must have decided that it was fifteen seconds too long, and some butcher of a sub-editor had chopped off the skyline and siren sequence, cobbling up my last words in the crudest possible fashion. No one had reflected, plainly, that this might be the final report of my life, or that I might have taken pride in the way it looked. I really think if I had been killed my affronted ghost would have haunted the *Nine O'Clock* desk forever. Some of these people, I reflected, had as much aesthetic sensitivity as Saddam Hussein himself.

There were seven of us in the BBC team, all committed to staying on no matter what happened. I had talked to them about it at intervals during the previous few days to make sure that they really wanted to be there, and that they knew they could leave at any moment. All of them had assured me they did. The team included Eamonn Matthews, who had had such an unpleasant time on our first visit to Baghdad, and Bob Simpson, the foreign news correspondent.

That evening, 16 January, the French and American organizations with teams in the Al-Rashid Hotel got in touch with them to say they had been told that the bombing would start that evening. We heard nothing from the British side; traditionally British governments regard British journalists as an unwanted burden, so it didn't surprise me. But the BBC too, seemed to have changed its mind about our being there, and had decided that we should leave Baghdad. One of the most senior figures in the Corporation, a good friend of mine, gave me my orders.

"You'll have to get yourself a new foreign affairs editor then," I said, my voice sounding harsh even in my own ears.

In the end he and I worked out a compromise. If I chose to disobey the instructions of the BBC he assured me that no disciplinary action would be taken against me.

"That's great," I replied. "We're about to face the biggest air bombardment in human history, so it's a real relief to know that there won't be any disciplinary action against us by the BBC."

While this conversation had been going on, though, another and rather rougher figure in the BBC hierarchy had been threatening some of the others much more effectively. They had been left with the clear impression that if they stayed on in Baghdad in direct defiance of his instructions, they would be regarded as having resigned from the Corporation. No compensation would be paid to their widows. Four of our team—including the entire technical staff, as it happened—decided that they couldn't disobey. By the time I came back into the room, they had made their minds up.

It was a serious shock. Here we were, about to face the biggest news event of my career, and our camera crew and picture editor were explaining to me that they wanted to leave the next morning. I could just about understand the reasoning of the camera crew, since they were both on the BBC staff and were both married. Yet I knew perfectly well that if the worst happened the BBC wouldn't really be able to cut their families off without a penny; opinion inside and outside the Corporation wouldn't stand for it. Anyway, the assurance I had received overrode the threats.

But I found the attitude of the picture editor quite incomprehensible. He was an Australian, young, tough and without a family, and he was a freelancer, hired in specifically to be part of the team that covered the war. Nothing had changed for him, except that he had contracted the general panic.

I felt personally let down, certainly—but the real problem was that I couldn't see how we could hope to compete effectively against ITN, if all these people left us. ITN had brought in a well-known cameraman, whose reputation was formidable. Perhaps he was a bit of a poseur—he had put bodybuilding stickers on his camera and was inclined to boast about having links with the Princess of Wales—but we would have no camera at all. What was the point of my staying, together with the television producer, Eamonn Matthews, when we would have nothing to work with? Yet there was no question about staying. I could see the same determination in the faces of Eamonn and Bob Simpson, and in some ways the defection of the others made the three of us all the more determined.

Eamonn and I hurried out to see if we could find anyone else who would work with us. We came across two disgruntled cameramen, both of whom had been badly treated by the organizations they were working for. Now, looking back, I regard them with great affection. One was a young man, Anthony Wood, who had been working for the now defunct breakfast television organization TV-AM. He had been sacked by them when, like me, he questioned his office's instructions to come home at once. His camera gear had belonged to the company and was being shipped out, but we had a small amateur video camera which he could use to get us some pictures. The other cameraman at a loose end was Nick della Casa, who was a freelancer and had been working for CBS. Poor Nick: he, his wife and brother-in-law were all murdered in northern Iraq a few months later when he was on a trip for the BBC.

Now, though, he was full of cheerfulness and a humorous resentment against CBS. They, like so many other organizations, had ordered him out, and when he had refused to leave they warned him that they would take no further responsibility for him. Nick had his own equipment, but it was designed for the American NTSC system (known without affection as "Never The Same Color") rather than for European PAL. Nor did he really like working with a group, to the instructions of a producer. Still, he and Anthony offered us at least the possibility of reporting on the world's most intensive bombing campaign. These considerations took up the last few hours of peace.

We had one other important advantage. I might be angry that the camera crew were going, but they had done us an enormous service, which in the end ensured the relative success of the BBC coverage of the early part of the war. When they had arrived in Baghdad, they had smuggled in a satellite telephone—strictly forbidden by the Iraqis. (The French and ITN had already imported satellite telephones legally.) The day before the war began, I had revealed the existence of our telephone at a meeting between the various English-speaking television groups and Najji al-Hadithi. It had had a gratifyingly explosive effect on everyone: Before my revelation, ITN and CNN both thought they had a major advantage over us, and Najji must have assumed that the BBC's broadcasts would be under government control.

It was obvious, though, that CNN had done a separate deal with the Iraqis, and soon afterward one of the main figures in the CNN group told me what had happened. (At that stage, when we were all facing an uncertain future together, there was a certain amount of mutual regard and solidarity in the air—not that it lasted long.) The CNN man explained to me that the Iraqi government had agreed to let them have use of a government communications system, a two-way telephone line called a four-wire, which ran in a protected culvert to the Jordanian border. It was likely to be immune to the general telecommunications jamming that the Americans were expected to carry out.

It was a Faustian pact, of course; the BBC certainly wouldn't have entertained such a thing. Nevertheless I don't believe CNN agreed to twist its reporting in any way in order to use the Iraqi four-wire. For Iraq it was enough to have an American television team operating in its capital during the war: anything Saddam Hussein wanted the outside world to know could be said via CNN, and the extent of the terrible destruction Saddam expected could be conveyed by its broadcasts.

It would be unfair to blame CNN for much of this, since it behaved exactly as any other commercial organization would. CNN's decision to stay in Baghdad and report from there seems to me to be perfectly reasonable; I would have wanted to stay there too, and when we were allowed to return to Baghdad I was a strong advocate of it. Since with the BBC, commercial interests aren't involved, I hope we wouldn't have tried to exclude CNN as CNN tried to exclude other Western news organizations. I hope too, that we wouldn't have tried to pretend that we were the only Western news organization in Baghdad. But these are small complaints, compared with the big issues at stake.

Later, ex-President George Bush and many of the newspapers on either side of the Atlantic were deeply critical of CNN, the BBC and other broadcasters who worked in Baghdad during the war. Yet even in wartime, broadcasters in a free society are not a co-opted branch of the military; their function is not and shouldn't be to keep up morale at home, nor to spread deliberate propaganda abroad.

If you are fighting in a good cause against those who wish to suppress truth and honesty—whether they are Nazis or the Iraqi government—it is the worst thing possible to suppress truth and honesty yourself. The results of the BBC's approach in the Second World War were of course remarkable. Not only did the civil population of Germany and the occupied countries listen to the BBC in preference to their own broadcasters, but the BBC's international reputation for honesty and unbiased reporting was established for the rest of the twentieth century.

The Gulf War was the making of CNN. Remaining in Baghdad when the world's other major organizations were forced to leave was a central—perhaps *the* central—part of that strategy. CNN denies strongly that it persuaded the Iraqis to throw everyone else out soon after the war began, and that it tried to stop them from being invited back some time later. In the absence of any other information, we shall have to accept CNN's word for it; though CNN has also denied that it used the Iraqi four-wire communication system. What we do know is that by establishing its preeminence in Baghdad, CNN became the television news leader in America.

After the long months of waiting, my war service in Baghdad was short and extremely violent. It began in the early hours of 17 January, soon after the crew had told me they were leaving and we had hired Anthony Wood and Nick della Casa. There was a yell of anger from Bob Simpson, the BBC radio correspondent, as his telephone line to London was cut. The Americans were starting to jam Iraqi communications: whatever was going to happen was just about to start. My mouth was dry, and I found myself picking at my fingers—a habit I thought I'd stopped. Remembering Saddam's forecast that there would be two enormously destructive waves of bombing, I felt distinctly nervous; but it was only the nervousness you feel before an important match, or a stage appearance.

At my suggestion, Anthony Wood and Eamonn and I headed out into the streets to film the start of the bombing. It was 2:32 A.M. We had two flak jackets among the three of us, and as the least useful person of the three I went without. I can't say it was much of a sacrifice. If Baghdad was about to be swallowed up in a tidal wave of high explosive, a flak jacket was about as much good as an extra pair of socks.

We ran across the crematorial lobby of the Al-Rashid. Outside it was cold and very silent. Most of the city lights had been switched off. Anthony had hired a driver for the night, but he turned out to be one of the most cowardly and feeble of them all. The rest, good and bad, had long since disappeared. We ran to his car, jumped in and slammed the doors.

"Drive! Drive! Drive!"

But drive where? We hadn't had time to work it out. Each of us shouted suggestions. I wanted to be in the heavily populated areas on the other side of the river, but I was afraid of crossing a bridge. All the bridges, we knew, would be bombed, and if we were stuck on the wrong side without any shelter we might well be lynched as spies.

We were still shouting when the darkness and silence exploded around us. There was an extraordinary racket, as the hidden guns and missile batteries started blasting off excitedly into the air. I remembered to look at my watch: 2:37. Red tracer flashed up in patterns beside us, lighting up the frightened, sweating face of our driver, and Eamonn peering through the window trying to see where we should go, and Anthony's face screwed into the side of the camera. Sirens started up everywhere. Our ears were besieged with waves of disorienting noise.

"I'm getting this, I'm getting this," Anthony yelled.

The car took a sharp turn into an underpass, its wheels squealing, and came out on the other side just as a battery of rockets exploded beside us.

I'm glad you are, I thought. I could see what was happening: the driver was so frightened, he was heading straight back to the hotel. We were going on a mile-long circle, with nothing to show for it but a few flashing lights in the sky and some spectacular noise. As for the bombing, it hadn't even started. This was just a display of nervousness by the Iraqi gunners. The driver, utterly consumed by panic now, screeched up to the front door of the hotel and ran in, leaving the door of the car open. We tried briefly to set up our camera in front of the main door, just as the first rumblings of aircraft—our aircraft, friendly aircraft—became audible over the excitability of the Iraqis. We were in for it now, I thought.

But we had no chance of staying outside. The big security guards of the *Mukhabarat,* vicious bruisers, many of them, hauled us inside. It was completely dark, and people were screaming. I lost touch with the others, and was forced at gunpoint down the narrow staircase that led to the underground shelter, shoved from behind into the crowd of people who were already pushing one another in an excess of panic. All I needed was for one person to slip, I thought. This was disastrous: my worst nightmare. Outside, now, you could hear the first bombs and missiles falling. The whole building juddered as they landed nearby. So far, though, nothing seemed to have hit us. Far better, I had said to the others, to be on one of the upper floors than to be packed down the basement. Especially if one of those concrete-burrowing bombs hit the hotel on its way down to find Saddam's bunker. This place would become a liquidizer, a people-blender. No, I thought, put images like that away, or you'll start shouting and pushing too. The heat and press of bodies and the darkness were horrible; and now the women, in particular, were starting to wail.

I tried to keep as calm as I could, allowing myself to be buffeted but refusing to start lashing out as some of the other men were doing. Down in the corridor, which was seething with people, there was a little emergency lighting. Fine, I thought, now you can see well enough to find Anthony. I craned over the heads of the frightened crowd, and saw him a little way ahead of me. When I caught up with him, all he was worried about was whether he'd got the pictures properly. Armageddon was going on outside, but he was worried whether his new employers would approve of his work.

We were swept past a short flight of stairs to a room, set a little higher than the corridor itself. On these steps stood the ITN correspondent and his cameraman. In this maelstrom of emotions and superb pictures, the cameraman's eyes were bright red and his camera was pointing at the ceiling. He wasn't filming anything. I needn't be worried anymore about the capability of the bodybuilding hero.

"You fucking coward," the correspondent was raging. He was a man I had good reason not to like, but there was nothing scared about him.

"I just can't," moaned the cameraman. I thought he might start weeping, but I was swept past them before I could hear any more.

I met up with Anthony again in one of the vast underground rooms that were being used as shelters. It smelled of fear. People were gathered all around the walls in little groups, lying or sitting, terrified or weeping or trying to come to terms with what had happened to them. The old rules that applied on the surface seemed not to work down here. I saw a young woman undressing in front of everyone, and neither she nor anyone else seemed to pay any attention. Children wept or defecated; old men and women sat looking at the floor, too frightened to do anything. And all the time, it seemed, the structure of the hotel, fifty feet above our heads, shook and shivered with the bombing.

Anthony and I fought our way out at last. Neither of us could stand to be in this living tomb any longer: we needed the cold air of the surface. A guard armed with a Kalashnikov tried to stop us, but I fought my way past him in the dark. We ran up the five flights of stairs to the BBC office, catching glimpses at each landing of the extraordinary battle that was going on outside. We couldn't stop: heavy footsteps showed that someone was chasing us.

The office was in complete darkness, and it was hard to find in the anonymous corridor. It was silent inside. The others, who were hiding there, had heard us and assumed we were from the *Mukhabarat*. The familiar room looked utterly different, lit up by green and white and red flashes from outside. Up here there was less vibration, and the missiles seemed to be landing a little way away from us. I crouched in front of the window and got one of the other cameramen to record a piece to camera for me. He had to shine his battery light on me, which was an alarming experience; any Iraqi soldier who saw it from the outside might think we were signaling to the planes, and might put a heavy round through the window. It had to be done; but I was relieved to get through it just the once, without needing a retake.

The man from the *Mukhabarat* must have heard my voice, and he started banging on the door. I thought I'd have to get out, so that the others could carry on with their work. I ran out, charging toward him along the beam of his torch, and dodged into a room that seemed to be empty. Once inside I locked the door, then went through several interconnecting doors till, in the light from the missiles and the anti-aircraft guns outside, I could see there was a bed. I lay down on it. Beside me was a little shortwave radio. I switched it on: whoever owned it had been listening to the BBC.

I heard the calm voice of the announcer in London telling me that the war had started, and the equally calm voice of President Bush explaining to me why it was such a good idea for so much high explosive to be dropped on my head. It's all right for you, I thought. Close by, a two-thousand-pound penetration bomb dropped and burrowed its way into the earth: the whole structure shook. One of the Americans had told me that when this happened all the fillings would be shaken out of your teeth if you were within a couple of hundred yards. I ran my tongue around the fillings: they were all there still. My watch said 5:45. I fell asleep.

Eamonn woke me up three hours later, beating on the door. He had been out on the hotel grounds, putting up our satellite phone. The guards were too demoralized to stop us going out, and we brushed past them as we ran. Thank God I won't be in vision, I thought, as I smoothed my hair down and did up the buttons of my shirt.

The gardens of the hotel were completely transformed. Little groups of journalists were gathered round the white umbrella-like dishes for satellite phones—three of them in all. This was no band of brothers: we were competing more fiercely with one another than at any time in the past few months. As for CNN, they were inside with their comfortable Iraqi four-wire.

For the time being, the skies were blue and empty except for occasional puffs of smoke from speculative ground-to-air missiles, and the gunfire was sporadic. I did a first telephone report about what I had seen in the night, but felt worried that I couldn't answer questions about what state Baghdad was in this morning.

So Anthony and I went out again; dodging the exhausted guards wasn't as difficult as I'd expected. We found a driver and went off across the still undamaged bridge to the center of the city. It was empty, quiet, and very strange. Our car was one of the very few in the streets, and there were scarcely any people to be seen: a woman trailing a weeping child, a few old men and women selling oranges. Here and there entire buildings had been snuffed out of existence—important government buildings, *Mukhabarat* centers or Ba'ath Party headquarters—and yet those on either side of them were mostly undamaged, and sometimes still had all their glass in the windows. A local telephone exchange, a smallish building opposite a hotel, was nothing more than a heap of rubble; the hotel was still completely usable.

A couple of hours later, a friend of mine who had been caught out in the darkness told me that she had seen strange red lights playing on the target buildings. British and perhaps American special forces had penetrated the city and were guiding in the missiles with infrared lamps; hence the extraordinary precision.

As we drove around, the driver spotted a *Mukhabarat* car.

"Allah! He see you take picture."

The unmarked white car picked up speed, overtook us and forced us to stop. I got out.

"Morning," I said. "Just looking around. I'm sure you don't mind."

He did mind. He ordered us to follow him. I could see Anthony was as determined as I was not to go. The unmarked car went ahead and we followed. We crossed the bridge as though we were going back to our hotel, but the police car signaled that it was going to take the right fork, to *Mukhabarat* headquarters: not at all a good destination.

Now, though, the sirens were wailing again, and the Defense Ministry a quarter of a mile away along the river bank vanished in a pillar of brown smoke. You couldn't hear the cruise missiles coming: You could only see the results.

"Go straight on, Ali," I hissed at the driver. "Don't turn. Go there."

I tried to look ferocious: Ali had to be more frightened of me at that moment than he was of the secret police. It did the trick. The *Mukhabarat* car turned right, and we sped straight ahead, the hotel only a few hundred yards away now. The missiles were falling again and the futile sound of anti-aircraft fire was everywhere. It must have taken the secret policeman a minute or so to realize what had happened, and another minute to turn; but as we raced into the car park the white car was already entering the hotel gates. Ali was safe enough: he told the police I had threatened to cut his throat. Technically it was a lie, but he had interpreted me right.

Upstairs I found the four BBC people who had decided to leave. I guessed by now that this was what the entire war would be like: fought out with weapons so accurate that unless our hotel was targeted we would be moderately safe. I hoped my colleagues would realize this too, and change their minds about going; but I wasn't going to beg them to stay. They didn't, even though the first night had been just about as dangerous as it got for us.

One of the four, who happened to be looking out of the window, called out in amazement. He had seen a cruise missile pass along the line of the road toward the center of the city, at about our level on the fifth floor. Some time later I saw one myself, which actually turned left at the traffic lights and followed the road that the white police car had wanted us to take. Maybe it hit the *Mukhabarat* headquarters itself; if so, it was even better that we hadn't gone there. Soon afterward I went down to the hotel garden, where the satellite dishes had been set up. I felt I had enough to say to the special program that was just starting on the BBC. It must have been around nine in the morning, London time.

TRANSCRIPT OF INTERVIEW FROM BAGHDAD, 17.1.91

Speakers: David Dimbleby, John Simpson

DD: We have our foreign affairs editor, John Simpson, on the line from Baghdad. John, what's happening there at present?

JS: I can hear quite loud sounds of gunfire or landings of rockets or missiles, I'm not quite sure what it is at the moment. The aircraft seem to be so high, and the missiles make remarkably little noise. An extraordinary thing happened, I suppose about an hour ago now. We were looking out of the window of our fifth floor room in the hotel, and a missile of some kind, a Tomahawk—I don't know, I'm not very good at these things—passed by on the line of the road on which the hotel stands, at about the level of our windows.

This is the first time anyone's seen a war like this. It wasn't what we expected, to be honest. I've covered quite a lot of wars in my time, but I thought this one was going to be horrendous; or at least I thought it was going to be last night. It's turned out not to be so horrendous, and it's the accuracy of the missiles and the bombs which makes it less threatening than one thought.

I didn't want to become an apologist for the war. But these words of mine were seen by both the pro- and anti-war factions as making the case for a new type of warfare, which was somehow neat and tidy and didn't cause much bloodshed. Until the terrible bombing of the al-Amiriyah shelter, in which hundreds of innocent women and children died, it's true that civilian casualties were minimal. I'm skeptical now whether it was worth fighting the Gulf War at all; though I am certain that the greed and carelessness of a number of countries, and particularly Britain, allowed Saddam Hussein to build up an unthinkably large arsenal of weapons before the war began.

But what is incontrovertible is that it was the first major war since 1918 in which killing ordinary people wasn't the main purpose. Those who disliked the war didn't want to hear this. Nor did they want to hear that when I went back to Baghdad after the war, and managed to get around most of the city thanks to the feebleness of the minders and the secret police, I counted only twenty-nine buildings destroyed; though those that had been targeted had been hit time and again.

The four BBC people left, together with about twenty or thirty others including the ITN cameraman. They even insisted on taking the two flak jackets, which were the only protection we had, on the grounds that having signed for them in London they might have to pay for them if they weren't returned. No one mentioned the circumstances under which they might not be returned.

So now there were fewer than forty of us left: a team from the Canadian Broadcasting Corporation, plus eleven British, eight French, three Italians, a Spaniard, an Australian, a New Zealander, a Turk, five Americans, and a couple of Jordanians. The French and the British were at loggerheads, and I scarcely spoke to the ITN correspondent. As for CNN, they rejected any request to use their broadcasting line with extraordinary ferocity.

We didn't feel safe, either. We knew now that we could survive the level of attack that had been directed at Baghdad so far, but that was all. On the second night the Americans told CNN that they were going to hit the Al-Rashid Hotel. Fortunately, if that really had been the decision, someone changed it. Even so, we all felt that we would rather die in our beds than end our lives in that terrible shelter with all those panic-stricken Iraqis. The other time I felt real fear was when I heard that Iraq had fired its Scud missiles at Israel. What if the Israelis retaliated with nuclear weapons? Yet there is a definite comfort in powerlessness. I had lost any great interest in surviving: I just wanted to see as much as I could and report it. There was absolutely nothing else I could do, so I might as well enjoy myself. I opened another tin of oysters, poured myself a glass of Laphroaig single-malt whisky, read a little Evelyn Waugh by candlelight, and woke up each morning to find myself unbombed and still alive.

The Al-Rashid had ceased to function as a hotel: there was no electric light, no heat, no power, no water, no food. You could tell which rooms were occupied by the smell coming from them. I moved from empty room to empty room, using a different lavatory each night. Out in the hotel garden where we had set up the satellite phones a large pool of sewage had formed, and every time a missile struck or a bomb landed the surface of the pool shook with the vibrations. Eventually you could tell when the planes were coming, because tiny ripples appeared round the pool's edges. Day and night the raids went on, but we scarcely bothered about them now. We realized that the missiles could loop around high buildings like the Al-Rashid.

We had established a kind of pattern now. Directly the air-raid sirens went, the minders and security men would run inside for the shelter of the hotel while we would run outside to start broadcasting without interference from them. We would usually pass them on the way, but they were too frightened and embarrassed to take any notice. One afternoon the sirens went while I was in my room. I ran down the corridor toward the emergency exit in the total darkness and cannoned into the sharp corner of a wooden desk. I cracked a couple of ribs, and lay there in the dark for a while. Then I managed to get downstairs. It was very painful.

Overhead a sensational battle was being fought between the American and British aircraft and the Iraqi ground-to-air missiles. There were explosions all across the sky. Chaff was thrown out, bombs fell, missiles exploded. I was desperate to get on air with an eyewitness account of it all, but a voice in the studio at the other end told me sharply that they had just begun a fourteen-minute report on domestic political reaction to the war and couldn't interrupt it. By the time the fourteen minutes were up and the local politicians had finished droning, the battle was over. The sky had cleared almost completely. When the moderator came on the line I was in a furious temper, both as a result of the pain in my ribs and the foolish waste of a wonderful broadcasting opportunity.

TRANSCRIPT OF INTERVIEW FROM BAGHDAD, 18.1.91

Speakers: David Dimbleby, John Simpson

DD: What's been happening?

JS: If you'd been able to join me a few minutes ago, I could have given you a description of an extraordinary overhead battle that's been going on here. As it is, it's completely over, I'm afraid.

DD: Do you have any information about casualties?

JS: I'm the only casualty I know about. I cracked a couple of ribs when I made contact with a rather large desk which someone had left in a darkened hallway in the hotel.

Some of the newspapers in Britain decided that this was a coded message to show that I had been beaten up by the Iraqis; and so, while an entire country's economic infrastructure was being blasted away, part at least of the British press was concerning itself with a mild injury to a couple of my ribs.

The Iraqis were only occasionally aggressive towards us. Most of the minders and security men were so reluctant to be out in the open with us that they didn't seem to care what we said. In fact it is my settled belief that most of them were praying that Saddam would be killed or overthrown as a result of the war. It seemed to me that the Coalition powers had a great deal to be grateful to the Iraqis for. If Saddam's army had fought in the way he had intended, there could have been large-scale losses for the Americans, the British, the Saudis and the French. As it was, they scarcely put up a token fight, because they didn't want to support him.

Sometimes, though, the security men could be rough. Once we were ordered inside while I was still broadcasting. I pretended that I was trying to close down the satellite phone, while in fact continuing to broadcast on it. The guard came over and started getting aggressive. I asked him if he could understand how to work it; and since he couldn't speak English I was able to get a few more sentences out before I thought he would start pulling his gun. Another time, as one of the minders was shouting at me to get inside, I told him to calm down.

"There's nothing to worry about," I said soothingly. "There's absolutely no danger out here."

At that moment there was a thick, spinning sound in the air, and a large-caliber bullet landed beside me on the steps.

"Huh—what do you think that is?" the minder said, and snatched it up angrily as a souvenir. It was still warm.

That afternoon the Information Ministry told us we would have to leave Iraq. The chief minder insisted that CNN would be going too, and it was only at the last minute that we realized for certain this was a lie. I tried to persuade the hotel doctor to say that I was in too much pain with my ribs. He gave me a note, which said in English:

TO WHOME IT MAY CONCERN. MR SIMPSON HAS TWO/ THREE CRACKED RIB AND MUSLE SPASME. HE CAN NOT DRIVE IN CAR FROM IRAQ.

Underneath he wrote in Arabic: "No problem—he can travel." So that was the end of another good idea.

Before we left, the area around the hotel was attacked by cruise missiles. Anthony got his little camera and started filming from the window of our room. Two of the missiles went around the hotel and hit the conference center opposite, which was one of the entrances to Saddam Hussein's bunker. Another was damaged by anti-aircraft fire and plunged into the hotel grounds. At the height of the action I recorded a quick piece to camera, with my back to the window. There was a terrible racket outside, but the people in the room were sitting here completely immobile and silent. Then Bob Simpson spoke.

"It went right behind you while you were talking. It was a cruise."

But there was no time to talk about it. Anthony and I went charging downstairs to film the damage done by the missile that had crashed. It had ploughed into the staff quarters, which were well ablaze by the time we got there. Fortunately no one had been in the huts at the time and there were no casualties. As we were filming, we were jumped on by four security men. We fought them for a while, but in the end one of them got hold of the camera and took the cassette out. I ran after him and almost got close enough to rugby-tackle him, but I was held back by the others and he escaped with the cassette. It didn't just contain the pictures of the crashed missile; it also had my piece to camera with the cruise passing behind my head. I felt as though I had lost a picture of the Loch Ness Monster.

At last we were forced to leave. For me, it was a long and very painful journey, not merely because of the ribs but because I was convinced that our material had not made it through to Amman, while ITN's had. I spent the ten-hour journey jolting around on terrible roads in some gloom, certain that I had been badly beaten on the most important story I had ever covered. A BBC reporter was sent out to meet me at the border, and I suggested to him that I should just slip into the hotel and go to bed. He seemed surprised.

We drove up to the Marriott Hotel in Amman, and I got out rather unsteadily. A dozen flashbulbs went off in my face; I couldn't really grasp it all. It turned out that, far from being in disgrace, we had done rather well. The BBC crew who had left Baghdad had successfully managed to smuggle our pictures through, while ITN's had been confiscated from their fleeing cameraman by the Iraqis at the border. And the telephone broadcasts in which I had been in turn excited, bad-tempered and deceptive to the security man had been broadcast to immense audiences. I hadn't just arrived in Amman; after a quarter of a century's reporting, I seemed to have arrived altogether.

11
The Mountain of Light

For never did chief more sorely need Heaven for his aid and stay
Than the man who would reign in this country, and tame for a day
Afghans.
— Sir Alfred Lyall, *The Amir's Soliloquy*, 1880

Foreign correspondents, like pilots and soldiers, have a tendency to superstition. They think that if they carry the right things in their pockets, or go through some private little ritual, they can protect themselves from violence, bad luck and the wrath of their editors. If they get shot, you can't say to them, "See, your system doesn't work," because they just reply, "It would've been far worse if I hadn't had my lucky coin, or worn my lucky white suit," or whatever.

I'm not superstitious. I may carry the occasional lucky stone or go through a little ritual or two when I leave for a difficult assignment; but if I leave the stone at home, or get distracted halfway through the ritual, I don't worry. I know that none of these things matters in the slightest, thanks to a journey I made to Kabul in 1989.

One rainy morning in London, in January that year, I had a call from the editor of the *Panorama* program inviting me to his office.

"Can we have a chat about Afghanistan?"

At that stage the Russians were just about to pull out of the country after ten years of a brutal war of occupation. I knew little about it, apart from what I had seen in the news bulletins. But I remembered a poem I had had to learn when I was eleven: *The Amir's Soliloquy*, written by a grand old Indian Civil Service poet of the nineteenth century, Sir Alfred

Lyall. It was probably the best background material I could want. It's all about the tribal divisions of Afghanistan and the impossibility of governing the place. In his palace at the Bala Hissar in Kabul the unfortunate amir who has to do it indulges in a gloomy soliloquy:

> I look from a fort half-ruined on Kabul spreading below,
>> On the near hills crowned with cannon, and the far hills piled with snow;
> Fair are the vales well watered, and the vines on the upland swell,
>> You might think you were reigning in Heaven—I know I am ruling Hell.
> For there's hardly a room in my palace but a kinsman there was killed,
>> And never a street in the city but with false fierce curs is filled
> With a mob of priests, and fanatics, and all my mutinous host;
>> They follow my steps, as the wolves do, for a prince who slips is lost.

A purist might complain about the scansion, but anyone who knows anything about Afghanistan could see that old Sir Alfred had got everything else dead right. The idea of going there appealed greatly to me; but as I opened the editor's door I found myself crossing my fingers. It was something I still did in those superstitious days.

Inside, sipping BBC tea from styrofoam cups, were two characters who looked like quintessential empire-builders. They were both cameramen in their early thirties who specialized in covering Afghanistan. One of them, Chris Hooke, was a tall, rangy Australian who had first gone there in 1984. The other, Peter Jouvenal, was fair-haired, English, and had a moustache straight out of a sepia regimental photograph. After serving in the army he had hitchhiked to Afghanistan in 1980, working first as a photographer and then as a cameraman. The two of them, together with several others of a similar kind, had based themselves in Peshawar on the Pakistani side of the Khyber Pass, and had produced the best coverage of the war.

The editor of *Panorama* handed me a document. *The Fall of Kabul*, it said. It was a program proposal by Chris and Peter.

> When the last Soviet combat unit crosses the Oxus and reaches the safety of home soil the Afghan war will enter its last phase. The Russians leave behind them a client regime, weak and divided, dependent upon a demoralized army of no more than 70,000. Set against this is a muja-heddin force, also divided, of roughly 200,000, whose morale has never been higher. Their final offensive will inevitably lead to the collapse of the Afghan army, the destruction of the Communist regime and the fall of the capital, Kabul. This film will document the mujaheddin's final offensive.

"I thought this might appeal to you," said the editor casually, as he fiddled with a pen on his desk. He didn't look at me.

He needn't have worried. The traveling I had done over the previous few years had mostly been pretty tame stuff, and I needed something a little stronger. Afghanistan was unquestionably it.

Chris and Peter weren't making us a cheap offer: television documentaries are expensive. Pinned to the back of the synopsis was a budget summary:

Salaries—production staff	£38,400
Salaries—technical staff	5,070
Equipment	29,880
Video stock	2,350
Travel and transport	9,210
Living expenses	4,880
Insurance	1,450
Location admin & expenses	1,200
Contingency 5%	4,622
Production cost total	£97,062

The total was approximately $135,000 in 1989 dollars. It would be a good deal more than that now, and it went well over budget. But it was money well spent. The BBC won prizes and a great deal of praise for the finished documentary, and sold it around the world. It became the standard work on the subject. Yet the subject proved not to be the fall of Kabul, but the reason why Kabul failed to fall.

As we sat there discussing the idea, Chris and Peter ran through the mujaheddin groups and their racial and religious origins. It would have been hard to keep all the savage-sounding names in my head without the help of Sir Alfred Lyall:

> And far from the Suleiman Heights come the sounds of the
>   stirring of tribes,
>   Afreedi, Hazara and Ghilzai, they clamour for plunder and
>   bribes;
> And Herat is but held by thread, and the Uzbek has raised
>   Badukshan;
>   And the chief may sleep sound, in his grave, who would rule
>   the unruly Afghan.

Not an awful lot had changed in Afghanistan since the 1870s, I could see. Except of course the firepower.

It sounded highly dangerous and highly romantic, in roughly equal proportions. I leaped at it, and a few weeks later, equipped with the best boots, anoraks and long silk underwear money could buy, we arrived in Peshawar, in Pakistan. There were four of us: Chris and Peter, myself, and a *Panorama* producer. It was Eamonn Matthews, who was to go to Baghdad with me the following year.

The snow did nothing to soften the sharp edges of the Hindu Kush as we flew in. I tried to imagine myself climbing those ridges and working my way through the passes, but the effort was too great. Yet merely looking up at them from the comfortable hotel I was staying at made my heart lift inside me. This was the North-West Frontier: the jagged lines of the landscape, the sharpness of the light, and the thin, pure air were a powerful lift to the spirit.

It wasn't just the landscape. When I went to the bazaar in Peshawar to buy some Afghan clothes, I found the muddy alleyways jammed with tall, hawk-nosed, villainous-looking characters in long robes and green and silver turbans, striding around with a characteristic rolling walk that made them look as though they owned the place.

This was a different world. There was a fiercer reality here, a sense of being beyond petty comforts like the rule of law, or British consulates, or insurance policies, or hospitals, or BBC administrators. These men weren't necessarily noble savages at all. Many were treacherous thieves, and outside the bazaar there were pathetic bundles of rags in the last stages of opium addiction, huddled over a one-rupee opium reefer. Life here was lived as it always had been: you were on your own, with only your strength and cunning to help you. That, like the cruel landscape, was where the real exhilaration lay. In contrast to the peaceable, safe life of the developed world, where most people never see a fight, let alone a dead body, I found it profoundly liberating.

Our expedition to Afghanistan was something Sir Richard Burton himself might have enjoyed. And since it was played out against a magnificent backdrop of mountains and villages that had scarcely changed since the days of *The Amir's Soliloquy*, it had a remarkably historical quality, as though it were all happening in 1889 rather than a century later, and we were players in the Great Game, the old competition between Russia and Britain in Central Asia. I probably enjoyed it more in retrospect than I did at the time; yet even then I knew I was experiencing one of the high points in my professional life, a period of sustained excitement and danger.

We traveled along the border between Afghanistan and Pakistan, to the high valley at Ali Mangal, where many of the Afghan mujaheddin groups had their base camps. Some, especially the fanatical Hezb-e-Islami, were hostile and mistrustful, and we had to be extremely careful even going near their camp. They had murdered several journalists, including a BBC cameraman. Our plan had been to join up with Hezbe and follow its subtle, treacherous leader, Gulbuddin Hekmatyar, in the race for Kabul. It soon became clear, though, that they would never agree to accept us and were best avoided. It didn't matter. Hezbe might be good at murdering journalists but they weren't much good at fighting, and their forces would play only a small part in the battles that lay ahead.

Other groups seemed to be rooted in exile, interested in picking up money and supplies from the Pakistani and American governments but not really in going back to take power. Others again were fawning and crafty; the BBC Pashtu and Farsi language services are listened to by just about every adult male Afghan, so there was huge kudos to be gained by any organization that took us with them in their search for power. We made our contacts with them and met their representatives, but I found it hard to know which to trust. We slept night after night in a barrack-like hut as the guests of men from a large middle-of-the-road organization: reliable enough, but not particularly noted as fighters and with no apparent interest in the race for Kabul. If there even was one.

One evening we came across a small Shi'ite Muslim organization called Harakat-e-Islami. There was something about the stocky little men who belonged to it that inspired trust. They looked very different from the usual tall, hawk-featured Pashtuns who belonged to the other groups: Harakat's people had Mongolian features, broad faces with high cheekbones, and they claimed descent from the Hazara, the thousand troops whom Genghis Khan had left behind to garrison Afghanistan as he made his way westward, conquering and destroying everything he found.

There was a particularly impressive figure among the group we met, who was treated with great respect by the others. They called him Mahmoud. He was taller and bulkier, but he had their high cheekbones and slanted eyes. He looked at you straight, and had an open, easy laugh. I sat next to him, cross-legged, on the floor of the mud-built hut that served as Harakat's headquarters, drinking little cups of strong, bitter tea. His English was basic but easy to understand.

"You know," he said quietly to me, "our people are everywhere in Kabul. They sweep the floors, they clean out the wastepaper bins. They find all the government's secrets." He paused for a moment. Then he added in a lower voice, "They are also inside the Khad headquarters. You know what is Khad?"

I did. Khad was the Soviet-trained secret police, which ran Kabul now that the Russians had withdrawn.

"If you come with us, we will show you everything Khad does. We will drive you through Kabul in the car which belongs to the commander of Khad. We will show you Harakat people who are in important positions in Khad. Will you come with us?"

The questions were still running through my mind as we climbed down the wooden ladder that was the only entrance to the hut. Could we trust Mahmoud? If Harakat had infiltrated Khad, couldn't Khad have infiltrated Harakat? On the other hand, how could we turn down this brilliant offer, to ride through the streets of Kabul in the Khad commander's car?

> Is it not passing brave to be a king
> And drive in triumph through Persepolis?

I had already decided that this trip would have to be undertaken in the spirit of Victorian travelers like Burton or Sir Samuel Baker. There was no point in holding back or in looking for safeguards here. Forget the mortgage, the children, the group pension scheme; if you got it wrong you would be lucky if someone scraped a hole for you in the stony ground and piled a few rocks over you. In these mountains, with these people, you had to rely on your judgment and your luck.

"I think we can trust them," I said to Eamonn, as we walked away.

There was no possible way of checking up: to have talked about Harakat's offer with any of the other Afghan groups, each of which was in a state of ferocious rivalry with every other, would have been to invite instant betrayal. I suppose what really decided me was the tough appearance of Harakat, Genghis Khan's men, and their romantic history. The sensible, responsible journalist in me, the BBC executive, finally bowed out at this moment, and the adventurer took over entirely. It wasn't really our job to infiltrate Kabul in disguise or to investigate the claims of any particular group; we were here to make a sober assessment of the mujaheddin's chances of seizing power once the Russians had left. It was just that I guessed this would make superb television; and in the long run I was right.

In the end, sitting on the floor of our hut and eating the MREs which the Americans had donated to the mujaheddin and which they had used contemptuously to fill in the holes in the road (Peter and Chris, always thrifty, had collected up the undamaged packs) we decided to split up. Since I was willing to trust Harakat I would go with them to Kabul, and Peter Jouvenal would come with me. Eamonn Matthews and Chris Hooke would trek off through the Hindu Kush to meet the legendary Ahmad Shah Massoud, the man who had defended the Panshir Valley for more than a decade against the most determined assault of the Soviet army. Our journey seemed likely to be more risky; theirs would be much more arduous.

We drove into Afghanistan as a group, and were quite close to Kabul when, a couple of mornings later, we shook hands in the snow and split up, two and two. The others watched us climb into the little pickup truck that Harakat had arranged for us. I turned round as we bucketed along the icy road: they were still standing there in the distance, waving. It didn't seem altogether likely that we would see each other again.

The more time I spent with Peter Jouvenal, the more I liked him. He could be taciturn and stiff-upper-lipped in an early Victorian kind of way, but he was good company too: just so long as you didn't tempt fate. If you said something careless like, "We seem to be getting on quite well now," Peter would get furious; and directly if things did go wrong it would be your fault.

I was pretty nervous anyway, because of something that had happened back in Peshawar just as we were leaving, at the very start of our expedition. I was sitting in the passenger seat of our vehicle, and the driver shoved the gear lever a little too roughly into reverse as we left the driveway of the house where we had been staying. The vehicle jerked backwards, and the glove compartment came open, shooting a book that had been inside it onto my lap. I looked down. The title of the book was *Kabul Catastrophe*. If someone were trying to give me a message, then this was undoubtedly it. I kept quiet and shoved the book back into the glove compartment, but there were moments over the next few weeks when I remembered the incident with a real feeling of discomfort.

For the time being, though, there was no catastrophe. We bundled along through the mountain passes and down into the plain that separates Kabul from the Hindu Kush. The stark, black rock of the mountain ridges showed through the brilliant snow, and the road lay yellow with mud before us. Nothing had changed here since Roberts fought his way north from Kandahar; not even the houses ringed with sallow trees and protected by high walls, all made of this same mud. They were primitive places (we stayed in a couple of them, lying on straw, and ate thin unleavened bread and dried apricots for dinner and breakfast) yet they were strong enough to withstand the violence of the late twentieth century. Russian tanks, passing this way, had often fired their big guns at the walls, but the sheer mass of packed mud absorbed the shock without cracking or crumbling.

There had been a lot of fighting. Beside every track, outside every shell-blasted house, there were little heaps of rocks surmounted by a bamboo pole with a few green and white rags fluttering from it: the graves of people who had died fighting the Russians, or perhaps just other Afghans. All very Alfred Lyall.

May he rest, the Amir Sher Ali, in his tomb by the holy shrine;
　The virtues of God are pardon and pity, they never were mine;
They have never been ours, in a kingdom all stained with the
　　blood of our kin,
　Where the brothers embrace in the war-field, and the reddest
　　sword must win.

As for people, they were few and far between: just the occasional Pashtun wearing a turban and *shalwar kameez*, with a blanket wrapped around him and the inevitable Kalashnikov automatic rifle in his hand. Sometimes we saw a few brightly dressed children in the villages we passed, but never a woman, not even an old one.

Mahmoud, the Harakat leader, brought us at last to a higher, snowier valley: Sanglakh. Our vehicle stopped, and swarms of stocky, willing men in mujaheddin uniform gathered round us, grinning and taking our equipment, and ran up the steep side of the mountain to a series of caves a hundred feet or so above us. It took me, in my mid-forties, rather longer to get there. When I arrived, I found myself in the literature of my boyhood. The main cave was full of dark, turbaned characters sitting in a line on blankets. There were pictures of the Prophet Mohammed and the Holy Shrine at Mecca on the walls, in between racks of guns. The turbaned characters were leaning against low wooden lockers that contained ammunition: tens of thousands of rounds of it.

"*Asalaam aleykum,*" I said politely, Peace be upon you, and once again had that feeling of being a character in a Kipling short story.

"*Aleykum asalaam,*" they murmured gravely: Upon you be peace.

By the light of hurricane lamps tea was passed round in an enormous enameled kettle, and from some unimaginable Pakistani source there were sweet biscuits. There were also questions, which Mahmoud translated.

"Why," asked an old man so deep in the recesses of the cave that I could scarcely see him, "does England allow the Holy Prophet's name to be insulted?"

It was said quite conversationally: there seemed to be no anger behind it. A week earlier there had been rioting in Pakistan over Salman Rushdie's book *The Satanic Verses,* and even here in their distant cave in the Sanglakh Valley the Harakat leaders had heard all about it from the BBC.

I explained as best I could the Western notion of free speech; not something your average Afghan warrior readily understands: there was a polite silence, then someone asked if I personally thought the book should be published. It was a difficult moment, but I thought they would be shrewd enough to realize if I merely soft-soaped them. So I gritted my teeth and went for it.

"A famous philosopher once said, 'I hate what you say but I will defend your right to say it with my life.' "

The friendly features turned disapproving, frowning in the yellow lamplight.

"After all," I added, searching for an argument they might appreciate, "you're Shi'a Muslims. You have no reason to love Sunni Muslims, yet you fought the Russians to protect them. It doesn't mean you have become more sympathetic to Sunni Islam."

A little murmur of surprise and pleasure went round the cave. If you talked approvingly about religion and fighting, I found, you could never go far wrong with Afghans. After that they were a little more inclined to give me the benefit of the doubt.

At four thirty in the morning, a few days later, I was awakened with a rough shake to the shoulder, and a whisper. I hadn't slept much, and even though we were in pitch darkness I knew instantly where I was: in a house in a village outside Kabul. Now we were going to be smuggled through the outer defenses and into the city itself. Feeling around, I grabbed one of the plastic bags I'd brought and quickly stuffed some essentials into it. Peter brought the little tourist video camera he was planning to use in Kabul. We made our way silently into the street.

Kabul was entirely ringed by small army posts, fifty or so yards apart, and all night long the sentries in them kept up a weird wailing to let the posts on either side of them know that they were still alive and hadn't gone over to the enemy. We crept forward in the darkness, Peter and I side by side, with Mahmoud just in front to guide us. As we were passing between two of the posts, the wailing died away; and in that instant of silence my wretched electronic wristwatch beeped: it was exactly five o'clock. The guards seemed not to notice; the next moment they were wailing as before.

We came out onto a road, with the darkness a little less intense. By the time we reached the first police post there was enough light to check our gear. I looked down. The plastic bag I had brought with me was blue and green, and looked disturbingly familiar. BOOKS FROM HEFFERS OF CAMBRIDGE, it announced in large letters. There was a policeman up ahead, standing at the barrier; how could he fail to spot the bag? However could he think that Peter Jouvenal and I were Afghans? What would he do?

We walked on. To waver or turn back would be to invite a bullet in the head. I gripped the Heffers' bag tighter. We were almost level with the policeman now. Somehow I couldn't avoid looking him in the eye. But his gaze faltered and fell away from mine: a mujaheddin sympathizer, maybe.

A red Kabul taxi was waiting for us farther on, and it drove us to one of the main roads of the city. We got out there and climbed into a large and very official-looking jeep with several aerials on its roof. The driver grinned.

"Car of commander of Khad," he said.

Peter and I looked at each other: Harakat, after all our doubts, had come up with the goods. We rattled along the road and stopped outside the British embassy, which was closed and empty, and our minder insisted that we get out and walk up and down while Peter filmed. Then we drove on, past the Russian embassy and the defense ministry and Khad headquarters itself, and I recorded a piece to camera as we rattled over the bumpy roads. Playing the videotape of it now, I can still hear the nervousness and surprise in my voice.

TRANSCRIPT OF *PANORAMA ON AFGHANISTAN*, 2.10.89

Speaker: John Simpson

JS: This is clear evidence of the degree to which the resistance movement has penetrated the system in Kabul. We have changed vehicles now, and the one we're in is a jeep belonging to the commander of the Afghan equivalent of the KGB, Khad. And the two men with us are both officers of Khad.

It was consummate cheek on the part of Harakat-e-Islami. They all knew they were endangering their lives by allowing us to film the jeep. But they thought it was worth it from the movement's point of view. To have the BBC show the secret power they possessed inside the enemy's capital was more important to them than their own lives.

That night we spent in a safe house, and were then moved on, again by taxi. Two men arrived and announced themselves as senior officers in Khad who were double agents for our mujaheddin group, Harakat. They wrapped their faces in their turbans and sat down to be interviewed.

Directly they had gone an older man with shifty eyes, completely different from the bold, smiling Mongolian types, arrived and announced he was going to make a rocket. There and then he started filling a big metal pipe with explosives and fiddled around with a watch, which was to act as the fuse. Peter filmed away, but we both had serious doubts about the ethics of all this. And about the wisdom of it too. Suppose Khad arrived and arrested us; wouldn't we be accessories in an act of terrorism?

The trouble was, these people had no concept of the function of journalism. We weren't just observers to them, we were fellow conspirators.

To have announced that we were no longer taking part in all this might have been suicidal. Anyway, it was so extraordinary that I think neither of us would have done it.

But worse was to come: our shifty-eyed minder insisted that we must also film the firing of his rocket. Yet another taxi, driven by yet another Harakat supporter, was already waiting outside. The bomb maker dumped his rocket in my lap and went and sat in the front seat. We drove along, jammed in together, with me nursing the rocket and feeling very much as though I didn't want to be there.

That was when our Kabul Catastrophe seemed likely to begin. First, the taxi driver panicked and stopped right beside a patch of open ground where a soccer game was going on. Twenty-two players plus a referee saw Peter climbing out with his camera and the shifty-eyed one carrying the rocket over to a group of men a hundred yards or so away, who were going to fire it. My job was to stay with Shifty Eyes and make sure he didn't try to get away. Meanwhile Peter realized that the target was to be the Khad headquarters, which loomed up at the far end of the open patch of ground where we were.

He shrugged his shoulders and started filming. The Harakat team walked across the open ground, pointed the rocket at it, and fired. Only the mujaheddin, we agreed afterward, could have missed a five-story building at that range; the rocket fizzed over the top and fell harmlessly on the other side. We made a run for it.

We spent that night in another safe house. But the next morning it became clear to us that things were going badly wrong. The deadlines our guides had given for picking us up came and went. We were prisoners, and it was getting claustrophobic. Peter and I told yarns to each other and laughed a lot—another sign we were nervous. From time to time Peter would peer through a narrow gap in the curtains to gauge the height and direction of the military planes that came and went overhead. He wanted to work out where in Kabul we were.

Suddenly, late in the afternoon, things started to happen very fast. There was the sound of gunshots, and Mahmoud appeared, shouting at us to get out. It turned out that Khad had known about us all along, even before we had arrived in Kabul. Their spies along the way had told them we were coming. Finally they had heard all about the rocket incident, and they knew we were using taxis to get around the city.

Now they had discovered our safe house. A few minutes earlier a colonel from Khad had reconnoitered it and was actually raising his walkie-talkie to his mouth to give an order when Mahmoud ran up behind him and shot him in the back of the head. We had escaped just in time.

As we drove off in the inevitable taxi I felt bad about the Khad colonel, but not too bad: a secret policeman that senior must have tortured and executed a lot of people. Things looked extremely black for us now, though. If we were caught we would have absolutely no defense against the charge that we were accomplices of terrorists and murderers; the chances were that we would be quietly executed rather than put on public trial. What had started off as an adventure had turned serious. Blood had been shed, and there could be more to come. I felt foolish and guilty: this hadn't been how it was meant to go at all. Out of the window now I could see groups of police and army stopping red taxis just like ours.

Peter was sitting bolt upright beside me.

"For God's sake," I said irritably, "can't you stop looking so bloody British?"

"Sorry," he murmured, and tried to slouch down. He wasn't very good at it.

We passed the InterContinental Hotel, where the remnants of the international press corps were staying, and I yearned to tell the driver to turn in and set us down there. But they wouldn't have been able to protect us, and might not have wanted to. We were outlaws, hunted like animals. It was an ugly feeling.

And then, somehow, we had passed through the most dangerous area. The police and army roadblocks became fewer and fewer. By the time we reached the edge of town, where the Pagman Mountains met the road, we were starting to feel we had a chance of escape. The winter's sun was going down redly over Kabul.

We shook hands quickly with the taxi driver, and walked fast for the hills with Mahmoud guiding us. Darkness fell quickly. We made our way through the ring of army watchtowers again, but this time one of them was unmanned. Mahmoud led us close to it so that we were out of sight of the others.

Only a few minutes later, the watchtowers erupted in a gigantic display of lights and tracer bullets. It was like Guy Fawkes Night and Chinese New Year all in one. We stood on a mountain ridge and looked back at the red and white lights shooting up into the sky. A thought struck me.

"It couldn't be for our benefit, could it?" I said.

"No," said Peter; "the government must be celebrating some kind of victory."

Mahmoud said nothing.

Hours later we stumbled in at the door of the Harakat headquarters in Pagman. Somehow I still had my Heffers of Cambridge bag with me. We were just drinking our first cup of tea when someone else arrived: a soldier who had just deserted from one of the watchtowers.

"Are you the ones?" he said, with respect in his voice. "We were ordered to fire every tracer bullet we had in the air in order to see you and catch you."

All the Harakat people crowded around to congratulate us, and in my relief I gripped their hands harder than I meant. Mahmoud winced.

"We will call you *Dast-e-gir*," he said, "the friend of the handshake."

It had happened to me in the past; now I was doing it to them.

Our Kabul Catastrophe had turned into an extraordinary, undeserved Kabul escape. I would never, I promised myself, enter a serious undertaking so lightly again. And I would never pay attention to omens either; good or bad.

In the years that followed the Soviet withdrawal, Afghans of all persuasions found it hard to understand why their country had been forgotten. Once it had been a significant piece on the international chessboard, but now the game had changed. The fighting was no longer against a superpower; it was a civil war.

When I went back to Kabul in April 1996 I found that things were much worse than they had been seven years earlier. The factions that Peter Jouvenal and Chris Hooke had wanted to follow had indeed captured

Kabul, though it took them far longer than any of us had expected. Once there, they had brought their rivalries with them. Soon it had turned into outright war.

The destruction was terrible. We filmed in a mile-long stretch of road leading to the outskirts of town. There had been two universities and five schools along this road. Now there was nothing but ruins and rubble. Sarajevo, by comparison with this, had got off lightly. The mud-brick, yellowish gray in color, had been smashed into piles of little more than dust. An occasional page from a textbook fluttered among the ruins. Everything else worth having had long since been looted, regardless of the danger from anti-personnel mines and unexploded shells.

None of this was done by the Russians. On the contrary, it had been with Russian help that the universities and schools were built up. Instead the destruction was the result of the fighting among the mujaheddin groups since the Russian withdrawal. With help and encouragement from Afghanistan's neighbors, who had no particular interest in seeing so difficult a country at peace, faction after faction had taken on the relatively moderate groups that form the government in Kabul.

Gulbuddin Hekmatyar had fought his way into the government coalition as prime minister, and then been ejected forcibly from it. His Hezb-E-Islami group had strong support from Pakistan, which fought out its proxy battles with India and Russia, backers of the Kabul government, on the territory of Afghanistan. General Dostam, with covert help from Russia, fought the government troops along this road and was responsible for the worst of the destruction. The Shi'ite groups, backed by Iran, flared up in occasional rebellion. Afghanistan had become a political black hole, without effective government, from which nothing emerged but heroin, and casualties too bad for the local hospitals to cope with.

Peter Jouvenal was with me again, but the other two were newcomers: Tom Giles from *Newsnight* and Garry Marvin, an academic who was researching for a documentary on newsgathering and occasionally acted as sound recordist. Directly we arrived in the center of Kabul we went to the compound of the International Committee of the Red Cross. It was obvious that something was up.

"We've got to hurry," one of the people there said, and he called for

his driver and his big white Toyota Land Cruiser. ICRC delegates work in style.

It sounded like some important national ceremony, but it was in fact a public execution. I suppose I should have been horrified, but my first reaction, like the ICRC man's, was to hope we wouldn't be too late for it. Working for television can do bad things to the soul. It makes you rejoice in the concept of "good" pictures, "good" meaning attractive or exciting. A public hanging would come high in the ranking of "good" pictures—a little above an earthquake or an erupting volcano, perhaps, though not as high as a political assassination on camera.

I am, of course, being satirical; yet which of us, if we were warned that something of the sort was about to be shown, would switch off the television in disgust? Why do people gather at scenes of violence and disaster, while even those who blame them for doing it take a look to see what is going on? Why do we read accounts of deaths or last words with such avidity? Because there is a terrible, slightly shameful fascination in the thought that a life, which is so strong and ardent at one moment, can be snuffed out the next. It could be us; in a way, it will be eventually, and perhaps we want to know what it looks like.

At this stage—April 1996—public executions were rare in Kabul. The relatively moderate mujaheddin coalition led by President Rabbani and Ahmad Shah Massoud was still in power, but its position was under serious threat from the Taliban. Within a few months the Taliban would put Rabbani and Massoud to flight and capture the city. Sensing the pressure from the Islamic extremists opposing them, the Rabbani government was keen to show that it too could behave with proper Islamic zeal.

In Saudi Arabia they behead criminals in public, but are outraged if pictures of the executions appear in the Western media. The Saudis like the essential savagery of their punishments to be a secret kept within the family. For the Afghans, on the other hand, the outside world scarcely exists. It is the place where weapons, foreign broadcasts, a little money and a little medical aid come from, and it is as distant to them as another galaxy. That foreigners might find a public execution degrading or unpleasant was both unimaginable and irrelevant.

We drove to the place of execution: a dreary open area in the center of the city, where modern buildings overlooked a large patch of scrubby grass. Hours beforehand, thousands of people had gathered in almost complete silence, waiting for something to happen. The crowd was entirely male. After the victory of the mujaheddin over the Communists, women were rarely seen in the city, occasionally showing themselves in shapeless *burka* of dull yellow or gray, their faces hidden behind a little square mesh of cotton or lace like a grille in a cell door, scurrying around as though they too wanted to rid the streets of themselves.

The gallows had been set up on a grassless knoll. Its shape was familiar from a thousand Westerns; yet it was still a shock to see it, like coming across a headsman sharpening his axe. The onlookers stood twenty deep at the closest point, and young boys hung in the branches of trees.

There was a sudden panic: People had climbed in such numbers onto the roof of a ruined building in front of the gallows that it seemed to be about to collapse, and men were jumping the twenty feet to the ground in fear. Some of them were injured, but no one cared: it wasn't injury they'd come here to see, but death itself.

The police, a ragged lot in old, stained blue uniforms, had broken branches off the trees around the gallows and were using them to beat the legs of the men and boys in the front row to keep order. It was essential. A couple of days earlier there had been a practice run for the executions, and the crowd had grown violent when it was clear no one was going to die. They turned on the police and the half dozen journalists who had turned out to see what was going on, attacking them with rocks and hunting them into the nearby buildings. One way or another, it seemed, there had to be death and violence.

It was clear the crowd wouldn't be disappointed this time. Three nooses of yellow plastic rope hung loosely from the cross tree, moving a little in the light breeze. A desk for the presiding mullah was set alongside, and a doctor with a dirty white coat over his mujaheddin fatigues checked his stethoscope nervously. I knew how he felt. I have seen people die in front of me many times, but none of them was put to death formally, by prearrangement, for the public good. I found myself swallowing a good deal.

For the small group of foreigners, most of them from aid agencies, it was a curiously social occasion. People like the ICRC man were greeting each other and grinning, as though they were going to watch a fireworks display. Someone ran over to me with a walkie-talkie, and a woman's voice, faintly familiar, squeaked from inside it. The voice said her name, and then I remembered: she was a rather glamorous UN official whom I had last encountered in Sarajevo.

"Look up!" squeaked the voice, and eventually I located her, waving from the fifth floor of the building opposite. She had binoculars: this was something she wasn't going to miss. Orange sellers and vendors of unpleasant-looking meats went through the crowds, shouting their wares, but there was still very little noise.

Then came the roar and grinding of an engine, and an armored personnel carrier ground its way up the slope in a fog of dark blue exhaust. A dozen guards and enthusiasts hung on to its upper works as it lurched up the slope to the gallows. This was the equivalent of the tumbril. A big crowd gathered round the rear of the APC as someone struggled to open the hatch at the back. Out of it, one after another, came the three condemned men. It was the first sighting, and the crowd made a little rustle of excitement.

Blinking in the light, their hands and feet manacled, they looked like any other mujaheddin: bearded, wearing flat *pukal* caps and camouflage fatigues, young, gawky, unremarkable in every way except that they had barely ten minutes left to live. Their feet were bare, and they stood around idly on the knoll in front of the gallows while the men in charge of the hanging directed all their attention to pushing our cameraman and the two or three other photographers back. As far as I could see, none of the condemned men even looked at the ropes which had been prepared to kill them.

Their crime was a savage one. They had killed a *kouchi,* or nomad, raped his wife, injured his sons, and stolen his sheep. The four crimes seemed to rank roughly equal in the eyes of Afghan law. As they stood there, waiting for the fuss to die down and the executioners to start their work, the smallest of the three, Farid Ahmad, said loudly that he was only being hanged because he had no money. It was probably true. Anyway, it sounded more like a statement of fact than a plea for mercy;

he must have known that there was no hope now. Once his outburst was over, he stood quietly enough in front of the middle noose. The man on his left, Nicmohammed, looked up at the crossbar and licked his lips. Zmarey, on the right, much taller and more bulky than the others, joked and laughed at the crowd opposite. They didn't respond; they were too curious at the spectacle of a man who would soon be beyond joking or laughing or any feeling whatever.

There was no ceremony. The whole affair was much uglier, more brutish and more careless than I had anticipated, and yet the first to die, Farid Ahmad, was strangling, disregarded, before we had realized that the noose had been tightened round his neck. It looked as though he had decided to get it over with quickly, and had put his weight into it immediately, slumping down like a sack of potatoes.

The executioner put the noose round Nicmohammed's neck. He took it quietly too, dropping down as the noose tautened but twisting round, his legs pointing and shaking dreadfully, his neck at an ugly angle, his eyes open as though he was trying to examine something very intently. As I watched, his hands and feet started to go a dull grayish blue.

Zmarey, who had played the fool, died the hardest. Although he was the tallest, he had been allotted the longest rope. His feet touched the ground and the rope throttled him slowly while the idiots in charge tried feebly to shorten it by twisting an iron bar across it, and then dug a hole under his feet. It was sickening to watch, and took a terrible amount of time before he, too, slumped, his head down on his shoulder and his feet at last pointing straight.

By comparison with a painful disease, or with what the three of them had done to the *kouchi* and his family, even Zmarey's death was mercifully fast. But what was lacking was any ceremony, any feeling that something of significance had happened here. There was no grand finale to the lives of the three murderers, none of the sense of occasion that we, who see so little of death, feel ought to accompany the irrevocable business of dying. Farid Ahmad, Nicmohammed and Zmarey should have been turned off like pirates at Execution Dock, with prayers and longwinded confessions and the sudden jolting of a cart. Instead, three bodies twisted in the cold wind and the crowd melted away, deeply dissatisfied, balked of a ceremony. The whole purpose, to teach society an Islamic lesson, had somehow been dissipated.

It took us a lot of effort to get the kind of pictures that would avoid showing the nasty reality of what we had observed. All we used when the pictures were edited were shots of the three standing in front of the gallows, but not having the nooses put round their necks; the cross tree bending under the weight of the first and second hangings; the eager faces of the onlookers; the shadow of Nicmohammed's feet on the ground; and a distant wide shot of the three hanging there side by side. Even so, there were complaints from viewers. There always are.

The people from the aid agencies who had started off by being such enthusiastic onlookers had gone very quiet. When they left, there was none of the earlier handshaking and backslapping. I had the sense that they all felt guilty and embarrassed and in some way diminished, as though they'd been carried away in some big crowd action like looting or burning someone unpopular out of their house; and now, when they thought about it, they didn't feel so good about what they had done. A Western photographer came to us quietly afterward and said he had a favor to ask.

"I'd be glad if you didn't show any shots of me up close, getting pictures of their faces."

We, at least, hadn't done anything to be ashamed of. We'd just been doing our job, and we'd put a lot of effort into making the hangings as inoffensive as we could. Even so, we ate our dinner quietly that night at the German Club, where we were staying. For once there were no jokes, no anecdotes about the absurdities of friends and colleagues. I brought out my bottle of Laphroaig single malt, and we each drank more than we usually would. With its aid I slept heavily that night, and remembered nothing until I woke up with the thin, gray light coming through the curtains. But I dreamt about it the next night, all the same.

The first time I came across Taliban soldiers, I couldn't tell the difference between them and any other mujaheddin group. And perhaps there wasn't any difference: a clever mixture of bribery and good propaganda had won over dozens of local warlords to the Taliban side. They were crouched behind a makeshift wall of piled-up rocks beside the road, and we had just made the nerve-racking journey by car between the two front lines, on the outskirts of Kabul. These men had no objection whatsoever to being filmed. Nor did their commander, though because he was still nervous about his new masters (he had only recently changed sides) he insisted that someone else should talk on camera for him.

It was only when we went south to Kandahar, the Taliban capital, that we found the real thing. They were very alarming indeed. Kandahar is famous for its homosexuality, and it was commonplace to find Taliban soldiers with mascara'd eyes, painted finger- and toenails, and high-heeled gold sandals. Also the AK-47.

"I've only seen one thing worse," Peter said.

In Liberia, it seems, he was filming a whole gang of soldiers looting the shops, when they came running down the street after him. They'd just hit a bridal shop and a lighting store, so they were wearing wedding dresses and lampshades on their heads. And they were angry.

The Taliban—the word means "religious students"—began in the refugee camps around the Pakistani border town of Quetta and swept across into Afghanistan in 1994, in rage at the failure of the government to impose the basics of fundamentalist Islam. They weren't particularly good fighters, but they were Pashtu speakers who had played intelligently on the linguistic divisions inside Afghanistan and had gained the support of many groups that disliked the lordly ways of the predominantly Tajik-speaking government in Kabul.

Some of the Taliban's greatest gains had been achieved through making deals, rather than on the field of battle. Now they controlled half the territory and almost half the population of Afghanistan, from Herat in the West to the border with Pakistan, and their forces were besieging the capital, Kabul, itself. The Taliban's main centers, Kandahar and Herat, were on the Pakistani telephone system, and Pakistani banks flourished in several of their towns and cities.

The Taliban were probably the most extreme Islamic fundamentalist group in the world. By comparison, Iran and even Saudi Arabia seemed positively liberal. There were even fewer women on the streets than in Kabul, and those few who appeared were covered from head to foot in the traditional *burka*. On either side of the road that led into the center of the city stood two rickety steel towers. The Taliban had strung up old televisions and videocassettes on them, hanging them with recording tape like the bodies of executed criminals from gibbets. Television was evil, because it presumed to capture the likeness of living creatures: something which, according to their interpretation of the Koran, was blasphemous.

Kandahar wasn't, therefore, the easiest place for a television team to work. An aggressive young mullah was appointed to chaperone us, and he had instructions to not even let us film the hanging television sets. Peter did it anyway, since the mullah had little idea of the scope a cameraman has for filming surreptitiously. On the flat roof of a nearby building, while our translator talked to the mullah, we recorded a piece to camera and at least got some pictures of people walking around in the streets.

But we had one sensational piece of good luck. On the morning after we arrived, Mullah Omar Akund, the one-eyed, reclusive leader of the Taliban, was to reveal the cloak of the Prophet Mohammed, donated centuries before to Kandahar, before the eyes of an expectant crowd. The cloak was only shown publicly at moments of great significance; the last time had been more than sixty years before. Now, as the Taliban prepared to open their great onslaught against Kabul, they took it out again.

Our driver, a fat, turbaned character whose young sidekick had some disgusting habits—we called him Ghastly Boy—edged the vehicle gingerly through the enormous crowd that had gathered in front of the building where the cloak was kept.

People gathered round us in large numbers, staring in through the windows. They weren't hostile; it was just that they hadn't seen Europeans before. It had happened the evening before as well, and that was quite alarming. The crowd looked particularly menacing, and men with terrible scars and one with an empty eye socket pressed their faces against the glass. It was very hot in the vehicle, and we were getting distinctly uneasy. Then Garry Marvin made the joke of the entire trip.

"Don't look now," he said, "but the crowd's turning ugly."

Now, with the ceremony of the Prophet's cloak to attract their attention, scarcely anyone noticed us. Peter Jouvenal was able to get some extraordinary pictures as Mullah Omar held up the ancient piece of pale brown material. The emotion of the crowd was intense. People wept aloud and tore the turbans off their heads to throw them up into the air and touch the cloak. Within a few months the Taliban had captured Kabul.

It seemed impossible to persuade any senior figure in the Taliban to record an interview with us on camera. One of them agreed to have his answers recorded, but wouldn't show any part of himself to the camera. He wouldn't even allow us to film the cup he drank tea from. Instead, the camera had to be on my face all the time as I listened to him—tough on the audience. Some Taliban leaders, more moderate, were sympathetic to the idea, but felt their position within the organization would suffer if it were known that we had made a graven image of them.

On our last day, we went to see the Taliban minister of health, Mullah Balouch. He had a fearsome reputation: a strong supporter of the punishments defined in the *Sharia,* or Islamic law, he tried to persuade the surgeons under his control to cut off the hands and feet of convicted criminals. If they refused, he did it himself. By all accounts he rather enjoyed it.

We found him in his office, surrounded by a couple of dozen petitioners. When he saw us he waved them away. With the camera running, I went over to him and asked him if he would consider giving us an interview. It never occurred to me that he might. Yet Mullah Balouch turned out to be a liberal; relatively speaking, that is.

"It is idolatry to show a person's face only, since a graven image can be made from that. But if you show me down to the waist, no graven image can be made from it."

"Absolutely," I said, not understanding a word of it; and we showed him, as he wanted, down to the waist.

He proved to be a frank interviewee, except on the question of his own involvement in the punishments. He absolutely denied cutting off anyone's hands or feet himself, even though what he had done was a matter of public knowledge in Kandahar. Perhaps he realized the effect it might have on a Western audience if he admitted it. But he insisted it wasn't in any way strange that a minister of health should try to persuade hospital surgeons to amputate perfectly healthy limbs. I wasn't going to

disagree with him. Liberals were in short-enough supply in the ranks of the Taliban without falling out with the only one we'd found.

Since 1989 Peter Jouvenal is the only cameraman I have worked with in Afghanistan. In the normal way I would tell the cameraman what I wanted to do, but in Afghanistan the pattern is rather different. In nearly twenty years Peter has made dozens of expeditions there, often in the most dangerous conditions. He knows almost every part of it. When we plan a trip, therefore, I don't tell him what we will do, I ask him what he thinks. And I take his advice.

His knowledge of military things is unrivaled. If you walk with Peter through the battlefields of Afghanistan he can tell you, not simply what each piece of rusting metal is, but what kind of gun or helicopter or military aircraft it comes from. He will know at a range of twenty yards which particular factory in which particular country the AK-47 in the hands of some louche *mujahid* was made. In Kabul he collects and restores the *jezails* and British muskets that can still be found there in large numbers.

Peter is a loner. His background is as odd as my own. His mother is German, and they lived with Peter's guardian, an old lady with a sensational Arts and Crafts house overlooking the Thames outside Henley. Then the old lady died, and the death duties forced Peter to sell the house. He tried unsuccessfully to raise enough money from the contents, and showed me some of the things that were there. His guardian's family had never thrown anything away, so there were copies of the *Times* from the 1830s, still in their unopened wrappers; medals; swords; letters from the famous; a cocked hat with a bullet hole in it that someone had worn at the Battle of Waterloo; endless mementoes from the Crimean War. It all went, and the house along with it.

Peter is a man who has everything carefully worked out: suppliers of goods, houses in the most unlikely places, unexpected comforts. At his house in Kabul, his cook had once been the French ambassador's chef. At the end of a long day's marching or riding, it is always Peter who pulls out the bar of chocolate, the restoring tin of bully-beef. The unexpected is his specialty. Once when we were staying at the German Club in Kabul, a large and rather pleasant compound where we could drink whisky and smoke cigars at the end of the day, he called us over to his room and pulled a couple of large metal trunks out from under his bed.

"Guess what's in there?"

We made a few wrong guesses.

"Couple of skeletons."

He started to open one of them and show us. Skeletons were exactly what you would expect to find in metal boxes under Peter Jouvenal's bed.

For some years he had run an organization that seeks to find information about the Russian and Afghan soldiers missing after the war in Afghanistan. From time to time he discovered the body of a Russian and dug it up, in order to be able to send it back to the family. It's typical of Peter: something no one else would do, extremely philanthropic, yet somehow weird. He is a thoroughly nineteenth-century character, buccaneering and highly principled. Sir Charles Napier, Sir James Brooke, Sir Henry Lawrence would all recognize him as one of their own, and John Buchan would have written a thriller about him.

One evening in 1989, as I sat in their house in Peshawar, Peter and Chris Hooke showed me a film they had made some time before in the remotest part of Afghanistan, the mountains in the far northeast. In the Kvajeh Mohammed range, where the Kowkcheh River runs parallel to Afghanistan's borders with Tajikistan and Pakistan, lies the world's best deposit of the dark blue semiprecious stone lapis lazuli. It may be the world's oldest continuously worked mine; lapis was being taken out of Sar-i-Sang for the jewelry of the Indus civilizations and those of Egypt and Mesopotamia as early as the fourth millennium B.C. According to Peter and Chris, the methods used now had improved very little.

Over the years that followed, I often thought about going to Sar-i-Sang—especially when I saw the lapis jewelry of Ur in the British Museum, or the inlaid eyes on the funeral mask of Tutankhamun, or an illustrated medieval manuscript where the Virgin's cloak was colored by the crushed lapis that the artists called ultramarine because it came from beyond the seas.

Some lump, ah God, of LAPIS LAZULI,
Blue as a vein o'er the Madonna's breast

So wrote Robert Browning. When I bought a set of lapis worry beads in the Grand Bazaar in Tehran, I felt a powerful desire to see the place where all this had come from.

Other mines, in Africa and South America, produce lapis lazuli of a sort. But the best quality, a deep, rich blue often flecked with gold, comes today as it did before the first dynasties in Egypt and China, from this one mountain in the Hindu Kush. Lapis isn't a precious stone; it is a rock. The blueness comes from the mineral lazulite, and the golden flecks are iron pyrites—"fool's gold." German, Japanese and American jewelers prize lapis highly, and rich Arabs encrust their bathroom scales with it.

It was difficult to persuade anyone that this would make a particularly good news story. Still, it seemed that the mujaheddin leaders in the area financed their war from the proceeds of the lapis that was dug out there, and the big drug dealers of Pakistan often used it to mask the profits from heroin. The BBC's initial doubts weren't so much editorial as practical: It seemed too dangerous. Sar-i-Sang was one of the hardest places in the world to get to. Robbers abounded, and the packhorse and mule were the only reliable means of transport.

It would take at least three weeks, and it wasn't easy for me to set aside a period as long as that. Things have a disturbing habit of happening in other parts of the world when you're locked into something like this. I was investigating human rights abuses in Argentina when Mrs. Gandhi was assassinated in India, and in the depths of the Peruvian jungle when sterling fell out of the European Monetary System. To be away from one's desk at such times is distinctly bad for business.

Still, it was merely a question of opening the diary at an empty page or two, and hoping that they would stay empty after I had written "Afghanistan?" on them. It had also become markedly easier to sell the idea to my colleagues. Our trip to Afghanistan in 1996 had won various awards in Britain and the United States, and I proposed that the same team—Tom Giles, Peter Jouvenal and I (Garry Marvin had now started a new job as a university lecturer)—should come to Sar-i-Sang with me now. We also invited a dealer in gems, Guy Clutterbuck, to go with us, since he knew the place and had been there more than once on buying expeditions.

On the last day of September 1997 we flew in to the small mountain town of Faisabad, two hundred difficult miles northeast of Kabul, in a UN plane. It was already starting to be cold. Horsemen skittered bravely on the dusty roads that wound round the mountainside, and went closer than was comfortable to the edge of the road, which fell away to the rushing green river half a mile below. The Hindu Kush range has a savage name; it means "Hindu Killer," because so many slaves captured in raids on India died as they were being brought through these high passes.

In Persian, though, it is *Uparisena,* "the peak too high for eagles to fly over," and Alexander the Great borrowed the name and turned it in Greek: *Paropamisus.* He passed through this region in 327 B.C., and the beautiful Persian woman he married, Roxane, daughter of Oxyartes, came either from the Panshir Valley or from Tajikistan, depending on your loyalties. Somewhere around the modern air base of Bagram, north of Kabul, Alexander founded a city, which he called Alexandria-in-the-Caucasus, with 7,000 local people and those of his own soldiers who were too ill, too old or too unwilling to go farther east with him. These are the mountains of Kipling's *The Man Who Would Be King,* whose two ex-army heroes come across the remains of an ancient Greek civilization.

> "See here!" said Dravot, his thumb on the map. "Up to Jagdallak, Peachey and me know the road. We was there with Roberts' Army. We'll have to turn off to the right at Jagdallak through Laghman territory. Then we get among the hills—fourteen thousand feet—fifteen thousand—it will be cold work there, but it don't look very far on the map."

It was an awful, long way on the ground, though. In the straggling market of Faisabad we bought everything we lacked: heavy blankets, some rotten little Chinese torches, a couple of elderly Russian sleeping bags, a gigantic ancient handmade padlock to protect the contents of my army surplus kitbag from pilferers. A leatherworker, squatting in the roadway, sewed thick leather patches on the tough-looking but easily torn Camel bag I had bought at Harrods; a lesson in the futility of Roughing-It chic. (On the other hand, my Barbour boots and my Drizabone topcoat, which I bought at the same time, proved to be superb in the most difficult conditions. Not everything cheap is good; not everything expensive lets you down.) We also paid a tailor to run up a couple of flags with "BBC" on them, blue on white. In a country where the BBC was so popular, and where there were so many brigands, we thought they might possibly do us a bit of good.

I was taking photographs in the market when Guy pointed out a small girl to me. She must have been about six, and had crept out with her friends to look at the extraordinary foreigners who were strutting round the market. Her hair was as gold as the brash necklaces that hung in the bazaars, her skin was lighter than mine, and her eyes were a startling blue. Directly I raised the camera to take a photograph, she and her friends ran off squealing in pleasurable terror. They came back again and again, of course, but I was never able to get a clear picture of this Roxane of the Hindu Kush.

In the meantime Tom and Peter had hired a pair of Russian-made jeeps, complete with drivers. The vehicles were brutalist in construction: The windows didn't open, and there were all sorts of flanges and unfinished edges of metal, one of which cut my leg and landed me in the hospital months later when the wound failed to heal. But they were the only vehicles tough enough for the journey. We left in the end, flags flying, waving, hooting our horns, while the children squealed and the mangy dogs barked and the old men laughed behind their hands at the spectacle we had made of ourselves and the amount of money we had parted with.

"I think we slipped out of there without anyone noticing," I said, echoing a joke which Eamonn Matthews had made on a similar occasion in the Peruvian jungle. What, after all, is the point of a good joke if you don't recycle it occasionally?

Before the fatigue of being constantly jolted up and down and sideways began to get to us, the journey was very enjoyable. Guy Clutterbuck was a good raconteur. One of his best stories was about how he had hidden a large, valuable and distinctively cut jewel up his backside for security when he was in a particularly difficult part of the world. After arriving in Britain and extracting it, he sold it to one of the big London jewelers. The next time he saw it, he said, was in a photograph on the cover of *Hello* magazine. Hanging round the neck of Diana, Princess of Wales.

We made a two-day detour to the front line to film the war between the Taliban and Ahmad Shah Massoud. It was just as war always is in Afghanistan, a mixture of absurd carelessness on the part of the fighters you are with, sudden sharp moments of considerable danger, and the strange lassitude that follows them. Tom and I, unused to the particular sounds that the weaponry of the mujaheddin made, tended to duck when there was outgoing fire and sometimes failed to notice when it was incoming. That caused a good deal of laughter. Years of working with Peter Jouvenal, though, had taught me that when he made for cover it was a good idea to follow.

Then it was time to begin the drive to Sar-i-Sang in earnest. It took another two days. A local warlord called Najimuddin Khan, loyal to Massoud, controlled the area, and a few days earlier we had managed to get his permission to go there.

It was given hurriedly, since a Taliban plane was coming in to dive-bomb us at the time.

"Go on, put anything in front of him and he'll sign it," Guy said. "Write out his will and he'll sign that."

"Or your expenses," said Tom, thinking perhaps of the administration that lay ahead of him when we got back to Britain.

I said nothing. I was watching the Taliban plane wheeling in the sky and coming toward us. Fortunately the pilot changed his mind.

Plenty of heavily armed men along our way owed no loyalty to anyone, and the threat of robbery was very real. Once a group of men fired shots to make us stop and pick them up; we didn't, of course. At night, as we slept, wandering groups of shepherds made their way through our camp with their flocks of sheep and goats.

There were occasional roadblocks, and the atmosphere was tense. Other groups of mujaheddin seemed to be trying to muscle in on

Najimuddin Khan's lapis lazuli. A piece of paper, scribbled by one of his junior commanders, got us through any problems, and maybe our BBC flags helped too. They certainly seemed to impress a lot of people as we drove through. But the worst part was the road itself, often nothing more than a boulder-strewn, dried-up river or a precarious track beside an abyss. Soon it was dark, but the track was too narrow for us to be able to stop and camp for the night, so the drivers decided to press on. They peered intently out into the darkness at the rocks and gray dust ahead, avoiding disaster by their instinct and the strength of their wrists. On our left was the solid gray rock wall of the mountainside; on our right there was nothing but darkness, where the edge of the road fell away into a precipice. Somewhere down there was the Kowkcheh River. When we stopped we could hear it rushing and foaming over the boulders in its bed.

We lit fires and ate a quick meal, then lay down to sleep. I stayed awake for what seemed like hours, listening to the strange sounds of the night. Some *kouchis* seemed to be camping nearby with their animals. Once there was a *crack* in the sky, as a shooting star hit the earth's atmosphere. I must have slept, though; each time I looked up at them, the amazing star patterns had shifted perceptibly.

We were on our way at five o'clock. It was Friday 3 October, and the journey I had waited eight years for was about to reach its climax. It had taken us fifteen hours to drive the last forty miles. Shortly after six our jeeps mounted the crest of a ridge and Sar-i-Sang lay in front of us. We got out and stood in the keen, cold air. It was a magical moment. Behind the mountain of lapis the rising sun's rays fanned out into the sky. "Like the crown of a god-emperor," I enthused a couple of days later, as I dictated my weekly column for the *Sunday Telegraph* by satellite phone. Then, thinking I had gone a bit over the top, I added, "or the letter-heading of a dodgy insurance company." The sub-editors, romantics despite themselves, disapproved and cut that part out.

We couldn't take our eyes off the mountain and its brilliant nimbus now.

"The Holy Grail," said Tom, and we shook hands silently as though we were Victorian explorers. And indeed only four Westerners had reached the mine in at least the previous quarter century. Two of them—Peter Jouvenal and Guy Clutterbuck—were here with us now.

The mountain was an isosceles triangle of yellowish granite a mile above us. The mining shift had just changed, and tiny figures ran down the steep paths, their feet throwing up clouds of dust, their backs bent under the weight of the lapis they had excavated, the overseers urging them on with sticks. They descended on a primitive village at the mountain-foot, which can't have changed in any essential for six thousand years: single-roomed huts made of piled stones, a few ill-smelling alleyways, shops selling vegetables, newly butchered goats' meat. There were no women here, and no children. Sar-i-Sang village exists solely to serve the mine, and the superstition goes that the mine is female. The presence of women here would make her jealous, and the supply of lapis would dry up.

The system of exploiting the mine is probably the same now as it always has been. Big dealers lease the workings for a month or so at a time, and the lapis that is dug out belongs to them. The miners are given wages. Long tradition allows them to pilfer a certain amount, and this is sold to small dealers who meet them on their way down from their shift; but the overseers are on hand to see that no really good-quality lapis is sold like this.

While we filmed a miner sitting on a rock and playing an intricate little tune on a handmade flute, one of our drivers nudged me. The man who ran the mine for Najimuddin Khan, Commander Malik, was coming down the little street between the stone houses toward us, accompanied by his lackeys and thrusting aside the donkeys and the little fringed and tasselled horses who stood in his way. The miners moved back quickly: Malik was the real power at Sar-i-Sang.

To us he was charming, and invited us to his house for tea and a meal. We sat on the floor and leaned against cushions as the tea kettle went round. A hurricane lamp hissed on the carpeted floor in front of us, and some very questionable meat on metal plates appeared. I ate the unleavened bread and a few gritty radishes, but declined the meat. I had seen a bloody goat's head lying in the alley close by, and assumed there was some connection.

Commander Malik had a crafty, intellectual face, with a high, domed forehead and ears that stuck out from under his turban. He looked as though he was always about to smile, but never quite did; and after he had said something his eyes scanned our faces to guess our reaction.

"How old do you think the mine is?" I asked.

"Well, I'm thirty-four and it was going when I was born."

I couldn't work out whether he genuinely didn't know, or was reluctant to give us any straight information. When I asked him about the profits from the lapis, he lied blandly.

TRANSCRIPT OF *NEWSNIGHT* REPORT, 5.11.97

Speaker: Commander Malik

CM: The money earned here is for everyone in Afghanistan. All over the country people come here to work, including those who are very poor. None of the money we raise here goes to the war or to the military commanders. It goes towards building roads, mosques and clinics, and helping the poor.

When an Afghan commander gets pious like that, you can usually guess he's lying. Still, he was hospitable enough, and invited us to climb up and see the mine for ourselves.

There are now four mines on the mountain, but only the Mardan-i-Yek, and the fourth, Mardan-i-Chahar, produce the jewel-quality lapis. The fourth mine was slightly easier to get to, but I was determined to see the workings that dated back before the early Egyptian and Chinese dynasties.

We set off shortly before noon. The entrance to Mardan-i-Yek was visible close to the peak of the mountain, but it was a long way up, at least a mile. The two-hour climb was one of the hardest things I had ever done, and I was soon the last of the group; though the rest, the oldest of whom was a good fifteen years younger than me, had problems too. In some places the path had been swept away by landslides, and we had to clamber over the bare rock. On the last and steepest part I looked down at the village, with the figures of miners and horses scarcely discernible, and tried to summon up the willpower to fight my way on. Tom leaned over from a little way above me, his face showing his anxiety.

"You are going to be able to make it, aren't you? We really need a piece to camera there."

I didn't want to let Tom down, and I didn't want to let myself down either. To have waited eight years and then give up so close to the mine was unthinkable. I gripped a fault in the rock, put one of my Barbour boots onto a tuft of some grayish green weed and the other on a little rivulet of small brown gravel, and pushed upward. Hands gripped me. As is so often the way, there was a path not far from us, and directly we found ourselves on that, everything was much easier.

It was a magnificent moment when the dark mouth of the mine yawned above us. We slumped down on a little platform covered with an old carpet, and one of the miners brought us tea. It was dark and bitter, but it tasted better than anything I had ever drunk. I sipped it and looked out over the superb river valley, southward in the general direction of Kabul.

The entrance to the mine was blackened by the smoke of six thousand years. In prehistory the sharp blueness of the lapis lazuli must have been discernible on the surface of the rock, and men must have lugged wood and water all the way up here, laid the wood against the rock face, set fire to it, and then dashed the water against the hot rock to crack it and get the lapis out. It was primitive and immensely strenuous, but it worked well enough to produce the material for Tutankhamun's funeral mask.

Until twenty years ago, the mining techniques were improving. Compressors and generators were installed, and experts of different kinds came in. The war ended all that. The miners had a few Swedish-made drills, elderly and small, with which they made holes in the rock face. One of the miners held the bit in his bare hand to direct it. Then they jammed explosives into the holes, lit the fuses, and ran like mad for safety. Peter and Tom, filming them, had no idea what was going to happen, and they ran for it too. We were just outside when a deep rumble shook the mountain, and dust drifted out of the mine entrance. But there was often a problem: if several sticks of explosive went off at once, they couldn't tell how many bangs there had been. That meant someone had to go back inside to see if all the explosives had gone off. Almost every month someone died like this. Once they were sure, the miners raced back in before the fumes had faded, to grab the best chunks of lapis for themselves.

It was about as dangerous a way to earn a living as you can imagine. And these must have been some of the worst-paid workers in the entire world, taking into account the value of what they produce. For a twelve-hour shift they earned £1.20—ten pence an hour. Each kilo of lapis lazuli they dig out is worth up to £12,000 when cut and polished: ten thousand times as much. The miners were essentially slaves of the mountain.

Worse, the brutal methods they used constituted a kind of rape. The lapis was fractured and spoiled by the explosives; and because it was being produced in such large quantities, and was so damaged, the international price for it fell. To have a unique source like this, and yet to sell it off more and more cheaply, was a sign of the most foolish wastefulness.

We interviewed one of the miners, a young man named Abdul Samad. What he said had the ring of truth to it, and contradicted everything Commander Malik had told us earlier.

TRANSCRIPT OF INTERVIEW FROM *NEWSNIGHT* REPORT, 5.11.97

Speaker: Abdul Samad

AS: Najimuddin Khan sells concessions to the mine to big businessmen in Pakistan. They give him the money, and he issues the orders from his base. Commander Malik keeps a check on it all for him. The commanders who have the power make the money. We blast the mine, but the commanders take over the big rocks and the rest of us get the left-overs. The commanders spend the money on themselves.

And the roads, the mosques, the clinics? Nonexistent, except for a short stretch of rough road running southward for a few miles along the line of the Kowkcheh River to the village of Skazar. The caravans of lapis, which once went to Kabul for cutting and polishing, now go over the mountains to Pakistan.

Commander Malik was as watchfully affable as ever when we left the following morning. There was a formal exchange of presents in front of everybody: he gave us a thousand pounds' worth of lapis, and I gave him my Sony Walkman. The crowd seemed to think it was a fair exchange. Everything was very pleasant; except that Malik warned our translator privately that we must never talk about the things we had seen at Sar-i-Sang. The purpose of television broadcasting seemed rather to have eluded him.

We headed off for the village of Skazar in a pleasant open valley at the confluence of the Kowkcheh and Monjan rivers. There we paid off our faithful drivers and their even more faithful Russian jeeps, and while I dictated my column to the *Sunday Telegraph* by satellite phone the others hired a team of horsemen at the caravanserai. On the map, the distance is short: twenty-five miles to the Pakistani border. But maps can be very deceptive. Some of the mountains around us rose to more than twenty thousand feet, and even the passes between them were extremely difficult.

Not, however, for the first leg of the journey. We merely headed along the river valley. My horse was rather good: a stallion that Ahmad Shah Massoud's chief of intelligence had once ridden in games of *buzkashi,* the ferocious version of polo that Afghans play with the headless body of a goat instead of a ball, while their mounts attack and bite each other. Now though, my horse's fighting spirit seemed to have been completely crushed out of him, and he merely plodded along, carrying my fifteen stone and a good part of our equipment. We established a good relationship. I found a noise that seemed to comfort him, and every time I made it he would turn his head and nuzzle my foot affectionately—alarming the first time, when I remembered his *buzkashi*-playing past, but fine after that. "Together," as Peachy Carnehan says to Rudyard Kipling, "we starts forward into those bitter cold mountainous parts, and never a road broader than the back of your hand."

The landscape was superb; and in the chill of the evening we came to a little mosque by the riverside and prepared to settle down there for the night. The drivers were simple men and very poor, and right from the start they seemed to show an unhealthy interest in the things we had: torches, gloves, penknives, food. By their standards we must have seemed unthinkably rich.

We were off by 5:30 the following morning, a penumbra of dust hanging over us in the golden morning sunlight and blurring the details like an impressionist watercolor. By eight o'clock we were climbing the mountains, and the difficult part had begun. The track curled in and out between rocks and over ridges, and whenever it got steep we had to get off our horses and walk. At this altitude the air felt fine and very thin, and we found ourselves taking thirsty gulps of it. The energy tablets I had bought at Boots before I left became very popular.

We often saw other caravans of horses or donkeys. This is the main trade route for all sorts of goods, smuggled or otherwise: lapis lazuli, emeralds, opium and heroin, guns. At midday, still without food, we came to a high plateau that served as a resting place for travelers. There were boulders everywhere, which were used to shelter small fires from the wind, and a half dozen or more groups of travelers had stopped to brew tea, smoke, gossip and rest. There was a kind of truce here. You could leave your bags of lapis or opium and go off, and no one would tamper with them.

A little farther off sat a group of men with six Siberian falcons, live and hooded, which they were giving a little air and exercise to. The falcons were more valuable than any lapis or emeralds. At the markets in Peshawar they would be bought by dealers and taken to Saudi Arabia, where they would fetch £100,000 each. Hooded, they turned their heads alertly to the sound of our voices, as though they were hoping to find out what was going to happen to them.

"Of course I know it's not right," the head of the group said. "These are our birds—Afghanistan's. Once there used to be lions here and all sorts of other animals. Now they've all gone. They've been hunted to extinction. I don't want that to happen to the falcons. But I'm a poor man. What else can I do?"

There was a characteristic whine in his voice, yet he was right in a way. Afghanistan has become a country which plunders itself for the benefit of others, and the most that Afghans can do is to get their cut—the smallest of all.

It was dark by the time we reached the border with Pakistan and found a couple of vehicles that would take us onward. In the confusion the drivers decided to steal some of our things: the lapis Malik had given us, and my Camel bag containing my passport, money, notebooks and my Psion organizer, which contains my entire life and is irreplaceable. Hunger, fatigue and cold drove me wild with fury. I grabbed one of the drivers by the neck and told our translator to go off and get a Kalashnikov. I'd shoot the driver with it, I said.

Maybe I didn't mean it, but the drivers thought I did. Even before the translator had started off in search of the AK, the lapis and the Camel bag had mysteriously been found. A superb golden moon climbed above the mountains and shone into the lake that lay between them. We still had twenty hours' traveling to do over the mountains into Pakistan before we reached Chitral, some of it as rough as anything we'd endured in Afghanistan. But the journey had been a success. I put my hand into my pocket and gripped the small piece of lapis I had picked up on the mountainside at Sar-i-Sang: as dark and rich as the blue of the Virgin's cloak, gently veined with a faint line of glittering gold like a vapor trail in the sky. It was true. I'd done it.

12
Bombing

*To a surprising extent the war-lords in shining armor, the apostles
of the martial virtues, tend not to die fighting when the time comes.
History is full of ignominious getaways by the great and famous.*
—GEORGE ORWELL, *Who Are the War Criminals?*, 1944

In March 1999 I went to Belgrade to report on the coming war.

It wasn't easy to get there. The Serbian authorities disliked the BBC,
and my reporting from Sarajevo during the siege by the Bosnian Serbs
had been regarded in Belgrade as anti-Serbian. Nevertheless in February
I had invited the foreign minister to be the guest on my program for
News 24 and BBC World, *Simpson's World*. I gave the minister a hard
time, and was worried at one stage whether I hadn't merely irritated
him further. Apparently not.

"No one else from the British or the American media has asked us for
our point of view," his adviser said afterward. "They just seem to want to
tell us what we think."

So we were able to be there for the big crisis after all. I flew into
Belgrade only two days before the airport was closed for good. The
situation looked bad; and now, with the benefit of hindsight, it is clear
that this was the intention. You do not have to be pro-Serbian—and I
am no more pro-Serbian now than I was anti-Serbian in Sarajevo—to
realize that the Kosovo crisis was a setup. President Clinton, badly
damaged by the Monica Lewinsky affair, had decided with his secretary of state, Madeleine Albright, that there would be only one outcome to this particular Balkan crisis: Milošević would have to back

down, or be bombed into submission. The draft agreement the Americans offered him at the Rambouillet conference at the start of February was packed with elements he could never have accepted. They wanted him to say no.

None of which makes Milošević or his backers in any way the innocent party. The latest crisis had erupted because Serbian paramilitaries had entered the village of Raćak in Kosovo on 15 January and murdered forty-five people. Milošević was the closest thing in Europe to Saddam Hussein: for a decade he had deliberately stirred up ethnic tension, ensuring thousands of deaths in the process, had lost every piece of territory he fought for, and had clung to power in an area of operation that was getting smaller with each new crisis.

Something, people felt, had to be done about him. President Clinton and Madeleine Albright thought that bombing his country was the best way. This had been Albright's solution to the Bosnian crisis; now it was her solution to the Kosovo one. She failed to notice that Bosnia was much less important to Milošević than Kosovo, which Serbs regarded as the cradle of their culture. It would all be over in a matter of days, she said. She turned out to be absolutely right: seventy-eight days.

President Clinton agreed, but insisted that there could be no question of putting American servicemen's lives at risk. In doing so he automatically sentenced five hundred or more Serbian civilians to death, since the bombing would have to be high-altitude and that meant it would inevitably be less accurate. Clinton's policy also ensured that large numbers of ethnic Albanians would lose their homes or be killed too, since there were to be no NATO ground troops to protect them, and the Serbs were thirsting for revenge. The British went along with all this, as did the other NATO allies. To have failed would have been to desert the United States at a critical moment. It would never have been forgiven.

As for me, I stayed in Belgrade throughout those seventy-eight days, plus a little more. Part of this time I spent with my leg in plaster, for reasons I shall explain, and I was thrown out, rather absurdly, after the conflict was over. I kept a diary, of which these are some extracts. I have interpolated some explanations to make it clearer, but I have resisted the temptation to embroider the facts in my favor.

Tuesday 23 March 1999

Richard Holbrooke, the American negotiator, is trying to persuade Milošević to do what Washington demands of him. I like and admire Holbrooke. I had lunch with him once, and was much impressed by the breadth of his reading and his knowledge of the business of diplomacy. From time to time he comes back to the Belgrade Hyatt, where he always stays and which has become the main press hotel. The dozens of television crews and reporters who are covering the crisis fall on him, shouting their questions. I hang around at the back on these occasions: You never get anything worth having under such conditions.

In the late afternoon I go round to the British embassy. The people there have the reputation of being the best informed of the Western diplomats.

"The signs aren't good," says _____. "If it all breaks down, the bombing will start pretty much at once. And it'll be hard."

How hard, I wonder? I reflect that diplomats like him will be long gone, but we'll be under it all and the Serbs will want to seek revenge on someone.

He explains. The infrastructure of the country will be progressively stripped away, giving Milošević the opportunity to stop it any time he chooses. The chances are that Milošević actually wants to back down now, and that he is looking for the opportunity to do it. If so, he will be able to tell his people after a few days that they have fought heroically, but that they simply cannot hold out against the greatest military alliance on earth indefinitely and must give in now.

"Does NATO have the nerve to keep on bombing until that point is reached? Or the cohesion?"

"I understand what you are saying, but we think it does."

I drive back through the quiet streets, looking at the gloomy buildings and wondering how many will still be standing in a few weeks. On the other hand, I tell myself, I have been through this before. Baghdad was hit with more high explosive than any city in the history of warfare, and yet we survived perfectly well. The trouble is, you never know beforehand how bad it is going to be this time.

Back at the Hyatt, Richard Holbrooke arrives, tired and gloomy. He is a servant of his government, but he is also a man who knew the former Yugoslavia well; I have the impression he would have liked to avoid a war if it were at all possible. It clearly isn't—not given the ultimatum Clinton and Albright have ordered him to give.

I corner him near the lifts:

"Our mission has failed. I will now be flying to Brussels to consult the alliance."

The war is about to begin; it simply requires the final agreement of the NATO countries, which is a foregone conclusion. The huge crowd of journalists breaks up and streams away. In the lift I grin at a producer from one of the American television networks, whom I remember from Baghdad.

"So we're in for it again."

He rolls his eyes.

"Food shortages, water shortages," I intone. "Soon we'll be able to tell which rooms are occupied because they'll smell so bad."

"So you'll stay?"

"Won't you?"

"Doubt it. The White House'll probably try to get us to pull out."

That, I reflect, is the reality for many American journalists now. When the big, dangerous stories come up, they are the first to leave. In Belgrade there are only one or two Americans who are prepared to stay. We'll no doubt be left, as we usually are in bad situations, with the old firm: the Brits, the Aussies, the French, and the occasional Italian or Spaniard or Dutchman. But for the most part you can forget the Germans, the Japanese and the Americans.

Wednesday 24 March

"The first bomb that falls on Serbia, you Westerners will suffer. And so will the Albanians. We'll kill them all."

It's just a hotel employee talking, but he reflects a genuine level of feeling here. Things could get very nasty directly the bombing starts. It gives me great pleasure not to give him a tip.

The government have been making their preparations in characteristic fashion. The independent radio station B-92 was closed down this morning. So was the satellite operation run by the European Broadcasting Union and Reuters Television. Several people were punched and slapped about, and Nikki Millard, a BBC cameraman, had his camera stolen by the secret police who carried out the raid. It won't be returned, of course; these people are a law unto themselves, and they'll sell it abroad somewhere.

Civilians who prepare for war always have a look of utter disbelief on their faces, and their preparations are half-hearted and badly done, as if they don't really expect that anything will come of it. In the security and familiarity of their own streets and houses they can't imagine what it'll be like to have huge quantities of high explosive falling out of the sky. Nor can I.

We are filming the arrangements which the shopkeepers are making in the center of town when my mobile rings. It is Jonathan Patterson, the BBC producer who is working with me.

"Can you talk?"

"Yes."

"We've just had word from Brussels that the first NATO planes have taken off."

"I'll be straight back."

It is a curious feeling to think of those immensely powerful bombers heading toward us at 500 mph, and that no one around me yet knows it. It reminds me of a family friend who worked in Military Intelligence during the War and had a nervous breakdown because she could not tell anyone about the V-1 and V-2 rockets which she knew would soon be landing on London.

We drive back over the main bridge toward the hotel. In the evening sunlight people are queuing as usual for their trams home. No panic, no sign even of nervousness. They don't know what is coming their way. If it's anything like Baghdad the bridges will go early on.

Dragan Petrović, our Serbian producer, is driving. He is a powerfully built man of thirty, with a head as shaven as that of any Arkan supporter, and no one messes with us if Dragan is there. His appearance belies his character entirely: he is a thoughtful, serious-minded and gentle man, and I have come to rely greatly on his advice and information. His English is superb, but he does a particularly good angry-Serb-speaking-English impression. "For why you criticize my President?" he asked an American correspondent who had been sounding off about Milošević. "Tell me your name." The correspondent almost went down on his knees to apologize.

Now, checking my watch, I ask Dragan to stop in a side-street near the hotel. The first bombs will fall very soon now, and I want to be out in the open when it happens, so that I can see them more clearly.

The sirens begin to wail, first one, then another, then right across the city: a sound I haven't heard for nine years. That was on a different continent. But the smart bombs and the missiles will be the same, and I'm not nearly as nervous about them as I was in Baghdad in 1991; then I thought we would all be killed in a savage indiscriminate carpet-bombing of the city. Instead, their accuracy was phenomenal, and there is safety in that. The real danger for us will be the reaction of the local thugs: their desire to revenge themselves on anyone from the countries that are bombing them.

Now we sit and wait: it is already some way past the time Jonathan told me to expect the first explosions. Then there are two flashes on the distant horizon, and the sound follows some seconds later. I call London on my mobile and go live into the six o'clock radio news: "The air attacks have started." But I am surprised that they are no nearer than a dozen miles from Belgrade. This is not going to be a savage all-out attack after all: the bombs will grind us down slowly.

That evening power-generating plants and some factories on the edge of Belgrade are hit, and the television cameramen stationed on the roof film the distant explosions.

"Not much of a shot," one cameraman grumbles, peering through the eyepiece at the sudden upsurge of fire on the horizon.

I record a piece to camera and take the cassette downstairs with me to edit. While we are still busy someone comes running into the room.

"They've arrested all the guys on the roof and taken them away."

Kevin Bishop, our other producer, was there, with Gig (Peter Gigliotti, an Australian cameraman who's working for us). It's a bad moment. There are at least forty other camera crews up there. We have no idea where they have been taken, nor what will happen to them.

Thursday 25 March

They spend most of the night at a police station, being questioned and having their full details recorded before being released. No one seems to have threatened them, perhaps because the hotel security staff went with them. They also brought them sandwiches and coffee at three in the morning. Modern warfare is a strange business: our countries bomb this city, we watch it, and some of the victims regard it as their first duty to make sure we're properly looked after.

The atmosphere has become a great deal nastier, all the same.

"We have to take certain measures," says someone at the Foreign Ministry warningly, when I ring to complain about the treatment of our staff and the theft of our camera by the police.

Arkan, the Serbian warlord and gangster, arrives in the Hyatt coffee shop with his gang of minders in black leather, and settles down to watch the foreign journalists with a menacing look on his pudgy young face. Christiane Amanpour, CNN's best correspondent, whose outspoken documentary detailing Arkan's crimes has just been rebroadcast and who is a strong advocate of bombing Serbia, is marched through the hotel lobby to the front door in the middle of a crowd of heavies. It was brave of her in the circumstances to have come here at all. She looks strained and frightened, and the heavies have been brought in by one of the Western embassies to get her to safety across the Hungarian border.

I panic though, thinking she has obtained an exclusive interview with Milošević and is being escorted off to do it. It is only when I see Brent Sadler, another of the CNN correspondents, celebrating that I realize she must have been thrown out of the country. I'm sorry she's gone, because I admire her and like her. But I'm also relieved, because she is serious competition. Things should be easier for us now.

All the other journalists crowd round to the Information Ministry. It's like Angus cows queuing up at the roast beef trolley in Simpson's-in-the-Strand. Vuk Drašković, formerly an opponent of Milošević but now his vice-premier, is flushed and his speech slurred: it is 11:30, and the day's first bottle of slivovitz must have been going around.

"You are all welcome to stay," he says.

But at another press conference elsewhere in Belgrade, the Serbian information minister, a nasty, pasty-faced little man who looks like a character out of Dickens and is a faithful supporter of the extreme nationalist Vojislav Šešlj orders all journalists from NATO countries to leave the country at once. There is panic at the Hyatt as the news spreads. The BBC group gathers to talk it over, and they all want to go. I would rather stay, but decide to go too; what can I do here, entirely on my own? The thugs would pick me off in ten minutes.

My stuff is already in the vehicle when I hear from Jonathan that Greg Wilesmith of ABC Australia is staying. On an impulse, I tell Jonathan I'll stay as well. At least I'll have company. I dig my case out of the vehicle again and say goodbye to the others, feeling scared yet oddly justified. "I think you're doing the right thing," says Kevin Bishop. It's nice of him—but I think the chances are I'm destined for some obscure and miserable fate. Even so, I feel liberated. It's a great feeling to be shot of all that pack journalism stuff and to be on my own.

I take over a suite—why not, under these circumstances?—and phone the office. Malcolm Downing, the foreign editor, sounds relieved. I also phone Dee to explain. She is calm and resigned, which makes me feel a lot better. She knows she's married to a lunatic, I suppose. I pour myself a generous slug of Laphroaig, light up a big, fat Upmann no. 2, and start broadcasting. This, I feel as I look out of the window, is the life. Let's hope it is.

Friday 26 March

As the bombing intensifies, so do the demands. I never knew there were so many BBC news programmes. By the evening I have done 167 live interviews. By the time the crisis finishes, three months later, I will have clocked up 190 hours of calls on my mobile. Any researcher wanting to know if this is dangerous merely has to give me a brain-scan. Our phoneline is cut several times: the security police are listening carefully to everything I say. If the questioner or I begin to criticize Milošević, they pull the plug. The hotel is entirely silent, though the nearest bombs are still a few miles away. This is not turning out to be anything like Baghdad, where I stayed in 1991 when the Gulf War bombing began. It's a lot lonelier, and a great deal more scary. There we were afraid of the bombs. Here I'm afraid a mob will storm the place and get me. And yet I still feel really good about staying. Even if something really bad happens, I think I will have done what I was paid to do.

At 2 A.M. the loudspeaker in the room orders everyone into the air raid shelters. I ignore it: this is my chance to get a couple of hours' sleep. Someone bangs on the door: "Open, please!" Convinced it's Arkan's Tigers, I leap out of bed stark naked and hide in the gap between the curtains and one of the windows. Pressing the cheeks of my backside against the window and holding my hands strategically in front of me, I prepare to sell my life dearly. It's only the hotel security men. They suspect I am around somewhere, and keep calling out variants of my name, going through the cupboards in the various parts of the suite, but for some reason ignore the curtains; though one man passes close enough to make the material move perceptibly.

They catch me later, by slipping into the room after I have fallen asleep. It is a relief to look up and find it's not a mobster dressed in black with a gun in his hand. Politely, the security men usher me downstairs. I find one or two other stay-behinds there, including Dave Williams of the *Daily Mail* and his equally relaxed and pleasant photographer: good company, I feel.

Saturday 27 March

I can't operate entirely on my own much longer. I need to know what Serbian television and radio are saying, and I can't find out because I can't speak the language. I also have a desperate need for some contact with life outside this hotel, in order to be able to report what is going on. Simply describing the explosions I can see from my window won't be enough soon.

I ring Dragan and Vlad Mirjanović, our other local producer, on my mobile. They are both entitled to be nervous and resentful, since I am breaking their cover and it could be extremely dangerous for them. Instead they are courteous and friendly. Surprised, though; they had assumed we had all gone. Dragan insists on coming straight round. He is a magnificent character: the best.

"It could be really dangerous for you, *Dragane moi.*"

"I'm coming anyway," he says gruffly.

We throw our arms round each other when he walks into the room.

Later the phone rings. It is Peter Gigliotti, our Australian cameraman, who travels on an Italian passport. (Italy is still regarded here as a friend.) He has managed to get back to Belgrade. Now we can start operating again in earnest.

Sunday 28 March

We drive out to see the wreckage of the US Stealth aircraft shot down near Budjanović. A wing lies in a field, and there is such competition to get a piece of the anti-radar fabric that a local photographer jabs his knife at me when I get in his way. Mostly, though, the Serbian journalists co-exist easily with us. An old woman brings out glasses of *rakija,* ferocious home-made brandy, and hands me one.

"If they drink this, they won't fight any more," she says.

I down it, and understand why.

The pilot has been rescued by an American helicopter team. This really is an extraordinary war. No doubt the Stealth aircraft had engine problems, and the bullet-holes we can see in it were inflicted when the plane was already coming down. But that isn't, of course, how the Serbs see it. Soon they will be printing stickers reading "Sorry, we didn't know it was meant to be invisible." They regard this as a sign that NATO is far from being invincible, and that if they can hold on and inflict a few more losses like this NATO's will to continue may start to fade.

If the British diplomat was right, and Milošević's real intention was to carry on resisting for a few days and then to hold up his hands and say, "They're just too overwhelmingly powerful for us," then that entire strategy has come a serious cropper. Now the Serbs think they're more than a match for NATO. We could well be in for the long haul here.

(Three years later, in the spring of 2002, I was having lunch in an extremely pleasant restaurant on the south bank of the Thames, opposite the Tower of London. My companions were my wife Dee, a close friend of hers, and an American named Matt who had previously been a pilot in the US Air Force. The conversation turned to his activities as a controller of bombing during the NATO campaign against Serbia. When I told him I had been out to see the wreckage of the Stealth aircraft, he laughed. It

seems he had had instructions to bomb the wreckage that morning, to prevent the technology from getting into Chinese or Russian hands; but, perhaps because the US military was anxious not to cause more civilian causalties than were necessary, the order was countermanded. The man who might have organized my killing and I sat opposite each other and laughed a lot about it. It was one of the more enjoyable lunches I have had; I'm just glad I was there to enjoy it.)

Monday 29 March

Dragan and I venture out for the first time to the center of Belgrade.

"Don't say anything and don't make eye-contact," he warns me.

I walk around with my eyes firmly on the ground. There are some very unpleasant-looking characters hanging around, and the cultural centers of Britain, France, the US, and Germany have all been comprehensively trashed and looted, with obscenities spray-painted on the walls. It makes me angry (bourgeois habits die hard, I suppose) and I start to exclaim and shake my head.

"John," Dragan hisses beside me, "you'll get us both killed if you don't shut up."

He's right; but I hate the sight of all those books burned and destroyed.

Tuesday 30 March

Mike Williams, from the *Today* programme, manages cleverly to get a visa back to Belgrade. He has a difficult and dangerous journey back in, and has to stop at the main army barracks outside Belgrade for a while. This is probably the worst-bombed building in Serbia.

Mike is excellent company, witty, sympathetic, widely read; he also takes a large share of the burden of radio and television interviews off me. "What's the mood on the streets?" and "What are the Serbian people being told about all this?" we are asked again and again. It is easier to bear now there is someone to complain to.

Wednesday 31 March

Things are still very dodgy: gangs of nasty characters hang around the hotel and the center of the city. Someone in London

won't take no for an answer and keeps asking me to go into the
RTS studio for a fatuous interview in good-quality audio instead
of doing it over the phone. To them it's nothing: just a matter of
the look of their programme. It could be really difficult for me.
But I'm in business to broadcast, not to stay silent; so in the end I
reluctantly agree.

I refuse to put Vlad or Dragan in the spot, so I decide to go on
my own, full of self-righteousness and not a little self-pity. Fortunately the spare car is sitting in the hotel car park, and the porters
have the key. I am quite scared as I drive through the empty streets.
If anyone catches me, I have no documents or passes and could be
in trouble. I reach a police roadblock. The cop peers in, and I pretend to struggle with the window then give up helplessly with an
"aren't-I-stupid?" gesture and a grin. He looks bored, and waves
me through. Outside the TV station I park carefully: I may need to
make a quick getaway. I remember the BBC correspondent in
Northern Ireland who was chased by an angry mob to his car, and
snapped the key off in the ignition in his anxiety. The army had to
rescue him.

The television staff are the same as ever: not friendly, but not
hostile either. I don't care about them; it's the gangs outside who are
the problem. I sit in the sauna-like studio (fan not working again)
and hear all the comfortable sounds and voices at the other end. The
technical staff in London are always friendly and jolly, at any rate.

Then on comes the questioner. There is testosterone in his
voice.

"How does Slobodan Milošević think he's going to get away
with committing crimes like this?"

I start to answer in emollient fashion. No good: the line is cut
by some angry Serbian control freak.

"Oh dear," says testosterone-voice, "we seem to have lost John
Simpson there in Belgrade."

"I wonder why," I think.

I sit there for a bit, listening to the line noise, but we're obviously
not going to be reconnected. I storm out into the control cubicle.

"Who the hell cut our line with London?"

Shrugs and embarrassment all round: oh, was it cut? Nothing
to do with us. Must have been some technical fault. Or maybe
the bombing. They know as well as I do that the censors were

listening, and would have pulled the plugs immediately if there was something they didn't like.

I'm too irritated to be nervous as I storm out of the studio and cross the road to my car. Three nasty-looking characters are hanging around nearby, but nobody had better mess around with me at a time like this. I glower at them and get in, remembering not to snap the key off. They take no notice of me anyway.

In the afternoon we visit the University Clinic, which lies right in the middle of four or five natural targets for NATO: the Security Police ministry, parts of the Ministry of Defense, etc. etc. The director and his staff tell us of their fears that if NATO attacks these targets the hospital will be hit. He is a gentle man, who has clearly watched the pictures of suffering refugees from the borders of Kosovo on Western satellite television and feels profoundly disturbed by them. "You must not think we are barbarians," he murmurs.

We meet several doctors, liberal-minded people with close links to British and American medicine, who tell me anxiously and with passion how their stocks of drugs have been depleted as a result of the outside world's sanctions against Serbia. How can the West presume to dictate to Serbia about humanitarianism when it restricts the supply of medicines to the sick?

In the end I can't keep quiet any more. "And what," I ask, "did you do when the Bosnian Serbs were besieging Sarajevo, and the main hospital was down to two surgeons who had to operate on patients without anesthetics by candlelight?"

There is bewilderment in their faces: this isn't a version of history they have come across; and to them it must just sound like the kind of arid point-scoring which habitually goes on here.

Thursday 1 April

I have arranged an interview with the warlord Arkan. It's going to be difficult, and I am determined that no one can accuse me of giving him an easy ride, as they did over CNN's interview with him yesterday. But it's one thing to be criticized for a feeble interview, and another to be criticized for doing the interview at all. Quite a lot of people in London seem to feel there is something wrong with interviewing those on the other side of the line. That,

I'm afraid, I simply don't understand. How can more information be a bad thing? Are we so insecure about our own approach, so scared of hearing anything else, that we dare not allow people to hear the response of an out-and-out thug?

Friday 2 April

NATO goes downtown. At 2 A.M. two MUP [interior ministry police] buildings are hit in the city center, right beside the University Clinic hospital where we filmed on Wednesday. We dress and run out of the hotel; by now there is no one to stop us. Dragan is driving. Mike, Gig and I stay very quiet when we reach a police roadblock. The policeman turns us back, but Dragan finds another way to the city center. We park, leaving Gig and his camera in the car for safety's sake, and tell him we will come back and get him if it's OK.

Mike, Dragan and I creep silently through the dark streets, avoiding police patrols. The flames light up the sky, and we have to be even more careful as we get nearer the MUP buildings. Now we are starting to get inquisitive looks from the people who have gathered to watch, and from the police. Not far from us, cameramen and photographers—all of them Serbs, working for Serbian organizations—are being roughed up and arrested. There is no question of getting Gig out of the car with his camera. While the others hang out in the street I dodge into the front garden of a block of flats and do a couple of live interviews for BBC World and News 24 on my mobile.

Afterwards we slip round to the University Clinic, to see if any damage has been caused there. We find the mothers in labor and those with young children have been moved into the basement— several dozen of them. A lot of fear and anger here. The director we spoke to—the one we interviewed on Wednesday, who was apologetic over what the Serbs were doing in Kosovo—hurries in from home to inspect the damage to the hospital. He shakes my hand almost with distaste. I ask if we can go in to film the women in the basement. He breaks away and hurries inside. "No, you may not," he calls out angrily over his shoulder.

Belgrade has been at the heart of ethnic cleansing and outright war for years, while scarcely suffering in any serious way. For the most part this city's people know only what their government has

chosen to tell them through the state media about the suffering which the rest of the former Yugoslavia has endured as a result of President Milošević's policies. Now, for the first time, they are suffering something of what their President has inflicted on everyone else, and they don't like it.

Wednesday 7 April

The army press center takes us to Priština, where NATO has hit a row of houses and killed some civilians. We drive for hours through the silent countryside of southern Serbia and Kosovo, looking at the torched houses and the paramilitary thugs lounging at the roadblocks. Priština is eerily empty, cleansed of most of its Albanian inhabitants. The Serbs mostly stay indoors. The only sounds are the crows in the trees and the barking of abandoned dogs. Terrible things have gone on here.

Friday 9 April

I start to notice something intriguing. Time and again, the Serbs seem to know where the next bombing is going to happen. Until now this has been just a suspicion, but today it becomes near-certainty when we receive information from Kragujevać, south of Belgrade, where the big Zastava car factory is situated. The workers in most big industries have been staging sit-ins in order to deter NATO from bombing them. This human shield tactic developed from the concerts held each night on Belgrade's main bridge.

Last night, representatives of the local authorities in Kragujevać went round to the Zastava factory and told the work-force there to end their sit-in, because NATO was about to attack. The workers moved out of the factory and into the car parks and waste ground beside it. Not long afterwards the bombers arrived. The plant was destroyed, and 124 people who had strayed too close were injured. The Kragujevác authorities, we're told, are delighted; their warning worked.

So how did they know? Either NATO is leaking information to the Serbs about what they're planning to hit, in order to minimize civilian casualties, or else there is a spy within NATO. This second possibility is completely outside my range of knowledge, but the first is certainly worth considering.

Since television news is not a good medium for floating theo-
ries, I decide to launch my trial balloon in my weekly column for
the *Sunday Telegraph*:

> A pattern is emerging which suggests that the Yugoslav
> government may be receiving prior warning from NATO
> about some of its planned air-strikes, in an attempt to min-
> imize civilian casualties. There are signs that as more and
> more Serbs join sit-ins to protect their places of work and
> their cities from air-strikes, Belgrade has had word before-
> hand so that the human shield can be lifted.

Not, perhaps, the strongest introduction to a story I have ever written, but it's as far as I can go without having any informed background
material or confirmation from this end.

(A year later, the BBC broadcast a documentary about the war, which
demonstrated from reliable sources in the US forces that the Yugoslav
government was indeed receiving prior information from NATO. But I
was wrong to suggest that NATO as an organization *intended* to give it to
the Yugoslavs: It came from a spy. There were various possibilities: the
Greeks and Italians, though members of NATO, maintained contacts
with Belgrade throughout the bombing; France was continually intervening to prevent air attacks that would cause particular damage or loss
of life; there was unprecedented doubt and dissension within the Alliance
about the entire strategy of bombing the Serbs, which may have led some
individual to a unilateral act of betrayal; and the Russians seem to have
begun their espionage efforts against NATO again, so that the leak could
have come from them. Or the Chinese, whose embassy was later
bombed, may have been monitoring NATO communications.)

Monday 12 April

We are allowed to film at a special session of the Yugoslav Parliament. Before it starts we can wander around on the floor of the
house, and I approach Vojislav Šešlj, who is in his seat with the
rest of his party members to the right of the speaker. I offer to
shake hands with him.

"Fuck off, BBC," he says, scarcely looking at me.

"Thank you," I say as smoothly as I can manage, "can I use that?"

Šešlj's men were some of the worst during the earlier fighting, and he remains the most dangerous figure in public life here; which in this gangster-ridden place is saying something.

We need to interview people in the streets: the voice of ordinary Serbs has so far been lacking. It is certainly going to be dangerous, because feelings are running so high. Just three of us will go: Gig, Dragan and I. We joke in the car, but we are all anxious.

"Let's just do it here," I say when we get to the main pedestrian area.

A couple of policemen stroll past. Dragan asks them if they'll hang around in case of trouble.

"BBC? Fuck off," the policemen say, and walk away laughing. It seems to be becoming a habit.

Already people are gathering angrily around us. I scarcely need to ask them any questions: they're shouting before I've got the words out. Spit lands on my face.

"We used to like everything from West. Now we hate you."

"We are all for Milošević now, even if we didn't like him before."

"You British are the fucking slaves of fucking America."

There is a real sense of violence here, yet in the end by listening to what these people are saying and arguing with them politely I find that I can talk them round. They don't really hate us at all; they are frightened and resentful of the bombing. I end up on friendly terms with one of the stall-holders who sells patriotic lapel badges and postcards of the bomb-damage. He loads me down with presents as we leave.

We have a powerful story, and we have escaped without getting our heads broken. I've never had so many "fucks" to blank out in a report before.

As we are editing in our hotel suite a couple of secret policemen arrive: big men. They are polite enough, but unyielding—Gig must get out of the country within 24 hours. I should have guessed: the Angel of Death was sitting in the hotel lobby when we got back. She is a big, blowzy woman from the security police, who dyes her hair a brilliant and unlikely red, and seems to come here as a back-up whenever someone is thrown out of the country. I ring a senior official in the hope of getting the decision reversed, but he is adamant. It's a punishment for our hostile reporting.

Tuesday 13 April

The foreign journalists have started coming back to Belgrade in large numbers, and the hotel is filling up again. I'm glad, in that it gives us a lot more protection: no one can just come round and pick us off now. Even so, I rather miss the quietness of the hotel and the sense of being free of pack journalism. Jacky Rowland, the BBC correspondent, has managed to get back too, and has taken a lot more of the burden of reporting off my shoulders and those of Mike Williams. I am fond of her, not least because she reminds me of my daughter Julia.

Wednesday 14 April

A column of Albanian refugees is hit close to the border. Various suggestions are proffered in Brussels: it was a military convoy; enraged Serbian soldiers shot the refugees; it's all an invention of the Milošević propaganda machine. Here the immediate assumption is that it's NATO. I say in a *Nine O'Clock News* interview that if the Serbs feel confident that NATO did it they'll take us down to see the place where it happened. If not, they'll quietly forget about it.

Thursday 15 April

Fury in Whitehall at my reporting—both the filming in the street and the 9:00 studio interview. Unnamed officials tell lobby journalists I have been guilty of accepting the Serbian version of events. I am gullible, I am being used by the Serbs for their propaganda purposes, I am pro-Serb. Tony Blair has told the Commons that I am working here "under the instruction and guidance of the Serbian authorities." Some MP (Labour, I think) called out "Shame!" God bless him. If Blair repeated that outside the privilege of the Commons, I would sue him and win; the Serbs aren't instructing me, and they certainly aren't guiding me; and I take it as the greatest insult. For his part, Alastair Campbell, the Downing Street press spokesman, apparently thinks our interviewees in the street only said what they did because they were frightened of the secret police. He should have been there.

But it had to happen: when the going gets tough in wartime (the Falklands, the bombing of Libya in 1986, the Gulf War) the

first instinct of British governments is to attack the people who are reporting the unpalatable. There's already been a harbinger of it all, a Labour MP called Ben Bradshaw. Downing Street have set him up to attack me because he was apparently a BBC correspondent—a stringer in Berlin, someone tells me—before he was elected to Parliament. It's a spiteful attack, quite personal. When someone from one of the British papers rings me for my reaction I say, grandly but perfectly truthfully, that I had never heard of him, either as a BBC correspondent or as an MP. The quote is taken up.

A phone call from a friend at Westminster: the Ministry of Defense had been much worse and more insidious than Downing Street; Alastair, whom I've always quite liked, was merely bluff and irritable. It was a couple of senior MoD people who were putting out the real poison.

This time, though, there is a big difference from all the other occasions in the past. The newspapers rally round, MPs object, support flows in. The BBC is more robust than I have ever seen it: I get calls of support from Sir Christopher Bland, the BBC chairman, Sir John Birt, the director-general, Tony Hall, head of news and any number of others. In the past the BBC would have caved in at once. Nowadays it's developed some real lead in its pencil. Maggie O'Kane, the *Guardian* correspondent in Belgrade, slips a note under the door: "For what it's worth, I've always thought your reporting was completely independent." It's worth a good deal at a time like this.

Friday 16 April

Interviews with Russian, Japanese, French, German, Italian, American, Swedish, Greek, Turkish, Dutch and Spanish journalists. By now the story, much exaggerated, has gone round the world: the British government is trying to silence the BBC. Opinion abroad is genuinely shocked, and I find myself defending Tony Blair and trying to explain the BBC's independence of the government; it doesn't sound very convincing, in the light of all this. The Serbs are jubilant, of course. That's the worst of all—they think we're as bad as they are. I refuse to be interviewed by their newspapers or television on principle, and explain why.

The fact is, I can say most of the things I want here. It is true that our videotaped reports have to be passed by the censor (by the end of the war my reports had been more censored than those of any other correspondent in Belgrade) but the security people no longer seem to be listening to our phones. Whenever the censors cut something out, I simply repeat it over the phone.

We have to be careful, all the same. There are passionate advocates of the Serbian cause listening in London to everything we say, and reporting back to Belgrade; especially a ghastly little man with a bald head like a penis who pops up all the time on BBC World and Sky. His name is Garsić, pronounced *Garsich*, but we call him Arsić. If you are sensible, and you do not go in for name-calling (Milošević a fascist dictator, etc. etc.), and can substantiate what you say, then you are likely to survive here. But if we find a good story that is likely to get us thrown out, I have made it clear to everyone here that we will use it, and damn the consequences.

Goran Matić, a smooth, cynical government minister and a confidante of Milošević's, is amused by my troubles with the British government. "They should have complained about _____," he says, naming another Western organization. "We call them Serbian Television." Interestingly, Downing Street has backed off completely. Now, apparently, they're falling over themselves to say they don't know how anyone got the idea they were critical of my reporting. Respected figure, doing a good job under difficult conditions, etc. etc. It's all very amusing, really. It just shows that if the BBC stands up for itself against the politicians, it will always win the day.

Sunday 18 April

Robin Cook, the foreign secretary, still hasn't got the message. Shrilly, he tells a commercial station I should get out of Belgrade. Clare Short, the overseas aid minister, compares my reporting from Belgrade with reporting from Berlin in the Second World War; that makes me a Nazi sympathizer as well as being pro-Serb, I suppose. A political friend of mine rings from his mobile without giving his name. "Watch George [Robertson]," he says. "You won't find him slagging you off. He's advising the others to stay cool. Cook and Short don't count for anything anyway, and they're only attacking you in order to show how super-loyal they are. As for Tony, he's really embarrassed about the way it's all back-fired. Your lot have come out of all this rather well, I thought."

Much more seriously, one of the last voices to be raised here against Milošević has been silenced. Slavko Curuvija and his wife came home this afternoon from a walk in the spring sunshine, and two gunmen shot Curuvija dead. He was a complex and interesting man; not an angel, certainly, but someone with real moral courage and an independent spirit. He had helped to found *Dvevni Telegraf*, The Weekly Telegraph. There is a gangsterish quality about this place: anyone can be shot at any time.

Monday 19 April

Dragan and I sit in our car in the car park of a dreary housing estate, watching out for policemen or other official busybodies, and wait for a tall, gangling young man in his early twenties to come and find us. "This is him now," says Dragan, and flashes the headlights. His name is Balša, and he is a young cameraman, recently out of film school. We have to be careful: even the fact that we are meeting him can turn out to be very awkward for him. If the Serbs throw out our accredited cameraman to punish us, what might they do to a young bloke who is just starting to make his way in the world?

"You'll like him," Dragan says, and I do: he's quiet and brood-ing, but there's an earnestness about him and a determination to do the job to the best of his ability which pleases me. He knows a picture editor, too: Bata, a sensitive and gentle man, also in his early twenties. They are very different in character, both from each other and from Dragan, the mainstay of our whole opera-tion here. But their company keeps me going in this depressing place: they lark around, and bring an air of real life into our reporting, something better and more decent than the gloom of Milošević's regime.

Tuesday 20 April

We set up shop in the hotel. Power cuts are frequent now, but one of the advantages of having a suite is that for some mys-terious reason the razor socket in the bathroom still works when the entire rest of the hotel is in complete darkness and the generator is at its lowest capacity. Bata and Balša think we can run our editing machines, which (thank God) I told Gig to leave behind when he was thrown out, from this socket. We hired the room next door to mine for the edit suite long before, and Bata and Balša sleep there each night. (Dragan has another room, which he shares with his girlfriend Daniela, a beautiful and delicate Montenegrin girl. He brought her here because of the bombing, their own flat being on the top floor of a nearby block and unpleasantly vulnerable to passing missiles.) So the wires snake their way across my suite, gaffer-taped down to prevent anyone tripping over them. The hotel security people have warned us not to run anything off the razor sockets in case there is a fire; but the work comes first. We successfully run about eight different machines off this tenuous link with civilization.

Balša suggests we should film at the KGB Café in central Belgrade. Young people, sick of the war and of their rotten government, come here as a refuge. Talking to them is deeply refreshing: like the Belgrade of the old days. It's a relief to find a bedrock of people here I like and can sympathize with. There are one or two older ones here too, getting away from all the hatred and stupidity outside. It feels like a real refuge. Thank God someone in this city is sane and decent.

Wednesday 21 April

We try to go to Curuvija's funeral, but are specifically told that if we do we will be thrown out of the country immediately. I don't like giving in to threats, but decide eventually not to go: staying here for the long haul is more important.

This week's edition of Curuvija's paper came out today: there were the usual nudes, a vicious attack on the BBC's reporting, a lot of rhetoric about gallant Serbs and neo-fascist NATO aggressors—and no mention whatever of Curuvija's murder. The press has learned its lesson.

At the funeral another brave man, Professor Jarko Korać of Belgrade University, told the mourners, "Slavko was the toughest critic of the government. His assassination was a political message, and some people are asking themselves if this has opened the process of settling scores with those who think differently."

Slobodan Milošević's Yugoslavia is a place where any dark crime can occur.

Thursday 22 April

At around 3 A.M. I have just got into bed when an explosion, terrifyingly close, almost knocks me to the floor. I bundle the blankets over my head and roll into the bathroom just as another gigantic explosion rocks the room, knocks things over, and makes every window in the place bulge inward. I wait a moment or two, but I know what it is: the Usce building, three hundred yards away. It's where the radio and TV station belonging to Milošević's family and friends is based: a great ugly sixties block which used to be the Communist Party HQ. I creep over to the window and poke my head through the curtains, as though that will protect me. Half the building is in flames; and just as I look, a third smart bomb hits the roof and drops down through the building. It's an extraordinary moment. The place is on fire throughout, and yet there are sections of the building where the electric lights are still on. At last they go out.

The transmitting tower stays upright on the roof of the Usce building, however. Some nights later there is a fantastic whirring sound overhead: the noise of a cruise missile's motor. It strikes the transmitting tower, which can only be seven or eight feet across, and knocks it over the edge of the building where it hangs like a crumpled wire coat hanger. The thought that a missile fired from five hundred miles away could be so accurate is extraordinary.

It's beginning to feel uncomfortable here: the bombs are close, and the threat of the murder gangs hasn't gone away.

"Oh, you'll be safe enough," says a colleague from London, rather patronizingly. "They won't hit your hotel with journalists there." Glad he thinks so; they managed to hit the Al-Rashid (in Baghdad).

Friday 23 April

I have just got to sleep when a tremendous explosion nearby rocks the room. It is 2:13 A.M. RTS, the State television service, has been hit. I turn the TV set on: just hash and line noise. NATO threatened to do this before, but Jamie Shea, the NATO spokesman, gave the strong impression it wasn't a target. I must say, I always assumed it would be. I've been going round there night after night with Vlad to satellite our material, and every time we walked out afterward I wondered whether the place would still be standing in the morning. We've had warnings from the BBC in London for two weeks now, advising us not to go there. What can you do? Here, you could get killed just lying in bed.

Some months later, one of the most senior people at CNN told me that he'd been called by the Pentagon and warned that the TV station was going to be hit that night. He rang everyone he could in Washington to advise them not to go ahead with the attack, and later heard that the plane in question was turned around half an hour before it reached the target. Afterward, though, the decision was reviewed, and the Americans decided to go ahead with the bombing.

Richard Holbrooke was a particular enthusiast: RTS was Milošević's main propaganda weapon and had to be taken out, he said. If only these people knew a little more about the way television works. The Serbs had planned everything out in the event of an attack on the TV station, and they were only off the air for a few hours. If NATO had had the wit to attack the transmitters, no one would have been killed and the TV service would have been off for much longer. [When they try that later, it works.]

We decide it is too risky to drive round to the RTS building right away; there will be gangs out on the streets. Instead we will go at first light. The sight of the place, still burning and with rubble strewn everywhere, is really depressing in the cold chill of dawn. Firemen are clambering over the heaps of rubble, listening for the sound of human voices.

A government minister arrives: he is remarkably sprightly and jolly with us, and his face only becomes serious when we interview him. I start to believe the stories which have been going the rounds, that the government told RTS to ensure that the station was fully manned every night. It makes excellent propaganda for them if people have been killed.

They let us in, and we walk along the corridors which have become so familiar over the weeks; only now they are smashed and burned, and our feet crunch on rubble and broken glass. We peer into a studio where I have done a lot of interviews: all wrecked.

"Somebody here," says our guide.

I know this little room: it's where the overnight make-up lady worked. Her foot is sticking out of the rubble at an angle. It is encased in a dusty shoe, and there is a razor cut over a bunion. Nothing I have seen in this city so far is worse than this.

What kind of war is it, where NATO targets a make-up lady, and the government is glad to see her killed? The television staff came here because they assumed they would be safe. They should have noticed that the top management never came in at night-time.

By 7 A.M. RTS is broadcasting again: it had cost fifteen lives to keep it off the air for four and three quarter hours. Serbian Television is indeed part of the central nervous system of President Milošević's control over this country, just as NATO says. It has made it far easier for him to ensure public complaisance over the stripping out of Kosovo's ethnic Albanian population. It has, by judicious editing and selection, managed to give its viewers the impression that only NATO's governments are in favor of the war, while ordinary opinion abroad supports "this small, brave country."

It has buoyed them up artificially with the belief that Russia is about to enter the war on their side, and has hinted that the Russians have been supplied with all sorts of secret weapons. It has assured them that dozens of NATO aircraft have been shot down. For years now it has hidden from them all information about the terrible crimes that people acting in Serbia's name have committed in the former Yugoslavia.

By any measure of honesty and decency, Serbian Television is the tame instrument of a nasty system. That made it a natural target for NATO bombs and missiles. But should the television station, as opposed to its transmitters, have been hit? Should the make-up lady have paid the ultimate price for the propaganda of people so high up in the system that she would never have been allowed to put powder on their foreheads?

Monday 3 May

I decide to make a move over the whispering campaign against me a fortnight ago. I write a fierce letter to Alastair Campbell, but make it clear I will take no legal action if he gives me an undertaking that the government has no criticism to make of my professional conduct here. The letter sits in my word processor for a while: this will really be a declaration of war, if he refuses to play ball. Then I e-mail it: let the chips fall where they may.

Thursday 6 May

Real signs of war-weariness by now. "If only this were over," someone says to us in a street interview. Later President Clinton, visiting Europe, says NATO can do a deal with Milošević. As a result Milošević gets a new lease of political life, ministers here are jubilant. Clinton, who promised there would be no ground war, has now given Milošević further reason to hold out.

Tony Blair says this is a war for international morality. People here call it the War of Two Penises—Clinton's and Madeleine Albright's.

Friday 7 May

Receive an emollient letter from Alastair Campbell. Not an apology, certainly, but then I didn't expect one: governments never apologize. But he's sorry it happened, and I get the impression he feels it was all a foul-up from their side. The assurance I was looking for is clearly there. Should I make the letter public? It's marked "private and confidential," so I can't. But in the afternoon I get a call from the *Sunday Telegraph*: somehow they've heard about it. I confirm the version they've received, correcting the odd detail. Strange feeling, being a spin-doctor on my own behalf against the headquarters of spin-doctoring. Stranger too to win.

Saturday 8 May

Wakened at two-fifteen by a God-almighty bang close by. Mike Williams rings: "They've hit the Chinese Embassy. We're going round there—are you coming?" To my great and lasting shame I say no. I've had only a few hours' sleep over the past week and I'm too lazy to roll out of bed once I've got into it. "Stupid bastards," I mutter. "Tell me what it's like when you get back." Serious dereliction of duty: this is of course one of the biggest stories of the war. While everyone is hanging round out-

side the embassy in the darkness there is another missile attack nearby. The hotel where Arkan's Tigers are based has been hit. Typically, NATO seemed not to have got any of them, while killing three poor Chinese people.

How can they conceivably have mistaken the Chinese Embassy for another building? It's right out in the middle of a stretch of open ground. It doesn't even look like anything except a Chinese embassy, with its curved gables and its typically Chinese surrounding wall.

Much later, a former American diplomat, who at one stage had close links with the CIA and the rest of the intelligence community, told me that the bombing was the work of a small rogue grouping within the CIA, who switched the maps which the US Air Force needed for bombing the ministry of military procurement in Belgrade. The ministry is near the embassy. Mistakes always happen in war, of course, and the Chinese were known to be passing information about NATO to the Serbs.

The conclusion the Americans draw from this war is that you can't fight an intelligent campaign with nineteen nations involved. My conclusion is slightly different: the stupidity factor in Washington is higher this time than it has ever been. That's saying something.

Sunday 9 May

I read the *Sunday Telegraph* front page on the Internet. "Downing Street Apologizes To John Simpson," says the headline. Not entirely true, but close enough to be satisfactory. I don't think this government will try to call the BBC to heel again. Maybe, if we're lucky, no future government will either. If you're weak and feeble, it's an invitation to these people to hit you again. If you punch back (and especially if you fight dirty, as I have) they'll look for another target.

But the day is a special one for other reasons. Dee arrives. She has battled her way through Romania in order to get to the Yugoslav border. Dragan warns me not to, but I can't resist climbing on a concrete bollard to wave to her. She waves back. The border police come running over and threaten me with all sorts of things. I'd forgotten quite how beautiful she is. She looks sensational in her pink sweater and coat. Dragan purrs approvingly beside me. We drive back to Belgrade, and I cannot stop talking, trying to show her everything as we go. She is amazingly gutsy about it all, viewing the ruins of the different government buildings and the Chinese embassy with a calm interest. We discuss at length whether we should take a safer room, further away from the bombs. Dee says no. Life for me has suddenly become a great deal better.

Wednesday 12 May

Cluster bombs land in the center of Niš. These are disgusting weapons, which should be outlawed along with landmines. Mike Williams describes the way they parachute down slowly and explode, killing and maiming people over a wide area. A BBC correspondent contradicts him flatly on air, sounding exactly like a NATO spokesman. What prats some of these people are: as though, just because the rules say cluster bombs can only be used under certain circumstances, NATO is only using them like that. My impression is that the Americans in particular are taking more risks with civilian lives now. Maybe they've noticed how quickly, once NATO has made its formal apology, the mistakes are forgotten. Every Serb you speak to believes now that civilians are being deliberately targeted. It's not true, but this war is already worse than the Gulf War in terms of casualties. As for Milošević, he must be delighted; loss of life among his own people has never held him back.

Friday 21 May

Not a good day. After a swim with Dee in the hotel I am walking down some steps near the pool when I slip on the wet tiles and land badly, rupturing the tendons that attach my left thigh muscle to the knee. It's much worse than breaking the bone, and pretty painful. A doctor comes and gives me an injection, which lasts for a while. Thank God for Dee, and Dragan too. He lifts me up as gently as a father.

Eventually an ambulance takes me to hospital: the University Clinic, where we have filmed before, and where we were turned away after the bombing of the secret police headquarters next door. Great place to be. As I am being lifted out of the ambulance in a certain amount of pain, an oafish paramedic starts haranguing me about NATO and Blair and the bombing: I tell him to fuck off, and feel slightly better.

As a couple of nurses take my details, the air raid sirens begin to wail. They glance at each other, and then at me. One seems about to say something unpleasant, but the other shakes her head.

The registrar explains what has happened: the tendons connecting the thigh muscles of my left leg have been ripped away from the kneecap. It's something to do with being in my fifties. People who are younger or older would have broken a bone. At my age, it seems, the tendons are briefly weaker than the bones. As I lie on the stretcher, trying to think what I should do, Dee uses her mobile to consult a specialist friend of hers in South Africa. (What a strange world, that she can ask someone in Jo'burg for advice in the middle of an air raid in the darkest Balkans.)

This will be a very difficult operation, he tells her, and if it goes wrong I won't walk again. His advice is to catch a plane for London at once. The trouble is, there are no planes here to catch. It will take a good twenty-four hours to get to London, probably more. We talk about it between ourselves about the advisability of having the operation done here, as rationally as though we are deciding where to have lunch, but both of us know how important our decision could be. I'm impressed by Dee's calmness. This moment will decide her life as well as mine.

The registrar listens to our discussion—what must he be thinking, given that if even he is injured he cannot leave the country?—and points out that if the operation is delayed the tendons in my leg will shrink and recovery will be even longer and harder. He explains the operation in the kind of detail I don't really want to hear: drilling holes in the kneecap and tying the tendons to it. It'll take me a long time to recover, he says.

There are two dangers: that the hospital, which has already been hit once and is right beside all sorts of NATO targets, will be hit again while I am here; and that the quality of the surgery won't be high. Then I remember what one of the specialists said when we filmed here a few weeks ago: "The only good thing about Yugoslavia's recent history is that all these wars we have been having have provided us with excellent experience." As for the hospital being hit, that's a danger everyone in the city faces. Only yesterday we filmed at the neurological ward of another

Belgrade hospital which had been hit during a NATO attack on an army barracks nearby. Three patients were killed.

"All right," I say, "we'll do it here." I feel better immediately.

I'm not leaving Belgrade at this late stage in the war: I want to see how it all ends. Dee and Dragan both seem relieved, and beam at me.

The operation takes place in the afternoon. I am determined to be as conscious as I can, and opt for an epidural injection. "Be nice to the anesthetists," said a medical friend of mine once. "They're the ones who kill you; the surgeons just maim you." It is easy to be nice to the anesthetist here because she is a very pretty blonde, and she is really nice back, which makes me feel better. Although groggy and moving in and out of consciousness, I manage to watch a surprising amount of the operation reflected in the shiny steel of the overhead lamp, as they slice open my knee and pin back the flaps. It lasts about 45 minutes. While it is going on, the charming young surgeon tells me afterwards, two people come up to him and say he shouldn't be wasting his time on a Brit when NATO is killing Serbs every day. Thank you, Hippocrates. Fortunately he tells them where to get off.

When it is over, I am brought into the intensive care ward for the night. This is far worse than being under the knife. To lie in a silent hospital ward in the blackness of a power cut, unable to move, watching anti-aircraft fire arcing into the air and listening to the engines of the NATO planes as they come in for the attack, is to share the fears of everyone else in this city. Up at the Hyatt we aren't particularly safe—windows have been broken, and some of the bombs have fallen uncomfortably close—but the thick double-glazing protects us from the noise of it all. Not here. Especially not here. This hospital has already been hit, and it is surrounded by military buildings which NATO has already targeted. Each of them is within fifty to a hundred yards of where I find myself tonight. And if something happens, I can't even get out of bed. I can scarcely even move.

Saturday 22 May

They shift me to another room, away from the other patients, many of whom have been injured in the bombing. I feel a bit of a fraud: all I did was to fall over in the swimming pool of a five-star hotel. I hadn't planned to write my *Sunday Telegraph* column this week, under the circumstances, but now I feel a bit clearer in my head I change my mind. I ring the foreign desk: they sound surprised. I scribble my report into a notebook and dictate it to copy. It runs easily enough, since I'm just telling the story of what happened to me. The key part was last night. Dominic Lawson, the editor of the *Sunday Telegraph,* once said to me, "You're the kind of person who'll be writing descriptive pieces on your deathbed." He was right.

Dee, Dragan and Mike Williams come round with food and presents. Mike has made something for me to illustrate the old First World War joke, which he taught me, about military communications at the front: "Send reinforcements, we're going to advance" becomes "Send two-and-fourpence, we're going to a dance." He's mounted coins to the value of 2/4d in pre-decimal money in a frame, with a little note. I'm very touched. To be able to look at the three of them and feel the warmth of their affection is better than any medicine. I sit here like a kid with my toys after they have gone, playing with each in turn.

At night, though, things don't seem quite so good. Dee, Dragan and Mike have left (I refuse to let Dee stay with me, in case the hospital is hit) and virtually all the specialists and doctors head for home. Just a few nurses are on duty. I can hear the other patients snoring or muttering in their sleep, or calling out "*Sestre!*", "Nurse!" But the nurses are exhausted, and usually sleep through the calls.

Pain and the discomfort of this fiendish cast keep me awake. The lights are switched off directly the air raid sirens sound, and I wait for the night's fireworks. If you are immobile, you feel especially vulnerable. Who will come to help me if a bomb lands on us? What will I do, given that I can't even shift this heavy weight, my leg?

The whoosh of the anti-aircraft rounds, the whining of the jet engines as the pilots search out their targets, the deep rumble and shake as the bombs hit—not far away, that one: these are noises I never heard at the Hyatt. Now I'm getting the *version originale,* as they say in the French movies.

The cause is just, I tell myself as I wait for one of the neighboring buildings to go up; those are our boys overhead. Somehow, though, lying in the darkness unable to move, it's hard to be convinced.

Friday 28 May

I've been back in the hotel for four days now, lying on the bed in our grand suite and trying every now and then to learn how to use crutches. A ferocious-looking but charming physio comes over from time to time to torture me.

"For you, Tommy, ze war is over," says Dee.

I'm determined it shan't be. I have put too much into it to leave now, and although my left leg is in plaster from ankle to groin and I stay in bed for large parts of the day, I shall soon be able to get up and go downstairs to record a piece to camera. I have scarcely told the BBC about my problems, nervous that they will go Auntie-like and try to medivac me out of here. Most of the program presenters who interview me over the phoneline clearly know nothing about it; though you would think they might read the newspaper. One presenter asks me what I see when I go out onto the streets. I answer as briefly and truthfully as I can, without saying "I've been lying in plaster for a week and can't even stand up, you daft bimbo." Which is, of course, what I would like to say most.

For the rest of my life I shall probably have a slight limp, and sometimes be forced to use a walking-stick. My knee will always remind me of my time in Belgrade. Still, my chances of playing rugby for England were getting pretty slight anyway, and there are worse things than limping. The memory of a poem about these things stirs faintly, but I won't be able to track it down until I get back to Dublin. It turns out to be by W. E. Henley, more excitably imperialist than most:

> What if the best of our wages be
> An empty sleeve, a stiff-set knee,
> A crutch for the rest of life—who cares,
> So long as the One Flag floats and dares?

Which has nothing to do with my emotions whatever, and anyway mine was a pretty ludicrous accident, scarcely glamorous or self-sacrificing. I did the job I was sent to Belgrade to do, and don't worry too much about my stiff-set knee as a result. After all, I could have done it coming out of Finnegan's bar on a wet Saturday night in Dublin.

The hotel management is a problem. The last time the ambulancemen carried me through the lobby on a stretcher, we were told we must go through the back route from now on. It upset the guests to see me, they said. Bastards.

I am, thanks to the efforts of Dee, Dragan, Mike, Balša, Bata, and Vlad, managing to keep going. I lie on the bed in the editing room, cutting my reports, and then Dragan wheels me down each night to the front of the hotel and props me up so I can do my obligatory piece to camera. Often I am standing at a slight angle, I notice; no one else seems to. I can watch ghastly Serbian television, and BBC and Sky and CNN, get BBC On-line on my laptop, and have room service to bring me anything I want, and enjoy the company of my wife and friends around me. Really, I have been in worse wars.

Thursday 3 June

At long last, it's coming to an end. It has lasted far, far longer than Madeleine Albright promised the Clinton administration it would take. In Washington they're calling it "Albright's War," and the knives are out for her. But she will of course survive, like some waddling turkey that has become a household pet and cannot be cooked for Christmas. Tony Blair was right to advocate the sending in of ground troops, because that was the only way the lives of innocent refugees could have been saved and the war brought to a speedy end. But Clinton apparently told him in as many words to shut up about it.

All that has happened in Albright's War is that NATO has expended vast quantities of money and much of its prestige dislodging the Serbian police militias and the MUP (Internal Ministry) troops so the Kosovo Liberation Army can take their place and start doing precisely the same thing to Serbian civilians that the Serbs have done to Albanian civilians: killing them, torturing them, forcing them to flee. This is a country where the tribe counts above everything. You are not an individual here, you are a representative of your people and therefore available for attack and murder in the event of trouble. Serbs who have grown up in the friendliest way with their Albanian next-door neighbors set fire to their houses and drive them out at gunpoint with nothing; and Albanians do it to Serbs.

"You are bombing us," people say to me every time I take a camera out into the streets. "What do you mean?" I reply irritably; "*I'm* bombing *you*? You're not getting bombed any more than I am."

What they mean is that my tribe is bombing theirs.

All Madeleine Albright did was to get involved in a nasty little local conflict, and then try to persuade the rest of us that one side was uniquely evil while the other was uniquely innocent. The wholesale clearance of ethnic Albanians from Kosovo was an act of wickedness, sure. But that's what the Serbs do: if they're being hit by someone they dare not hit back at, they will take their revenge on some weaker party. We set it all up for them so that they would take out their anger on the ethnic Albanian civilians of Kosovo.

This has not been a moral crusade, it's been a practice exercise for bombers which were in no danger themselves and took insufficient care about the lives of others. And since those others didn't count in terms of American politics—they were foreigners, after all—then no one was counting. As for NATO's claims about destroying Serbian military equipment, they have turned out to be absurdly wrong. Finally, the man who's responsible for the whole evil mess in the former Yugoslavia, Slobodan Milošević, is bound to be left unchallenged in power at the end of it. NATO has not scored a lot of points out of three.

Anyway, it won't last much longer. Today the Serbian Parliament has accepted NATO's terms. It is a beautiful sunny day, and I am far too excited to stay indoors. Dragan carries me down to the car and we drive to the city center, where I sit at an open-air café reporting to London on my mobile. People around about me listen, but no one interrupts me or threatens me; those days are long gone. No one here cares about anything any longer, except just to get it over with as fast as possible. While I sit here in the sun, Dee, Dragan, and the crew are interviewing people in the street. Again and again the interviewees say they want to get rid of Milošević. In the new climate here, we won't even have any problem satelliting this kind of thing tonight.

Tuesday 8 June

The bombing ends, but no cars drive through the streets, honking their horns. No flags are waved. No one is holding a street party. The headlines in the newspapers and on television faithfully report what they have been instructed to: that this is all a remarkable achievement by Serbia, that Belgrade has succeeded in keeping *de jure* control of Kosovo, that its army is undefeated. In some ways, depressingly, it's true.

In the open-air cafés people sit and read *Politika* and *Blic,* and draw their own conclusions about who has won. People here are going through the motions, exactly as though nothing has happened. Their feelings and emotions are on autopilot. The girls saunter along in their skimpy summer clothes, the young men laugh with their friends, the older people hurry to jobs they are lucky enough to have kept, or worry about finding enough food to buy.

I am taken to the hospital, where one of the surgeons examines my leg. I ask him how he feels, now that there will no longer be any bombing to disturb his operations. He goes over to the window, looking out at the sublime summer's day.

"I don't know whether to be relieved or depressed," he says, and there are tears in his eyes.

The last victims of this war were three poor so-and-sos killed on a farm in rural Serbia which NATO hit by accident. By this stage, no one seems to care. The journalists in Brussels do not ask NATO for an explanation, and there is no apology.

In the evening, Bata, thoughtful and long-haired, is sitting at the editing machines, putting the final touches to our report about the end of the bombing. Dee sits on one of the beds directing him. I am lying on the other bed, my left leg in plaster from ankle to mid-thigh, recording the track on a microphone like a radio commentator at the Derby.

There is a knock at the door. Two secret policemen, the politest I have ever met, are standing apologetically in the doorway.

Dragan goes over to speak to them, and listens to them gravely, while I shout into the microphone as though the Derby is in its last furlong.

"They've come to throw you out, John," Dragan says when the

race is over. After thirteen weeks in Belgrade without a single day off, my temper, never particularly good, is at a record shortness.

"Tell them to bugger off. We're busy."

It doesn't faze them. Polite as ever, they offer me all sorts of indulgences: someone else can bring my passport to be stamped with a 24-hour exit visa, and it can wait until tomorrow morning. But it will have to be done. I have apparently upset the Serbian Information Service in London—those experts on objective reporting—by something I have said about Milošević. Maybe it was Mr. Arsić, the man with the head like a penis.

For the next few hours we argue and pull every string we can collectively think of; and by emphasizing the medical problem we manage to get the deadline extended by a week.

Tuesday 15 June

Dee and I leave at 9:30 A.M. for the long drive to Hungary. After eighty-eight days I wave goodbye to Dragan, Mike, Balša, Bata, Vlad, and the rest. They have become like my own family.

We stay overnight in an expensive hotel in Budapest, where the food is a great deal better than anything we have had for months, and watch a video. We should be extraordinarily relieved and happy; instead we both feel a little low.

Wednesday 16 June

The boss himself comes to Heathrow to welcome us back: the BBC's equivalent of getting the Victoria Cross.

It doesn't come as an enormous surprise when we get home to read in the newspapers that after seventy-nine days of bombing, 40,000 or so sorties and untold tens of thousands of tons of bombs, smart and stupid, NATO managed to hit only 13 Serbian tanks in Kosovo. It claimed, of course, to have knocked out up to 40 percent of the 280 or so tanks which the Serbs were believed to have deployed in Kosovo, plus nearly 60 percent of their artillery and mortars.

What NATO really hit were canvas and wood replicas. Colleagues of mine reported seeing some of these in Kosovo after the bombing was over, together with old armored personnel carriers,

broken-axled and rusting, which the Serbs had carefully left out in the open for NATO's pilots to target.

As for me, I always knew I would get a lot of grief for sleeping with the enemy; or at any rate living, working and to some extent suffering with them. When I go through the mail, I find the full extent of it: large amounts of hate-mail from people who didn't want to be told what it was like on the receiving end of NATO's bombing. The clinching argument always seemed to be the same: would the BBC have had a correspondent in Berlin from 1939–45?

Well, of course we would, if only it had been possible. What's the problem about wanting to know more, rather than less, about what is going on? That, surely, is what we should all want. Slowly, as I go through the letters, I understand that what these people dislike is the reminder that under NATO's bombs there were ordinary men and women like themselves. They would much rather not know; they wanted to believe that every bomb reaches its target, that every casualty is someone who deserves it. Well, I'm here to tell you it ain't true. Sorry.

The hate-mail merchants will probably say I am the victim of the Stockholm Syndrome, whereby prisoners come to love their captors. But lying in my hospital bed, listening to the groans and snores and the cries of "*Sestre!*," I understood that we were all in this together. If a bomb had hit the hospital during the nights I was there, we would all have suffered: the English patient along with the Serbs. When it really counts, your tribe doesn't really mean anything. But try telling anyone in the former Yugoslavia that. Or the people who write me hate-mail, for that matter.

13
Finishing the Job

Stephano: Flout em and scout em,
And scout em and flout em!
Thought is free.
Caliban: That's not the tune.
      —WILLIAM SHAKESPEARE, *The Tempest*, ca. 1611

It took me a month to return to Afghanistan after 11 September. For a long time I tried to get in from Pakistan but was stymied. It was partly my own fault. Against the advice of Peter Jouvenal, the cameraman I was working with, I insisted that the two of us get across the Hindu Kush mountains into Afghan territory, helped by a group of smugglers. The smugglers insisted that if they were to help us, we would have to disguise ourselves as they thought best. And so Peter and I, dressed in the all-encompassing burka of Afghan women, were driven up through the Khyber Pass and into Afghanistan, where we did some filming and some broadcasting.

It caused a mild sensation, and had every one of the malign effects Jouvenal had forecast. A grand religious council was held in the tribal area along the Pakistan–Afghanistan border to decide whether a *fatwa* should be issued against me for breaking the religious code of Islam; fortunately for me, an elderly tribal leader argued successfully that while I had no doubt broken the civil code, nothing I had done could be condemned on religious grounds.

The Pakistan provincial government in the North-West Province was predictably angry, and went to some lengths to stop our crossing into northern Afghanistan. So at considerable expense of time and money we had to make a large circle through Asia and the Gulf in order to reach the former Soviet Central Asian republic of Tajikstan, which neighbors Afghanistan to the north. That took time too, but eventually we got clearance to cross the border into territory occupied by the Northern Alliance, enemies of the Taliban.

Then began the hardest journey not just of my life, but also of the lives of most of the other journalists and cameramen who undertook it: five or six days of grinding through the mountains and near-desert of northern Afghanistan. There was scarcely more than twenty miles of recognizable road, and that came only at the end; the rest of it was merely a track that ran over boulders or along riverbeds. My colleagues and I slept out in the open, or in inns and private houses. Our tough Russian jeeps broke down continually, and only one of the four we started with reached our destination: the town of Charikar, only twenty-five miles north of Taliban-occupied Kabul and a mile or so away from the front line, which ran across the sensationally beautiful Shomali Plain.

We were a good twenty miles closer to the action than the rest of the press corps, who were penned up by the Northern Alliance at the town of Jabal Saraj, and while they were heavily controlled, we were able to do exactly as we wanted. Our good luck began with Peter Jouvenal's selection of a building in Charikar, which had been built during the Soviet occupation for the city administration. This was important for us because, although it had been hit several times by mortar shells and all its windows had long since been blown out, it boasted several Western-style toilets. This has not helped much in the past, since they were all heavily blocked and people had been using the rooms instead. The stench was so overpowering when we first arrived that I doubted whether we would ever be able to use the place. Yet a bit of British drive and efficiency—and money, of course—had the building cleaned up within a day; and we lived there in moderate comfort for an entire month. We called it Bin Laden Mansions.

The best piece of luck came on our first morning. As we were inspecting the building a group of angry soldiers appeared, led by a short,

stocky man whose eyes were red with anger. We might have thought the
building was empty, but in fact it was the headquarters of the local mujaheddin commander. We had moved our equipment into the empty part
of the building without asking his permission. For all I know, we had
deprived him of his toilet as well.

Recognizing the value of the place to us, I went into auto-grovel and
was quite gruesomely pleasant to him. It was an uphill struggle for a bit,
until it occurred to me to suggest that we were of course more than
happy to pay for our accomodation there. It was the magic key that
unlocked everything. From then on, Commander Hajji Bari was our
landlord, our transport officer, and the quartermaster who made sure we
had all the food and other supplies we needed. For a consideration, of
course. Yet our luck didn't end there. Hajji turned out to be the commander in charge of most of the Shomali Valley sector of the front, and
gave us blanket permission to film there whenever we wanted. He even
gave us his personal jeep and driver, so no one would stop us.

And so we began a month of waiting. No one had better access to
the front line than we did, and as a result we were able to broadcast what
I think may have been the first genuinely live television report with pictures from a battlefield, via a curious and still quite primitive machine
called a videophone. Tank shells were passing us in both directions, and
the U.S. Air Force obligingly bombed the Taliban front line a couple of
hundred yards away. We got it all, and I shouted down the line to London in answer to the questions of the studio presenters.

It was a cold and uncomfortable month, and we spent each night on
concrete floors in rooms with plastic sheeting at the windows. But we
got on very well with each other, and drew rather sad pictures of the
things we didn't have on the walls: a hi-fi set, a piano, and an extremely
well-stocked drinks cabinet with bottles of excellent French brandy,
some good vintage champagne, and the best single-malt Scotch. Since
we were entirely without alcohol of any kind, we sometimes found ourselves standing in front of the imaginary drinks cabinet for long periods
of time. It didn't even help to quote W. C. Fields in *My Little Chickadee*:
"Crossing the Afghanistan desert, we lost our corkscrew. We were forced
to exist on food and water for days."

At last, though, the slow-moving process of the American bombing, which was often surprisingly light, even though plenty of journalists allowed themselves to use expressions like carpet-bombing, achieved its aim: the Taliban forces in the lines opposite us were sufficiently weakened to make an attack by the Northern Alliance possible. I had ruffled a few feathers in Britain by maintaining that the Taliban were feeble soldiers, who would scarcely resist a determined assault by the Northern Alliance. They would, I said, crack like an egg; I was thinking of the little, stunted eggs that our head cook, Rahman Beg, brought in for us every morning. Having seen the Taliban operate, though, I knew they wouldn't put up a fight. Even so, I was determined that the BBC should be up in the first wave of the attack; and here again our luck held. Hajji Bari, our landlord, was appointed to command the assault on Kabul, and he promised to take us with him.

Five o'clock on the morning of Sunday, 12th November 2001: I woke up believing that, at long last, the big attack was going to happen. Hajji Bari had told us the previous afternoon to be ready to leave for the front line at six. I switched on the radio: at the United Nations, President George W. Bush and President Musharaf of Pakistan had both called on the Northern Alliance not to enter Kabul. Some commentators were interpreting this as a warning to the Alliance not to *attack* Kabul; they forgot that in politics and diplomacy you have to look at the use of words very carefully. The Northern Alliance had already said quite clearly they wouldn't enter Kabul; so Bush and Musharaf were merely telling them not to do something they weren't planning to do anyway.

But it all seemed deeply confusing, and the mood among the journalists based at the Foreign Ministry in Jabal Saraj was gloomy. Some of them, indeed, had decided that nothing was going to happen until the following spring, and had left for home a couple of days earlier. I didn't think they were right, but nothing that was happening sounded like the prelude to an immediate attack.

At six o'clock there was no sign of Hajji. He eventually turned up at around ten, complaining that we had hired a new driver from someone other than him. He didn't even mention the possibility of an attack. We covered our deep disappointment as best we could.

A couple of weeks earlier we had hired a new translator and local fixer, Khair Mohammed. This had brought us a lot of grief from the Foreign Ministry, who claimed the sole right to hire out translators to foreign journalists. We suspected that any translators we hired from them would be useless, and would only be there to keep an eye on us and report back. Khair Mohammed, anyway, had other advantages: His father was the top man in Northern Alliance military intelligence, and seemed to be passing on messages to us via his son.

Now Khair Mohammed arrived, as neat and well-groomed and quiet-spoken as always. I walked up and down the corridor with him for greater security, as he told me the latest.

"My father say, America only seeming to say no to Northern Alliance to please Pakistan. Attack will take place tomorrow, as I told you. Don't have worries."

It was true: Khair Mohammed had told us the attack would happen on Monday; it was just that Hajji Bari had seemed so certain it would be today.

We had been invited to lunch by General Anwari, the head of the mostly Hazara Harakat-e Islami group. He greeted us with considerable warmth at his headquarters, a little way from Jabal. Peter Jouvenal and I had, after all, put his organization on the map back in 1989 by going with them to Kabul, and Anwari had been a senior figure in the *mujaheddin* ever since. We owed him and his top men a great deal, too. Abu Faisal, whose courage and toughness had saved our lives back then in Kabul, was there too, and our meeting became quite emotional. You could see the effect of the injuries he had suffered as a result of helping us. He was still a big man, but he seemed thinner and slower and quieter than before.

We all sat round the tablecloth on the floor, which was covered with good things: fresh vegetables, fruit, yogurt, bread, great mounds of rice flecked with berries and spices, and a dozen different dishes of varying heat and ferocity. After the scanty diet at Bin Laden Mansions it was unforgettably good. Anwari still had many complaints about the Americans—their closeness to Pakistan, the suspicion with which they continued to regard the Northern Alliance, their unwillingness to throw everything into the attack on the Taliban, their unceasing caution and slowness. But the Northern Alliance, under General Dostam, an Uzbek leader of great ferocity, had recently captured the vital town of Mazar-e Sharif from the Taliban, and that was clearly the beginning of the end. Anwari was a very happy man.

So, by the end of lunch, were we. I had learned to believe everything that Khair Mohammed told me, because it invariably came true; but it was good to have Anwari's endorsement of his assurance that the big attack would take place tomorrow. The food cheered us up, too, and so did the English of one of Anwari's top assistants, who did the translating. In particular, he found it difficult to say the words terrorism and terrorists; they came out as tourism and tourists.

"Anwari says absolutely essential to stamp out tourism from the world. Any tourists should be arrested and put on trial. He says tourism is the great evil of modern times."

"I absolutely agree with him," I answered. "I don't feel that Western governments are nearly tough enough on tourism. They should stamp it out once and for all."

It was turning into a good day altogether. As I sat writing in my room at Bin Laden Mansions, there was the roar of a lorry engine outside, and a good deal of hooting and excitability. I kept on writing because I had a deadline, but when I heard the sound of loud, cheerful conversation and some new voices, I went out to see what it was all about. The satellite gear had arrived from Northern Afghanistan, with its Russian engineers and its BBC producer. The timing of the dish's arrival was as good as it could have been. The engineers were able to get everything up and running just in time for the big assault. It was an extraordinary success for us.

The new arrivals had brought all sorts of things with them: cold-weather clothes, gadgets like head-torches and tin-openers, some medicine I needed, some really powerful painkillers, some excellent Cuban cigars, and—best of all—sizeable quantities of alcohol. Somebody, knowing my weakness for Laphroaig single malt, had put a bottle in for me: an act of great thoughtfulness and charity. There were also some books, which I had urgently asked for: Dickens and Trollope; but, through a rather charming misunderstanding, the Trollope wasn't by Anthony, as I had expected, but by Joanna. No matter: I read that too, and enjoyed it.

At this point, when it seemed that Christmas had come early, General Gul Haidar, the one-legged commander who had been put in overall charge of the campaign, came bursting into Bin Laden Mansions, shouting greetings, accepting all sorts of food he had never eaten before, and eyeing up the bottles of booze speculatively. It was, he said, all on for tomorrow; and the Northern Alliance had been approached by a very senior commander on the Taliban side, who promised to come over to them directly the fighting began.

That night those of us who were going to Kabul with the attackers got all our things ready for the morning, and left them in the corridor outside our rooms. I was just taking a rucksack and my flak jacket. Everything else I had with me—carpets, a London-made flintlock in perfect condition, and the heavier gear—would be shipped down to Kabul once we arrived there. Nobody doubted that we would. There was only one problem: Joe Phua, the charming, piratical cameraman from Singapore, had broken a bone in his foot a few weeks before, and could only keep on filming on a diet of pretty heavy duty painkillers. But he was determined to finish the job, and I couldn't find it in my heart to tell him to stay behind. At around one in the morning I lay down on the floor and went straight to sleep, too tired even to speculate about the coming dangers or where I might spend the following night.

At five-thirty I was up. We loaded our gear into the jeeps and headed down to the front line. There were already columns of smoke going up, and we could hear violent, jolting explosions. We got as close as we could to where the actual fighting was just starting. Joe and I went into a bombed and wrecked farmhouse to set up the camera. The half dozen Northern Alliance troops who were based there were too stoned to stop us, or even take much interest. We hoped they weren't typical of the rest of the army.

Joe found a niche on the top floor, overlooking the front line, with a wrecked piece of wall to lean against. But after two bullets went by so close that we could hear them crack nastily in the air as they passed, I told him to pack up and go down again. This was going to be a long day, and an important one. I didn't want anything to happen to him or me which might stop us reporting.

A major rocket and artillery duel was starting up. The Chinese rockets of the Northern Alliance were seeking out the Taliban's Russian rocket-launchers, and vice versa. They arched through the sky over our heads and crashed into the hilltops a couple of miles or so on either side of us. Then the tanks opened up. The Taliban tanks, which were mostly being used as mobile artillery, had taken a considerable beating from the American bombing, yet there seemed to be plenty of them around still; as the Iraqis had proved in 1991 and the Serbs in 1999, air power alone cannot take out everything.

By now we could hear the deep rumbling of aircraft engines coming down the valley. It was a sound we had become thoroughly used to over the past few weeks, and soon the silver crosses of a couple of B-52s showed in the sky, leaving their huge four-track vapor trails three miles above us. They wheeled majestically around, and brown and gray smoke boiled up out of the ground quite close to us, mounting into the sky, and the shuddering sound hit us again and again. More American planes were flying down from Uzbekistan to join them, their vapor trails crossing one another, and the smoke went up and we were jolted by more explosions, and then more. Joe and I walked past Peter Emmerson and Kate Clark, our radio colleagues, as they were trying to put over a report to the BBC World Service—notorious sticklers for good sound quality. I could hear Kate apologizing to the studio engineers down the satellite phone.

"It's just that it's very noisy here," she was saying.

They had asked her to do it again, without the unacceptable background sound.

Fortunately, the television bulletins were rather more in favor of that sort of thing, and we were able to supply it. We set up the videophone on the lip of a trench, and started broadcasting. At the end of our last interview the program presenter said, "Enjoy yourself!" He was a former foreign correspondent, and I knew how much he would have enjoyed it too, if he had been there alongside me.

Later, some of the more politically correct elements rebuked him, on the grounds that it was unacceptable to suggest that anyone should enjoy reporting on a war. That seems to me like Pecksniffian humbug. I don't like wars in the slightest, and regard them as fundamentally evil—especially when the people who are being killed are mostly civilians. But this was, by contrast, a very different kind of war, in which the casualties were numbered in dozens rather than hundreds or thousands, and very few civilians died.

It would be dishonest to deny that there was a certain excitement at being so close to the action, and at getting such magnificent front line pictures; and the presenter understood that. It wasn't the prospect of blood that was attractive: far from it. But there was an undeniable excitement in the air, now that the culmination of all our efforts had arrived; and the personal risk involved in getting the results we wanted gave me, and I'm sure the others with me, a heightened sense of anticipation and—yes—enjoyment. I don't think there is anything to be ashamed of in that.

We needed to get on now; the Northern Alliance forces were starting to push forward and take some Taliban positions. In order to make our way forward we had a long and rather nerve-racking walk of a quarter mile along the road that ran through no-man's-land, parallel to the Taliban front line. We were outlined clearly against the sky, but no one shot at us; maybe they were too preoccupied by the American air raids and the continuing rocket attacks. We set up the videophone in seven different places altogether that morning, reporting each time for three or more programs.

Not all our live shots were successful. Once, nervous that we might be in the way of a Taliban counterattack, we dodged into a decayed vineyard which had largely been taken over by wasps. They buzzed angrily around my head as I answered the questions, and during one interview one of them landed on my face. I had to brush it away on camera without letting it sting me. Not at all easy.

Afterward we were moving cautiously forward down a lane with the characteristic high mud walls of the vineyard on either side of us. Ahead lay what seemed to be the foremost point the Northern Alliance had reached; a couple of armored vehicles had come to a stop there. As we got nearer, some of the soldiers came running back toward us.

"A tank is breaking out! A Taliban tank! It's coming this way!"

That, at least, is what I assume they were saying, since these were the facts of the situation; but I couldn't really understand their nervous, excited babble. They ran into one of the vineyards, and it wasn't clear to me whether they were trying to escape from the tank, or looking for a position from which they could ambush it. Maybe they weren't sure either.

The group of seven or eight of us felt distinctly vulnerable. If the tank came down this narrow lane, as it seemed it might, its crew would certainly take us for American special forces and fire on us. We had to be under cover, but able to get shots of the tank at the same time. We jogged back down the lane with our gear, looking for somewhere to hide, and at last found an entrance to a vineyard where the walls had been broken down.

Peter Jouvenal, looking back at the Northern Alliance lines, thought he saw some men on the rooftop of a nearby farmhouse, looking in our general direction. Someone else, peering through his binoculars, said he was sure they were American forward spotters.

"As far as I can see, they've got fair hair and light skins."

We didn't want them to see us, any more than we wanted the Taliban tank to. In war, soldiers have an understandable tendency to attack first and identify the bodies later. There were so many American planes circling in the sky and coming down into the attack on call that it would have been very easy for the spotters to have summoned an air strike to get rid of us. Every few minutes another column of dirty smoke would go up in the air, and another explosion would assault our ears.

Then the Taliban tank made its run. I thought it was an act of great courage, to attack an army that was so far superior in weapons and air power. As it turned out, the tank was a little way away from us as it broke through and made its way across no-man's-land, and we weren't in any danger from it. Peter Jouvenal got an excellent shot of the forward spotters on the rooftop pointing at it and shouting into their walkie-talkies, and a few minutes later an American plane came screaming down above us, quite low, and dropped a bomb on it. The tank exploded in a sheet of flame. It was the last act of serious resistance by the Taliban.

We made the long walk back through no-man's-land to find our vehicles. It was 12:15 P.M. It seemed clear that the Taliban resistance had crumbled here in the Shomali Valley, and that the Northern Alliance would soon start the big advance on Kabul. But for the moment the pounding still went on. On the edges of the valley, American planes were bombing the Taliban positions in the deserted villages, which protected the flanks of the main Taliban force. Joe and I were in one vehicle, Peter in the other. Peter headed off in one direction, Joe and I another. We had to force our unwilling driver to head off the road on a small track that led across no-man's-land to a position that seemed to be in Northern Alliance hands now, but that had until a few minutes ago been a key part of the Taliban front line. We could see the soldiers standing on the roof, waving with joy.

In the time it took us to get there, the victorious troops received orders to head on to the next position. I looked at my watch: The 10 A.M. news bulletins would require something from me in fifteen minutes, and up here, on the Taliban front line, seemed the best place to do our next set of two-ways. So Joe and I sat on the rooftop and waited, uncomfortably aware that the Northern Alliance army was sweeping forward fast and we were in danger of being left behind. A couple of buses arrived to take the troops farther forward, and we still had to wait where we were. Finally the minute hand reached the hour, and we were able to do the two-ways we had been waiting for.

Directly they were over, Joe packed up the videophone gear and we jumped into the jeep with Khalil, the medical student we had found on our journey through the mountains. Just at that point a column of jeeps containing Northern Alliance troops came sweeping through the dust and down the track into Taliban-held territory; and we slotted ourselves into the back of the line and followed through, indistinguishable from them. At this stage we were, I suppose, about twenty-five minutes behind the first wave of attack troops, but Peter was with them. And we had the satisfaction of being way ahead of the other journalists.

The dust cleared a little way through the line. We drove fast along the little lanes until we came to a village where the Northern Alliance spearhead had halted. It was twenty minutes to the hour: enough time to do some filming, then set up the videophone and do some more two-ways

for the next round of news programs. There was laughing; a group of soldiers came running toward us, carrying an assortment of things they had looted from the Taliban: rolled-up carpets, a chair, clothes, a cardboard suitcase.

"Taliban!" they shouted into the camera lens, laughing and gamboling around like kids.

Almost immediately afterward we heard groaning, and saw a large Northern Alliance soldier staggering along under the weight of a man's body, which was draped across his arms like the looted carpet we had just seen. He set his burden down with some care under a tree, and Joe moved in to film the injured man. He had taken a shot, or perhaps a piece of shrapnel, in the chest, and the dark stain was still spreading. He wheezed, and his eyes rolled up. Enthusiasts recklessly tried to hold him up for the camera. Standing behind Joe, I waved at them to let him lie flat: who knew what damage might have been done to his internal organs?

Not that there was any chance whatsoever of getting medical care for him; the Northern Alliance might be allied to the Americans, but they got no help from them except for the Russian weapons they carried, and which the Americans had paid for. No field hospitals, no surgeons, no care beyond what the other soldiers could give him—which was nothing at all. And yet such is the magnetic force of television that the man lifted his head to take a look at Joe, then sank back, dying, into the arms of his friends, like Nelson on the Victory. I imagine he was dead within minutes.

We had seen Peter's vehicle abandoned by the side of the road at the entrance to this little village called Singid Darra. He, meanwhile, had followed a group of soldiers who were hunting down the Taliban from the garrison here. They had caught up with them in the fields outside and slaughtered them out of hand. If they had been Afghans, they would certainly have spared their lives. Instead they were Pakistanis, and the Northern Alliance, like a clear majority of Afghans, regarded Pakistan and its people as the source of their country's disasters.

Peter didn't film the deaths; they would have been quite unusable in television terms. But he did film the Northern Alliance soldiers going through the pathetic loot they found on the bodies: pens, a few useless Pakistani rupees, letters from home, passports.

"Pakistani! Taliban!" screamed one of the executioners into Peter's lens. He was still almost hysterical with the excitement of having done the passport's owner to death.

A little later, Peter came across General Gul Haidar, the overall commander of the attack—the man whose prosthetic leg Peter had paid for. Gul Haidar had just gotten out of his car to examine a group of prisoners from Singid Darra, including an elderly Turk.

"You old fool!" Gul Haidar shouted at him, partly for the benefit of Peter's camera and partly for his men's. "What are you doing, coming here to ruin my country like this?"

He grabbed the old man by the beard and shook his head like a cat shakes a bird, while the Northern Alliance soldiers laughed sycophantically. The old man reacted rather well, I thought: he resisted, and shouted something in Turkish. Gul Haidar clipped him round the ear and laughed. He must have thought this was what our viewers wanted to see. The old man was bundled off with the other prisoners onto the back of a truck and driven away. Once they were arrested, though, they would all survive the experience. Afghans can be appallingly brutal in the heat of the moment, but after a while, when the Northern Alliance men cooled down, they would remember that there was credit to be obtained for capturing prisoners, and perhaps some reward too. Soldiers must have been like this in the Hundred Years' War, I thought.

Joe, Khalil and I threw the gear into the jeep and raced on. The light was fading fast, and we would have to hurry if we were to do another piece to camera. I felt that it was important, because the one I had done earlier, when Peter had driven off rather than wait for us, wasn't only out of date, it was clearly wrong. Khair Mohammed had told me the day before that the Northern Alliance were planning to capture the front line, then regroup and attack the second Taliban line of defense. But that was all entirely out of date now. The front line had indeed broken like an egg, as I had suggested it would, and the Taliban hadn't stopped to defend their second line of defense in front of Kabul. They were on the run everywhere.

Ten minutes later we reached the second line: a single trench, impressively dug and well defended with sandbags, which stretched east-west right across the southern part of the Shomali Valley. It was entirely empty. No one had done any fighting here at all. We stopped, and I did a piece to camera about the speed with which the Taliban had abandoned it, and the fact that there were no longer any serious defenses between the Northern Alliance and Kabul.

The words were right, but the whole atmosphere was completely wrong. The trench was so empty, the absence of fighting so obvious, and I looked so neat and tidy—even my hair was neatly arranged—that it looked as though we had just ambled along, way after the Northern Alliance shock troops, and come across the second line of trenches by surprise. It looked, in other words, very much as though we were just part of the general group of journalists instead of being far ahead of them. I should have done the piece to camera back in Singid Darra, when it was obvious that we were right up with the action, and the crowds of looters and the injured would have been all around us. Ah well—*inutiles regrets*. The real problem was having two things to concentrate on at the same time—the live broadcasts via the videophone, and filming for our edited report, to be satellited to London later.

We drove on in the thickening darkness. The American bombing had stopped soon after the Northern Alliance broke through the Taliban front line, but there was the continuing danger of unexploded bombs all the way along the road, together with the certainty that the Taliban had mined the fields around their positions. Now, though, the landscape changed, as the vineyards and farms gave way to moorland. We had reached the low hills that had obstructed our view of Kabul when we were still in Charikar, and that we had often stared at speculatively through our field glasses. Soon we got to the main Kabul road, down which, from Bin Laden Mansions, we had so often watched the Taliban trucks bringing up reinforcements and supplies, their headlights cutting through the unpolluted darkness of the Afghan night. And now it was all over. Those Taliban who had not surrendered, been captured, or secretly betrayed to the Northern Alliance had fallen back on Kabul; whether to defend it or to surrender, we had no way of telling.

In the darkness we found our way down the main road to the village of Qarabagh. Here the thrust toward Kabul had petered out from sheer exhaustion; and here, as a result, we met up with the whole scattered BBC contingent: the radio team, whom we had last seen that morning, well before the Taliban front line was broken, and Peter Jouvenal.

We all wandered around together, looking for pictures in the darkness. We soon found them. An Afghan Talib lay on the back of a truck with a group of Alliance soldiers gathered around him. He had been injured in the foot. I asked Khalil to whisper to him quietly and find out if he was being badly treated. No, he whispered back. He would be safe now; he just needed treatment for the nasty bullet hole in his foot. By the light of a torch, I asked him what had happened when the attack had taken place.

> We were taken completely by surprise. It never occurred to us that they could attack us so fast. I suppose we were fools, really. We believed what the Taliban told us. They said the enemy would never dare to fight us. We were very shocked, and we scarcely put up any resistance at all.

Afterward I wandered up and down trying to decide what to do. There was no doubt that we could edit our pictures, as good as anything I had ever seen from a war, and transmit them better if we went back to Bin Laden Mansions, especially now that the dish had arrived and was fully operational. On the other hand, Afghans were capable of anything, whatever arrangements you reached with them; and just because General Gul Haidar assured us now that he would keep his men here all night and attack again at first light in the morning, it didn't mean things would necessarily happen that way. It would be a disaster to miss the next morning's attack on Kabul itself.

Perhaps, I thought, we should make the difficult journey back down the road (during the evening, a bus carrying soldiers hit an unexploded bomb in the roadway, and eight people on board were killed) and then drive back in the early hours of the morning and doss down by the roadside with the soldiers. I looked at Joe Phua: his broken foot was clearly giving him great pain, and he was exhausted. And the more he protested that he would be happy to drive back, edit our report, and then drive back again, the more I knew I shouldn't really put him through all this.

And then, as so often happened when we really needed him, we came across Hajji Bari. His eyes were red, but with exhaustion now rather than anger. If we stayed with him, we couldn't go wrong, since he was to lead the attack on Kabul tomorrow.

"I shall go back to Charikar," he said slowly, as though even the words were too heavy to say. "And I shall take you to Kabul with me in the morning. I promise it."

Our decision was made. We loaded up the gear and headed back down the road to Bin Laden Mansions.

The last shot we took that night in Qarabagh before we left was a timeless scene by the roadside, as a group of seven or eight soldiers sat around a fire, happy and exhausted at the victory they had obtained, the red-gold light flickering on their beards and fierce, hawklike faces. The AK-47s and the camouflage uniforms aside, they could have been Alexander the Great's Macedonians.

Twelve hours later, shortly before eight on the morning of Tuesday, 13th November, we were in Kabul. And that evening Joe Phua and I were sitting in our edit suite (which doubled as his bedroom) in the InterContinental Hotel, starting to compile our report on the events of that extraordinary day. At six minutes, it was to be the longest piece I have ever done for television news; it contained the best pictures I have ever been fortunate enough to use, and it was seen by more than 400 million people around the world. ABC News in America, NTV in Russia, and NHK in Japan were among the television organizations that broadcast it in its entirety.

I say this merely to marvel at the strange universality of television. The efforts of three very tired men, one of whom was suffering the pain of having walked for two miles with a broken bone in his foot, were seen within a few hours by a substantial proportion of the entire human race. For us, of course, it was no different from any of the other reports we had compiled in our careers; apart from the length, and the extraordinary satisfaction we felt at the job we had done. It happens quite often, of course, that people who are thinking and acting in the most restricted terms—politicians, say, or criminals, or rock stars, or sports heroes—find to their amazement that their names and what they have done are being broadcast around the world, and have become known in the farthest recesses of the globe. It's not the action itself that counts, so much as the medium of communication that makes this universality possible.

Joe and I had no opportunity for such philosophical considerations. We had three hours available for a task that, by the usual rule of thumb for television news, required twice as many. Fortunately, Joe played on the keys of an edit machine like a pianist playing Rachmaninov—I'd often marveled at it over the previous weeks—and he always kept his nerve. He sat there now with his painful foot propped up, an electric fire to keep us warm in the dank atmosphere of the InterContinental, and a regular flow of drinks and snacks, which our producer, knowing how important these small things are, kept bringing in like room service; and we reveled in the pictures Joe and Peter Jouvenal had shot that extraordinary day. And as Joe sped through the pictures, looking for the best sequence to open up with, I knew I scarcely needed to look at them myself; Joe was, if anything, better at matching pictures to words than I was.

Reading my words now, they seem pretty dull and uninspired. Leaving aside the natural poverty of my phrase-making, though, and the tiredness, and the speed with which we had to work, I found myself deliberately under-writing. The pictures were so good that I didn't want anything to distract from them. We left a great many gaps too, so that the natural sound the camera had recorded could come through: the background noise, the voices, the guns.

This was the opening sequence.

It was just before dawn that the wild dash for Kabul developed: thousands of soldiers intent on capturing the capital. It seemed to take no time at all to cover the twelve or so miles. As we drew nearer to Kabul, the grim evidence of battle. These were former supporters of the Northern Alliance who had switched sides and joined the Taliban. No mercy for them. Then we saw they had captured another man. The

presence of our camera probably saved his life. He was paralyzed with
terror. By now there were no Taliban left to resist.

From the *Six O'Clock News,* Tuesday, 13 November 2001

That morning at Bin Laden Mansions, everything was ready to go
before five o'clock. Those of us who had been covering the break-
through of the Taliban front line and the advance to Qarabagh the previous day had managed to get only three or four hours sleep. But we
were buoyed up by the tension and excitement of the day ahead. You
could see the signs: loud voices, noisy laughter, the nervous checking
of watches.

I spoke to Joe privately: What was the state of his foot now?

Oh, fine, fine.

I could see he was worried that I might tell him he mustn't come.
Three or four times during the previous week a bone setter had come in
from the town—an old man with a long white beard and a large green
turban—and manipulated the broken bone in Joe's foot. When it was
really bad you could hear the gasp of pain from the corridor outside, but
Joe always insisted that he felt fine. I knew what he was thinking: If this
got back to London, the foreign desk would go into auto-Auntie mode
and order him out.

"I feel this is our story," Joe had said to me once before, when he
resisted the desk's demand that he should hand over to another cameraman and go home.

It was even more our story now, after we had covered the battle the
day before. I simply couldn't find the words to tell Joe he mustn't come.

All right, but on one condition. My doctor has sent me some really
strong painkillers, just in case. They came with all the stuff the night
before last. You must take the proper dose, and I'll feed them to you.

They were big horse tablets, and you felt just by looking at them that
you could have confidence in them.

Hajji Bari came storming down the corridor, shouting and waving
his arms: It was time to get going. Today, as yesterday, we would use his
jeep and he would lead the entire assault on the capital in a little red

Japanese-made car. The entire road from Charikar to Kabul was paved, after a fashion, so this was possible.

Sitting in the jeep, our flak jackets holding us erect and upright like Victorian corsets, we drove very fast down the road we had followed yesterday. Now it was completely open. Even the unexploded bomb that had caused us to take a long and tiresome detour on our way back last night was gone: It was this that had killed the eight soldiers on their bus. We just edged our way around the fatal crater and sped on. Joe was sitting in the front, and got some sensationally beautiful pictures of the scarlet-and-purple dawn, with the headlights of the convoy piercing what was left of the darkness. Qarabagh was entirely empty as we drove through it—just the ashes of the previous night's campfires. The army was ahead of us. The driver jammed his foot down on the accelerator.

They had already done the killing by the time we caught up with them, soon after we had passed through Karez-e Mir. The bodies lay by the roadside. These were men of the Northern Alliance who, about a year before, had defected to the Taliban. By and large, Afghans show a reluctance to kill other Afghans in battle; but in this case they had made an exception. It was pretty clear from the way the bodies lay huddled together that they had surrendered, had been herded together, and shot down as a group. If we had gotten there a little earlier, it wouldn't have happened: the Northern Alliance, even the ordinary soldiers, demonstrated a certain savviness when it came to the media. This had been a massacre, carried out in cold blood.

We stopped a little further on, and I could see, up on a spur by the side of the road, that a group of Northern Alliance soldiers had captured another of the defectors. I suppose I felt that we had been partly responsible for the other deaths because we weren't there when it happened. I couldn't bear it to happen again. Joe and John Jennings and I ran up the slope to where the group had gathered, and Tony Davis, our Australian friend, came with us. Joe was first: the painkillers seemed to be working well.

The man they had caught was young, bareheaded and utterly terrified. They were dragging him around by his arm, kicking him and hitting him with their guns. As we ran up, one of them gave him a terrible kick in the back, enough to injure him badly. The next thing would be to start shooting. Joe and I waded in, shouting. They laughed, and left him alone. For a time he just lay there, stupid with fear. Then he crawled away like an injured animal.

It was getting near the top of the hour, and I got on my mobile phone: the type called a Thuraya, the handset of which connected directly to the satellite. I spoke to the BBC's international radio arm, the World Service, where the producer and presenter both showed the flair and courage to let our interview go on and on for a remarkably long time. Often, in the heat of the moment, I would forget about the audience, and shout out instructions to Joe and Peter Jouvenal while I still held the phone in my hand. I even tried to persuade a Northern Alliance commander to take us into Kabul, ignoring the World Service altogether and feeling quite surprised when a distant voice reminded me they were still there. I used a lot of bad language, because at times like this you do. It didn't seem to faze the people in the studio. Having been, years before, a radio producer myself, I could see that if you had the guts and the imagination, it could make good broadcasting.

> Then came the critical moment: would the Northern Alliance simply race on and pour into Kabul itself, even though they had undertaken not to? The commander in charge was determined not to let it happen. He ordered the armored vehicles to block the way; the great advance was stopped in its tracks.
>
> But Kabul lay temptingly close below us now. The small BBC team decided to head on into the city, on our own, and on foot so no one would think we were soldiers. We plowed on, radio side by side with television.
>
> From the *Six O'Clock News*, Tuesday, 13 November 2001

That is how I dealt with this part of the story in my report.

Looking down the road, where Kabul lay below us, it was clear to me that the Northern Alliance wouldn't take us there. If we wanted to go, and we did, we would have to walk. Hajji Bari drove back up the road in his bullet-riddled red car after trying to negotiate the Taliban's surrender. Gul Haidar reluctantly agreed to let us walk in. The others in the BBC team, having endured so much to get there, were in no mood to stop here and look at Kabul. As for me, I was absolutely determined that the BBC would get there ahead of the rest of the world's journalists, and link up with the three BBC people who were already there. It had suddenly become more important than anything else. I knew it was dangerous, but there are times when that ceases to matter so much. This was one of those times. I fed Joe another pain-killer, and we started off.

> Well, this is it: we're walking into Kabul city. We don't seem to have any problems around us. There are only people who are friendly—and chanting, I'm afraid, *Kill the Taliban*. As I understand it, though, as we walk in here, there aren't going to be that many Taliban anyway.
> From the *Six O'Clock News*, Tuesday, 13 November 2001

We were well on our way down the steep hillside before I even thought about doing a piece to camera. In fact I was so wrapped up in the excitement and nervousness of it all that I might never have thought about it. It was Joe, white-faced with the strain of keeping up with me, who called out to me over the noise of the cheering and excited crowd that had gathered around us.

"Maybe we'd better do a piece to camera as we go."

There was nothing to be said in it, other than to talk about what was going on. No philosophical reflections, no military or political judgments. These things would have sounded foolish. It was enough, at a time like this, to state the obvious. On the words 'As I understand it', an excited kid tried to grab me, and, concentrating on the camera and what I was saying, I elbowed him thuggishly aside. Every time I have seen it since I have winced at the sight, and a little titter goes around the audience I am showing it to. It was a relief to have gotten the piece to camera done, and fortunately I only needed the one take—unusual for me. But as I walked on I remembered thinking to myself, I wonder if I'll live to do another one.

It was 7:53 A.M., local time. Kabul was a free city, after five years of perhaps the most extreme religious system anywhere on earth. Under the Taliban, girls could not be educated, men could be whipped for shaving, all music was banned. It was forbidden to play chess, to sing, to possess a picture of any living creature. No wonder they were happy.

From the *Six O'Clock News*, Tuesday, 13 November 2001

The post in the middle of the road that marked the city boundary of Kabul was directly ahead. I could see Peter Emmerson walking a little ahead of me, and I sped up, my legs aching with the strain, in a childish effort to get there first. The crowds were huge now, and the cheering and shouting made it impossible to hear anyone else. It was now that I lost contact with Joe and Peter Jouvenal, without noticing. Joe had to stop to rest his foot, Peter fell over a bicycle in the crush and cracked the lens of his camera. Joe got one last shot of me as I was swallowed up in the huge crowd of joyful, celebrating people.

John Jennings and I stopped a taxi and explained to the driver why we needed it. With the usual generosity of Afghans, the passengers got out and gave us their seats. They were excited to be handing over their vehicle to the BBC anyway. The driver edged his way through the crowd in a U-turn, and headed off with us toward the center of Kabul. I was disturbed about losing contact with the others, but I knew they'd be safe; it was obvious by now that the Taliban wouldn't be shooting at us. We had made an arrangement with the others to head for the InterContinental, and they were all resourceful, experienced people.

I fished out my mobile phone again and tried to get through to London. For some reason it didn't work: there was no signal. Maybe, I thought, it was because we were on the move, so every few minutes I asked Jennings to tell the driver I want to stop to call the BBC in London. The same thing happened each time: the phone refused to work, and a crowd gathered round us, heard we were from the BBC and started the noisy business of congratulation all over again.

It wasn't all rejoicing, though. The word was already going round that the Taliban and their Al Qa'ida allies were finished, and people were hunting down the foreign volunteers who had come to Afghanistan to fight with them—chiefly Arabs and Pakistanis. When they found them, they killed them brutally.

> But there was an ugly price to be paid for so much repression. In the streets, in the ditches, foreign volunteers for the Taliban, especially Arabs and Pakistanis, ended up dead, lynched or shot. They were particularly loathed.
>
> From the *Six O'Clock News*, Tuesday, 13 November 2001

We drove past one bloody heap lying in the gutter, an arm flung out in useless self-protection, a small crowd of peering, celebrating people standing around it. Then we passed another. In Afghanistan, power rarely seemed to change hands without blood being shed. All over this city, it was being shed now.

> In the surroundings of the InterContinental Hotel, in the center of Kabul, we caught side of Arab and Pakistani Taliban trying to escape the vengeance of the people of Kabul. A group of soldiers is hunting them down.
>
> From the *Six O'Clock News*, Tuesday, 13 November 2001

We reached the private road that leads to the InterContinental Hotel— the only decent hotel in Kabul—which looks out over a wide expanse of parkland toward the snow-covered hills. A group of soldiers was jumping out of a truck by the entrance to the road. They didn't look like Taliban, but I didn't see how they could be from the Northern Alliance either. John asked them who they were; they said they were allies of the Northern Alliance, and had just arrived from somewhere west of Kabul.

Getting to the InterCon was an important part of our plan, since we would need a sizeable number of rooms when the second wave of BBC people arrived from Charikar with the satellite equipment. Getting to Kabul was only the first phase of the operation; we would need to establish a broadcasting center in the hotel for weeks to come.

We drove up to the main entrance, sixty-four days after I left it, and

I searched my pockets for money to pay the driver. He was the luckiest man in the city: all I could find was a hundred-dollar bill, so I gave it to him with my thanks. When I asked him for a receipt he looked helpless, and I decided not to waste any more time over it.

The place was silent and empty as John Jennings and one of the soldiers got out with me. The vast, ugly 1960s lobby was dark: the power, as ever, seemed to be cut. I was more than a little nervous. The Taliban often operated from the InterCon, and could still be here. Two figures were sitting huddled together in the gloom, but since they weren't wearing turbans I assumed they weren't dangerous. I turned to the man behind the counter.

"I'd like to book some rooms, please."

"It's already been done."

The voice was familiar, and I looked round at the two figures. Peter Emmerson and Ian Pannell were laughing at the success of their trick. I suppose I was faintly annoyed that they had gotten here first, but mostly I was relieved: they at least were safe.

They had had a more glamorous entry into the city than John Jennings and I. They had gotten ahead of us in the crowd by hitching a ride on the backs of two bicycles, and then, when they fell off, abandoned them for a taxi, which had brought them here. It must have been a superb moment for them, speeding through the welcoming crowds on the bikes, and they were still elated by the whole episode, laughing and reminding each other of the things they had done.

The entire hotel was empty, and the lift, inevitably, was out of operation. The five of us—Emmerson, Pannell, Jennings, the Afghan soldier and I—made our way through the dark, empty kitchen and up the back stairs to the rooms where our BBC colleagues Rageh Omaar, William Reeve, and the American Fred Scott (the three who had persuaded the Taliban to let them come to Kabul a short while before) were staying. But there was no answer when we banged on the doors. An old man I recognized from my previous visits here shuffled up in hotel uniform and produced a key. Were there still Taliban here? The old man shrugged.

We searched the three rooms for a satellite phone—our mobiles still weren't working—because we were anxious to call the BBC: no point in being here if we couldn't broadcast. But the three of them seemed to have left, taking their satellite phone with them. We found out later that they had gone to the BBC office, and had had a dangerous time of it, being fired at and stopped by a Taliban patrol. They were lucky to have escaped with their lives.

It was the third piece of luck they had had. The night before, the Americans had bombed a house close by the BBC office just as William was in the middle of a live broadcast to London. The explosion propelled him out of his seat: the image became one of the most celebrated of the entire fall of Kabul. What was more: although he was still on camera he managed not to swear, which is more than I could achieve that morning, when I was doing my live with the World Service. The three of them, William, Rageh and Fred, had decided that there could be further bomb attacks, and they must get out. It was dark, and in the streets they found that the Taliban government and the remnants of Al Qa'ida were escaping from the city, together with any Talib who could get out with them. Curiously, the Taliban leadership seemed to have the same unconcern as their soldiers, refusing to believe that the Northern Alliance could capture the city.

The BBC team were stopped at a roadblock manned by frightened and jittery Taliban, including one unpleasant character with a black turban who, a day or so before, had threatened to kill them. Fortunately he seemed to be so unnerved by the danger that he didn't remember to carry out his threat. With characteristic courage Fred Scott, the quietest, wittiest and most thoughtful of cameramen, switched his camera on and left it running while they were caught at the roadblock, holding it down by his side. The pictures, dark and skewed as they were, gave a vivid sense of the danger and the chaos of the last hours of Taliban rule. If anyone had realized that Fred's camera was running, they would all have been murdered for certain.

As for us, we were still trying to work out how to get in touch with them when we heard voices outside in the corridor. There was an instant of fear, until I recognized Peter Jouvenal's characteristic tones: he and Joe Phua had arrived. It was a good moment, as we shook hands. The team was now reunited except for Kate Clark, who had gone directly to her old office—the one that had been blown up—in order to start broadcasting from there. And now that Joe was here we had a satellite phone again.

At that moment the soldier who had come with us put his head around the door and spoke urgently to John Jennings.

"He says there's a group of Arab Taliban heading for the hotel."

The soldier took us to the window at the end of the corridor and pointed. I got a shock: seven men, clearly not Afghans, in uniform and with AK-47s, were edging their way around the wall of the hotel right below us. Since we were only two floors above them, all they had to do to see us was to look up. It was a reasonable assumption that they'd heard we were here and had come to kill us. The Arabs who volunteered for the Taliban and Al Qa'ida were notorious for their hatred of Westerners.

It seemed safest to go to the top floor of the hotel, in the hope that they would get bored with searching the other floors before they found us. Joe decided, despite his ankle, to film the whole business. This gave us a strange, reassuring feeling, as we plowed our way up the emergency stairs, carrying all the gear, and gathered breathlessly on the fifth floor. Another ancient in a hotel uniform appeared. I told him what I thought was going on, and he agreed to hide us in the rooms if necessary.

Time passed. I was increasingly anxious to start broadcasting. In the end we went rather sheepishly downstairs again, with Joe still filming so he could catch the moment when we were all blown away. There was another moment of anxiety while I tried to get through to London from the balcony of one of the rooms, and the Arabs passed close to us on the grounds of the hotel. I lay on the floor of the balcony for a while, but finally got bored with waiting and dialed London anyway.

Jouvenal, though, had noticed what I failed to: the body-language of these Taliban showed that they weren't hunting, but being hunted. It turned out that the soldiers we had seen near the entrance to the InterCon were making a sweep through the hotel grounds and were searching for them. Peter announced that he was going out to film what happened.

"Just be careful," I told him feebly. He paid as little attention to that as he could without actually being rude, and borrowed Joe's camera.

> Another soldier is bringing up some grenades to flush them out. They are trapped inside this building. But some local people have caught another one of the Taliban. He's an Arab. They make him call the others to get them to come out and surrender. Eventually, it works: they are brought out as prisoners. This man is a Pakistani. The Arab gets particularly brutal treatment.
>
> From the *Six O'Clock News*, Tuesday, 13 November 2001

It's always hard to get really good action footage. Partly, it's a matter of luck: you have to be on hand, with your camera running, at precisely the right moment. But, equally, everyone seems to want to keep the cameras away from what is happening, either because they are worried about your safety or—more likely—because they think something reprehensible might happen.

Afghanistan is different. Safety never seems to be a matter of concern, and no one seems to have the slightest awareness of television's needs, or of the results of broadcasting a particular story. There is an innocence about Afghanistan which makes it a cameraman's paradise.

This was to be one of the finest sequences Peter Jouvenal had ever filmed. He headed straight out into the hotel grounds where, in an ancient building, six members of the Taliban group had gone to ground. The Northern Alliance soldiers surrounded it. A couple stood by the entrance and fired their automatic weapons several times through the open door. As Peter was filming this, he heard some excited shouting behind him, and turned to find that some local people had captured the seventh member of the group and were coming to the Northern Alliance soldiers to hand him over.

They roughed him up and made him stand at the entrance to the building and shout to the others to come out. Slowly, they emerged one by one out of the darkness, their hands in the air. Watching the pictures, you had the sense of being a spectator to the whole thing; so unusual is it to see events unfolding in this way. An elderly Pakistani Talib with a long gray beard emerged first through the open doorway. The Northern Alliance soldiers searched him and stripped him of his few belongings: the perks of war.

One of the soldiers walked up to the Arab who had been captured first and hit him a terrible blow on the back of the head with a rifle wrapped in cloth. It was an act of completely gratuitous brutality; but Afghans of all kinds felt that, bad as the Taliban were, the volunteers who had come from other countries to fight for them were far worse. Soon the people would be handed over to the United States, who shaved their heads and beards forcibly and flew them across the world to the American base at Guantanamo Bay in Cuba. Scarcely anything was achieved by this, and only two or three pieces of really useful information were obtained from the prisoners.

> In the jeep there are other Taliban prisoners. This one is an Arab, perhaps an Egyptian. The other two are Afghans. This is the end of the Taliban in Afghanistan.
>
> From the *Six O'Clock News*, Tuesday, 13 November 2001

Jouvenal followed the soldiers to a vehicle that contained three other Taliban prisoners. One looked like an Egyptian, with a bloody and swollen nose. He tried to keep his face covered, and as one of the soldiers reached in and pulled his arm away from his face the man glared at Peter's camera with a mixture of fear and defiance. Peter had no sympathy for him.

"They came here to someone else's country to kill people," he said as we watched the pictures on our edit machine. "They can't complain now."

True, of course. Yet, stripped of their guns and their organization, these people were just human beings like the rest of us; and like Peter and me, they had taken a chance in coming here. We happened to be on the winning side, but maybe next time it could be Peter or me sitting there with the broken, bloody nose.

While he was away I settled down at the end of the empty second-floor corridor in the InterCon. The satellite phone was set up, and I even managed to get one of the ancients to bring us some coffee—the first thing we had had to eat or drink since four thirty this morning. It tasted good, and after a month of roughing it in our barracks at Charikar the grubby white cloth on the metal tray, the teaspoon and the battered silvered pot almost made it seem as though we had found civilization. I was in touch with London again.

That proved to be a mixed blessing, since not long afterward I made a foolish joke on air, which went around the world and caused me a certain amount of grief. A program presenter in London said she didn't quite understand what was happening; the Northern Alliance had stopped at the gates of Kabul, but the Taliban had been driven out. Who, therefore, had liberated the city? I said I supposed it was the BBC. Big mistake. The British tabloid press, which is the most ferocious on Earth, has no sense of humor and for the most part detests the BBC. From that moment on the received version was that I had boasted on air that I had liberated Kabul personally.

At the time, though, while the tabloids were preparing to explode in ersatz righteousness and indignation, there were more important things for us to think about. Peter Jouvenal and I had often talked about what we should do when we got to Kabul. There were three or four places we wanted to get to quickly when we arrived: an Al-Qa'ida base not far from the InterContinental; the house where one of Osama bin Laden's wives lived, and which he used to visit quite often; and a training center we had heard about. Over the next couple of days we went to all these places, and each time we were the first people to go to them.

> It's the end, too, of this country's links with international terrorism. We went to a house where a senior Arab member of Osama bin Laden's Al-Qaida organization had lived and worked. There were explosives in one room, anti-personnel mines in another. Notices on the wall were all connected with Al-Qaida, including a training certificate and an organizational chart. Upstairs, there's a manual in English, with notes in Arabic, for sabotage and causing explosions. There were all sorts of guides about timing mechanisms and booby traps.
> From the *Six O'Clock News*, Tuesday, 13 November 2001

The morning wore on. Extraordinarily, the next group of people to arrive at the hotel weren't the reporters from newspapers or some other television organization, they were from the BBC too. Our satellite dish,

complete with engineers, had made the long and difficult journey down the road from Charikar. They had talked their way past the Northern Alliance position at the entrance to Kabul, and got here through the dangerous streets of the city to the hotel. I shook hands with Nick Springate, the producer who had managed all this, and told him I thought it was the BBC's best achievement yet. I still do. A camera team is quick and mobile; a three-ton truck full of equipment is ponderously slow. And yet here they were, long before anyone else. It was a triumph of planning, but it took a sizeable amount of courage too. Nick had even better news for me: the engineers thought they could be up and running by the time of our *One O'Clock News* in London. We would get our pictures of the morning's extraordinary events in satellite quality on the first available news program. Not bad.

It's been my good fortune to watch the overthrow of all sorts of hated regimes over the years: in Iran, in Berlin, in Czechoslovakia, in Romania, in Russia, in South Africa, in Indonesia, in Serbia, and now in Afghanistan. There is a purity about the joy at such moments, as people give themselves over entirely to the happiness of the moment. It rarely lasts, of course; and sometimes the new system turns out to be every bit as bad as the old one, and occasionally worse. But the moment of revolution itself is always magnificent. There is nothing so brave, nothing so generous, nothing so fierce, nothing so sentimental as a revolutionary crowd. When the cause demands it, people will give their houses, their cars, their money, their lives. Everything is heightened; and the moment is one that lives in the minds of everyone who witnesses it forever.

In the streets of Kabul, people were savoring their new freedom. Friends were out in the streets, shaving off the beards they'd all had to wear if they wanted to escape a savage beating. Women were walking around and showing their faces for the first time in five years. There was a kind of mass ecstasy, as the things people had longed for secretly for so long came suddenly true. No one in the streets seemed to have expected their liberation; only the previous night the continuing American bombing of Kabul had added to the misery of people who felt they had been abandoned by the entire world to their fate.

In 1989, when the Russians hastily withdrew from the only country that had resisted them militarily over a period of years in any serious way, it seemed to be a liberation. True, Moscow left its puppet ruler behind them: Najibullah, who strove courageously to unite the country behind him and leave behind the irrelevancies of Marxism–Leninism. But the foreign politicians who had made the most noise about the Soviet occupation of Afghanistan started to go quiet. We no longer heard anything about the horrors that were taking place in Afghanistan from Margaret Thatcher or Ronald Reagan or George Bush or Helmut Kohl. Suddenly, because the Russians were no longer there, it didn't matter. It was just a faraway Third World place of which we knew little and cared less.

Najibullah was swept away by the combined force of the *mujaheddin* in 1992, and for the next four years corruption and civil war and covert foreign intervention reigned in Kabul; and still nobody cared. In 1996 the last, worst twist of the downward spiral brought the victory of the Taliban and the cruel lynching of Najibullah. Even now nobody cared. Afghanistan had become the worst and most lunatic state on earth, but no one did anything about it. It was only when America was attacked that the Taliban, Osama bin Laden's reluctant hosts who had done very little to support him, were discovered to be uniquely evil. It was hard, even at a time like this, to feel too much enthusiasm for the responses of the Western world toward this half-destroyed, half-savage, half-civilized country.

There was only one question left. Having discovered that Afghanistan mattered, would the United States forget it once again and withdraw into its shell; or would it, and the other powers that are in a position to help, understand that countries like Afghanistan aren't simply adventure play-grounds for geopoliticians, but places where real people live, and where real suffering needs to be averted?

But for the moment now it was all over. As I wrote the final words of my script, I felt a powerful sympathy for these people whose misery I had observed over the years: brave and loyal people, who hadn't deserved the disasters that had overcome them. It was an unalloyed pleasure to see them free once again.

If all that is finished now, so is the system which intruded in every-one's lives. Suddenly you don't have to wear a beard any more if you don't want to. Shaving is a way to show your liberation; so is showing your face if you are a woman. And there's one thing more: children can fly kites again. Freedom is in the air here.

John Simpson, BBC News, Kabul.

Epilogue

Of course, completing a book gives one a sense of crossing a frontier, of finality. As Pushkin put it, Why this strange sadness troubling me? At the same time, there is an awareness of the powerful flow of life, which began before us and will continue after us.
—ANDREI SAKHAROV, *Moscow and Beyond*

The BBC has changed utterly and out of all recognition since the day I first went to work there on 1 September 1966. And yet at the same time it remains essentially the same organization, with the same set of basic values that it has always had. I don't believe that, as plenty of people will tell you in Britain, it has lost its way, or lost its ideals; I think they're still there, just as strong as ever. What has changed is that the BBC has finally gotten its act together. Not everyone in Britain—governments, political parties, newspapers—likes that.

Of course it remains a big, slow-moving bureaucracy, taking an infuriatingly long time to respond and to pay its bills, patronizing, self-congratulatory (well, you can see that from this book) and occasionally treating its own with breathtaking cruelty. But its programs are as excellent for 2002 as they were for 1966, and define our times as they defined those.

This quality has spread into areas no one could have conceived of in 1966. Some years ago a friend of mine told me he was giving up his job as a television correspondent to become the boss of a new on-line news service that the BBC was planning to start up. I congratulated him, of course, because he had already taken the plunge; but I remember thinking he was making a terrible mistake to give up one of the best jobs in television for some weird, nerdish experiment that would probably be closed down after a year or two.

Now BBC News Online has become the most successful website in Europe, and half of all the hits on it come from the United States. I have a feeling that it will soon be one of my main employers; the other being BBC World. Neither of these services existed more than a decade ago. The BBC's ability to reinvent itself and continue leading the field is extraordinary, given that it is such a large, varied and often quite slow moving organization. Yet at the same time it hasn't lost its hold on the affection of the British public. When shortly before the epoch-making fireworks display at the famous pop concert at Buckingham Palace in June 2002, which marked the Queen's jubilee, the Prince of Wales thanked the BBC for arranging and broadcasting the concert, it was noticeable that the applause was loud and sustained; only the applause for his tributes to the Queen herself and to the country were louder.

In other, lesser ways the BBC has remained exactly its old self. When on the evening of 1 September 1966 I came home after my first day's work and met my then wife and my father for a celebratory meal, they asked me what it was like.

"Everyone there seems amazingly polite," I remember answering.

It was true. The tweed-jacketed characters who seemed to fill its corridors were always holding doors open for one another and saying please and thank you and would you mind? Now nobody ever seems to wear tweed, and in the summer quite a few people wear T-shirts and shorts; some even pad around on bare feet. But they still all say please and thank you and would you mind?, and they are positively obsessive about holding doors open for one another. Recently a politeness initiative was launched, whereby you mustn't bully the people below you, or be insulting, or—a serious challenge to the corporate ethic, this—blame other departments. As a relatively infrequent visitor to Television Centre, I found it hard to see why any of this (except the business of blaming other departments) could conceivably be thought of as necessary.

Its strange, unstructured approach to broadcasting is prefigured in its buildings. As you arrive at the entrance to Television Centre in Wood

Lane, you can see that there have been at least six different building-stages added onto the original round building, four of them in reddish brick. Yet each section has a different shade of reddish brick. It is, when you come to think of it, quite an achievement to find non-matching bricks quite so unerringly. With luck, by the time of my fortieth anniversary with the BBC in 2006, if I haven't died, been sacked, or stormed out in a rage, the News division will be getting ready to move from the East German wastelands of Wood Lane back to Broadcasting House, near Oxford Circus, where my BBC career began.

Nothing in this career of mine has ever required such sustained physical and mental effort as reporting on the impending fall of Kabul at the age of fifty-seven, with all the hard driving, climbing of mountains, dressing up, sleeping on hard floors, taking cover on front lines and general physical effort that it called for. But it was all thoroughly worth it, both in personal terms and in the sense that it helped to set the seal on the BBC's dominance in international news broadcasting. The whole experience was a delight, a joy. Working closely with people you like and admire, enduring hardships with them, and having something to show for it at the end seems to me to be as satisfying an activity as you could imagine.

There are few things as good as having excellent pictures to write to, and enough time to do justice to the business of editing them. I'd go further: the moment when you sit there in the edit suite, watching the pictures for the first time and working out how to enhance them with words, is one of the most enjoyable moments the job has to offer.

Best of all is the pleasure of the news hunt. There is, I think, nothing better than to work out what your story requires in the way of pictures, and then to launch out into the complexity of events and bring those pictures back. It is, I suppose, your way of making sense of things, of setting an understandable mark on great moments and small ones: You become the novelist who brings out the characters, the playwright who reveals the plot, except that the materials you are working with are unalterable facts rather than creatures of the imagination. It's not easy: it wouldn't be worth doing if it were. But if you feel, after you have finished the editing process and you sit back to watch what you and the picture editor and the producer have labored away at for the past couple of hours, that you have captured something of the essence of the subject, that is an unbeatable sensation.

And the subject doesn't have to be a gloomy or depressing one, by any means. Let me give you one last example. It begins back in 2000, when my old college at Cambridge awarded me an honorary fellowship. It was a charming gesture on the college's part, and on 1 May, Dee and I turned up at Magdalene together with the Irish poet and Nobel Prize–winner Seamus Heaney, an infinitely worthier recipient, to receive it. And because there wasn't really any great tradition attached to the awarding of honorary fellowships, they decided to make one up. Everyone wore academic gowns and someone went to the trouble of composing a pleasant rigmarole in Latin, along the lines of "Inasmuch as it hath pleased." Some of the dons were friends of mine from my days as an undergraduate. My old tutor was there, with a beard as superb as Charles Darwin's. The former chaplain, now a bishop, had performed the ceremony at my first marriage. My one-time director of studies was the one who wrote a letter to the BBC, recommending me for a job.

The British, as the former U.S. ambassador Ray Seitz affectionately pointed out, like dressing up and having ceremonies. I knew Seamus from my Irish past, and every now and then during the occasion I caught his eye and we exchanged schoolboy grins, as though to say, "What are a couple of outsiders like us doing in a place like this?"

(A couple of years later Dee and I were in Dublin, buying something from a Grafton Street vendor for our young nephew Sagan, who was staying with us. A familiar, growling voice broke into the transaction.

"Is this any way for an honorary fellow to behave?" Seamus Heaney asked.

And when Dee told Sagan that this was the most famous poet in the world, the most famous poet in the world said, Now stop that sort of thing at once.)

Magdalene is a small college, neither wealthy nor particularly famous, and you usually have to tell people its name is pronounced "Maudlin." Samuel Pepys studied there in the 1650s, and there were close associations with a wide range of figures: including Kipling, Parnell, the Everest climber George Mallory, T. S. Eliot, C. S. Lewis, and in latter years a slew of media people. The college has always contained a streak of the unexpected. In the eighteenth century it became one of the main centers of the anti-slavery campaign, thanks to a campaigning Master of the day, Dr. Peter Peckard. At the turn of the century another Master, A. C. Benson, turned the college into the intellectual and social powerhouse of the university.

Throughout the nineteenth century and well into the twentieth it produced colonial administrators who were famous for their liberal attitudes and their sympathy for the people they governed. Somehow, in our own time, it began to have a connection with South Africa, thanks to a couple of leading alumni; and the master, the geneticist Sir John Gurdon, and the senior tutor, Dr. Mark Billinge, a particular friend of mine, hatched up a daring proposal: to invite Nelson Mandela to visit Magdalene and receive an honorary fellowship.

When I heard about it, I was sure it wouldn't happen. Mandela was getting frail, and on a previous visit to Britain the vice chancellors of a half dozen universities were summoned to London to give him honorary doctorates in one combined ceremony so as not to tire him. The idea that he would go all the way to Cambridge to visit one small college seemed pretty unlikely. A first attempt was aborted in November 2000, because Mandela was ill.

And then I started getting messages from Mark Billinge that it was looking good for the following May. The college offered to let me cover it for the BBC, and I grabbed at the chance. On 1st May, the anniversary of my own honorary fellowship, Dee and I stayed in the fellows guest room, a medieval monk's chamber furnished with chairs, chests and other equipment belonging to Samuel Pepys; and after a night spent on two narrow monkish beds we woke up early on the morning of Wednesday, 2 May.

I was nervous, and wouldn't have slept well in any bed. This might have seemed like a piece of cake: everything was laid out for us, and there was no question of having to fight anybody or take risks or struggle to get this story. We had it to ourselves, since the college wanted it that way. And yet there were so many problems; not least that it is difficult to broadcast about these things without offending someone—and these people, who had been generous to me, were the last ones on earth I wanted to offend.

Then there were real procedural difficulties. The South African High Commission in London had made it clear they didn't want Mandela to be interviewed; there were political problems in South Africa, and they were worried that someone might lure Mandela into criticizing his successor, Thabo Mbeki. And yet I knew it wouldn't be sufficient merely to hear and see the formal business of the day: We needed an interview. Dee and I were also determined to turn the whole event into a *Simpson's World*—and that would certainly require me to speak to the great man. I had promised the BBC to get these things, and didn't like to fail. It wasn't going to be easy.

But there were positive aspects as well. I had explained all these things to Mark Billinge the night before, and had a pretty clear idea that the college would support me in getting an interview with Mandela: We even arranged precisely where and when it would take place. I also had a good team. Chris Marlow, a friend of mine for twenty years, was the cameraman—a sharp, mordantly witty man with whom I had always enjoyed working. I knew he would do a first-class job.

But I was still nervous. We sat at a coffee shop across the River Cam from the college and made our plans, and I cursed the weather. The sky was leaden, and we ideally needed some spring sunshine on this day of days. Magdalene is a small gem of a place, built from the warmest and mellowest of medieval brick, and the sun brings out its best qualities. We did a good deal of standing about with the leading dons of the college before the off, all of us nervous and awkward. Then we moved into the Fellows' garden at the back, where Mandela's helicopter was to land.

From here, standing on the grass of the beautiful lawn, I could see the windows of the room I had occupied on the night before my entrance exam to the college, thirty-eight years before. Even then, hunched in front of an inadequate gas fire and doing some pointless last-minute revision, I knew this would be one of the turning points of my life; and now, at the farther end of my life and career, I reflected how comforting it would have been on that cold night if I had only been able to catch a glimpse of my future self, burly, gray-haired, and almost as nervous at this age as I had been as a skinny, ignorant eighteen-year-old. Now the college had become an important part of my life again. I looked around the lovely gardens—where I once danced till four in the morning and partied and played croquet—and shivered, cold in spite of my long cere-monial gown.

There was the faint sound of a helicopter in the cloud bank above us. Two scarlet-robed figures, the master and the college president, scanned the sky as anxiously as we did; and soon the equally scarlet tulips in the sacred flowerbeds were blowing around wildly, and the helicopter was sinking into the damp lawn to half the circumference of its wheels. The door opened. Slowly and with dignified care the latest honorary fellow of the college stepped out. The scarlet figures moved forward to shake hands and welcome him. Then there was a pause.

"Isn't anyone else going to say hello to me?" asked the slow, familiar voice.

Dee and Gina stepped out from behind the camera and shook Man-dela's hand with great reverence, and he spoke to them in his courtly, fluent Afrikaans. I knew from my own experience how good he was at making *you* feel good; now it was happening to them too.

Helped by his aides, looking distinctly frail, Mandela walked toward the college buildings: two delightful fifteenth-century squares of cherry-colored red brick, built around beautifully kept lawns and flower-beds, as pretty and intimate a place as you can find anywhere on earth. The college staff, the students and anyone else who could wangle an admis-sion ticket were waiting on the grass to see him. Mandela stopped and talked and joked with them. If it had been anyone else you would have said he was working the crowd. But this was no mere politician: you could see that on the faces of the people he spoke to and smiled at, as he made his way to the college chapel.

The college's Mandela scholars, drawn from all the main population groups in South Africa, were drawn up there to greet him. One was a young man from the poorest part of rural South Africa, who suffered from polio as a boy. His mother, who was a servant, was determined to get him a good education; and eventually, through the triumph of their combined wills, he came to Magdalene, a world away from the bitter poverty of his childhood home.

Magdalene is a surprising place. When I was an undergraduate there I never thought there was anything particularly remarkable about the college dons; yet when it started to come out in the 1970s that Britain had broken the German Enigma code during the Second World War, it turned out that several Magdalene dons had played an important part in this.

The atmosphere has always been friendly, even though for years Magdalene kept up the old male-only tradition, and was the last college in either Oxford or Cambridge to resist the arrival of women students. Yet the first woman to teach there told me that on her first night at dinner in the college hall, her neighbor was particularly charming and invited her back to coffee afterward. It was only afterward that she found out he'd been the leader of the college's anti-women movement.

After the ceremony in the chapel, Mandela was brought into a grand room nearby to meet the originators of the Mandela scholarship scheme. It was here that we were waiting. Mark Billinge had organized it cleverly so that I, as an honorary fellow, introduced them to Mandela—and then, as a BBC correspondent, was able to ask him some questions. His press minder, a tough, blonde Afrikaans woman, started to get angry, and urged the high commissioner, who was also a woman, to move in and stop me. The high commissioner, embarrassed, tweaked my jacket. I took no notice; after all, I once did an interview with President Mikhail Gorbachev while one KGB man wrestled with the cameraman and another twisted my arm to make me stop. A job is a job, and it wasn't exactly going to do Nelson Mandela any harm if I asked him a couple more questions. Often these officials get too big for their boots.

The interview secured, we all felt a lot more relaxed. Which was good, since the climax of the ceremony was about to take place in the college hall, a charming, intimate, wood-paneled place with ancient portraits looking down at us and coats of arms glowing in the stained-glass windows. At night the dons and undergraduates dine here by candlelight, and it was here that, in October 1963, I was first inducted into the college and met the people who are still among my closest friends. I acted in plays here, sang, made speeches and got mildly drunk celebrating my honorary fellowship. And now I was here in the presence of this mythic figure, whose prison sentence in his native country had only just begun when I was a student.

He felt, he said, looking out at his audience, rather nervous about being here.

"This is for three reasons. Firstly, I am an old-age pensioner."

There was some mild, deprecatory laughter.

"Secondly, I am unemployed."

The laughter was louder and more confident.

"And thirdly, I have a ba-a-a-d criminal record."

A huge wave of laughter and applause followed that.

The finale was nothing short of magical. The college choir, up in the musicians gallery, began singing a familiar African song, and Mandela was soon on his feet, moving in time to the music, grinning as he did so. And one by one, some enthusiastically, some embarrassed, but all irresistibly, the dignified figures in their scarlet and blue and black gowns stood up too and danced sedately in time with him, while the voices of the choir filled the hall. And, I kept telling myself, I was there to see this moment and broadcast it. I was so choked with the joy and emotion of it, and what it meant to me, that I could scarcely speak.

But I had to. Dee nudged me.

"You've got to do a piece to camera before everyone leaves."

She was right. I ran up and joined Chris Marlow in the musicians' gallery. There was just one thing I needed to know.

"How long since the college was founded?" I called down to one of the dons, a particular friend of mine. He did a quick calculation, and gave me the answer. I turned to the camera.

"This college has been in existence for five hundred seventy-three years," I said, "but we can safely assume it's never seen anything remotely like this."

When I talk to audiences in Britain and abroad, it's obvious they tend to associate me primarily with wars, death and pestilence: trouble of all kinds. The questions they ask are often about how I manage to cope with these things, and whether it all makes me cynical about human affairs.

Not a bit of it. How could it, when I have also been on hand for the release of a Nelson Mandela in 1990 after twenty-seven years in jail, for his election as president of South Africa in 1994, and for his induction as an honorary fellow of Magdalene College, Cambridge, and have had the opportunity to try to capture the essence of these superbly uplifting moments for television news?

But this is only the day job. Like everyone else, I go home occasionally; though in Dee's and my case home is a moveable concept. We live in various places, each of which feels like home whenever we get there.

Our main home is in a village on the Irish Sea, just outside Dublin—only fifty yards up the road from where I lived when I was based in Ireland in the 1970s. What I hadn't realized was that during the twenty intervening years it had become one of the most expensive places to live in the entire British Isles. Dalkey is now home to a half dozen singers and rock musicians who are known the world over, plus writers, actors, and (for some reason) a Formula One driver or two.

It was once the medieval port of Dublin and is now a superb little place, with a couple of castles on the main street and sensational views over the sea. There are two particular pubs, the Queen's and Finnegan's, which compare favorably with any watering-holes anywhere; and although everyone is perfectly aware of the famous show-business names who go and drink there, no one takes any notice of them whatsoever. Dalkey has rock stars like other places have football supporters.

The place has changed in other ways too. A quarter of a century ago, it still had the last vestiges of the Pale town it once was. A guidebook of 1876, which I found in a Dublin bookshop, said you could still occasionally hear Shakespearean English spoken there; and once, when a Dalkey carpenter came to mend an old armchair I had bought, he said, "I'm afraid I shall have to take this asunder." I don't suppose anyone uses words like that in Dalkey anymore. It has become gentrified, and nice little bistros are elbowing out the old grocery shops.

Dee and I, not being in the celebrity category, live in a small flat on the sea, looking out at the birds and the boats and the occasional seals. Entire days pass in which nothing happens, and only the passenger ferries from Britain and the house martins swooping out from their nests under

the eaves attract our attention. I think it is the most peaceful place I have
ever lived.

By contrast, we spend other parts of our time in Paris. The street outside our flat in the 7th is noisy and full of life, and no one there takes any
notice of us either. Thirty-four eating places of real quality are within a
ten-minute walk of us, including a restaurant that specializes in the food
and wines of southwestern France, and does things in the traditional way.
That means putting lace curtains up at the windows, having proper cloth
napkins of red and white check, and producing one of those cyclostyled
menus where the handwriting is reproduced in purple ink.

Every morning we slip out and have our café crème and croissants in
one of the nearby places, with the Eiffel Tower looming over us in the
distance. Recently, though, we switched cafés after an incident in which
I developed a craving for ham and eggs, and told the waiter precisely
how I wanted them done: a mistake in France, of course.

En principe, monsieur, le chef comprend son travail, he said grandly: in
principle, sir, (a menacing phrase which begins many a devastating
French put-down) the chef knows his job. That is, there is a right way
and a wrong way for serving fried eggs, as with so many other things in
France, and I had just selected the wrong way. But the pleasure of having an argument in French is that you can be devastatingly rude in ways
that would be unthinkable in English, and no one ever seems to care.
That too brings peace of mind of a sort.

So does the other place where I like to go after returning from somewhere difficult. It's neither a house nor a flat nor a restaurant, but a
church: Chelsea Old Church, in London. I don't in general think much
of organized religion, having seen the bad side of so much of it; but when
I came to the Church of England—what Americans would call the
Episcopalians—relatively late in life, I found its gentle, non-prescriptive
ways very much to my liking.

After seeing some unpleasant sights or encountering some particularly hostile people in my work, there are few more calming experiences
than sitting in the place where Sir Thomas More used to worship every
Sunday and may even be buried (minus his head); where John Donne
delivered his sermon about no man being an island, and where his friend

and fellow-poet George Herbert sat and prayed and thought up rhymes in his head:

> Let foreign nations of their language boast
> What fine variety each tongue affords:
> I like our language, as our men and coast;
> Who cannot dress it well, want wit, not words.

And slowly, when you think about it, you start to understand that the things that have disturbed and frightened you are not necessarily so very different or new or threatening after all, but are simply part of a wider, longer, more obscure, and elaborate pattern than you had previously appreciated.

Not long ago someone asked me whether all the bad things I had seen, the thirty-plus wars and revolutions, and all the bomb explosions and deaths and injuries hadn't made me despair of human nature. In casting around for an answer I happened to remember a little four-line squib I had once read by the poet John Masefield, who isn't very fashionable nowadays but who also used to hang out occasionally at Chelsea Old Church. He called it "Epilogue," and although it isn't in any way serious it sums up very much what I feel about this strange life of mine:

> I have seen flowers come in stony places,
> And kind things done by men with ugly faces,
> And the gold cup won by the worst horse at the races.
> So I trust, too.

Exactly.